Matters of Life and Death

ELLIOT N. DORFF

Matters of
Life and Death

A JEWISH APPROACH TO MODERN
MEDICAL ETHICS

For Beth and Howard,

1/30/05

With warm regards.

Elliot Dorff

THE JEWISH PUBLICATION SOCIETY

 Philadelphia 5764•2003

Publication of this book was made possible
by a generous gift from Rabbi Benjamin Z. Kreitman
in honor of his grandchildren
Jared Pierce Rosenfeld
and
Sydney Bree Goldstein
עטרת זקנים בני בנים

© 1998 by Elliot N. Dorff
First paperback edition 2003. All rights reserved

The Jewish Publication Society
2100 Arch Street, 2nd floor
Philadelphia, PA 19103

Manufactured in the United States of America

03 04 05 06 07 08 09 10 10 9 8 7 6 5 4 3 2 1

LIBRARY OF CONGRESS CATALOGING-IN-PUBLICATION DATA

Dorff, Elliot N.
Matters of Life and Death: A Jewish Approach to Modern Medical Ethics / Elliot Dorff

    p. cm.
Includes bibliographical references and index.
ISBN 0-8276-0768-7
    I. Medicine - Religious aspects - Judaism. 2. Health - Religious aspects - Judaism. 3. Medical
laws and legislation (Jewish law). 4. Medical ethics. 5. Ethics, Jewish. I. Title
BM538.H43D68 1998
296.3'642 - dc21

For MARLYNN

לִבַּבְתִּנִי אֲחֹתִי כַלָּה

You have captured my heart, my sister, my bride.
—Song of Songs 4:9

לֹא אִישׁ בְּלֹא אִשָּׁה
וְלֹא אִשָּׁה בְלֹא אִישׁ
וְלֹא שְׁנֵיהֶם בְּלֹא שְׁכִינָה

A man is not complete without a woman.
A woman is not complete without a man.
And both of them are incomplete without God.
—Genesis Rabbah 8:9

Table of Contents

Preface   xiii
Acknowledgments   xviii

Part One   Matters of Method and Belief   3

Chapter One   Consulting the Jewish Tradition for Moral
              Guidance   5
              The Revolution in Medical Science
                 and Its Moral Problems   5
              Assumptions of this Book   7
              The Impact of the Reader   9
              The Purpose of this Book   11

Chapter Two   Fundamental Beliefs Underlying Jewish
              Medical Ethics   14
              The Body Belongs to God   15
              Human Worth Stems from Being Created
                 in God's Image   18
              The Human Being Is an Integrated Whole   20
              The Body Is Morally Neutral and Potentially
                 Good   24
              Jews Have a Mandate and Duty to Heal   26

The Community Must Balance Its Medical and
   Nonmedical Needs and Services   29
Jews Must Sanctify God's Name   30

Part Two   Moral Issues at the Beginning of
           Life   35

Chapter Three   Having Children with One's Own Genetic
                Materials   37
                The Roles of Sex Within Marriage   37
                   Marital Companionship   37
                   Procreation   39
                Infertility in Jewish Sources   42
                The Range and Costs of Available Infertility
                   Treatments   45
                Traditional Sources on Nonsexual
                   Insemination   47
                Artificial Insemination Using the Husband's
                   Sperm   51
                IVF, GIFT, and ZIFT   53
                Surrogate Mothers   58

Chapter Four   Having Children Using Donated Genetic
                Materials   66
                Artificial Insemination with a Donor's Sperm:
                   Legal Concerns   66
                   Adultery and Illegitimacy   67
                   Unintentional Incest in the Next Generation   69
                   The Identity of the Father   72
                Artificial Insemination with a Donor's Sperm:
                   Moral Concerns   80
                   Licentiousness   80
                   The Impact on the Marriage and on the Parent-
                      Child Relationship   81
                   Racism   93
                   Demographic Concerns   95
                   Compassion   96

Using Donated Eggs   98
    Balancing the Risks of Egg Donation
      with the Alternative of Adoption   98
    Moral and Psychological Issues in Egg
      Donation   98
    The Identity of the Mother   100
    The Problem of Selective Abortions   101
    The Obligation to Procreate   102
Donating One's Sperm or Eggs   103
    Donating Sperm   103
    Donating Eggs   106
Adoption   107
Single Parenthood   111

Chapter Five   Preventing Pregnancy   116
Masturbation   116
Contraception   120
    Male Forms of Birth Control   121
    Female Forms of Birth Control   122
    The Broader Context Affecting Decisions to Use
      Birth Control:
      Social, Religious, and Personal Matters   123
Sterilization   125
Abortion   128

Chapter Six   The Social Context of Generating Life   134
Education in Sexual Morals for Teenagers and
    Adults   135
Homosexuality   139
Genetics   151
    The Theological Underpinnings of Issues in
      Genetics   151
    Genetic Screening and Counseling   152
    Gene Therapy and Genetic Engineering   161

Part Three   Matters at the End of Life   165

Chapter Seven   Preparing for Death   167
                Advance Directives for Health Care   168
                Material and Ethical Wills   172

Chapter Eight   The Process of Dying   176
                Suicide, Assisted Suicide, and Active
                    Euthanasia   176
                    The Medical and Legal Context of These
                        Questions in Our Day   176
                    Suicide   180
                    Assisted Suicide   183
                    The Contemporary Circumstances That Sully
                        Arguments for Euthanasia   186
                Letting One Die: Passive Euthanasia   198
                Effective Versus Beneficial Therapies:
                    Rules Versus Policies   202
                Removal of Artificial Nutrition and Hydration
                    from the Terminally Ill   208
                Removal of Nutrition and Hydration from
                    Those in a Persistent Vegetative State   213
                The Use of Animal or Artificial Organs
                    and Other Hazardous, Experimental
                    Therapies   217
                Hospice Care   218

Chapter Nine   After Death: Cremation, Autopsy, and
                Organ Donation   221
                Cremation   223
                Autopsies   224
                Organ Donation   225
                    Living Donors   226
                    Cadaveric Donors: The Permissibility of Using
                        the Body for Donation   226
                    Cadaveric Donors: Defining the Moment of
                        Death   228

Cadaveric Donors: The Issue of Ḥillul ha-
    Shem   229
Cadaveric Donors: Factors Impeding Jews'
    Willingness to Donate   230
Cadaveric Donors: Donating One's Body to
    Science   239

Part Four   The Communal Context of Medical
            Care   243

Chapter Ten   Preventing Illness   245
    Personal Measures to Prevent Illness   245
        Prevention in Preference to Cure   245
        Personal Measures to Preserve Health   246
        Personal Measures to Avoid Hazards to
            Health   249
    Communal Measures to Prevent Illness   252
        Social Steps to Preserve Health   252
        Social Measures to Avoid Health Hazards   254

Chapter Eleven   Linking Mind and Body   255
    Visiting the Sick   255
    Mental Health   264
    Tattooing and Body Piercing   267
        Tattoos   267
        Body Piercing   269
    Cosmetic Surgery   270
    The Disabled   272
        Disabled Newborn Infants   273
        Children and Adults with Disabilities   274
        Disabilities Late in Life   276

Chapter Twelve   Nonmedical Aspects of Medical Care   279
    The Distribution of Health Care   280
        Five Classical Criteria for Triage   282
        Applying These Principles: A Specific Case   291
    The Cost of Medical Care   299

Lessons from the Sources and Jewish Historical
Practice   299
A Contemporary Jewish Synthesis on Managed
Care   306
Medical Research: The Case of Cloning   310
Moral Issues   313
Theological Issues   318
Recommendations for Morally Guiding
Research   322
Epilogue: An Imperative to Choose Life   325
Notes   327
Appendix: The Philosophical Foundations of My Approach
to Bioethics   395
Religion and Morality   395
The Role of Religion in Making Moral
Decisions   395
The Relationship Between Religion and
Morality: Four Theories   396
The Contributions of Ethics to Religion   398
The Contributions of Judaism to Moral Theory
and Practice   400
Legal Versus Nonlegal Methods of Accessing the
Tradition   404
Rules Versus Principles and Policies   408
Balancing General Guidelines and Individual
Cases   411
Weighing the Applicability of Precedents   412
The Impact of the Reader   416
A Traditional, Dynamic Ethic for Our
Time   416
Notes to the Appendix   418
Bibliography   424
Index   443

Preface

JEWS LIKE TO THINK OF THE JEWISH TRADITION AS A WAY OF life. That phrase describes the all-encompassing nature of Judaism, with concepts, values, stories, and laws articulating a point of view on virtually everything, from the most trivial to the most sublime. Depicting Judaism as a way of life also conveys its ever-developing nature, for just as the conditions of human life continually change, so too do Jewish views and patterns of action.

In each age, however, Judaism must earn the compliment of being valued as a complete way of life by remaining relevant to new sensitivities and circumstances. In the service of attaining that end, Jews who know and love the tradition must ever be willing to stretch it to address the old problems that now appear in new guises and the completely new problems produced by changed contexts, moral awareness, and technologies. Rabbis and other learned Jews who refuse to expand the scope of Judaism in that way do a disservice to both Jews and Judaism; in the name of preserving the tradition that our ancestors have passed down to us, they make it irrelevant or, worse, morally blind and harmful.

On the other hand, Jews who ignore their tradition altogether or identify it with whatever they happen to think at the moment also do a disservice to both Jews and Judaism. After all, Jews throughout the ages have cherished their tradition—even died for it—because it has constituted a fount of wisdom for their lives, the road to holiness, and their understanding of the will of God. For individuals to identify it cavalierly with whatever they think is right is to abandon it for their own limited wisdom. A large part of the tradition's value is precisely that it is normative, that it challenges us to think and act in ways that we would not otherwise imagine.

The trick, then, is to find a way to balance tradition with change, to learn how to hone one's sense of judgment so as to be able to apply the tradition wisely to modern circumstances. Sometimes that means adhering to the ancient ideas and laws, even against modern trends; sometimes it means finding ways to apply traditional Jewish law or thought to new circumstances; and sometimes achieving a proper balance between tradition and modernity requires revising Jewish tradition to meet the demands or incorporate the advantages of new needs and circumstances. Deciding how to respond appropriately to specific issues is definitely not an easy process. Indeed, no individual can rightfully claim total wisdom or moral sensitivity; only God can. The best that we humans can do is to engage in serious discussions with others in order to refine our own thinking and practice. I personally consider myself fortunate in having the Conservative movement's community in general, and its Committee on Jewish Law and Standards in particular, as my fellow travelers in our mutual attempt to discern what is good and holy in life, what, to the best of our knowledge, God would have us do.

If the need to continually discover the proper balance between tradition and modernity is true for life in general, it is especially true for Jewish bioethics, the topic of this book. While many things have changed during the twentieth century, the way doctors practice medicine has undergone the most radical of changes. Questions about engendering and saving lives arise in ways today that our ancestors could not even imagine. This produces major problems of method, for how do you gain guidance from the tradition on questions it never contemplated? I state and address some of these issues in Chapter One, but due to the philosophical nature of these matters, I have reserved the more extensive discussion of them for the Appendix. Chapter Two then grounds the rest of the book in the fundamental Jewish concepts and values that affect all matters of bioethics.

After the two chapters of Part I, "Matters of Methods and Belief," I turn, in Part II, to moral issues at the beginning of life. I include discussions of generating pregnancy in infertile couples with their own gametes (Chapter Three) as well as with other people's genetic materials (Chapter Four), and, conversely, I discuss preventing pregnancy (Chapter Five).

One continuing theme of this book, however, is that these matters do not occur in isolation, apart from the conditions and pressures of life. It is, therefore, misleading and ultimately unhelpful to think of bioethics as if decisions were made by individuals or couples in the rarified context of the doctor's office; the problems they face, and the decisions they make, are very much influenced by what they have been taught to value, what they expect of themselves, what others expect of them, what they can afford, etc. In Chapter Six I address some of the social issues affecting the beginning of life, to return at greater length to the social aspects of health care in general in Part IV.

Part III addresses issues at the end of life — preparing for death (Chapter Seven), the process of dying (Chapter Eight), and medical procedures after death (Chapter Nine). If new technologies to generate pregnancy exert some pressure on infertile couples to try everything rather than acquiesce to their infertility, that type of pressure is even more in evidence at the end of life, where patients and their families must face the often excruciating decisions about when to withhold or withdraw treatment. In recent decades, we have come to realize all the more keenly that just because something *can* be done technologically does not necessarily mean that it *should* be done, and it takes honed skills of judgment and grounding in the values and concepts of a tradition like Judaism to make decisions about these matters wisely.

Finally, in Part IV, I address the communal context of health care. This includes preventing illness through both individual and communal measures (Chapter Ten); issues that arise from the linkage of mind and body (Chapter Eleven)—issues like the effects of visiting the sick, defining and treating mental health, tattooing and body piercing, cosmetic surgery, and our treatment of the disabled; and the distribution and cost of health care in modern times, when neither most individuals nor society as a whole can afford to supply everyone with everything that might be used beneficially (Chapter Twelve). In this age of costly medical procedures and small, nuclear families who often are scattered and sometimes broken, these soft issues in medical ethics—"soft" only in the sense that they do not deal directly with the treatment of the body—have become at least as significant as the "hard" issues of when to apply specific treatments.

This book, then, is my formulation of how Jewish law, morals, and concepts should be applied to current bioethical issues. It comes out of the distinctive approach most closely associated with the Conservative/Masorti movement in Judaism, in which Jewish law is understood to be binding but is to be interpreted and applied with the full weight of both traditional and modern scholarship in mind. This approach requires also that Jewish law be interpreted and applied with attention to moral, social, and economic concerns, just as the Rabbis who formed the tradition from the time of the Mishnah did. A reader may certainly disagree with my specific judgments, but the approach I am taking is authentic to the methods and sources of Judaism as it has developed historically. As such, from a theological point of view, this book represents one use of the procedure our ancestors have always employed to discern the will of God.

While many colleagues in the rabbinate, in medicine, and in law and many other good friends have helped me immeasurably over the years to learn about the issues treated in this book and to refine my thinking about them, I especially want to thank Doctors Brenda Fabe, Michael Grodin, Cappy Miles, Michael Nevins, and Neil Wenger, esteemed physicians and, in some cases, professors in medical schools; law professors Vicki

Michel and Arthur Rosett; the members of the Conservative Movement's Committee on Jewish Law and Standards, particularly the members of its Subcommittee on Bioethics during my tenure on that subcommittee now and in the past—namely, Rabbis Kassel Abelson, Amy Eilberg, David Feldman, Aaron Mackler, Avram Reisner, Joel Roth, and Elie Spitz; and ethicists Louis Newman and Judith Wilson Ross. As usual, none of the people mentioned here is responsible for any of the errors or judgments of my work, but they all have contributed immensely to my own thinking on these complicated issues, and they have my sincere appreciation as colleagues and as friends.

Finally, and most especially, I want to thank my wife, Marlynn, to whom this book is dedicated. Aside from tolerating my time spent reading, at conferences, on the telephone, and at the computer in the process of writing this book, she has helped me distinguish good arguments from bad in many areas of life, including a number treated here. I am writing this Preface in the week after we have read in the synagogue the opening chapters of Genesis, and so I am most mindful of the Torah's description of Eve as Adam's "fitting helper" (Genesis 2:18). Marlynn has certainly been that and much more—the sweet music and love of my life for these past thirty-six years.

Elliot N. Dorff
University of Judaism
Los Angeles, CA
October 30, 1997

Acknowledgments

M Y THINKING ABOUT BIOETHICS HAS SPANNED MANY
years. It is, therefore, not surprising that some of the
sections of this book have appeared in an earlier form
in various places. I would like to thank the sponsors and publishers of my work for their kindness in giving me the opportunity to develop my own thinking in these matters through exposure in their projects and publications and for their permission
to reprint some sections of the articles that they published.

Several of the chapters in this book are based on the rabbinic
rulings (*teshuvot,* or responsa) I wrote for the Conservative
Movement's Committee on Jewish Law and Standards—specifically, the chapters on techniques to overcome infertility, on end-
of-life matters, and on assisted suicide; and on the *Rabbinic
Letter on Intimate Relations* that I wrote with and for the Rabbinical Assembly's Commission on Human Sexuality—specifically, the section on the role of sex within marriage. I would like
to thank the Rabbinical Assembly for creating those forums, for
inviting me to participate in them, and for permission to reprint
parts of those materials that were subsequently published in the
journal, *Conservative Judaism,* and in the *Letter*—specifically,
from "A Jewish Approach to End-Stage Medical Care," *Conservative Judaism* 43:3 (Spring, 1991), pp. 3–51; "Artificial

Insemination, Egg Donation, and Adoption," *Conservative Judaism* 49:1 (Fall, 1996), pp. 3–60; and *"This Is My Beloved, This Is My Friend:" A Rabbinic Letter on Intimate Relations* (New York: Rabbinical Assembly, 1996), 64 pages. Much of that material has been rewritten or reformulated for purposes of this book, but what I have written here is largely based on the research I did for those assignments.

I would also like to thank the Park Ridge Center in Chicago for involving me in their projects on organ transplantation and euthanasia, for the tremendously enlightening conversations I had with the members of three of their research teams, and for permission to reprint parts of the articles I wrote as part of two of those teams. They appeared as "Assisted Death: A Jewish Perspective," in *Must We Suffer Our Way to Death? Cultural and Theological Perspectives on Death by Choice*, Ronald P. Hamel and Edwin R. Dubose, eds. (Dallas: Southern Methodist University Press, 1996), pp. 141–173; and as "Choosing Life: Aspects of Judaism Affecting Organ Transplantation," in *Organ Transplantation: Meanings and Realities*, Stuart J. Youngner, Renee C. Fox, and Laurence J. O'Connell, eds. (Madison: University of Wisconsin Press, 1996), pp. 168–193.

Part of the thinking in Chapter Twelve appeared in my article, "Paying for Medical Care: A Jewish View," *Kennedy Institute of Ethics Journal* 7:1 (Spring, 1997), pp. 15–30. Finally, part of my treatment of methodology in the Appendix appeared in its first form in "A Methodology for Jewish Medical Ethics," in *Jewish Law Association Studies VI: The Jerusalem 1990 Conference Volume*, B. S. Jackson and S. M. Passamaneck, eds. (Atlanta, GA: Scholars Press, 1992), pp. 35–57. These materials, too, have been largely reformulated in this volume, but I would like to thank these publishers for the opportunity to develop my thinking in these matters through their publications and for their permission to republish any sections that have remained the same.

Matters of Life and Death

PART ONE

Matters of Method and Belief

CHAPTER ONE

Consulting the Jewish Tradition for Moral Guidance

*The Revolution in Medical Science
and Its Moral Problems*

PUBLIC HEALTH AND MEDICINE HAVE MADE IMMENSE strides in the twentieth century. One measure of that is a simple one: in 1900, life expectancy in the United States for both men and women was approximately forty to forty-five years of age; now it is almost twice that. Most of that difference can be attributed to public health measures such as washing hands before meals, indoor plumbing, covered and treated sewage, vaccinations, and health education. Antibiotics account for another significant percentage of that increase. What we read about most—the latest forms of surgery and the newest drugs—are, statistically, only a tertiary source of our longevity, but they too have contributed.

Some of the preventive measures we use today are already documented in ancient and medieval Jewish sources. The Torah knows about the preventive significance of quarantine. The Talmud proclaims, as a general rule, that "physical cleanliness is conducive to spiritual purity," and the talmudic rabbi, Samuel, declares that "washing one's hands and feet in the morning is more effective [in securing health] than all the lotions in the world." Water left standing uncovered was considered unfit for human consumption, and water suspected of being contaminated had to be boiled before use. Maimonides teaches which foods are best eaten with which, and he cautions that one should not eat too much in the first place and that one should exercise—advice with a remarkably modern ring![1]

Curative medicine before the twentieth century, however, was much less effective. Though usually unhelpful, bloodletting was a technique commonly in use. Surgery was attempted when a leg had turned gangrenous or a fetus had to be delivered by Caesarian section. Since antibiotics were not known, though, the patient often died from infections in the open surgical wound, if not from the surgery itself. Set against this background, the advances in curative medicine in this century must be regarded as nothing short of revolutionary.

With new capabilities, however, come new moral problems. When one *cannot* do something, there is no moral question of whether one *should*. When one *can* do something, however, then whether one *should* do it is often not only an apt question but a critical one. Thus our new abilities to save and sustain life or alter its conditions raise concomitant questions about when and how we should do so.

It is for this reason that bioethics has become a significant concern in our day, not only for physicians and hospitals but for government, employers, and indeed everyone. As a result of the advance of medicine, many decisions must be made: by individuals for their own health care; by businesses and insurance companies regarding whom and what they will cover and at what cost; and ultimately by government, which must decide whether health care is a right for all citizens (and perhaps noncitizens too) that constitutes part of the government's mandate "to provide for the general welfare," or whether it is a privilege that individuals may use if, and only if, they can afford it. In other words, in addition to the "micro" issues in contemporary bioethics—that is, those that affect disease prevention, treatment, and care of the individual—there are also many "macro" issues—namely, the social aspects of health care, including its distribution, extent, and cost.

In making these decisions, people look to several sources of authority for guidance. For micro issues, most will seek the advice of their family physician and, if necessary, specialists. Some will also consult summaries of research or speak to others who have faced the same decisions.

Decisions on the macro level require expertise not only in medicine but in economics, social work, social planning, public policy, and politics. Before a rational decision can be made in planning health care for the present and future, experts in these fields must determine costs of alternative therapies, their effectiveness, and the relative difficulty of making them accessible. So, for example, even though a given procedure is medically ideal for curing a given malady, it may be ultimately considered much less than ideal if it is prohibitively expensive or if it can be delivered only in highly sophisticated hospital settings. Similarly, research probing the effectiveness of given procedures ("outcomes research"), very little of which is done now, will increasingly become a necessity, not only to cure patients more effectively but also to keep costs down.

Assumptions of this Book

The very subject of this book, *Jewish* medical ethics, assumes that Judaism can guide us in moral questions generally and questions of medical ethics in particular. That is not an obvious assumption, for religion has nothing to contribute to some issues (for example, which baseball team to root for, or which economic policy will best balance growth with inflation); and religion has sometimes led people to commit totally immoral acts (for example, Yigal Amir's assassination of Prime Minister Rabin or the medieval Catholic Church's Inquisition). Implementing Jewish medical ethics thus calls for an examination of the various interactions between religion and morality to demonstrate how religion can nevertheless contribute to morality.

Furthermore, the Jewish tradition places great trust in resolving moral dilemmas through legal methods. Some contemporary Jews, as a result, depend solely on Jewish law to make their moral decisions. Others, however, ignore Jewish law entirely, thinking it too far removed from modern perspectives and circumstances to be helpful and believing that in any case, in a modern, free society it has ceased to be law in any meaningful sense. This book assumes that moral issues *can* be profitably treated by using Jewish law, but only if the law is applied intelligently—that is, with attention to the difference between principles and policies, the nuances of specific cases, the historical development in the meaning of legal texts, and the impact of the reader in discerning their meaning and applicability—as well as with constant and full recognition of Judaism's moral and religious purposes.

These are critical matters, for the way in which one understands and applies the tradition will often determine the outcome. In fact, this book differs fundamentally from Orthodox and Reform treatments of the same issues on the basis of the ways in which it perceives the relationship between religion and morality and the methods it uses to interpret the tradition and thereby apply it to modern circumstances.

Discussing how and why to understand the tradition in one way as opposed to others, however, is highly philosophical and does not directly address the concrete bioethical issues explored in this book. For these reasons, such questions are briefly treated in the Appendix for the benefit of those readers interested in the theoretical basis for this approach. All others are invited to proceed directly to the heart of the book.

Readers are urged, however, to try their hand at the material in the Appendix. The arguments there, after all, form the logical foundation for the rest of the book. Although logic demands that we first describe the assumptions and methods that underlie and inform all of our specific examples—that is, that we go from the general to the particular—concrete examples often enable us to understand the general discussion of principles and methods. Readers not accustomed to philosophy, then, may find the arguments in the Appendix easier to understand once they have seen the methodology applied to particular issues throughout the book. Moreover, I want to argue not only for my specific decisions on particular issues but also for a general approach to these matters that can enable us all to probe and apply the tradition authentically, intelligently, and wisely.

The Impact of the Reader

There is one matter of method, though, that must be addressed here. Recent theorists of literature and law have increasingly pointed out the role of the reader in identifying the meaning of a text. Radical deconstructionists have even suggested that a text does not control meaning at all but rather that the meaning of a text is totally and exclusively what the reader wants it to mean. More moderate—and, I think, more accurate—understandings of this process draw attention to the crucial impact of the reader's background and goals in his or her understanding of a text but also acknowledge the role of the text in evoking and delimiting that meaning. Thus any given literary interpretation is generally and properly subject to critical evaluation based upon the degree to which it preserves the language, context, thrust, and apparent purpose of the text.

Legal texts are no different. Karl Llewellyn was probably the first to demonstrate the elasticity of legal texts and the corresponding effect of the reader in determining their meaning, and Ronald Dworkin and others have expanded on this point in recent times.[2] Ultimately, in legal texts as in others, what readers bring to the text is crucial in defining its meaning for them—at least as crucial as the text itself.

Lewis Newman has astutely and correctly applied these considerations to Jewish medical ethics. Acknowledging the critical role of the reader, he argues for semantic, methodological, and conceptual adjustments in contemporary Jewish bioethics.

Semantically, we should not, according to Newman, talk about what "Judaism" teaches on these matters, but rather what we, given our particular interpretive assumptions and our particular way of construing the coherence of the tradition as a whole, find within the traditional sources. That is, each rabbi can only offer *a* Jewish position, not *the* Jewish stance.

Methodologically, proponents of any given Jewish position must not simply state their reading of the tradition but must argue for it against other possible readings and, more broadly, describe how their ruling on a given issue fits into their own view of the tradition as a whole. They must, in the language of American jurisprudence, present "a *reasoned* opinion," not just an opinion.

Conceptually, Jewish bioethicists who adopt a legal mode must reflect greater knowledge and understanding of contemporary theories of legal reasoning and judicial interpretation. On the other hand, those who choose a nonlegal methodology should explain why; should demonstrate awareness of other modes in medical ethics; and, I would add, should articulate how their approach is identifiably Jewish.[3]

Only when these elements affecting any decision in Jewish medical ethics are made manifest can one fully understand the role that moral sensitivities can and should play in arriving at a ruling. Reform writers often speak as if contemporary moral sensitivities should replace traditional Jewish legal sources in shaping current policy. At best, they maintain, classical texts should be cited to reinforce what the writer thinks best on independent grounds. Orthodox rabbis, on the other hand, generally refuse to admit contemporary moral sensitivities as an independent source of authority; they deem authoritative only that which somehow can be deduced from the classical texts. Even those few Orthodox writers who openly speak about a moral component in halakhic decision making do so defensively, trying to justify why such components are legitimately considered.[4] Authors affiliated with the Conservative movement have been much more aggressive than their Orthodox colleagues in asserting a major role for ethical concerns, but unlike their Reform counterparts, Conservative rabbis use moral values as an integral part of the Jewish *legal* process by which contemporary decisions should be made.[5]

As a Conservative rabbi, I suppose it is no accident that I embrace this last approach,[6] but I would also argue that contemporary literary and legal theory can augment the usual arguments in favor of it. For it is not only that rabbis over the centuries have shaped the tradition with a conscious eye toward making it meet the highest moral standards; it is also that *any* reading of a text will involve the values and concerns of the reader. Thus moral considerations are quite properly part of the process of making decisions in contemporary Jewish law. We, as the interpreters of our tradition, have been taught by it to strive for the right and the good; and our understanding of what that means, although surely influenced by our tradition, is not exclusively shaped by it. We also bring our own contexts, with their inherent complexities, to our understanding of classical Jewish texts, and so our interpretation of those texts will inevitably—and properly—reflect those contexts and thus possibly differ from the readings of our ancestors. The point is that in reading our own concerns and our own moral sensitivities into the texts, we are no different from our ancestors; this is how texts must and should be read.

The Purpose of this Book

This book, then, like any other, is the product of its author's particular reading of the materials presented and his judgment of how best to apply them to contemporary circumstances. I speak, though, as a Conservative rabbi, one who has served for over a decade as a member of the Conservative movement's Committee on Jewish Law and Standards and is currently vice chair of that committee. Significant portions of the material in this book—specifically, the chapters on using donor gametes to generate life, on end-of-life issues, and on the distribution of health care—are based on responsa that I wrote for the committee and that were approved by it as a valid stance within the Conservative movement. Other parts of the book articulate positions that were approved by the committee based on responsa by other Conservative rabbis (for example, on abortion and on tattooing and body piercing). On one topic, homosexuality, I wish to state explicitly that the book articulates my own view and that it is, at least as of this writing, a minority view within the Conservative rabbinate. The rest of the book, I honestly think, represents views widely held among Conservative rabbis, even if they are expressed here for the first time. Nevertheless, while a number of the positions represented here have been officially validated by the Conservative movement's Committee on Jewish Law and Standards, the book as a whole does not represent the official views of the Conservative movement.

I am writing, however, not simply as an individual Jew, nor merely as an individual rabbi, but specifically as a Conservative rabbi with a doctorate in secular ethical theory who has spent the better part of his life integrating the worlds of Judaism and philosophy, with special emphasis on ethics. The judgments made in this book, then, are intended to be normative judgments, ways in which I believe Jews *should* live out their Jewish commitments in these matters.

In a free, pluralistic society, each person, of course, is at liberty to make his or her own moral choices, and the same freedom applies to the way in which Jews may practice their Judaism. The normativity with which I write, then, is surely not that of rules that can be enforced by the police. My judgments are normative rather in another sense. Their authority for people other than myself comes from the fact that I am basing my positions on the Jewish tradition and that I am putting forward arguments as to how I think that tradition should be read.

The Jewish tradition consists of many things: law and lore; peoplehood and history; music, art, and dance; Hebrew and attachment to Zion; ethnic patterns of behavior; and memories, associations, and hopes. We also look to the Jewish tradition, however, for moral guidance. This book, which takes a number of stands on Jewish bioethics, seeks to provide that guidance in this area of concern.

As Louis Newman correctly says, however, any reading of the tradition will be *a* possible interpretation, and thus every reading must provide its *reasons* for interpreting and applying the tradition as it does. Since I base my reading on traditional texts, and since I explain how I interpret them and why I think my reading is appropriate and better than other possible understandings, Jews, I dare say, should take these arguments seriously. People may surely disagree with me, but the burden of proof is on those who do to show why their reading of the tradition is reasonably identified as a Jewish interpretation and why it is more compelling than mine from the perspective of Judaism and/or morality. The authority of the moral judgments in this book, then, stems from the inherent cogency of its arguments and, for Jews, from their ties to the Jewish heritage. For I seek to articulate nothing less than what I take to be the import of Judaism for critical decisions in our lives.

CHAPTER TWO

Fundamental Beliefs Underlying Jewish Medical Ethics

JUDAISM IS NOT A DEDUCTIVE, PHILOSOPHICAL SYSTEM; IT is rather a religious civilization that developed over time. As a result, it has all of the logically haphazard pushes and pulls typical of historical growth. One cannot point to a clear statement of Jewish beliefs regarding health care that was formulated and adopted by some authoritative body at some time in Jewish history and has governed all decisions since. The tradition just does not work that way.

At the same time, with all of its diversity, Judaism embodies a coherent worldview that is markedly different, in kind and/or degree, from secular and other religious ways of understanding life and of acting in it. These beliefs directly and profoundly affect what rabbis have to say on specific issues in health care, sometimes explicitly and sometimes implicitly.

It is important at the outset, then, to articulate some fundamental Jewish beliefs relevant to health care so that the individual bioethical decisions described in the rest of this book may be intelligible in the context of Judaism's broader convictions. Because Judaism lacks an official formulation of such tenets, I have created this list myself, but I will quote a number of statements within the tradition or cite them in the endnotes to indicate that these are, indeed, Jewish affirmations. In the chapters that follow, I will then spell out what these beliefs imply about the moral issues involved in health care.

The Body Belongs to God

For Judaism, God owns everything, including our bodies.[1] God lends our bodies to us for the duration of our lives, and we return them to God when we die. Consequently, neither men nor women have the right to govern their bodies as they will; since God created our bodies and owns them, God can and does assert the right to restrict how we use our bodies according to the rules articulated in Jewish law.

One set of these rules requires us to take reasonable care of our bodies. Just as we would be obliged to take reasonable care of an apartment on loan to us, so too we have the duty to take care of our own bodies. Rules of good hygiene, sleep, exercise, and diet are not just words to the wise designed for our comfort and longevity but rather commanded acts that we owe God. So, for example, Hillel regards bathing as a commandment (mitzvah), and Maimonides includes directives for good health in his code of law, considering them just as obligatory as other positive duties like caring for the poor.[2]

Ultimately, Jews have the duty to preserve their own lives (pikuaḥ nefesh). When interpreting Leviticus 18:5, which says that we should obey God's commandments "and live by them," the rabbis deduce that this means that we should not die as a result of observing them. This tenet is so deeply embedded in Jewish law that, according to the rabbis, it takes precedence over all other commandments except murder, idolatry, and incestuous or adulterous sexual intercourse. That is, if someone's choice is to murder someone else or give up one's own life, one must give up one's own life. So, for example, if someone were to force Jews to bow down to idols, as did the Greek king, Antiochus, in the Hanukkah story, they must choose instead to give up their lives; and the same choice would be required if Jews were forced to commit acts of incest or adultery, as they were by the Nazis (although rabbis living in the death camps found ways retroactively to excuse women who were raped by the Nazis on the grounds that these women were not even given the choice of dying instead).

If, however, Jews need to violate Sabbath laws or steal something to save their own lives or the life of someone else, then they are not only permitted but *commanded* to violate the laws in question to save that human life. In fact, Maimonides specifies that even if the emergency requires violations of other commandments, the rabbi and other leaders of the community should not get non-Jews or less well educated Jews to take care of it; they should tend to it themselves, for saving a life is the most sacred of obligations. If, in the process of responding to such an emergency, the rescuers stole something (that is, if they violated a law regarding the relationships between one person and another), they would have to restore the lost object or its equivalent when the emergency had passed and they could safely compensate the owner; but there would be no culpability, and therefore none of the usual fines involved, if they had stolen in a medical emergency for the purpose of saving a life. If they violated the Sabbath (that is, if they violated a law governing the relationship between Jews and God), God would forgive the transgression, for, as the rabbis say, "better that he [the victim] should violate one Sabbath so that he can observe many Sabbaths [once his life has been saved]"—and the same excuse applies to those who act on his behalf.[3]

Jews are commanded not only to do virtually anything necessary to save their own lives; they are also bound by the positive obligation to take steps to save the lives of others. The imperative to do so is derived from the biblical command, "Do not stand idly by the blood of your neighbor" (Leviticus 19:16). This means, to take the Talmud's example, that if you see someone drowning, you may not ignore him or her but must do what you can to save the person's life.[4]

What happens, though, when you can only save your life *or* someone else's? Whose life takes precedence? The Talmud[5] tells the story of two men in a desert who discover that they have enough water for only one of them to reach civilization alive. Should they divide the water between them, acting on the principle of human equality, even though they know that then both of them will die? Should the decision be made on the basis of property rights, so that whoever owns the water should claim it (and if they own it jointly, they should divide it accordingly)? Or should the matter remain at its status quo position, so that whoever has possession of the water when they discover the shortage should retain it?

The opinion that ultimately wins the day in Jewish legal literature is that of Rabbi Akiba, who takes the last of these positions. He argues on the basis of textual analysis and moral concerns. The Torah says that one should not exact interest from a fellow Jew "so that your brother may live with you" (Leviticus 25:36). That requires, though, that you must be alive before you care for your brother, for otherwise he cannot possibly live *with you*. Consequently, according to Rabbi Akiba, "your life takes precedence *(ḥayyekha kodemim)*."

On a moral plane, this means that the two people should leave the water with whoever has it at the time they discover their shortage, for to do otherwise would involve both in either suicide or murder. One or both of them may die if they follow Rabbi Akiba's ruling too, but at least it will be nature that determined this outcome rather than their voluntary choice. In other words, in morally impossible circumstances that will produce an untoward result no matter what one does, Rabbi Akiba directs us to remain passive and let nature take its course so that we are at least not morally responsible for the outcome.

In the course of this discussion, then, the principle is established that your life takes precedence. In the case of the drowning person, therefore, you must not immediately jump into the water to save him or her; indeed, unless you are trained as a lifesaver, you must not do so. You should instead seek the help of others or do what you can from the shore. Even if you have lifesaver training, Red Cross lifesaving procedures demand that you stay out of the water if you can save the person's life by doing so—for example, by throwing a rope to a conscious and nearby victim and pulling him or her in—and thereby refrain from endangering your own life, and Jewish law would concur. Protecting your own life comes first.

Just as we are commanded to maintain good health, so we are obligated to avoid danger and injury.[6] Indeed, Jewish law views endangering one's health as worse than violating a ritual prohibition.[7] So, for example, anyone who can survive only by taking charity but refuses to do so out of pride is, according to the tradition, shedding his or her own blood and is thus guilty of a mortal offense.[8] Similarly, Conservative, Reform, and some Orthodox authorities have prohibited smoking as an unacceptable risk to our God-owned bodies.[9]

Judaism also teaches that human beings do not have the right to dispose of their bodies at will (that is, commit suicide), for to do so would totally obliterate something that belongs not to us but to God.[10] In contrast, the laws of most American states permit suicide but prohibit aiding and abetting a suicide.[11] In secular terms, it is frankly difficult to construct a cogent argument that it is in the state's interest to prohibit suicide, especially if the person is not leaving dependents behind. Indeed, even though the U.S. Supreme Court ultimately overruled their decision, two federal appellate courts recently voided such state statutes, holding that mentally competent, terminally ill patients have the constitutional right to use the services of physicians and "others whose services are essential to help the terminally ill patient obtain and take" medication to assist them in dying.[12] In Judaism, however, the theoretical basis for this prohibition is clear: we do not have the right to destroy what is not ours.[13]

Human Worth Stems from Being Created in God's Image

In marked contrast to this Jewish position, the American way of thinking is thoroughly pragmatic: a person's value is a function of what that person can *do* for others. It is this view, so deeply ingrained in American culture, that prompts Americans to value those who have unusual abilities, who *succeed*—and, conversely, to devalue those who are disabled in some way, even to the extent of questioning whether someone with severe disabilities should continue to live. Such utilitarian criteria for judging the value of a given person's life are often embedded in "quality of life" discussions in America, not only when others are making the judgment but even when the disabled person is doing so.

In sharp contrast, the Torah declares that God created each of us in the divine image: "God created the human being in His image, in the image of God He created him; male and female God created them."[14] Exactly which feature of the human being reflects this divine image is a matter of debate within the tradition. The Torah itself seems to tie it to humanity's ability to make moral judgments, that is, to distinguish good from bad and right from wrong, to behave accordingly, and to judge one's own actions and those of others on the basis of this moral knowledge.[15] Another human faculty connected by the Torah and by the later tradition to divinity is the ability to speak.[16] Maimonides claims that the divine image resides in our capacity to think, especially discursively.[17] Locating the divine image within us may also be the Torah's way of acknowledging that we can love, just as God does,[18] or that we are at least partially spiritual and thus share God's spiritual nature.[19]

Not only does this doctrine *describe* aspects of our nature; it also *prescribes* behavior founded on moral imperatives. Specifically, because human beings are created in God's image, we affront God when we insult another person.[20] More broadly, we must recognize each individual's uniqueness and divine worth because all human beings embody the image of God:

> For this reason Adam was created as a single person, to teach you that anyone who destroys one soul is described in Scripture as if he destroyed an entire world, and anyone who sustains one soul is described in Scripture as if he sustained an entire world . . . . And to declare the greatness of the Holy One, praised be He, for a person uses a mold to cast a number of coins, and they are all similar to each other, while the Sovereign of all sovereigns, the Holy One, praised be He, cast each person in the mold of the first human being and none of them is similar to any other. Therefore each and every person must say: "For me the world was created."[21]

Consider also the traditional blessing to be recited when seeing someone with a disability: "Praised are you, Lord our God, *me-*

shaneh ha-briyyot," "who makes different creatures," or "who created us different." Precisely when we might recoil from a deformed or incapacitated person, or thank God for not making us like that, the tradition instead bids us to embrace the divine image in such people, indeed to bless God for creating some of us so.[22] Treating others as images of God thus has significant moral implications.

The Human Being Is an Integrated Whole

Western philosophical thought and Christianity have been heavily influenced by the Greek and Gnostic bifurcation of body and mind (or soul). In these systems of thought the body is seen as the inferior part of human beings—either because it is what we share with animals, in contrast to the distinctively human mind (Aristotle) or because the body is the seat of our passions and hence our sins (Paul in Romans and Galatians[23])—whereas the soul can be saved. Even though the Greeks glorified the body in their art and sculpture, it was only because developing the body was seen as a means to an end, a necessary prerequisite to cultivating the mind (as, for example, in Plato's pedagogic program in *The Republic*). Similarly, Paul regarded the body as "the temple of the Holy Spirit,"[24] but only because it serves to sustain the soul so that it can accept faith in Jesus; the body per se, he believed, "makes me a prisoner of that law of sin which lives inside my body."[25]

The views articulated in Western and Christian classics have shaped these traditions from ancient times to our own. In Christianity, Augustine, Luther, and Calvin, following the lead of Paul, all maintain that the body's needs are to be suppressed as much as possible; indeed, asceticism has been a recurring theme in Christian history. In secular philosophic thought, "the mind-body problem" (how is it that the two, presumed to be so obviously different and separate, are related in some ways to each other?) continues to be a "stock" issue in philosophic literature.

Since Jews in ancient and medieval times lived among, and interacted with, Greeks, Romans, Gnostics, and Christians, Judaism was inevitably influenced rather heavily by these conceptions. Two of the most prominent Jewish thinkers to reflect these influences are Philo, a Jew writing in first-century Alexandria— a city avidly pursuing Greek thought—and Maimonides, a twelfth-century Jewish philosopher who effectively translated Aristotle into Jewish terms. Such Jewish thinkers echo the widespread Greek and Christian notions that the soul is divine and the body animal; Philo even calls the body the "prison house" of the soul, as do many of his Hellenistic contemporaries in Alexandria. Philo and Maimonides also draw some of the same moral conclusions as their non-Jewish counterparts, defining the ideal person as one who cultivates the soul and abstains from the pleasures of the body as much as possible.[26]

Biblical and talmudic literature, however, do not share in this understanding of the human being. The Bible speaks of a person's *nefesh,* which translators often render as "soul" but which actually has many meanings (including bodily parts like the throat). Even when the word specifically refers to the inner being, it stands in contrast not to a person's body but to his or her identity within the outside world. In this sense, the relevant correlatives in the pair are *shem*—that is, a person's name, or public identity within the community—and *nefesh,* his or her inner being, self-identity, private thoughts, and so on. Another Hebrew term often translated as "soul" is *neshamah,* which in its narrowest meaning denotes "breath" but more broadly means one's inner being, roughly equivalent to *nefesh.*

According to the Talmud and Midrash, our souls are, in some senses, separable from our bodies. For example, when the Torah describes God as breathing life into Adam's body, rabbinic sources understand the text to mean not only physical life but also consciousness. God repeats that process each day when taking our souls away during sleep and returning them to us again when we awake. Moreover, at death the soul leaves the body— only to be united with it again at the time of resurrection. So, for example:

> Our Rabbis taught: There are three partners in [the creation of] a person: the Holy One, blessed be He; his father; and his mother. His

father supplies the source of the white substance [probably because semen is white] out of which are formed [white things like] the child's bones, sinews, nails, the brain in his head, and the white in his eye. His mother supplies the source of the red substance [probably because menstrual blood is red] out of which are formed his skin, flesh, hair, blood, and the black of his eye. And the Holy One, blessed be He, gives him breath [ruah] and spirit [neshamah], beauty of features, eyesight, the power of hearing, the ability to speak and to walk, understanding, and discernment. When his time to depart from the world approaches, the Holy One, blessed be He, takes away His share and leaves the shares of his father and mother.[27]

Similarly, when the following morning prayer, "Elohai neshamah," thanks God for returning us to life after death, it is equating sleep with death and the return to consciousness with the renewal of life within "dead corpses" (the Hebrew words are deliberately redundant):

My God, the life-breath (soul; Hebrew, neshamah) You have given me is pure. You created it, You fashioned it, You breathed it into me, You preserve it within me [that is, You keep my body and soul together], and one day You will take it from me and return it to me in the future that is to come [after death]. So long as this life-breath is in me I thank You, Lord, my God, and God of my ancestors, Ruler of all creation, and Sovereign of all life-breaths (souls). Praised are You, Lord, who returns life-breaths to dead corpses.[28]

Rabbinic sources conflict, however, as to whether the soul can exist apart from the body, and even those who say it can depict the soul in physical terms, capable of performing many of the functions of the body.[29]

In any case, in sharp contrast to the Greek and Christian traditions, classical rabbinic sources maintain that the soul is definitely not superior to the body. Indeed, one rabbinic source speaks of the soul as a guest in the body here on earth: one's host must accordingly be respected and well treated.[30]

Moreover, since the rabbis regarded the human being as an integrated whole, the body and the soul are to be judged as one:

Antoninus said to Rabbi [Judah, the president, or "prince," of the Sanhedrin], "The body and soul could exonerate themselves from judgment. How is this so? The body could say, 'The soul sinned, for from the day that it separated from me, lo, I am like a silent stone in the grave!' And the soul could say, 'The body is the sinner, for from the day that I separated from it, lo, I fly like a bird.'"

Rabbi [Judah] answered him, "I will tell you a parable. What is the matter like? It is like a king of flesh and blood who had a beautiful orchard, and there were in it lovely ripe fruit. He placed two guardians over it, one a cripple and the other blind. Said the cripple to the blind man, 'I see beautiful ripe fruit in the orchard. Come and carry me, and we will bring and eat them.' The cripple rode on the back of the blind man and they brought and ate them. After a while the owner of the orchard came and said to them, 'Where is my lovely fruit?' The cripple answered, 'Do I have legs to go?' The blind man answered, 'Do I have eyes to see?' What did the owner do? He placed the cripple on the back of the blind man and judged them as one. So also the Holy Blessed One brings the soul and throws it into the body and judges them as one.[31]

Not only is this fundamental integration manifest in God's ultimate, divine judgment of each of us; it is also the rabbinic recipe for life. Although the rabbis emphasized the importance of studying and following the Torah, even placing it on a par with all of the rest of the commandments,[32] they nevertheless believed that the life of the soul or mind by itself is not good, that it can, indeed, be the source of sin:

An excellent thing is the study of Torah combined with some worldly occupation, for the labor demanded by both of them causes sinful inclinations to be forgotten. All study of Torah without work must, in the end, be futile and become the cause of sin.[33]

Thus, while the rabbis considered it a privilege to be able to study Torah, they themselves—or at least most of them—earned their livelihood through bodily work, and they also valued the hard labor of the field worker who spends little time in the study of Torah:

A favorite saying of the rabbis of Yavneh was: I am God's creature, and my fellow [who works in the field and is not a student] is God's creature. My work is in the town, and his work is in the country. I rise early for my work, and he rises early for his work. Just as he does not presume to do my work, so I do not presume to do his work. Will you say, I do much [in the study of Torah] and he does little? We have learned: One may do much or one may do little; it is all one, provided that the person directs his heart to Heaven.[34]

The Body Is Morally Neutral and Potentially Good

The body is neither bad nor good. Rather, its energies, like those of our other faculties, are morally neutral. But they can and should be used for divine purposes as defined by Jewish law and tradition. Within these constraints, the body's pleasures are God-given and are not to be shunned, for to do so would be an act of ingratitude toward our Creator. The body, in other words, can and should give us pleasure to the extent that such pleasure enables us to live a life of holiness.

Here Judaism differs markedly from both the American secular view of the body on the one hand and Christianity on the other. In the American media, the body is often portrayed as a virtual pleasure machine. In contemporary films, commercials, and music, we are encouraged to derive as much pleasure as possible from the body, that being its primary purpose. The only restriction inherent in this ethic is that *I* may not deprive *you* of pleasure in the process of getting it for myself. Yet even this limitation is not absolute. Characters in American popular culture, such as Rambo, are "cool" precisely because they do not care about how they injure others. In contrast, Judaism teaches that the body's pleasures are indeed to be enjoyed, but only when experienced within the framework of holiness delineated by Jewish law and theology.

At the other end of the spectrum is Christianity, which depicts the body as a negative part of us to be suppressed as much as possible. Thus in Catholic and many Protestant sources, the ideal Christian is the ascetic, who eschews the pleasures of sex, food, and possessions as much as possible. Of course, not all forms of contemporary Christianity embrace this ascetic way of thinking in its entirety, but Roman Catholicism, by far the most populous Christian faith, still does, and to some degree so do many Protestant sects.

The closest Jewish parallel to this attitude are the rules governing Yom Kippur and historical fast days like Tisha b'Av, on which we are to "afflict our souls" through fasting, sexual abstinence, and other forms of physical self-denial. But in each case such abstinence is restricted to that day alone and is designed to call attention to the spiritual theme of the day; deprivation itself is not expected to effect atonement or historical memory. In fact, if a person's life is endangered by fasting, the law not only permits but *requires* him or her to refrain from fasting and to take appropriate measures to ensure life and health.[35]

As Jews, therefore, we attain holiness not by enduring pain but rather by using all of our faculties, including our bodily energies, to perform God's commandments. For example, though we eat, as all animals do, our eating takes on a divine dimension when we observe Jewish dietary restrictions and surround our meals with the appropriate blessings. Some bodily pleasures are even commanded. Thus we may not fast on the Sabbath (with the exception of Yom Kippur), and we must eat three meals to celebrate it. We should also bathe and wear clean clothes in honor of the day.[36] Sexual intercourse in marriage is commanded not only for purposes of propagation but also to enhance the spouses' mutual enjoyment.[37] Marital union thus simultaneously produces the next generation and strengthens the couple's bond to each other, a benefit not only for the couple but also for their children, for partners in a strong marriage are more likely to have the emotional strength needed to nurture and educate their children, both emotionally and Jewishly.

According to the rabbis, it is actually a sin to deny ourselves the pleasures that God's law allows. Just as the Nazirite was to bring a sin-offering after denying himself the permitted delight of wine, so will we be called to account in the world to come for the ingratitude and haughtiness involved in denying ourselves the pleasures that God has provided.[38]

According to Maimonides, bodily pleasures are most appropriately enjoyed when we have the specific intent to enhance our ability to do God's will:

> He who regulates his life in accordance with the laws of medicine with the sole motive of maintaining a sound and vigorous physique and begetting children to do his work and labor for his benefit is not following the right course. A man should aim to maintain physical health and vigor in order that his soul may be upright, in a condition to know God . . . . Whoever throughout his life follows this course will be continually serving God, even while engaged in business and even during cohabitation, because his purpose in all that he does will be to satisfy his needs so as to have a sound body with which to serve God. Even when he sleeps and seeks repose to calm his mind and rest his body so as not to fall sick and be incapacitated from serving God, his sleep is service of the Almighty.[39]

The medical implications of this teaching are clear. We have the obligation to maintain our health not only to care for God's property but also so that we can accomplish our purpose in life, namely, to live a life of holiness. Moreover, since pain is not a way to attain holiness, it is our duty to relieve it.

Jews Have a Mandate and Duty to Heal

Because God owns our bodies, we are required to help other people escape sickness, injury, and death.[40] We are to do so not out of some general (and vague) humanitarian motivation or anticipation of reciprocity. Nor are physicians obliged to heal the sick to honor a special oath they take, to pay back the society that trained them, or to fulfill a contractual promise that they make in return for remuneration. Rather, we have a universal duty to heal others because we are all under the divine imperative to help God preserve and protect what is God's.

This is neither the only possible nor the most obvious conclusion to be derived from the Bible. Since the Torah says, on the one hand, that illness is one of the divine punishments for disobedience and since, on the other, God announces Himself as our healer in many places in the Bible,[41] we might conclude that medicine is an improper human intervention in God's decision to cause illness or cure it, indeed, an act of human hubris.

Although the rabbis were aware of this line of reasoning, they counteracted it by pointing out that God Himself authorizes us to heal. In fact, they maintained that God requires us to do so, basing their assertion on two biblical verses: Exodus 21:19–20, according to which an assailant must ensure that his victim is "thoroughly healed," and Deuteronomy 22:2 ("And you shall restore the lost property to him"). The Rabbis understand the Exodus verse as giving *permission* for the physician to cure. (They further argue that the command to "love your neighbor as yourself" in Leviticus 19:18 even permits curative measures that require inflicting a wound in the process.) On the basis of an extra letter in the Hebrew text of the Deuteronomy passage, the Talmud declares that this verse imposes the *obligation* to restore another person's body as well as his or her property, and hence to come to the aid of someone else in a life-threatening situation.[42] That obligation also stems, as indicated earlier, from Leviticus 19:16, "Do not stand idly by the blood of your neighbor."

Yet even though each Jew is obligated to come to the aid of a person in distress and assailants are obligated to cure their victims, Jewish law also recognized that medical expertise was usually necessary in such cases. Thus here, as in other similar cases, laypeople are permitted to hire an expert to carry out their obligations. The Talmud acknowledges the limited expertise of physicians of its time (even declaring, "The best of physicians deserves to go to hell!"), and some later Jewish authorities were particularly wary of physicians' abilities to practice internal medicine (in contrast to surgery and healing external wounds and diseases); but the Talmud nevertheless prohibits Jews from living in a community in which there is no physician. This returns us to the first principle described above, for only if a physician is available to care for our bodies can we carry out our duty to preserve that part of God's property.[43]

Medical experts, in turn, have special obligations because of their expertise. Thus Rabbi Joseph Caro (1488–1575), the author of one of the most important Jewish codes, the *Shulḥan Arukh*, teaches:

> The Torah gave permission to the physician to heal; moreover, this is a religious precept and is included in the category of saving life, and if the physician withholds his services, it is considered as shedding blood.[44]

The following rabbinic story, though acknowledging the theological challenges involved in medical care, clearly affirms that the physician's work is legitimate and, in fact, obligatory:

> It once happened that Rabbi Ishmael and Rabbi Akiba were strolling in the streets of Jerusalem accompanied by another person. They were met by a sick person. He said to them, "My masters, tell me by what means I may be cured." They told him, "Do thus and so until you are cured." The sick man asked them, "And who afflicted me?" They replied, "The Holy One, blessed be He." The sick man responded, "You have entered into a matter which does not pertain to you. God has afflicted, and you seek to cure! Are you not transgressing His will?"
>
> Rabbi Akiba and Rabbi Ishmael asked him, "What is your occupation?" The sick man answered, "I am a tiller of the soil, and here is the sickle in my hand." They asked him, "Who created the vineyard?" "The Holy One, blessed be He," he answered. Rabbi Akiba and Rabbi Ishmael said to him, "You enter into a matter which does not pertain to you! God created the vineyard, and you cut fruits from it."
>
> He said to them, "Do you not see the sickle in my hand? If I did not plow, sow, fertilize, and weed, nothing would sprout."
>
> Rabbi Akiba and Rabbi Ishmael said to him, "Foolish man! . . . Just as if one does not weed, fertilize, and plow, the trees will not produce fruit, and if fruit is produced but is not watered or fertilized, it will not live but die, so with regard to the body. Drugs and medicaments are the fertilizer, and the physician is the tiller of the soil.[45]

How remarkable is this concept, for it declares that God does not bring about all healing or creativity alone, but rather depends upon us to aid in the process and commands us to try.

We are, in the talmudic phrase, God's partners in the ongoing act of creation.[46]

The Community Must Balance Its Medical and Nonmedical Needs and Services

The duty to provide health care applies not only to the individual physician; the community itself is charged with making it available. On the basis of Leviticus 19:16 ("Nor shall you stand idly by the blood of your fellow"), the Talmud expands our obligation to provide medical aid to include expending financial resources for this purpose. Rabbi Moses ben Naḥman ("Naḥmanides," fourteenth century) explains that this duty derives from the Torah's principle, "And you shall love your neighbor as yourself" (Leviticus 19:18).[47]

The community, however, is also responsible for providing other necessities of life and of Jewish living. The Talmud, in fact, specifies ten things that a community must provide its members if it is to be fit for a rabbi to reside there:

> It has been taught: A scholar should not reside in a city where [any] of the following ten things is missing: (1) A court of justice which can impose flagellation and monetary penalties; (2) a charity fund, collected by two people and distributed by three [to ensure honesty and wise policies of distribution]; (3) a synagogue; (4) public baths; (5) toilet facilities; (6) a circumciser *(mohel)*; (7) a surgeon; (8) a notary [for writing official documents]; (9) a slaughterer *(shoḥet)*; and (10) a schoolmaster. Rabbi Akiba is quoted [as including] also several kinds of fruit [in the list] because they are beneficial for eyesight.[48]

Note that the list includes several items relevant to health care. Since there was no indoor plumbing then — actually until the nineteenth or even twentieth century in many places — it was important for purposes of public health to have public baths and toilet facilities. If the latter were not available, raw sewage in the streets would attract disease-bearing flies and rodents, a menace to public health as one can see to this day in many parts of the developing world. These facilities were also important, of course, for the general aesthetic quality of the environment;

urban conditions lowered the quality of human life. The "surgeon" mentioned in the list was the person who could perform the most important form of curative care known at the time, namely, letting blood. (The surgeon might also try other forms of curative care, but since the medicines available were largely ineffective, the list refers to the strong suit of medicine at the time rather than using the more general term "physician" [ro-feh]). Finally, Rabbi Akiba's addendum concerns the availability of healthy foods in the town, a recognition that our choice of food plays an important preventive role in assuring health.

The list, however, also includes a number of items not directly related to health care, such as a court of justice, a synagogue, and a schoolmaster. Moreover, since the non-Jewish government during talmudic times provided defense, security, roads and bridges, and other governmental services for the Jewish community, these were not included in the Talmud's list. In a sovereign Jewish state, however, these too would undoubtedly appear in any list of communal needs.

In Chapter 12 we shall address the question of how to balance these various needs. Suffice it to say here that health care cannot be the sole service the community provides, and that communal resources spent on health care must therefore be balanced against those expended on other social needs.

Jews Must Sanctify God's Name

Finally, all of these concepts and duties related to health care are rooted, in the Jewish tradition, in the obligation to sanctify God's name. The Torah demands that our actions and words sanctify God's Name (kiddush ha-Shem) and that conversely, we do not desecrate it (ḥillul ha-Shem). These concepts have most commonly been applied to cases of martyrdom. As we have discussed, the Talmud establishes the rule that if one is forced to murder someone else, engage in incest or adultery, or bow down to idols, one must choose to die rather than commit any one of those three offenses; with regard to any other commandment, however, one must violate the commandment if that is necessary to save one's life, for the Torah declares that we should live by the laws, which the rabbis interpreted to mean that we should not die by them. After announcing this principle, though, the Talmud goes on to introduce two other factors that can either broaden or narrow the occasions on which one must give up one's life. If the action demanded of Jews is in private and only for the heathen's own pleasure, then they may even bow down to idols to save their lives. On the other hand, if the demand is specifically to cause Jews to violate Jewish law, or if the heathen's demand requires Jews to transgress Jewish law in public (even if only for the heathen's pleasure), then one may not even "change one's shoe strap from white to black" (that is, violate even a Jewish custom) but rather choose to die in defense of Judaism.[49] During the Middle Ages, when Jews were forced to convert to Christianity, some Jews did not wait for the Church authorities or the Christian mobs to torture and kill them if they would not convert but rather took their own lives ("and fathers slaughtered their children with their own hands"). In those circumstances, some people feared that they might succumb to the Christians' demands to convert under torture, and at least some rabbis permitted such people to murder their children and then commit suicide instead.[50]

The requirement for sanctifying God's Name, then, sets the limits of the Jewish commitment to preserve life. *Kiddush ha-Shem*, though, does not only apply to dire circumstances where martyrdom may be required; it applies much more broadly to other areas of life as well. Specifically, Jews are always supposed to act in such a way that brings honor to themselves, their people, and the God Jews worship; they thereby enhance God's reputation (Name). Conversely, Jews are never supposed to act in a way that will sully the standing and repute of the Jewish people or God, for that would tarnish God's name *(hillul ha-Shem)*.[51] This imposes an immense burden of acting honorably at all times in life, a burden that is probably impossible for fallible human beings to meet at all times but nevertheless goads Jews to aspire to high moral standards.

This latter understanding of *kiddush ha-Shem* also affects Jewish bioethics. First, it requires Jews to participate in general, communal efforts to promote health and well-being, for if non-Jews perceive Jews to be shirking a clear social responsibility, that would sully God's name. This concern will directly impact our discussion of, among other things, Jewish participation in organ donation for transplantation and in contributing to communal health care facilities. Moreover, this broader meaning of *kiddush ha-Shem* sets the proper stage for understanding the entire Jewish effort to care and cure, for it makes the motive for Jews to engage in health care nothing less than an opportunity to serve and sanctify God. This links Jewish endeavors to promote health with Judaism's challenge in all aspects of life.

These seven principles of Judaism will reappear over and over again in our discussion of Jewish medical ethics. Sometimes they will take specific legal form, mandating that we do *x* or refrain from doing *y*. At other times they will guide the discussion more generally, determining the list of considerations taken into account and guiding the weighing of conflicting values. On still other occasions, they will appear as ideals toward which we should strive.

At no time will these theological tenets disappear completely from view; they will always play a role in one way or another in making Jewish bioethics distinctively Jewish. That is because Judaism is a rich religious tradition, weaving together thought, values, law, and custom; individuals and communities of the past with those of the present and future; and the wisdom of the ages with current expertise. Any discussion of a specific aspect of Jewish bioethics, then, may temporarily concentrate on one particular part of the tradition, but it must take account of all the others as well. Only such a depiction can be faithful to the abundance of the tradition, producing an authentic response to it.

Moreover, these tenets will guide us both in providing historical and philosophical depth and in widening the scope of our discussion. As a quick look at the Table of Contents will make clear, Jewish medical ethics must consider the person not just as a physical machine but as a whole human being; consequently, it must pay attention to the mental and emotional aspects of medical care. Moreover, contrary to so much of contemporary medicine and bioethics, we dare not pretend that people live in isolation; Judaism's communitarian base warns us to think of people and their health as products of the complicated and complex interactions among individuals, their society, and their environment. Inevitably, then, an adequate discussion of Jewish medical ethics must consider how the presence or absence of social support affects a person's health and how society's decisions about the distribution and cost of health care, as well as its treatment of the environment influence health and illness. Any discussion narrower in scope would be neither an adequate account of the factors in our health nor a faithful representation of Judaism's views and concerns.

In the chapters that follow, then, the treatment of issues at the beginning and the end of life will sometimes look familiar as we analyze the specific elements of the medical circumstances, but that will quickly change as we deepen and widen our discussion based on the principles described above in order to provide increased conceptual and moral vision. Moreover, at various points along the way we shall consider the emotional, social, and environmental aspects of our subject, paying special attention to those matters in the last section of the book. This approach will make our discussion more thoroughly Jewish than any strictly legal or moral treatment of specific issues could be, for it will respond faithfully to the many elements of Judaism — legal, moral, theological, and social—that make its treatment of these matters as sensitive and wise as we would expect and hope it to be.

PART TWO

Moral Issues at the Beginning of Life

CHAPTER THREE

Having Children with One's Own Genetic Materials

The Roles of Sex Within Marriage

FROM THE EARLIEST SOURCES OF THE JEWISH TRADITION, sex was understood to have two primary purposes: procreation and marital companionship. The Torah thus includes two positive commandments with regard to sex: "Be fruitful and multiply" (Genesis 1:28), and the prescription that when a man marries a woman, "her food, her clothing, and her conjugal rights he may not diminish" (Exodus 21:10). God thereby consecrates—indeed, commands—each of those roles separately. Even when sex cannot be procreative, it is still regarded as contributing to the companionship that God intends marriage to afford. Conversely, even when procreation occurs without sex, that is, through artificial means, it still may fulfill the commandment to propagate.[1] Each of the roles sex plays within marriage, then, is independently valued and has an important function in the Jewish conception of the human being, the family, and the community.

Marital Companionship

Adam and Eve, the progenitors of all humanity according to the biblical story, were specifically created for each other, "for it is not good that a person be alone, . . . and therefore a man leaves his father and his mother and clings to his wife so that they become one flesh" (Genesis 2:18, 24). The Torah thus recognizes the basic human need for intimate companionship and seeks to satisfy that need through the institution of marriage.

Indeed, chapter 2 of Genesis portrays Adam as created by God first as a solitary human person, endowed with all the possibilities of life. Since, according to that story, God eventually created both Adam and Eve, why, we wonder, did God not create them simultaneously? One modern rabbi suggests that God wanted the first person to experience, not just to imagine, what it is like to have every-*thing* but no-*body*. Only after Adam had experienced the pain of aloneness, despite all his possessions, would he be ready to appreciate the need for companionship and interdependence as the essential path of personal fulfillment.[2]

Sex is one of the ways in which this companionship is expressed. Sexual intercourse is, of course, a source of physical pleasure and release, and the Jewish tradition does not look down on that; on the contrary, within the bounds of modesty, a married couple may, according to Jewish law, have sex in any way they wish so as to maximize their physical pleasure.[3]

The tradition understood, however, that sex not only involves physical enjoyment; it is also an intense form of communication through which a husband and wife convey their love for each other. It is precisely because this communicative aspect is essential to human sexuality that licentious sex is effectively a lie, for here the couple clearly do not mean to undertake the fundamental commitment to each other conveyed by their sexual union. Even if two people verbally declare to each other that their sex act is only for physical pleasure with no intention of further commitments, what they are conveying with their bodies belies what they have said with their lips. Such a situation, in other words, is rife with the potential for miscommunication, misunderstood intentions, and deeply hurt feelings. Undoubtedly, that is one reason that the Jewish tradition wants sex to be restricted to marriage.

The Torah recognizes that both men and women desire the physical and emotional fulfillment that sex provides. While we might take this mutual desire for granted, we need to recognize that most other societies in the ancient world—and, for that matter, in the medieval and the modern world as well—assume that only men have sexual appetites. According to this theory, women tolerate the sexual advances of their husbands only because they want children and economic security. In sharp contrast to this widespread view, the Torah and the rabbis who later interpreted it structured the laws of marriage so that both spouses have rights to regular sex within marriage.[4]

However, when sex becomes a tool for control, the marriage ceases to be the partnership that it is intended to be. Jewish sources specifically proclaim that coercive sex is never allowed,[5] and they disdain either spouse's "rebelling" against the other by denying sex.[6] Although one need not agree to engage in sexual relations each time one's spouse wants to do so, and although occasional refusals must be respected, the tradition does not approve denial of a spouse's sexual rights over a long period of time without due reason, for then the spouse who wants to have sex is being denied the sexual expression of companionship to which each partner is entitled in a marriage.

Yet marital companionship is only partly sexual. In the Jewish wedding ceremony, the only explicit reference to the couple describes them as *re'im ahuvim*, loving friends. This description appropriately portrays the companionship of marriage as far-reaching; husband and wife are not only lovers but friends, sharing the tasks, joys, and sorrows of life together. Their friendship is indeed as strong an element in their relationship as their sexual partnership.

Procreation

Marriage is also theologically important because of its potential to produce children. Procreation provides an opportunity to enjoy the riches that children bring to life and also enables the Jewish tradition to continue through the generations. The potential for these blessings makes marriage itself, and sex within it, nothing short of holy.[7]

While both husband and wife are obviously necessary to procreate, the Mishnah, basing its rulings on exegetical and, probably, economic and/or physical grounds, claims that only the man is subject to the biblical commandment to procreate,[8] and that to fulfill this duty a man must father at least two children.[9] Here the Mishnah typically specifies only the minimum needed to fulfill one's obligation under the law. Jewish practice at that time and subsequently, as well as later Jewish law itself, makes clear that one should have as many children as one can, for, as Maimonides says, "whoever adds even one Jewish soul is considered as having created an [entire] world."[10]

This is an especially important teaching in our own time, when low reproductive rates among Jews, caused in part by their extended education and the late age at which they marry and attempt to have children, have combined with assimilation and intermarriage to create a major demographic crisis for the Jewish community. Nothing less than the future of the Jewish community and of Judaism depends upon fertile Jews having three or four children per couple.[11]

Children are not only an obligation; they are a blessing. God's blessings of the Patriarchs promise children as numerous as the stars; and later on, Leviticus, Deuteronomy, and the Book of Psalms include children prominently in their descriptions of life's chief goods.[12] Children, of course, are not an unmitigated good: the children in the biblical stories bring plenty of anguish to their parents, and modern parents too inevitably worry about their children, get angry with them on occasion, and experience their frustrations and missteps together with them. Parents, though, also get to share in their children's accomplishments, and through them to renew their own sense of the adventure of life and its joy and hope. Experiences with their children also contribute to the parents' own psychological growth.[13]

Moreover, children are both our heritage and our destiny, perhaps our strongest ties to both the past and the future. They connect us to "the great chain of being" and thus give us both roots and hope. Biblical sources affirm that we live on after death in primarily two ways: through the influence we have had on others during our lifetime, and through our children.[14] These doctrines reflect the fact that we are, after all, linked to both past and future generations, and that children are one primary form of that bond. They also make it possible for the Jewish tradition to be passed down from one generation to the next.[15] For all of these reasons and more, Jews historically have had as many children as they could, and in fact Jewish law stipulates that they do so.[16]

Three other points should be noted about the tradition's requirement that we procreate. Both during and after the years during which a couple are having their children, the duty to have conjugal relations for the sake of companionship continues. God's desire, according to the Torah and the Talmud, is that people should, if at all possible, live in marital partnership, regardless of their ability to procreate.[17]

Second, parents of "special needs" children bear extra burdens—physically, financially, and especially emotionally—as they help their children manage the process of fitting in to a society that often does not accommodate or even recognize their special needs. The American Jewish community, through programs like Tikvah at several Ramah camps, has finally begun to provide some services for these children, and more needs to be done. Even with increased financial and educational support, though, parents of such children may understandably find it beyond their emotional capacity to have the three or four children I am recommending to other families, and they should feel no guilt in having fewer.

Third, *if a couple cannot have children, the commandment to procreate no longer applies*, for one can be commanded to do only what one is capable of. The religious commandment to generate children, which in any case traditionally is incumbent only on the male, ceases to apply to those men who cannot have them, and there is no guilt or shame involved in that.[18] That is just the way God created some of our bodies. Under such circumstances, couples may consider adoption or use modern technologies in an attempt to overcome their infertility, as detailed below. They are, however, under no obligation to do so from the point of view of Jewish law, for the duty to procreate devolves only upon those who can do so through sexual intercourse with their spouse. Indeed, all Jews should try to alleviate the immense frustration infertile couples feel by offering a supportive, listening ear and by reassuring them of their value as human beings and as Jews.

Infertility in Jewish Sources

In many ways, the emphasis on children in Judaism exacerbates the frustration and alienation that infertile Jewish couples suffer. So, for example, when the Psalmist wants truly to bless his listener or reader, he says:

> Happy are all who fear the Lord, who follow His ways. . . . Your wife shall be like a fruitful vine within your house; your children, like olive saplings around your table. So shall the man who fears the Lord be blessed. May the Lord bless you from Zion; may you . . . live to see your children's children. May all be well with Israel![19]

As this passage indicates, such positive feelings about children are, at least in part, due to the tradition's conviction that children are an expression of God's blessing of those who abide by the conditions of God's covenant with Israel. As the Torah explicitly says:

> If you obey these rules and observe them faithfully, the Eternal, your God, will maintain for you the gracious covenant that God made on oath with your forbears. God will love you and bless you and multiply you. . . . There shall be no sterile male or female among you.[20]

While these words sound warm and loving to those who have children, they have a very different ring to those who do not. As one infertile Jewish woman has written,

> Fertility, it seems, is an integral component of the covenant. Is barrenness, then, next to godlessness? If you who are fertile have received a sacred blessing, have we who are not received a divine curse?[21]

The Bible includes stories of a surprising number of people who cannot have children, and the people involved in the biblical stories of infertility include no less than the Patriarchs and Matriarchs, who are depicted as being in very good graces with God. Sarah, Rebecca, and Rachel all have trouble conceiving and bearing children,[22] which, in the biblical stories, adds to the preciousness and theological import of the ones they ultimately do have. The merits of these women and their husbands and the oath God swears to them are the reasons God forgives the seriously erring Israelites after the molten calf incident and the motive for God's choosing the People Israel in love.[23] The Torah is thus explicitly ambivalent about claiming that piety produces fertility and that fertility is the mark of piety.

As in the biblical stories, modern couples often experience their inability to have children as frustrating and degrading. Why can they not do what their bodies were designed to do and what most other people's bodies enable them to do? When all their married friends are having children, partners in an infertile marriage often feel not only unlucky and deprived but embarrassed and defensive as they continually feel the need to explain why they do not have children too. Infertility even challenges people's feelings of adequacy as men or women—and as mates. Some marriages fall apart due to the tension engendered by continued, unsuccessful attempts to have children. To add insult to injury, Jewish couples who seek to make Judaism an important part of their lives—and even those who do not—often *feel* that they are letting down not only each other but also their parents, the Jewish people, and God.

It is therefore crucial to underscore that while children are critical for the future of the Jewish people and a blessing to their parents as well as to their community, a person's *value*, according to the Jewish tradition, is *not* a function of his or her ability to produce children. Rather, human worth derives from being created in the image of God, which is true of each of us from the moment of our birth to the moment of our death, whether or not we produce children in between. (Note that, in contrast to many religions of the ancient past, God in the Bible and in the Talmud and Midrash specifically does *not* engage in sexual union to create us or anything else, and so imitating God does not require procreation through sexual union.) As Jews, we gain additional divine worth through our covenant with God, but one's status as a Jew depends *not* on the ability to procreate but on being born Jewish or being converted to Judaism in accordance with the requirements and procedures mandated by Jewish law. Thus one's status and value as a human being and as a Jew, according to Jewish sources, are both totally independent of the ability to produce children, a Jewish teaching that needs to be affirmed again and again in this age of massive infertility among Jews.

Moreover, as indicated above, the command to procreate, like all other commandments, does not apply to those who cannot fulfill it. "In cases of compulsion *(ones)*, the All-Merciful One exempts him," the rabbis say.[24] Thus men who cannot impregnate their wives should not see themselves as thereby failing to obey Jewish law, for their inability to procreate frees them of the responsibility to do so. In that way they are legally in a better position than a man who has had many children but all of the same gender, for such a man presumably could still fulfill the commandment of begetting a boy and a girl but has not done so.[25] Even here it seems only fair to credit a man with fulfilling the obligation to procreate once he has fathered two children, regardless of their gender, because no man can control the gender of the children he begets. In the same vein, it seems all the more justified to exempt from this duty a man who cannot have children at all.

The context, then, for the entire discussion below on methods to overcome infertility must be made clear at the outset: it applies only to those couples who *choose* to use them. Jewish law imposes no obligation on infertile couples to employ any of them. Such methods do enable approximately half of infertile couples to bear children. As such, they offer new hope to such couples, and we certainly rejoice with them, both personally and communally, when they succeed in having the children they want. Whenever we *can* do something new, though, the moral and legal question of whether we *should* do so then arises, and the new methods of achieving conception come with some clear moral, financial, communal, and personal costs that will be described below and must be acknowledged and balanced against the great good of having children.

The Range and Costs of Available Infertility Treatments

One in seven couples in the United States is infertile. (A couple are defined as "infertile" when they are actively trying to have a child over the period of a year and cannot conceive or when the woman repeatedly miscarries.) Although in developing countries like those in sub-Saharan Africa, infertility afflicts the lower socioeconomic classes the most and primarily results from tuberculosis, venereal disease, infections, and malnutrition, the case is quite different in industrialized countries, where it is the higher socioeconomic classes and those of advanced reproductive age whom infertility hits hardest, and for very different reasons.

In only 25 percent of cases is one factor alone the cause of infertility. Ovulatory dysfunction is a factor in between 25 and 45 percent of cases, spermatozoal disorders (mostly unexplained) in 20 to 35 percent, tubal disease in 15 to 30 percent, pelvic endometriosis in 10 to 50 percent, poor sperm-mucus interaction in 5 to 15 percent, and antispermatozoal antibodies in 5 to 15 percent (with some 5 to 10 percent being totally unexplained).[26] Overall, in approximately 20 percent of the cases the cause cannot be determined.

Since Jews attend college and graduate school in percentages far exceeding the national norm, they generally marry comparatively late and do not even try to have children until their late twenties or thirties. That compounds the problem yet further for Jews as a population, for infertility increases with age: 13.9 percent of couples are infertile where the wife is between thirty and thirty-four; 24.6 percent where the wife is between thirty-five and thirty-nine; and 27.2 percent where the wife is between forty and forty-four. Despite all of our modern technology, physically the ideal age for a woman to become pregnant is still twenty-two, "after her body is fully mature and before she is subject to the diseases that can come with aging." While some men as late as their sixties or seventies can father children, male fertility and potency also decrease with age, and so for men too the ideal age to procreate is in their early twenties.

As many as 1.2 million patients are treated annually in the United States for infertility problems, with approximately one billion dollars being spent each year on their care. Even so, for as many as one in five infertile couples, a cause is never found, and as many as half the infertile couples seeking treatment are in the end unsuccessful, despite trying various avenues of treatment.[27]

The other side of that statistic, of course, is that currently about 50 percent of infertile couples are ultimately treated successfully (up from about 20 percent before 1960[28]). About 85 to 90 percent of those are helped through conventional medical and surgical therapy. Medical treatment ranges from relatively simple techniques like teaching the couple to time their intercourse to take place shortly after the time of ovulation to more sophisticated treatments like artificial insemination or drug therapy. Surgical treatments also vary in complexity, from ligation of testicular veins for eliminating varicocele to delicate microsurgical repair of reproductive tract structures in both men and women.

Ovulation induction, surgery, and artificial insemination are the most widespread and the most successful approaches to overcoming infertility; some seventy thousand births per year in the United States result from artificial insemination alone, compared with three thousand from more technologically sophisticated procedures.[29] Drug therapy with Clomid for stimulating ovulation and artificial insemination are successful in slightly less than 50 percent of the cases in which they are tried, and they generally cost $300 or $400. (If Pergonol is used instead of Clomid, the cost is considerably greater, amounting to $2,000 to $3,000 per cycle.) Corrective surgery, of course, is also expensive, but where it is appropriate, it holds out the hope of a permanent solution to the couple's infertility problems. Approximately half of all the women who are artificially inseminated become pregnant, on average after seven inseminations over a period of 4.4 cycles at an average cost of $953 for the entire procedure.[30] Since 37.7 percent of the women inseminated ultimately give birth to live infants, this technique too is successful in overcoming infertility for many couples.[31]

When for some reason it is not possible to use any of these methods, or when none of them has worked, three more complicated and more expensive reproductive technologies can be tried: in vitro fertilization (IVF), gamete intrafallopian transfer (GIFT), and zygote intrafallopian transfer (ZIFT). Together, these techniques account for the other 10 to 15 percent of the 50 percent of couples who are successfully treated.[32] These procedures, however, are much more costly ($8,000 to $10,000 for each try), have a much lower success rate (estimated at somewhere between 10 percent and 17 percent for each attempt), and raise gnarly legal, moral, and psychological problems.[33] Another option for the couple is to enlist the help of another woman through ovum surrogacy (also called "traditional surrogacy") or gestational surrogacy.

In the remainder of this chapter, then, we shall focus on the ways in which couples overcome infertility with their own gametes. They include, first, artificial insemination by the husband (AIH) and then the more invasive and technologically sophisticated techniques of IVF, GIFT, and ZIFT. The first cases of surrogacy used the surrogate mother's eggs ("ovum surrogacy" or "traditional surrogacy"), but IVF now enables a couple to use their own gametes ("gestational surrogacy"); we shall therefore treat surrogacy in this chapter as well. In Chapter 4 we will turn to the use of donor gametes through donor insemination and egg donation and, finally, to the alternative of adoption. Along the way, we will also address the Jewish legitimacy of volunteering to be a sperm or egg donor or of becoming a single parent through these new technologies.

Traditional Sources on Nonsexual Insemination

Artificial insemination is the oldest method couples and physicians have tried in their attempts to overcome infertility. Because it is the least invasive, the least dangerous, and the least costly technique available, it is still the first one used today when a couple cannot conceive through sexual intercourse because of sexual dysfunction, insufficient or abnormal sperm, or inadequate motility of the sperm.

Four sources within the tradition discuss insemination of a woman without sexual intercourse. Even though they do not reflect modern methods of insemination, they are commonly invoked in present-day Jewish discussions of artificial insemination.

The first occurs in the Talmud:

> Ben Zoma was asked: "May a high priest [who, according to Leviticus 21:13, must marry a virgin] marry a maiden who has become pregnant [yet who claims she is still a virgin]? Do we take into consideration Samuel's statement, for Samuel said: 'I can have repeated sexual connections without [causing] bleeding [i.e., without the woman losing her virginity],' or is the case of Samuel rare?" He replied: "The case of Samuel is rare, but we do consider [the possibility] that she may have conceived in a bath [into which a male has discharged semen], and therefore she may marry a high priest. . . . "[34]

However implausible such conception may seem to us, this talmudic source clearly contemplates the possibility of conception without sexual intercourse. Its simple meaning is that artificial insemination neither invokes the prohibitions nor leads to the illegitimacy connected with adultery or incest. Some medieval and early modern rabbis had trouble imagining such a situation, let alone basing their legal decision upon it, and so they chose instead to interpret the passage metaphorically.[35] Others, though, accept the possibility of such conception and interpret the passage at face value. Rabbi Moshe Feinstein, for example, cited this source as one justification to permit donor insemination.[36]

The second source generally cited is a medieval midrash regarding Ben Sira, a second-century B.C.E. author of a book of the Apocrypha cited in the Talmud. This legend, first mentioned by Rabbi Jacob Moellin Segal (1365–1427) in his work *Likutei*

Maharil, claims that Ben Sira was conceived without sexual intercourse by the prophet Jeremiah's daughter in a bath, the father having been Jeremiah himself who, coerced by a group of wicked men, had emitted semen into the water. The midrash is undoubtedly based on the fact that the Hebrew spellings of "Jeremiah" and "Sira" have the same numerical equivalent, 271.[37] This legend subsequently appears in many medieval texts as well as most, if not all, of the rabbinic responsa dealing with artificial insemination.[38] This story supports three contentions: that conception without sexual intercourse is possible; that, unlike sexual intercourse, it does not make a child conceived by a father and daughter a *mamzer* [illegitimate]; and, since the legend asserts that Ben Sira was the child of Jeremiah, the sperm donor is apparently to be considered the legal, as well as the biological, father of the offspring.

The third source commonly quoted is the comment of Rabbi Perez ben Elijah of Corbeil in his work *Haggahot Semak*, who states:

> A woman may lie on her husband's sheets but should be careful not to lie on sheets upon which another man slept lest she become impregnated from his sperm. Why are we not afraid that she become pregnant from her husband's sperm and the child will be conceived of a menstruating woman [*niddah*]? The answer is that [we are not concerned about the child being the progeny of a menstruating woman] since there is no forbidden intercourse, [and so] the child is completely legitimate [*kasher*] even from the sperm of another, just as Ben Sira was legitimate. However, we are concerned about the sperm of another man because the child may eventually marry his [own half] sister. . . .[39]

Whether or not a woman can, in fact, be impregnated by sperm on a sheet (presumably shortly after the man has left the bed), Rabbi Perez clearly assumes that she can, and thus we have another source within the tradition that contemplates insemination without sexual intercourse. As in the legend cited above, Rabbi Perez assumes that the child so conceived is legitimate, even if the sexual union of the biological parents would have been prohibited—here, because the woman was (or might have been) menstruating. He also mentions a concern that will arise in cases of artificial insemination by a donor (and also in cases of adoption), namely, the worry that the child will later have intercourse with a half sibling, an act classified by Leviticus 18:9 as incest. The people involved would presumably be acting unknowingly, of course, and one must then ask whether the prohibition would apply, but this source assumes that it does.

Finally, Rabbi Moses ben Naḥman (Naḥmanides), in explaining the verse, "One may not have intercourse with one's neighbor's wife for seed [or sperm]" (Leviticus 18:20), points out that the last two Hebrew words of that verse seem unnecessary. He then raises the possibility that they were included in the text to emphasize one reason for the prohibition of adultery, namely, that society will not know from whom the child is descended. On this basis, Rabbi Yoel Teitelbaum rules that donor insemination is biblically prohibited, for as with adultery, the identity of the biological father (in this case, the donor) is usually unknown. Rabbi Eliezer Waldenberg goes even further: he uses Naḥmanides' interpretation as forbidding the very act of injecting a donor's semen into a married woman's womb as an act of adultery, regardless of the absence of sexual contact involved.[40]

As stated in Chapter 1 above and in the Appendix, I maintain, as a matter of general policy, that we should use the precedents within our tradition to guide us in our own rulings as much as possible, even when such sources are scant in number and considerably different in context from the questions we are asking, as long as we keep in mind the ways in which these sources differ in a relevant way from the case at hand as we weigh such precedents and draw conclusions from them. Even Rabbi Teitelbaum, however, acknowledges a problem in basing his opinion on the commentary of Naḥmanides, for it is debatable whether biblical commentaries were ever intended to be sources of law.[41]

Moreover, current infertility treatments differ from all four of the above sources in two significant ways. First, when these modern techniques are used, all parties involved *intend* conception to take place; and second, the *probability* of conception is considerably greater than it is in the situations described by the above four sources, where it occurs by sheer happenstance. In fact, these sources are so unlike the contemporary conditions in which the question of the permissibility of artificial insemination arises that one wonders whether they can seriously serve as a legal resource for our questions.

Artificial Insemination Using the Husband's Sperm

In what is a common chronological order of treatment, couples having fertility problems are normally first advised to time their intercourse to coincide with the woman's most fertile time. Rabbis do not object to this technique, since ovulation usually occurs at the beginning of the time when the couple is permitted by the laws of family purity *(tohorat ha-mishpahah)* to have conjugal relations following the end of the woman's menstrual period. Even when the woman routinely ovulates so early in her cycle that she cannot have intercourse at her most fertile time without violating these laws, rabbis have been willing to find ways to permit intercourse during her fertile time despite these laws to enable the couple to have children.[42]

Sometimes drug therapy is required to stimulate the woman's ovaries. Even though there is evidence that such drugs to some extent increase the risk of ovarian cancer, high blood pressure, and strokes, the demonstrated risk is not so great that such therapy must be prohibited because of the overriding Jewish concern of Jewish law to preserve the woman's life and health.[43] On the other hand, because the woman's own health is not threatened by her infertility, and because in any case she is not subject to the command to procreate, she is not required by Jewish law to use such drugs.

The next most common method of reproductive therapy is artificial insemination by the husband (AIH). The first successful case of using AIH in humans was reported by the Scottish surgeon Dr. John Hunter in 1790,[44] but since AIH does not require the assistance of doctors, women probably performed artificial insemination on their own for some time before then and still do so today. About half of all artificial inseminations are done to overcome fertility problems in the husband,[45] and the other half serve to circumvent problems in the wife[46] (or in both partners).

Most rabbis who have written about AIH have not objected to it.[47] Because Judaism appreciates medicine as a divinely authorized aid to God, AIH is not prohibited among Jews, as it is among Catholics, merely because it is artificial.

Some rabbis, though, worry about the means by which the husband's sperm is obtained. To ensure that there is no "destruction of the seed in vain," in violation of the rabbinic interpretation of Genesis 38:9–10,[48] these rabbis advocate collecting it from the vaginal cavity after intercourse. However, an obstetrician I consulted, who has many observant Orthodox and Conservative patients, told me that collecting sperm in that way is simply "unrealistic." Moreover, the vaginal pH kills the sperm, since it is more acidic than cervical mucus.

Other rabbis permit the husband to use a condom (clearly, one without spermicide) for the purpose of collecting his semen for AIH. Some of these rabbis insist that the condom have a small hole in it so that there is still some chance of conception through the couple's intercourse.

While I have no particular objection to couples using such constraints, it does seem to me that they are unnecessary, for producing semen for the specific purpose of procreating cannot plausibly be called wasting it. Even some Orthodox rabbis agree and therefore permit a man to masturbate to produce semen for the artificial insemination of his wife.[49] I endorse this last approach.

In the same spirit, the Conservative rabbi Morris Shapiro has argued that where the husband is the donor, he should be credited with fulfilling the mitzvah of procreation, for the mitzvah is to produce two viable children for which both intercourse and artificial insemination are merely preparations.[50] Although AIH severs the command to procreate from sexual intercourse, I would agree with Rabbi Shapiro for three reasons: (1) The sperm involved is the husband's, and the child is therefore the husband's according to all understandings of Jewish law.[51] (2) The husband, by hypothesis, cannot fulfill the commandment in any other way. By going through the expense and trouble of artificial insemination, he has clearly demonstrated that he wants to obey the commandment, and the Talmud says that if one tries to fulfill a commandment but cannot, God nevertheless counts it to one's merit.[52] Finally, (3) the husband generally goes through considerable humiliation, pain, and perhaps depression in coming to terms with his inability to impregnate his wife through sexual intercourse, and we should do all we can to make him feel good about the process and the child that results.

IVF, GIFT, and ZIFT

As discussed above, when the husband cannot provide sperm capable of impregnating his wife, he ceases to have any obligation to procreate. A Jewish couple faced with this situation, then, should pause, seek counseling, and think carefully about whether they want to use donor sperm or engage in costly and often frustrating attempts to have a child through some of the new reproductive technologies. Once again, *there is no Jewish obligation to use any of these new techniques.* On the other hand, as I shall argue below, the couple *may*, with certain restrictions, choose to use them.

In vitro fertilization (IVF) is the fertilization of an ovum outside the body; the term "in vitro," literally "in glass," refers to the petri dish in which the sperm and eggs are combined. This technique was first used successfully for reproduction by British researchers Robert Edwards and Patrick Steptoe, leading to the birth in July 1978 of Louise Brown with the gametes of her parents. Originally developed to circumvent the woman's damaged or absent fallopian tubes (which connect the ovaries to the uterus), this method is now also used in response to other female infertility problems such as endometriosis or ovulation dysfunction, male factors, and "unexplained infertility."[53] The Society for Assisted Reproductive Technology and the American Fertility Society report that in 1992, IVF and related procedures were performed for 45,801 cycles, leading to 7,355 deliveries (a 16.06 percent success rate); the success rate was 16.9

percent when the recipient's ova were used without embryo freezing, when there was no male factor involved in the couple's infertility, and when the woman was under age forty.[54] For the sake of comparison, if a sexually active couple is not using contraception, the average monthly likelihood in the general population of fertilization leading to a live birth is between 20 and 25 percent.

As IVF is typically practiced, a woman preparing for it receives hormones to stimulate the ovaries to produce several eggs, rather than the usual one. Shortly before ovulation would normally occur, a physician uses ultrasound to guide a needle through the cervix to the ovaries to gather or "retrieve" developed ova. After inspecting the ova to make sure that they are not defective and after appropriate preparation, the ova are combined with the prepared sperm. The resulting embryos are allowed to develop in the petri dish for a few days, reaching the stage of two to eight cells; they, or a portion of them, are then transferred on the third or fourth day to the woman's uterus through a catheter inserted through the cervix. If more than enough embryos are produced through this process, they may be frozen ("cryopreserved") for use in further, future attempts.

Similar techniques are employed in two related, alternative procedures. In GIFT (gamete intrafallopian transfer), ova and sperm are mixed and placed directly into the fallopian tube, thus imitating the natural process of fertilization more closely and therefore, hopefully, increasing the odds of leading to a live birth. With ZIFT (zygote intrafallopian transfer), the embryo produced in vitro is transferred to the fallopian tube rather than to the uterus, again in an attempt to imitate natural fertilization more closely. Both of these procedures require laparoscopy, a somewhat more invasive procedure than the transcervical procedures used in IVF. The success rate with them has been less than with IVF and certainly not as promising as originally theorized and projected. IVF therefore remains "the gold standard" of these technologies, and GIFT and ZIFT are generally used only as a last resort, after IVF has been tried several times unsuccessfully.[55]

These procedures can be used with donor sperm, donor eggs, or both, but most often it is the husband's and wife's gametes that are used. Under those circumstances, most rabbis who have thus far ruled on these procedures, including Rabbi Aaron Mackler in a responsum approved by the Conservative movement's Committee on Jewish Law and Standards, have generally permitted them, for after all, they hold out the promise of enabling an otherwise infertile couple to have children.[56] I would agree with that assessment.

Some issues, however, need attention. Because doctors can now be guided by ultrasound to the ovaries so that they can remove eggs vaginally, surgery is no longer necessary to harvest eggs. However, to minimize the number of times that a woman must undergo the procedure and to maximize the possibility of pregnancy, the woman must be treated with drugs to produce more than one egg. (Eggs cannot yet be frozen.) The hormones necessary to hyperovulate a woman subject her to an increased risk of several maladies, including even stroke and heart attack, and a recent study found that "women who had used fertility drugs had three times the risk of invasive epithelial ovarian cancer compared to women without a history of infertility . . . [and] four times the risk of ovarian tumors of low malignant potential (borderline tumors) seen among women lacking a history of infertility." On the other hand, as of 1988, 1.9 million women aged fifteen to forty-four were estimated to have taken fertility drugs, and only a very small percentage of those had contracted ovarian cancer. The authors of this study therefore concluded:

> At present, there is no need to change medical practice regarding use of fertility-enhancing drugs. There is enough cause of concern, however, to slightly alter the physician's approach to counseling patients. We suggest advising patients receiving fertility drugs as to the possible increased risk of ovarian cancer.[57]

Although Judaism regards having children as a great good, preserving the woman's life and health clearly takes precedence. We are permitted to take some risks in life, however, even for entertainment and certainly for the sacred goal of producing children. Since current medical research affirms that the risk involved in hyperovulation is not prohibitively high, infertile Jewish women may undergo that procedure, assuming, of course, that no other factor in the woman's medical history would make that unwise.

In 1979, Rabbi J. David Bleich objected to IVF on the grounds that at that time we did not know whether children produced through the procedure would suffer greater risk of defects or diseases as they grew older. Almost two decades of using the procedure, however, have not borne out that fear.

A more serious objection that Rabbi Bleich raised then is the problem of selective abortion. Because the rate of success with IVF, GIFT, and ZIFT is currently as low as 10 percent and only as high as 17 percent, depending upon many factors, the standard practice in North America among infertility specialists is to implant four or five sets of gametes (GIFT) or zygotes (IVF or ZIFT) each cycle in the hope of raising the odds of success to 25 percent or so. In most cases, the couple are lucky if even one of the implants "takes"—indeed, they are then beating six-to-one (or maybe even ten-to-one) odds—but in some instances all four or five attach themselves to the uterus and begin to develop. Women can generally safely carry up to three healthy children; but a pregnancy with more than three fetuses poses a substantial threat to both the life and health of the mother and fetuses.[58] Therefore, the common practice is to abort all but three fetuses if more than that successfully implant in the uterus.

This practice is problematic on three counts. The Jewish tradition requires abortion when the mother's life or her physical or mental health is at stake. Judaism also sanctions abortion when the mother's physical or mental condition makes pregnancy more of a risk than it normally is. Generally, however, abortion is prohibited, and the burden of proof is always on the one who wants to abort. We therefore do not want to create situations where we know ahead of time that we may have to abort one or more fetuses.

Moreover, from a psychological perspective, abortion commonly leaves feelings of guilt for terminating a potential person's life, even when the procedure is necessary to preserve the mother's life or health and thus morally right. The psychological trauma is likely to be all the more severe for a couple with fertility problems in the first place.[59]

Even the physical facts seem to argue for a limitation on transferred zygotes. A Belgian study found that "limiting the number of embryos transferred to only two did not influence the take-home baby rate but eliminated triplet and quadruplet gestations. Moreover, the number of patients with good quality supernumerary [extra] embryos available for cryopreservation increased." The American Fertility Society has issued a similar recommendation of transferring two, or at most three, embryos.[60]

Despite these concerns, some Orthodox rabbis have permitted selective abortions on the grounds of the mother's mental and/or physical health when more than three embryos implant in the uterus,[61] and Conservative rabbis would undoubtedly do so as well. However, to avoid the need for selective abortions as much as possible, Jews in the first place should have only two, or at most three, zygotes implanted for IVF or ZIFT and should use only two, or at most three, eggs for GIFT.

IVF, GIFT, and ZIFT raise the possibility of other legal, moral, and psychological problems. Since multiple eggs are usually harvested each time to minimize the risks and costs of extracting them, and since they are then inseminated and frozen for later use in further attempts at having a first child or for additional children, a number of questions arise as to the status of those frozen embryos. Who, for example, owns them if the couple later divorce or if one of them dies? May such embryos be morally and legally sold to other infertile couples? Are frozen embryos, in other words, property in the usual sense and therefore subject to the laws governing the ownership and transfer of property, or does their status as potential human beings put them into a different category, with presumably more restrictive rules?

Jewish law, as I understand it, would affirm what American courts have said, namely, that if both members of the couple are alive, both have a right to restrict the use of their embryos; neither may do that alone. If their original attempts at having children with IVF succeed and if they do not want any more children, they may discard the remaining embryos; Jewish strictures on abortion do not apply because these embryos exist outside the uterus, where they have no chance of developing or even of remaining viable on their own once thawed. Because of that, I would permit the couple to donate their embryos to an infertile couple, but only subject to the cautions and restrictions described in Chapter 4 in regard to any use of donated gametes.

Surrogate Mothers

When the couple cannot conceive in the first place or the wife cannot retain a pregnancy for any of a number of known or unknown causes, the couple may try to find another woman to bear their child. This can be done with six different combinations of gametes: (1) those of the husband and wife; (2) the husband's sperm and a donated egg; (3) the wife's egg and donated sperm; (4) donated sperm and donated eggs from a woman other than the wife or the surrogate mother; (5) the surrogate mother's egg inseminated by the husband's sperm; or (6) the surrogate mother's egg inseminated by donated sperm.

Since the first attempts to use a surrogate mother involved the relatively simple technology of artificial insemination of the woman acting as a surrogate, using her own egg for the embryo together with either the husband's sperm or donated sperm (combinations 5 and 6 above), that is called "traditional surrogacy" or, more recently, "ovum surrogacy." When IVF and later GIFT and ZIFT were developed, it became possible for the surrogate mother to bear children with the sperm and eggs of other people—any of combinations 1, 2, 3, or 4 above. That is called "gestational surrogacy," for the surrogate mother is allowing her womb to act as the fetus's incubator during the nine months of gestation without contributing any of her own genetic materials to the fetus. Because the whole point of surrogacy is to enable a couple to have children bearing the genes of at least one of them, the fourth and sixth options listed above, where donated sperm would be used with either the surrogate mother's eggs or a donor's eggs, are seldom chosen.

Ovum surrogacy is used when the wife lacks either healthy ovaries or the ability to produce ova for retrieval, or when she is unable to carry a baby to term. Gestational surrogacy is used when the wife can produce eggs of her own but has one or more fertility problems: a malformed or absent uterus; a medical condition that would make pregnancy dangerous, such as severe hypertension, diabetes, or lupus; or a condition that would endanger the fetus, such as phenylketonuria.[62] Despite the many diagnoses that would suggest using surrogacy, the procedure is still rare: only four thousand children had been born to surrogates by 1991. The present pace is estimated at one thousand new agreements a year—but of course not all of those result in children.[63]

Since gestational surrogacy uses IVF, GIFT, or ZIFT, our examination of those procedures above applies to surrogacy as well—especially the need to limit the number of zygotes to be implanted at any one time to three so as to avoid unnecessary abortions. In addition, if anything but the sperm of the husband and the eggs of the wife are used, all of the moral, legal, and psychological questions addressed in Chapter 4 regarding donated gametes apply to surrogacy as well.

In ovum surrogacy, though, the problems concerning the surrogate mother's relationship to the child are as complicated as they ever get, for after all, she is biologically bound to the child not only through bonding with the fetus during the months of pregnancy but also through genetics. This fact would argue for even more extensive counseling than other donors, recipients, and progeny would need, and for careful planning by the couple and the surrogate mother as to how they are going to live through the pregnancy and birth together and how they are going to manage relationships with the child once born.

In a small minority of cases, the surrogate has refused to give up the child. Of the estimated four thousand children born to surrogates from the late 1970s to the early 1990s, only twelve surrogacy-related cases have been filed in American courts, and in every case except one, custody was awarded to the intended parents.[64] Still, since surrogacy already involves complex emotional ties, everything possible should be done at the outset to avoid the complications of court challenges—yet another reason why those contemplating surrogacy must engage in careful counseling and planning.

Even if the psychological pitfalls and the contractual legalities of surrogacy can be managed, the procedure raises serious moral questions. Specifically, should surrogacy be banned altogether because it is inherently degrading for a woman to rent out her uterus? Does the morality of surrogacy depend to any significant degree on the fact that usually the woman is paid? Does it matter that in some cases surrogate mothers from the lower economic classes carry babies for well-to-do couples?

Most of the rabbis who have written about surrogacy to date have disparaged it on such moral grounds—to the point that one Orthodox writer claimed in 1991 that regarding surrogacy "the rejection is almost universal."[65] That is still true for the Orthodox (although there are isolated exceptions),[66] and even among Conservative and Reform analysts, opinion is mixed.

The major argument in favor of surrogacy, of course, is that it enables infertile couples to have children with the gametes of at least one of them. Not only is surrogacy thus a response to the pain of infertility for the couples involved; it is also a way for that couple to fulfill an important Jewish value and hope.

Those arguing against surrogacy on moral grounds (rather than, or in addition to, the American legal and psychological issues noted above) have raised several objections. Some, like the Orthodox rabbi Immanuel Jakobovits, find it inherently demeaning: "To use another woman as an incubator . . . for a fee . . . [is a] revolting degradation of maternity and an affront to human dignity."[67] In like manner, the Conservative rabbi Daniel Gordis holds that surrogacy is degrading because it involves a "commodification" of the surrogate woman's body, that is, a transformation of the woman's reproductive abilities into a commodity that can be traded on the market. Further degradation comes from the limits imposed on the surrogate: Gor-

dis cites feminist Carole Pateman as pointing out that "since surrogacy contracts typically limit a woman's sexual activity after
insemination, govern the drugs and foods she can consume, and
have attempted (in some cases) to remove her option of abortion, surrogacy verges on the enslavement of women."

Rabbi Gordis also worries about the social effects of surrogacy. Surrogacy will, in his view, accentuate the social and economic differences between the relatively rich couple and lawyer as against the relatively poor surrogate mother. A *New York
Times* article he cites reported a typical surrogacy agreement in
1987 that provided $10,000 for the surrogate mother, $10,000
for the lawyer, and $5,000 for the medical expenses involved
and for maternity clothes. (Surrogacy has become more expensive since then: the cost for a typical ovum surrogacy in 1994
had risen to $42,000.[68]) The couple's joint annual income ex-
ceeded $100,000, whereas the surrogate's annual income was
$8,000.

Moreover, the costs of surrogacy mean that only the rich will
be able to pass down their genes in this way, and that is effectively saying that the rich are more entitled to reproduce than
the poor. Indeed, if surrogacy were legitimized, Rabbi Gordis
fears, women on welfare might have to explain why they would
not be willing to earn money as surrogates, another aspect of
the inherent slavery involved. Since that burden could be imposed only on women, it would serve further to degrade wom-
en vis-à-vis men in our society, in this case women on welfare
versus men on welfare.

The sharpened social differentiations engendered by surrogacy between rich and poor, whites and blacks, and men and wom-
en will negatively affect not only the people involved in the specific surrogacy, Rabbi Gordis claims, but the rest of society too,
for people think of themselves not only in terms of their absolute economic gains and losses over time but relative to what
other people have ("relative deprivation"). Few of us can afford
everything we might like, but the desire for children is considerably more intense and personal than most of our other desires.
Thus if surrogacy were to be permitted, infertile couples who

cannot afford surrogates would feel all the worse for their inability to have children of their own. Surrogacy also widens the gap between the races and classes of women who are willing to be surrogate mothers, for "in a 'womb/pregnancy market,' white women will generally command a greater fee than will blacks." In sum, then, surrogacy, in Rabbi Gordis's view, will have the deleterious social effect of deepening the divisions and inequities between rich and poor, whites and blacks, and men and women.[69]

Reform Rabbi Marc Gellman expresses yet another moral concern. While surrogacy may not technically be adultery, introducing a third party into the couple's reproductive process may *feel* dangerously close to that and may ultimately undermine the couple's relationship altogether. Furthermore, in ovum surrogacy using the husband's sperm (the most common type of surrogacy), the wife is being asked to raise a child who is genetically her husband's but not hers—and one carried by another woman to boot. "The sanctity of family life requires a single husband and wife."[70] Along the same lines, Israel's Health Ministry outlawed surrogacy in 1987 on the grounds that "the practice was just unacceptable," in addition to the resulting uncertainty as to the identity of the parents of the child.[71]

These moral concerns are real. In a landmark responsum adopted by the Conservative movement's Committee on Jewish Law and Standards, however, Rabbi Elie Spitz responds to many of them, and I think that the others can be satisfactorily addressed as well.[72]

Let us speak first to Rabbi Gordis's social concerns. It is indeed true that only the rich will be able to afford such a procedure, and that will amplify the differences between rich and poor. The United States, though, is not a socialist country, and while Americans have considered it important to provide basic medical care to the elderly and to those who cannot afford it through programs like Medicare and Medicaid, even the most liberal stances in American politics do not endorse making surrogacy available at public expense. Indeed, even those countries that have enacted government-sponsored, universal health care, like Canada and the United Kingdom, do not pay for surrogacy. Moreover, while surrogacy is economically beyond the reach of the poor, it is hardly the thing they covet most. It is, after all, still a rare procedure and thus not likely to be a privilege of which they feel even comparatively deprived. One certainly must create social safeguards to ensure that the gap between rich and poor will not deprive the poor of essential services or make the society politically unstable, but surrogacy does not seem to fall into either of those categories.

The degradation of the woman, an issue raised by both Rabbis Jakobovits and Gordis, is a more serious issue, but that fear has been substantially allayed by the brief history of surrogacy. Rabbi Spitz reports that at least eight doctoral dissertations and other professional studies probing surrogacy have been conducted, and all of them belie the early predictions and concerns about the procedure. Surrogate mothers, the studies found, are not generally black and poor; on the contrary,

> the typical surrogate mother was twenty-eight years old, married with children, employed full-time, and had thirteen years of education. Her husband was supportive of her decision to serve as a surrogate. Most were Caucasian, middle-range in income bracket, in good health, and had positive experiences in past pregnancies. While money was a factor in choosing to become a surrogate, it rated consistently lower than the desire to help another couple.[73]

Since surrogacy is rare and the surrogate mother is generally not poor, Rabbi Gordis's worries about women on welfare being forced to serve in this capacity have proven unfounded.

Moreover, these studies should allay the fear that surrogacy is inherently disgraceful. The money involved certainly makes it less than totally altruistic, but to deny the altruism of surrogate mothers simply because it is not pure is to misunderstand the complex nature of human motivation in general and the conscious and real feelings of these women in particular. This predominant motivation makes their act not morally degrading but, quite the contrary, morally praiseworthy. (The same arguments apply to the vast majority of sperm or ovum donors.)

The concern that surrogate mothers might be virtual slaves has largely been allayed by developments in American civil law. According to William Handel, an attorney with special expertise in surrogacy, the items often contained in a surrogacy agreement include (1) complete freedom of choice for the surrogate to withdraw from the agreement prior to conception; (2) a guarantee of the surrogate's right over her body during pregnancy, including the right to abortion and operations to protect her health; (3) a commitment on the part of the intended parents to accept the newborn, regardless of his or her condition; and (4) payment to the surrogate of all medical costs, psychological counseling, attorney's fees, and living expenses in addition to her fee. As in any contract, there are some responsibilities that the surrogate must also assume, namely, not to abuse her body in a way that would likely cause damage to the fetus (e.g., by taking drugs) and to turn over the baby to the intended parents once born.[74] Thus even though the biblical precedents for surrogacy depict Sarah and Rachel as using their handmaids for the procedure, the provisions in modern surrogacy agreements detailing both parties' rights and duties make them clearly contracts between free agents.

Improved surrogacy contracts and new laws governing surrogacy in some states also help to prevent the social rancor that would result from a long string of broken surrogacy agreements. Very few court cases on surrogacy have in fact occurred.[75] The highly publicized cases—in particular, the Baby M case in 1987–1988 and, to a somewhat lesser extent, the Marriage of Moschetta case in 1993[76]—inevitably caused great pain, but the incidence of such failed surrogacy agreements (.025 percent) is much lower than the frequency of failed adoption agreements, where the chances of the biological mother changing her mind are commonly put at between 5 and 15 percent, and in one study were as high as 38 percent.[77]

Some judges and some state laws have complicated matters by analogizing surrogacy to adoption and then seeing paid surrogacy as forbidden baby selling; indeed, four states have made it illegal for a surrogate to receive any payment, and five more have allowed "expenses" only.[78] As Rabbi Spitz argues, though, the analogy is faulty for several reasons: contrary to adoption, in surrogacy (1) the intended father is in most cases the biological father; (2) through their surrogacy contract the intended parents accept responsibility for the child from the moment of conception, thus protecting the interests of the child in having a secure home regardless of impairment in the child or of any changes of circumstances among the adults involved—a state of responsibility parallel to that embedded in Jewish law for all of a parent's children;[79] and (3) there is less duress on the woman who agrees to give up the child, since she makes her decision even before conception and is typically a married, secure woman with children of her own.

In contrast, the woman who gives up a child for adoption is most often an unmarried teenager for whom this is her first pregnancy, who regrets the pregnancy (as does the biological father), and who lacks the financial resources to take care of the child. Adoption law therefore rightfully seeks to protect such a vulnerable, pregnant teenager from baby brokers who offer her some money in exchange for the unwanted child. This is significantly different from surrogacy, where the goal of all concerned is to produce a child for parents who want one through the surrogate mother's pregnancy.[80]

The state, then, has a real interest in transforming the provisions now commonly included in surrogacy contracts into legal requirements. It need not, however, protect the surrogate mother from the kinds of abuse to which unwilling teenage mothers are subject by making payment to the surrogate illegal. On the contrary, if it does that, it will, except in a few cases of family members serving as surrogates, effectively make surrogacy unavailable to those infertile couples who cannot have a child in any other way with the gametes of at least one of them. In Rabbi Spitz's view, which I endorse in light of the arguments above, outlawing payments to surrogates would be an unnecessary and unwarranted ban that would unjustly prevent infertile couples from having the child they so desperately seek.

CHAPTER FOUR

Having Children Using Donated Genetic Materials

Artificial Insemination with a Donor's Sperm: Legal Concerns

So far we have investigated techniques using the genetic materials (gametes) of the couple trying to have a child. These techniques, however, can also be used with donor gametes. The American Fertility Society estimated in 1991 that as many as fifty thousand couples each year use a third party in an attempt to have a child, most through sperm donation, some through ovum donation, and some through surrogate mothers, and more recent estimates have put that number at well over a hundred thousand.

Before delving into the complex legal, moral, and psychological issues involved in these techniques, it is important to remind couples considering these options once again that Jewish law does not require the use of any of them. Moreover, since the financial and psychological tolls are considerable, couples considering these procedures are well advised to learn about the pitfalls and to make plans to cope with their own psychological strains in advance.

The first successful DI (donor insemination) was reported by Dr. Pancoast in 1884, but until the 1970s there were only intermittent reports of DI in European and American medical literature.[1] Since the procedure of artificial insemination is not difficult, the paucity of discussion of DI was undoubtedly due primarily to the legal and moral problems it raises, some of which will be discussed below. Nowadays, however, about 45 percent of all artificial inseminations use donor sperm, and since the 1950s, donor insemination alone has been responsible for at least 300,000 births in the United States, with 10,000 to 20,000 new DI births each year.[2]

Frozen semen was first used successfully for DI in 1953,[3] but the technique did not become common until the mid-1970s. Now almost all DI programs use frozen sperm exclusively. Frozen sperm succeeds in producing conception at about the same rate as fresh sperm does, and freezing sperm enables DI programs to test the donor over a six-month period for AIDS and other diseases before using his sperm. We shall treat donor insemination first and then consider the additional concerns raised by egg donation. The objections raised by various rabbis to both these procedures are legal and moral. I shall treat the legal issues posed by DI in this section and the moral ones in the next, although, as noted in Chapter 1 and in the Appendix, moral and legal concerns often overlap. Since this chapter is based on a responsum I wrote for the Conservative movement's Committee on Jewish Law and Standards, and since it was approved unanimously by that committee, my interpretations of Jewish law in this chapter are officially held positions of the Conservative movement.[4]

These, then, are the predominantly legal objections to DI that rabbis have raised:

Adultery and Illegitimacy

Since in DI a married woman is being inseminated with the sperm of a man other than her husband, some rabbis construe DI as adultery. This would make any child born through DI illegitimate (a *mamzer*); according to the Torah, such a person and his or her descendants may not marry a Jew for ten generations. Rabbi Eliezer Waldenberg, for example, takes strong exception to donor insemination on these grounds:

> The very essence of this matter—namely, placing in the womb of a married woman the seed of another man—is a great abomination

of the tent of Jacob, and there is no greater profanation of the family than this in the dwelling places of Israel. This destroys all the sublime concepts of purity and holiness of Jewish family life, for which our people has been so noted since it became a nation.[5]

This, in my view, misreads the prohibition against adultery. The Torah forbids it, along with incest and some other forms of sexual behavior, to make the Israelites holy and pure as a people. Holiness, as the literary and historical contexts of the Torah's prohibitions indicate, means that the Israelites must be different, separate, apart (the meaning of the Hebrew root *kadosh*) in moral character and action from the ancient Egyptians and Canaanites, and purity entails avoiding pollution of the land of Israel through licentious sexual practices.[6]

The Canaanites and Egyptians of old no longer exist, and most of the world's Jews live outside the land of Israel. The question, then, is whether modern artificial insemination violates our contemporary understanding of holiness and purity in a marital relationship, as adultery does; that question in turn leads us to identify which aspects of adultery make it abhorrent. Adultery is repugnant primarily because it violates the trust between husband and wife that must be the foundation of their relationship.[7] The woman has "cheated" on her husband, or vice versa. In standard cases of artificial insemination by a donor, however, the husband not only knows about the insemination but deeply wants it so that he and his wife can have children.[8] Contrary to Rabbi Waldenberg, then, artificial insemination by a donor is not an "abomination" or "profanation" that destroys all Jewish concepts of holiness and purity but rather a desperate attempt to have children—an undisputed good in marital relationships for the Jewish tradition—in a context of mutual openness and trust.

On a more technical level, the Talmud, Maimonides, Rabbi David Halevi (the "Taz"), and the majority of recent authorities maintain that the legal category of adultery is incurred only when the penis of the man enters the vaginal cavity of the woman.[9] That is clearly not the case when insemination takes place artificially. The lack of contact of the genital organs in donor insemination thus means that it does not legally constitute adultery, and the child conceived by DI therefore does not suffer from the liabilities of a *mamzer* (child conceived in adultery).

Another factor differentiates DI from adultery: the intent to have an illicit relationship is missing. When the Temple stood, a couple who mistakenly committed an act of incest or adultery (for example, a brother and sister who did not know each other as such, or twins who had married twins and erroneously had sex with their siblings' spouses) would still have to bring a sin-offering, but they would not be liable for the more serious penalties of extirpation *(karet)*, death at the hands of the court, or lashes.[10] Thus the intent of the couple is an important legal consideration, and it is an even more important moral consideration. In the case of DI, the couple's intent is the exact opposite of adultery, for they are going through expensive and emotionally taxing procedures expressly to affirm their love for each other through having and raising a child. Thus DI should not be construed as adultery either theologically, legally, or morally.

Unintentional Incest in the Next Generation

If the identity of the donor is known, the people born through his sperm donation can and should avoid mating with his offspring through marriage so as to avoid incest, for their common father makes them, after all, half brothers and half sisters. Usually, though, the donor is anonymous, and that raises the possibility of unintentional incest in the next generation. That is, the person produced by artificial insemination might happen to marry one of the children of the donor and his wife, and since the children share a father, they would each be marrying their biological half sibling. Both members of the couple and their families would be completely unaware that the relationship was incestuous, for just as recipients do not generally know the identity of the donors whose sperm they use, so, too, donors do not know the identity of the recipients.

If the donor has not been identified but it is known that he is not Jewish, sexual intercourse between the people born through his sperm donation and those born through his marriage would not technically constitute a violation of Judaism's laws prohibiting incest, even if the non-Jewish donor's wife is Jewish and thus his children are Jewish, for Jewish law does not recognize family lineage among non-Jews through the father's line.[11] On that basis, Rabbi Moshe Feinstein permitted DI if the donor was not Jewish, although he was later pressured to withdraw his responsum.[12] However the incest question is resolved, some Orthodox rabbis object to using a non-Jewish donor for fear that this will pollute the purity of the Jewish genetic line and will transfer non-Jewish qualities of character (whatever that means) to Jewish offspring. Rabbi Feinstein's original position, in any case, has led to a curious result. Physicians report that while traditional Jews who use DI prefer non-Jewish donors for fear of incest in the next generation, liberal Jews want Jewish donors. The motivations for that tendency may be many, but undoubtedly for some people insemination by a non-Jew smacks of intermarriage, and others probably hold an ethnic notion of Jewish identity and want a Jewish donor for reasons not unlike the Orthodox arguments against polluting the Jewish biological line.

Whether used by the Orthodox or the more liberal groups within Judaism, this line of reasoning is clearly rooted in exclusivist and frankly racist understandings of Jews and non-Jews, views to which contemporary Jews should not be party.[13] Indeed, they should feel embarrassed for even thinking such things, let alone using them in their decisions about overcoming infertility.

There is another factor, though, that makes it imperative that the identity of the donor, or at least substantial parts of his medical history, be known. Jewish law puts great emphasis on maintaining health. To uphold this value, we must strive to prevent the serious genetic defects and diseases that consanguinity of the couple can cause. This is clearly a concern if we know that the donor is Jewish, but in our own day, with rampant intermarriage, it is even a worry if the donor is not Jewish, for a child born through DI may some day marry a non-Jew who is his or her natural half brother or half sister—or have intercourse with such a person outside marriage. This concern is all the more worrisome because sperm banks are largely unregulated by state law, and many use the same donors for numerous inseminations.[14]

All these factors would argue all the more strongly that a child born through DI should know the identity of his or her natural father—whether Jewish or not—or at least enough of his medical history to avoid people with similar medical histories as mates. The same, incidentally, would be true for an adopted child. In light of the much larger numbers of non-Jews than Jews in North America, this concern would not be as great if it were known that the natural father (or, in the case of adoption, the natural parents) were not Jewish, for in this case the chances of such an unwitting, consanguineous union occurring are much, much smaller. The day is probably not too far off when such unions can be prevented through DNA analysis of the child and his or her potential mate without revealing anything about the identity of the donor.

There are yet other physical reasons to disclose as much as possible about the donor to the social parents and child. In the future, a health condition may arise in the child whose proper treatment requires more information from the donor than he provided on the initial questionnaire; conversely, a genetic condition might appear in the child that could have health implications for the donor, his children, or his family. Therefore, responsible sperm banks keep donor and patient files and continue to track the whereabouts of donors and patients, and state laws should require that.[15]

Disclosure of the identities of donors and recipients, then, is preferable for the physical reasons described above and the psychological reasons delineated below. Nevertheless, the strong recommendation of the American Association of Tissue Banks-Reproductive Council, the practice of most sperm banks, and the preference of most sperm donors and recipients are all that the parties involved remain unknown to each other, largely for the psychological reasons described below.[16] That confidentiality is permissible from the point of view of Jewish law *if* the sperm bank keeps thorough records on all its donors and recipients and conscientiously updates them as necessary. Furthermore, as much as possible of the donor's medical history must be revealed to the child in order to prevent possible genetic diseases in that child's own offspring.

The Identity of the Father

The identity of the father is potentially an issue in four matters: the child's Jewish identity, priestly status, and inheritance rights; and the father's duty to procreate. The first three of those are, in most cases, fairly easily resolved, but the last is more troublesome.

With regard to Jewish identity, it does not matter whether the donor of the semen is a Jew, for Jewish law determines a person's Jewish identity according to the bearing mother. Since we are talking about the artificial insemination of a Jewish woman, her offspring are automatically Jewish, no matter how she came to be pregnant. Where a Jewish couple will be raising the child, he or she may be known in Hebrew as the son or daughter of the social parents.[17] The more complicated questions of personal status regarding the possibility of incest in the next generation have been treated above.

Priestly status is determined by the biological father, for it is, according to the Torah, "the seed of Aaron" who are to perform the priestly duties.[18] Therefore, if the donor is known to be, respectively, a *kohen, levi,* or *yisrael,* the child has that status as well. If the donor's priestly status is not known, which is usually the case, the child is treated as a *yisrael* on a default basis. Over 90 percent of Jewish men are not priests or Levites, and so for the vast majority this will not be an issue. DI (and adoptive) fathers who themselves are priests or Levites, however, will undoubtedly find it jarring not to be able to pass their priestly status on to their sons (and, in some circles, their daughters). In Orthodox and some Conservative synagogues, this will mean that each time the Torah is read, the father and son will realize once again that they are not like most other fathers and sons, for the father is eligible to be called to the Torah for the first honors, whereas the son is not. In many Conservative and Reform synagogues, though, the first two to be called to the Torah are no longer necessarily a *kohen* and *levi*, and so the father and son need not feel the bite of this difference between them each time the Torah is read.

As for inheritance, would the child of DI inherit from the sperm donor, the husband (the social father), neither, or both? While significant claims of justice, deep emotional feelings, and serious sums of money can all be at stake in deciding who is legally the father of a DI child, matters of inheritance are governed in the Americas and in Europe by civil law, not Jewish law. In the United States, thirty-one American states have passed laws making the child of a married couple who use DI the legal child of that couple. Unlike adoption, no court order or other official action is required for this to be the case, but some states restrict this parentage to cases in which a physician did the procedure, and twenty-six require that the husband's consent to the donor insemination be in writing. Eighteen of these thirty-one states have adopted some form of the Uniform Parentage Act, which defines the donor as *not* being the father with regard to either rights or responsibilities, as long as a physician was involved in the insemination.[19] Donors who want to protect their property, though, may want to remain anonymous in states that have not enacted such a law, where a physician was not involved, or where the husband did not provide written consent to the procedure (or the donor has no way of knowing whether the husband did). In any case, since state law governs inheritance, the implications of DI for inheritance within Jewish law need not concern those who live in any of those areas. In Israel the matter is more complicated, depending upon whether the family chooses rabbinic or civil courts to adjudicate the disposition of the estate, but since the vast majority of Israel's Jews choose the civil courts, even there this issue is largely moot.

What Jewish law does determine, though, is whether a Jewish man fulfills the commandment to be fruitful and multiply if he consents to have his wife impregnated with another man's semen, if his own semen is artificially implanted in his wife's uterus, or if he himself is a semen donor. By and large, rabbis who have ruled on these matters thus far have maintained that for the purposes of this commandment, the father is the man who provides the semen. That would make a man who impregnates his wife through artificial insemination (AIH) the father of his child in Jewish law, and it would also make a semen donor the father of any children born through the use of his semen. On the other hand, it would deny the status of fatherhood to men who consent to have their wives impregnated with donor semen. These last two results are clearly alarming for donors and disappointing for social fathers.[20]

The first point to mention in evaluating these rulings is that donor insemination stretches our understanding of fatherhood. We normally assume that the same man who sired a child will be the one who raises him or her. When that does not happen, the legal category of fatherhood and the concept underlying it must be applied to circumstances not contemplated when the concept and the law were first formulated. In light of that, we should not be surprised if the traditional concept of fatherhood does not fit exactly right, no matter how we classify the new forms of procreation.

In our case, several factors would lead us to call the semen donor the father for purposes of the commandment of propagation. Unless there has been a formal, legal act of adoption, in American law we call the man who brings up a child but who did not sire it "the foster father" or "the stepfather," depending upon the circumstances. That usage, which exists in rabbinic law as well *(apotropos)*, would argue for seeing the biological father alone as the one official "father."

Moreover, as I shall describe in more detail in the section on adoption below, while the Jewish tradition applauded adoption as a way of providing parental support and education for orphaned children, it never ascribed legal parentage to the adoptive parents, seeing them rather as the agents of the child's natural parents. That precedent would seem to apply to a child born through DI as well, making the social father the agent of the biological father and not his legal substitute.

Underlying both the linguistic usage and Jewish law on adoption is the incontrovertible genetic fact that it is the natural father's DNA that the child inherits, not the social father's. Modern research has made us increasingly aware of the impact of our genes on who we are as people, not only biologically but in a number of character traits as well. The donor's genes influence the medical history of the child, and they determine the identity of the people whom it is genetically dangerous to marry, lest the children born of that marriage suffer from diseases rooted in their consanguineous union. Moreover, the donor's genes will affect the child's intelligence, height, general physical appearance, susceptibility to specific diseases, and even personality traits such as the tendency to get angry quickly or to laugh often. The genetic contribution of the semen donor, while modified by the child's upbringing, is thus ultimately indelible.

On the other hand, there are other factors that would lead us to classify the social father as the one who fulfills the command to propagate. According to the biblical law of levirate marriage, when a man dies childless, it is the duty of his brother to have conjugal relations with the widow so that a child might be born bearing the parentage of the deceased brother. That precedent would argue that the semen donor is not the father.[21]

Moreover, one classical rabbinic source ascribes fatherhood to the man who raises a child, not to the one who provided semen. It is a homiletical *(aggadic)* source, and therefore not one intended to announce law, but it does speak of a legal context, namely, the writing of a marriage contract. Moreover, it specifically proclaims the guardian the father and does not regard him *as if* he were the father. Based on Isaiah 64:7, "But now, O Lord, You are our Father," the Midrash says:

> The Holy One, blessed be He, said: "You have abandoned your ancestors, Abraham, Isaac, and Jacob, and you are calling Me father?" They said to Him: "We are recognizing You as [our] father." Parable: An orphaned girl grew up with a guardian *[apotropos]*, and he was a good and faithful man who raised her and watched over her as is fitting. He wanted to marry her off, and the scribe

came to write her marriage contract. He said to her: "What is your name?" She said: "So-and-so." He said to her: "And what is the name of your father?" At first she was silent. Her guardian said to her: "Why are you silent?" She said to him: "Because I know no father except you [the guardian]," for the one who raises [a child] is called father and not the one who begets [a child]. Similarly, these orphans, Israel, [have God as their father,] for Scripture says, "We were orphans without a father" (Lamentations 5:3), [but] their good and faithful Guardian is the Holy One, blessed be He, [and] Israel began to call Him "our Father," as it says, "But now, O Lord, You are our Father" (Isaiah 64:7). The Holy One, blessed be He [said]: "You have abandoned your ancestors and you call Me 'Our Father'?" as it says, "Look back to Abraham, your father, [and to Sarah who brought you forth]" (Isaiah 51:2). They said to Him: "Master of the world, the one who raises [a child] is the father and not the one who begets [him/her]," for it says, "For You are our father, for we have not known Abraham" (Isaiah 63:16).[22]

Furthermore, according to Jewish law, a gentile who renounces the idolatrous status of a given idol thereby converts it into a mere statue.[23] Similarly, it could be argued—although obviously with no implications whatsoever that a child is an idol!—that the donor's explicit intention to have someone else raise the child amounts to a renunciation of his status of fatherhood and a transfer of it to the social father.

Yet another precedent that argues in this direction is that of Jacob, who adopts Joseph's sons, Ephraim and Menashe, as his own. Their descendants thus become two of the twelve tribes of Israel, along with the descendants of the rest of Jacob's sons.[24] This example too identifies the father as the man who took on the responsibilities of fatherhood (here, inheritance) rather than the one who sired the child.

Aside from these arguments based on facets of Jewish law and other classical Jewish texts, a number of contemporary realities would argue in this direction. American law, as we have seen, construes the man who raises the child to be his or her father for all legal purposes. With the exception of the physician who asks for a medical history of the child's family, all of the people who come into the child's life see the social father alone as the father. That is right and proper, for the social father, after all, invests a lifetime of energy, love, and substance in the child, whereas in most cases the donor never even meets the child. Jewish law generally awards privileges only to those who bear concomitant responsibilities, and that principle would certainly suggest in this case that the man who raises the child, rather than the man who merely ejaculates, should merit the status of fulfilling the commandment of propagation. Such a ruling would accord with both the intentions and the actions of both men involved.

Whichever man is deemed the father, then, some aspects of the decision will seem counterintuitive, for in some ways the semen donor is clearly the father, and in some ways the social father is. Moreover, identifying exclusively one or the other as the father hides important aspects of the child's being. To be true to the identity of the child and to the roles that both men involved play in forming it, then, the fatherhood of both must be recognized for the distinctive ways in which each is the child's father.

For the purposes of the commandment of propagation, the semen donor must be seen as the father of the child. In part this is because of the precedents cited in the section on nonsexual insemination in Chapter 3 — although, as I indicated there, those stories are not really on point as analogies for the modern practice of DI. More substantively, however, it is the ultimate fact that the child's genetic heritage is that of the semen donor that justifies this classification. Jewish law abhors incest, counting it among only three prohibitions that one may never violate, even at the cost of one's life.[25] As indicated earlier, I believe that sexual intercourse between the donor's other children and the child produced by his donation of sperm should not count legally or morally as incest, since there can be no intent of incest, due to the couple's lack of knowledge that they are actually half siblings. Nevertheless, genetically such a union would be incest, and that fact must lead us to declare the semen donor as the father with regard to the physical act of procreation. As noted below, this imposes upon a Jewish donor some duties from which American law exempts him, and that must be part of his understanding and undertaking when he agrees to donate his sperm.

This is not to deny the critical input of the social father in the raising of the child. In some ways, the fact that the social father is not legally the father in Jewish law gives the man who assumes all the obligations of raising the children conceived through DI an even more honorific status. As the Talmud says,

> "Happy are they who act justly, who do right at all times" (Psalms 106:3). Is it possible to do right at all times? . . . Rabbi Samuel bar Naḥmani said: This refers to a person who brings up an orphan boy or girl in his house and enables them to marry.[26]

Thus while the social father is not technically the father in the biological sense and therefore does not fulfill through DI the specific commandment to procreate, he is the "real" father in some of the most significant ways for the child and "does right at all times."

Following my suggestion, the Conservative movement's Committee on Jewish Law and Standards has gone yet further. According to traditional sources, one who raises another person's biological child is not subject to the biblical prohibitions that apply to one's own child. Thus intercourse between an adoptive parent and the adopted child is not a violation of the biblical laws of incest,[27] and adopted children raised in the same home may, according to the Talmud, marry each other.[28]

Even though there is no biological relationship between the social father and the child adopted or born through DI, and despite the fact that the Talmud permits adopted children to marry each other, the emotional and educational relationships among the members of the family are sufficiently strong to apply the category of secondary relations (sheniyot) to DI children, and also to adopted children. That is, in most cases of DI, the wife's eggs are used for all of the couple's children, and then sexual relations between two of the children, who are biologically half brothers and half sisters, are prohibited according to the Torah itself. But even if a couple has a girl and a boy who were both born using another woman's eggs and another man's sperm, sexual relations between them should be seen as incest of the second degree, and consequently their marriage to each other would be forbidden as a rabbinic enactment. The same would be true for two adopted children, even if their biological parents are four separate people, all different from the social parents. Moreover, intercourse between adoptive parents and their adopted children, or between the social father and the donor-inseminated child he is raising, should also be seen as prohibited incest of the second degree. That is a stringency beyond the traditional sources, but one that the close relationship created in raising a child warrants.[29]

In sum, the social father does not fulfill the commandment of propagation through either DI or adoption, because the child's genetic heritage is not the social father's and because traditional sources define an adoptive parent as the agent of the natural parent. Jewish marital law, though, must recognize the strong bonds that social parents create between themselves and the children they raise and among the children themselves, whether they became the social parents' children through donor insemination, egg donation, or adoption. Consequently, sexual relations between the parents and children or between the children themselves are prohibited in the second degree.[30] Furthermore, the social father's name may be invoked when the child is being identified by his or her Hebrew name, as, for example, when called to the Torah.[31] Similarly, children of donor insemination should consider the Torah's commands to honor one's parents (Exodus 20:12; Deuteronomy 5:16) and to respect them (Leviticus 19:3) as applying to their social parents, and conversely, the social parents should consider themselves responsible for fulfilling the duties that the Torah and the Jewish tradition impose upon parents vis-à-vis their children.[32]

This approach openly recognizes the relationship to the child of both the semen donor (i.e., the biological father) and the social father. Donor insemination has real import for both men involved and for the child, and both men must be seen as the "real" father of the child in the critical, but different, ways in which they both are.

Artificial Insemination with a Donor's Sperm: Moral Concerns

Licentiousness

Since the strictly legal concerns discussed above can be resolved, most rabbis who have objected to donor insemination have done so on moral grounds. In my own view, positive law and morality are one undifferentiated web, in which each can and should influence the other. That is especially true in a religious legal system like the Jewish one, where a fundamental assumption is that the law must express the will of a moral—indeed, a benevolent—God. Thus the moral concerns raised by donor insemination are not, for me, "merely" moral, but fully legal.[33]

It is especially interesting to note, though, that rabbis who usually shun moral arguments in their legal decisions have invoked them to deny the legitimacy of donor insemination. Thus Rabbi J. David Bleich, for example, reminds us that according to Jewish law, the provider of the semen is the father, and therefore the social father does not fulfill the mitzvah of procreation by consenting to have his wife impregnated by another man's seed, even if he subsequently assumes all of the responsibilities of parenthood. In Rabbi Bleich's view, this reduces donor insemination to a matter of the personal desire of the social parents to raise children, and that must be weighed against the potential legal problems of adultery, wasting of seed, and incest in the next generation. Despite this, he hesitantly permits it under certain circumstances.[34]

Others have similarly voiced concern about the morality of using someone else's body or semen in this way, and still others worry that artificial insemination will increase the prospects of widespread licentiousness. Rabbi Jakobovits voices these moral concerns in strong language:

> If Jewish law nevertheless opposes A.I.D. [artificial insemination by a donor] without reservation as utterly evil, it is mainly for moral reasons, not because of the intrinsic illegality of the act itself. The principal motives for the revulsion against the practice is [sic]the

fear of the abuses to which its legalization would lead, however great the benefits may be in individual cases. By reducing human generation to stud-farming methods, A.I.D. severs the link between the procreation of children and marriage, indispensable to the maintenance of the family as the most basic and sacred unit of human society. It would enable women to satisfy their craving for children without the necessity to have homes or husbands. It would pave the way to a disastrous increase of promiscuity, as a wife, guilty of adultery, could always claim that a pregnancy which her husband did not, or was unable to, cause was brought about by A.I.D., when in fact she had adulterous relations with another man. Altogether, the generation of children would become arbitrary and mechanical, robbed of those mystic and intimately human qualities which make man a partner with God in the creative propagation of the race.[35]

I take a much more positive attitude toward donor insemination. After all, people who want to be licentious will find many ways to do so without artificial insemination. Indeed, donor insemination is so onerous a mode of illicit sex—if it be that at all—that it is downright implausible that people would go to the trouble and expense of using it for such purposes.

Furthermore, the couple is, by hypothesis, using DI when they have no other way to achieve a precious goal in Jewish law and thought, the bearing of children. Even if the social father does not technically fulfill the obligation to procreate through DI, we should applaud the couple's willingness to use DI for three reasons: the Jewish tradition has always valued children; in their efforts to have children, couples who use DI will undergo hardships that other couples need not endure, as described below, and they consequently need every encouragement they can get; and, finally, having and raising Jewish children is a demographic imperative for the Jewish community in our time.

The Impact on the Marriage and on the Parent-Child Relationship
Rabbi Jakobovits's point about severing the tie between generation and parenting is more serious. We clearly do not want to transform the generation of human beings into stud farming,

we certainly do want to acknowledge the importance of fathers in the rearing of children, and we do want to preserve the tie between children and loving families.

These concerns should not, however, lead to a prohibition of donor insemination. We shall treat the special issues raised by DI of single women in the last section of this chapter. The vast majority of donor inseminations, though, take place in the context of infertile marriages, and so to weigh the morality of donor insemination we must analyze what it does to the relationship between husband and wife and between parents and child.

In a philosophically penetrating article probing the nature of parenthood, Paul Lauritzen, a man whose own wife was artificially inseminated with donor sperm, notes that one need not deny the significance of genetic relationships to affirm that the more important parental relationship to a child is that of caring for it.

> Caring for, nurturing, and nourishing a child in the context of an ongoing social, emotional, and loving relationship is more important than physically begetting a child, however ineradicable and significant the physical/biological connection that is created thereby. . . . While genetic connection may foster relational bonds, it is the bonds that are crucial, not the genetic ties.[36]

Lisa Sowle Cahill has argued against artificial insemination (and adoption) on the ground that biological relation offers children greater moral protection from abandonment than the parental bonds to which individuals freely consent, but Lauritzen points out that that is not necessarily so.

> While it may be true that biological relation will often, in Cahill's words, "undergird and enhance" the interpersonal relation between parent and child, this biological relation is not necessary to the development of an intense, ongoing social relationship; nor does the existence of a biological relation ensure a social commitment to care. . . . Parental responsibilities are, in a sense, inalienable, but it is not genetic connection that makes them so; rather it is the intense, person-specific nature of the interpersonal bonds constituting the

parental relation that makes parental responsibility largely non-transferable.[37]

The real moral problems in donor insemination for Lauritzen, then, are those that threaten the purpose of parenthood and the relationship between husband and wife. Chief among those are secrecy and the genetic asymmetry donor insemination creates in the relationship between each of the parents and the child.

SECRECY.   The secrecy that often surrounds artificial insemination is sometimes justified as a protection for the child, sometimes as protection for the husband, and sometimes as protection for the donor. We shall consider each in turn.

Children, the argument goes, may feel perplexed and odd if they know they were conceived in an unusual way, especially as they approach puberty. Moreover, when they have their inevitable quarrels with their parents, children born through artificial insemination, like adopted children, may feel and say that they would not be having such problems if their *real* fathers were there. Secrecy presumably shields children from such feelings and helps them accept their social parents, even in times of tension.

Secrecy about how a child was conceived, though, undermines the trust that must be at the very core of a child's relationship with his or her parents—especially on a subject as critical to a child's identity and self-image as his or her genetic origins. Since secrecy almost definitely will require one or both social parents to lie to the child on a number of occasions, the potential damage is even worse. As Sissela Bok notes in her book, *Lying*, lies are particularly corrosive and contagious within families. "The need to shore up lies, [to] keep them in good repair," she writes, "the anxieties relating to possible discovery, the entanglements and threats to integrity—are greatest in a close relationship where it is rare that one lie will suffice."[38] Indeed, as Lauritzen points out, this is possibly the most egregious case of "living a lie," for when the truth about a child's origins through donor insemination is kept from the child, everything about the parent-child relationship is based on a presumed or explicit lie. That surely is "incompatible with the commitments that responsible parenthood entails,"[39] not only theoretically but practically, for it engenders in both children and parents shame, guilt, fear, and suspicion.

Secrecy does not protect the husband's ego either. It is perfectly normal for men who cannot impregnate their wives to feel angry, inadequate, ashamed, and even guilty. The only hope of coping with such feelings over the long run is not through denial but rather through expressing them (literally, pushing them out) through open communication with those who are likely to be sympathetic and supportive.

If a man can talk about this with his wife, she can reassure him that she still considers him a manly mate, whatever the number or motility of his sperm may be. Furthermore, he will soon discover, if he does not already know, that marriage is not based exclusively on the ability to procreate, that it includes, more importantly, sharing life together. Moreover, through artificial insemination or adoption infertile couples can raise children together, which, after all, takes much more time, energy, and commitment and offers a much more sustained basis for sharing than procreation alone does. If the man is sufficiently self-assured to talk with his male friends about this too, he may well find that he is not alone, that some of his friends may be experiencing the same problems or know of others who are, and that in any case they will not abandon him as a friend and will not think less of him as a man.

If the man cannot muster enough self-confidence to have such discussions, he ironically cuts himself off from the very strengthening he so desperately needs. Secrecy about his wife's donor insemination will thus only compound his problems in making the necessary adjustments in his thoughts, feelings, and plans. As Lauritzen says,

> Unfortunately, to mask a problem is not to resolve it, and the secrecy only serves to delay an acknowledgment of the emotional and psychological effects of sterility. Infertile individuals need to mourn and grieve the children they will not produce; they need to resolve

any feelings of inadequacies that sterility may engender, and secrecy is an obstacle to meeting both needs.[40]

Moreover, the secret of a woman's donor insemination can be revealed at any time in an angry moment, and that cannot but add stress to a marriage. Furthermore, relatives and friends who do not know about the donor insemination will quite innocently add to the man's pain when they talk about whom the child resembles. All of these factors mean that the husband's manliness is much better protected if he does not keep the donor insemination of his wife a secret.

In addition to these psychological and moral considerations, Jewish law would also encourage the husband to avoid secrecy. As we have noted above, if one *cannot* procreate, one ceases to be obligated by the commandment to do so. Therefore, an infertile man should not feel any shame or guilt for failing to fulfill this commandment, since it does not apply to him. Moreover, procreation is not the only duty we have regarding children. Social fathers surely fulfill many commandments to their children in supporting them, educating them, and caring for them, and they act with real, ongoing *ḥesed* (lovingkindness, fidelity) to the children who are, in most significant ways, their own sons or daughters. An infertile Jewish man whose wife is artificially inseminated with donor sperm or whose children are adopted therefore has nothing to hide—and nothing to gain—by secrecy.

That leaves the donor. Secrecy surrounding donor insemination is most often justified to protect the potential pool of donors, for if the donor's identity were known, it is feared, he might be held financially, morally, and perhaps legally responsible for the care of the child or the mother. This responsibility might include not only child support and a claim on the biological father's estate when he dies but also monetary compensation for any disease or disability that passed through the semen from the donor to the child, especially given the general lack of regulations governing sperm banks.[41] Moreover, according to Yeh and Yeh, "many potential donors would be reluctant to give specimens if they knew that their names would be given out publicly," and S. Cooke reports that when Sweden passed a law in 1985 requiring that the identity of the semen donor should be recorded to enable the child at eighteen years of age to contact the biological father, "this resulted in the almost total disappearance of DI in Sweden and frequent referral of couples to other parts of Scandinavia."[42] Conversely, the social parents may want to keep the identity of the donor secret to prevent unwanted intrusions by that man into their lives and into the life of their child.

Some of these are real concerns, and some are not. As noted above, since the 1970s most American states have enacted the Uniform Parentage Act or other legislation making the husband, not the donor, the legal father of the child, with most of these states requiring that the husband agree to the procedure in writing and that there be a physician involved in the insemination. (Similar legislation has been passed in the United Kingdom, Canada, and Australia.[43]) It is only in jurisdictions that did not pass such a law, then, or in cases where the requirements of the law were not met that the donor has any legitimate legal concerns with regard to inheritance or child support.[44]

Potential liability for genetic diseases that later manifest themselves in the child is a more serious reason for donors to remain anonymous. Indeed, three recent law review articles argued that legal notions of warranty should be invoked or legislation should be passed to prosecute such claims, at least if the donor knowingly hid important genetic information or lied about it.[45] This is especially important in light of the fact that donors are usually paid, and even though the sums are modest ($34 on average for each donation paid by public facilities and $44 by private sperm banks, often partly for transportation as well as for the donation[46]), the money may encourage donors to answer questions about their physical histories carelessly or evasively, or perhaps even to lie. Only three states—California, Florida, and Indiana—have enacted legislation going beyond the required testing of sperm donors for the HIV virus, and no state has statutorily imposed regulations sufficient to meet the recommended guidelines of the American Fertility Society.[47] This is undoubtedly because in-depth testing of donors and their sperm could cost recipients an additional $800 to $900,[48] virtually doubling the current costs.[49] But of course this expense is nothing compared with the cost of caring for a genetically defective or diseased child. No legal action has yet been brought against a donor on these grounds, but one could understand why a donor might want to remain anonymous to avoid any such risk.

The social parents may also want to preserve the anonymity between the donor and the recipient in order to keep him out of their lives and the life of the child. Of course, those states that passed the Uniform Parentage Act or its equivalent have thereby established protection against such intrusions, since the sperm donor, according to such statutes, is not legally the father in any way. Courts have given donors paternal rights, though, where the requirements of the law have not been fulfilled and where the donor has evidenced through his actions that he wanted to serve as the child's father.[50] Thus, even in those states with laws governing this issue, and all the more so in those without such laws, the social parents may want to guarantee their freedom from the donor by concealing the identity of all the parties involved.

It is interesting that Australia, where open adoptions have become the norm, has also enacted laws mandating that in cases of DI, donors, donors' spouses (if married), and infertile couples be counseled *not* to preserve anonymity before participating in donor programs. A registry identifying donors is open to children at age eighteen, equivalent to the law on adoption.[51]

American states, however, have uniformly protected the identity of donors and recipients, and even those that keep records of the donation allow them to be opened only for "cause" or "good cause," some requiring a court order to do so. This was the position incorporated into the Uniform Parentage Act as well.[52] Thus American states apparently do not want to go as far as Australia has gone in revealing donors, social parents, and children to each other.

As S. Cooke has said, though,

> There are two situations where most counselors would agree children *must* be told: first, where many members of the family and friends already know and the child might find out from someone other than his parents; secondly, where DI is preferred because of hereditary disease in the husband's family, or because a previous child has died of a genetic disease which carries a high risk of recurrence.[53]

Moreover, our experience with the laws governing adoption should pose a caution about the wisdom of secrecy with regard to DI. Once adopted children reach the age of eighteen, they now have the right, according to the law in many states, to trace their biological parents. Children born through donor insemination currently do not have that right, but DI children as a class may well gain it in the future, especially since the medical and psychological needs that propelled the change in legislation for adopted children are similar in DI children. Thus, despite the experience of Sweden described above, such needs on the part of the child should prompt couples using DI to make sure that the sperm bank they are using keeps careful and current records of their donors and recipients so that that information might be made available in the future should policies change.[54]

In the meantime, one can protect the *confidentiality* of the donor without keeping the fact of the donation a secret. One can even divulge to the child many facts about the donor without compromising his privacy, an important point given that children often want to know—and, one might even say, have the right to know—many genetic characteristics of their biological fathers. At present, only three states (California, Illinois, and Ohio) require the physician to keep records of the attributes of the donor, and fifteen states require that some state agency have such records.[55]

The Jewish tradition's demand that we preserve life and health and therefore avoid the genetic complications of consanguineous unions, together with its high standards of honesty, should encourage Jews to lobby for legislation requiring disclosure at least of the donor's medical history and, if possible, of other personal characteristics that would help his biological children understand themselves. Short of that, Jews should try to use sperm banks that follow such procedures as a matter of policy, even without legislation requiring them to do so. As Mahlstedt and Greenfeld say, "Considering donors real people with specific interests, skills, and family histories enables the donor children to identify positively with their genetic heritage."[56] For both psychological and physical reasons, then, if the donor insists on confidentiality, his sperm may be used for insemination within the bounds of Jewish law only if information about his medical history and, preferably, salient facts about his character and interests are made available to both the social parents and the child.

The above approach to matters of secrecy is based on the best advice available in the psychological literature to date. That, in turn, is based on the experience of many, many people involved in donor insemination, including couples, donors, and children. Still, even with all of this input, some couples may choose to keep the donor insemination a secret from their children, family, and friends in order to make themselves and their child feel as close to them and as "normal" as possible. Social parents should be informed of the advice that has emerged from those who have dealt with donor insemination extensively and the reasons for that advice, as described above, but ultimately the parents' decision in these matters must be understood and respected.

This is especially the case because of the couple's interaction with one other party to DI, namely, the community. Inappropriately and most unfortunately, various elements of the Jewish community attach genuine social stigmas to infertility. In Orthodox circles this attitude manifests itself in the negative remarks and accusations concerning the couple from both the community at large and, even more intensely, from their families. In more liberal circles, competition among families over the intellectual and economic success of their children can besmirch couples who adopt or "borrow" genetic material from others, thus "unfairly" trying to surpass others.

These pressures on infertile couples are both misplaced and cruel, and they must be stopped. Especially given the strong emphasis on procreation within the Orthodox community, Orthodox Jews should presume that couples without children or with a small number of them cannot have more and should therefore demonstrate compassion rather than pressure and disdain. Liberal Jews should stop worshipping the idol of their children's success and should definitely not accuse others of using DI or other techniques to overcome infertility as ruses to pass others in the eugenics race, a race that is the imaginary product of an unhealthy obsession in the first place.

Since couples by themselves cannot engender these changes in social attitudes, though, those subjected to them — and those who know they will be — may retain secrecy about their use of DI or other techniques to overcome infertility in order to avoid such unwarranted and hard-hearted pressures. They should, however, get help in coping with the risks of secrecy described above for the sake of their relationship with each other, with their child, and with their families and community.

ASYMMETRY.   The fact that a child born through donor insemination is the biological descendant of the mother but not that of her husband makes for an asymmetry in their relationship to their child. That can cause problems in their spousal relationship if the husband never works out his feelings of anger, impotence, shame, or perhaps even guilt at not being able to father a child. Every time he sees the child, he may be reminded of his own infertility and, in contrast, his wife's ability to procreate. He may once again resent his predicament and, through psychological transference, his wife. The asymmetry involved in donor insemination may also cause problems in the father-child relationship. In Lauritzen's words,

> When the child is young, there will be the inevitable speculation about whom the child resembles. For the father this is likely to be painful and to frustrate rather than further the parent-child bond. If the child develops in ways or with interests different from the

father's, or if the child is particularly close to his mother, the father may well feel left out, an outsider in the family. If the child is told about the conception, he is likely at some point to wield this information to inflict pain. He may shout in anger that he hates his mother, but only to his father will he say that he, the father, is not his real parent. So the absence of genetic relation is likely to be painful and isolating, and in this pain the mother cannot fully share.[57]

Adoption engenders some of the same feelings; adjusting to them in cases of adoption is in some ways easier and in some ways harder than in cases of donor insemination. On the one hand, since neither of the parents can see an adopted child as their biological progeny, the problems for the husband-wife relationship caused by the asymmetry of donor insemination do not apply. On the other hand, though, the parent-child relationship may be more difficult, for in donor insemination the child knows that at least one of the social parents (the mother) is also his or her biological parent, whereas in adoption both biological parents are unknown. Thus the adopted child's genetic uncertainty and the lure to blame the parents' lack of biological connectedness in moments of tension are doubled.

While these dangers in both donor insemination and adoption should not be minimized, they should not be exaggerated either. We do, after all, have many "blended" families today where children are raised by one biological parent and one non-biological parent. That may not be ideal for the same reasons of asymmetry that artificial insemination is not ideal, and yet we know that committed spousal and parent-child relationships based on honesty, trust, and respect most often overcome the difficulties. Indeed, according to a 1987 study by Goebel and Lubke that followed ninety-six couples for seventeen years after their DI treatment, in cases where the DI was successful or when, having failed, adoption was successful, 10 percent of the couples had divorced. Where neither DI nor adoption had been successful, on the other hand, 35 percent of the couples had divorced.[58] While this is a small study, it indicates that the asymmetry involved in DI is much less of a problem to overcome than the lack of children is.

Furthermore, a 1990 Australian study compared the psycho-social behavior of twenty-two DI children, twenty children conceived naturally, and ten adopted children (all matched by gender and age) and found no differences—except that the fathers as well as the mothers of the DI and adopted children participated in the interviews for the study, whereas in the case of the children conceived through sexual intercourse, only the mothers appeared for the interviews. "This might suggest," S. Cooke comments, "that the fathers of children conceived by DI, contrary to what might be imagined, have much more commitment and involvement with their children than many natural fathers appear to have."[59] Cooke may be stretching things somewhat, for this too is, after all, a small study, but the result does at least give some measure of evidence that DI fathers are no less committed to their children than biological fathers are.

One must remember, too, that marriages with no infertility problems are not always ideal; each marriage and family has its difficulties, and the asymmetry of artificial insemination is just one of many challenges. The couple and child *will* need to talk out the issues fully, however, perhaps with professional help, and such discussions will undoubtedly have to be revisited as the child matures.

The same point applies to grandparents. As Mahlstedt and Greenfeld point out, grandparents who remain distant from grandchildren conceived through donor insemination are generally not reacting to the means of conception but rather to their poor relationships with the social parents on other grounds entirely. It is those other personal problems that must be addressed before the special issues deriving from donor insemination can be successfully confronted.

It is very important for the social parents to recognize this point, for family support is critical to meeting the challenges posed by the asymmetry inherent in donor insemination. As Mahlstedt and Greenfeld say,

> the social attitudes which concern infertile couples most are *not* those of the church or the law, but those of their families. . . . It is

their support that most effectively enables confidence, conviction, and courage to emerge in the couple's experience with donor conception. Couples who receive family love and support reflect less ambivalence about their choice, more comfort in sharing their means of conception with others, and more confidence in their abilities to cope with negative social attitudes.[60]

Thus with grandparents, other family members, and friends, as with the social parents themselves, good relations apart from this issue will help everyone deal with it, and bad relations will make that task harder. Within a reasonably strong network of relationships, however, especially the couple's own, the asymmetry inherent in donor insemination need not become an insurmountable obstacle to a strong marriage and to good parenting, and the procedure therefore should not be prohibited in Jewish law on that moral ground.

Racism

Even if the identity of the semen donor is kept secret, couples considering DI often want to make sure that he is like them so that the child will resemble them. That, for some, is a racist attitude, and DI is objectionable on those grounds. (The same issue arises in egg donation and adoption.)

If the couple's rationale for preferring a child who looks like them is indeed because they value one race over another, that view is, by definition, racist. It would be immoral to use DI simply to propagate one race over another or to circumvent the necessity of adopting a child of another race, and it would also be immoral to restrict donors to one's own race for racial motives.

Moreover, for a Jew such an attitude is both theologically and legally problematic. Theologically, the Bible proclaims that God created all people, with no race inherently more worthy than any other. Legally, membership in a particular race is neither a necessary nor a sufficient condition for being Jewish: the plethora of races among Israel's Jews amply attests that membership in any one race is not necessary for being Jewish, and conversely, the large number of non-Jews of all races shows that membership in any given race is not a sufficient condition for being Jewish either.

Couples, though, generally prefer a child who looks like them for other reasons that are not inherently racist. Specifically, if the child resembles them, it will be easier for the parents and child to bond with each other. Moreover, it will minimize the awareness of family, friends, and others that the child became the couple's through any process other than their own sexual intercourse. To desire these things is understandable. After all, for all of us, part of the lure of having children is that they represent one of the ways for us to gain eternity; children are a piece of us that remains after we die. Moreover, preferring children similar in looks to oneself is morally legitimate, for the child stands to benefit from his or her likeness to the social parents. The parents and family, after all, often find it easier to bond with the adopted child if they look alike, and other children and adults are less likely to be aware of the DI, egg donation, or adoption and therefore less prone to comment on it (or, in the case of children, taunt the child about it).

Because they recognize the moral validity of parents desiring children who look like them, sperm banks generally will match donors with social parents in physical characteristics such as height, weight, eye color, hair texture, and body type as well as race, ethnic group, or national origin. Twelve of the fifteen surveyed by the Office of Technology Assessment of the United States Congress in 1987 were also willing to link parents and donor by religion, and eleven of the fifteen would match educational attainment, special abilities, hobbies, or interests. Only a few would ensure that the age of the donor approximately corresponded to that of the couple, and even fewer would screen for similar income levels.[61] As long as these measures are taken to benefit the child's acceptance into the family, such choices are morally legitimate.

DI is sometimes used, however, for eugenic purposes. Indeed, that same study reported that "When asked if they agreed that 'there is nothing wrong with sperm banks that specialize in donors with intellectual, artistic, or athletic gifts,' 58 percent of the fertility society practitioners and 49 percent of the cross-sectional physicians strongly or somewhat agreed."[62] From a Jewish perspective, it would be permissible to screen out, as sperm banks usually do, donors with genetic disorders or other diseases like HIV, syphilis, hepatitis, gonorrhea, and chlamydias,[63] for those characteristics of the donor are likely to affect the physical health of the child; but it would not, in my view, be permissible to choose only those donors with outstanding mental or physical traits. That would be a step toward creating a master race; it would no longer be assisting God in maintaining creation but would rather be playing God in an attempt radically to change it. I shall embellish further on this distinction in the section on genetic engineering below.

While discrimination among donors may thus be acceptable in the name of enabling the couple and child to overcome some of the psychological problems inherent in DI, egg donation, or adoption so that the parents and child can bond all the more effectively, it is certainly also legitimate morally and Jewishly to use a sperm or egg donor, or adopt a child, of a different race. Jews should understand that DI, egg donation, and adoption are all possible and fully valid within Jewish law with donors and children of any race or physical type, as long as conversion takes place when necessary.

Demographic Concerns

In addition to these moral issues that affect couples of all faiths involved in donor insemination, specific Jewish issues must be considered in judging its morality. Rabbi Jakobovits cited adultery and diminution of the role of the father as reasons to oppose donor insemination, despite his inability to find legal grounds to do so. For the reasons discussed above, I have rejected his contentions. There is one important moral factor, though, that argues, on the contrary, *for* permitting donor insemination. That factor is the demographic context in which this question is being asked.

As indicated earlier, the contemporary Jewish community suffers from a major demographic crisis. This factor must enter into the moral evaluation of donor insemination, because a Jewish examination of any moral issue cannot adequately address Jewish concerns if it only narrowly considers the specific legal issues involved. Any tradition based on law *must* grapple with its sources if it is to be true to itself and if it is to reap the many benefits inherent in a legal system,[64] as I have argued in Chapter 1 above and in the Appendix. Interpreters of the law, though, must be fully cognizant of the broader context of the issue before them, for otherwise they risk two opposite dangers: the law could either be ignored and thus dishonored, or else—perhaps the greater danger—it could be obeyed despite the personal, social, and moral havoc it wreaks on the situation it was meant to guide with sensitivity and wisdom. Certainly, since Jewish law tries to delineate the will of God as we understand it, those responsible for interpreting and applying it in our day must, like their forebears, pay attention to the welfare of the Jewish community and of the specific people involved—just as God would. Moreover, the Conservative movement's commitment to historical analysis means that Conservative interpreters like me must not only recognize the influences of historical circumstances on the legal judgments of the past but must also take on the responsibility of meeting the needs of Judaism and the Jewish community through their responses to the moral dilemmas of the present.

In our case, then, when the demographic statistics are as threatening as they are for the continuity of the Jewish tradition and the Jewish community, any opening in the law to enable Jews who are otherwise infertile to have children must be used. This concern, in other words, decisively tips the moral and halakhic scales in favor of donor insemination when the couple cannot have children in any other way.

Compassion

These communal considerations stand quite apart from, and in addition to, the compassion one must surely have for couples who have tried to have children and cannot. In such situations, both members of the couple suffer immensely. In addition to experiencing the frustration of being unable to have children when they deeply want them, infertile couples often have feelings of inadequacy as men or women. Infertility certainly requires people to alter their understandings of what it means to be a man, a woman, and a couple, for one important part of all of those concepts is no longer true. Thankfully, the greater publicity about infertility in our time, including its frequency, and the availability of support groups and helpful publications have enabled many couples to overcome the emotional hurdles involved; but more than a few couples have broken apart because of their inability to have children. In addition to our communal concerns mentioned above, then, attention to the needs of Jews who are trying to actualize Jewish ideals, as well as our interest in preventing divorce to the extent that we can, all argue for endorsing donor insemination, egg donation, and adoption when the couple are made aware of the issues described above through appropriate counseling—and that we do so with appreciation and encouragement.

Compassion in these cases, though, goes in two directions. Just as we want to be responsive and affirming to the couples who choose to use these new techniques to have children, we also want to recognize that some couples will opt not to engage in these procedures. In some cases, the cost will be a factor; in others, the psychological problems engendered by the asymmetry of donor insemination and egg donation pose too much of a threat to the marriage. For these and other reasons, couples may legitimately refuse to use either donor insemination or egg donation, and they should not be made to feel that they have let down the Jewish people, their partner, or potential grandparents. The commandment to procreate, after all, does not apply to a couple who cannot have children through their own sexual intercourse, and there are many commandments to fulfill and plenty of opportunities in life to do good deeds. Thus, as much as we may individually and collectively support those couples who decide to use DI or egg donation, we must also be sensitive to the good reasons motivating other couples not to try those options.

Using Donated Eggs

Balancing the Risks of Egg Donation with the Alternative of Adoption

The parallel phenomenon to donor insemination in the female is egg donation. In cases where a woman cannot produce eggs but can carry a fetus, eggs of a donor woman may be fertilized in a test tube with either the sperm of her (that is, the infertile woman's) husband or of a semen donor, and the zygote then implanted in her uterus for gestation. Moreover, even if a woman over forty can produce eggs, the success rate of IVF in such women is so dismal that doctors generally recommend the use of a younger woman's eggs instead.

One can understand the benefits of egg donation. Unlike adoption, the woman will go through pregnancy, an experience many women want to have. Moreover, in most cases the husband's sperm is used, so the child will bear the genetic imprint of at least one of his or her parents—the same advantage that leads couples to use DI when necessary.

One critical factor that makes egg donation less acceptable than donor insemination, though, is the extra measure of danger for the donor. While the risks to the egg donor are not so great as to require a total ban on the procedure out of concern for her life or health, they are significant enough to say that a Jewish couple may ask a woman to undertake those risks only when the couple have seriously considered all other options for having children, including adoption, and when the donor has been assured by her physician that she can donate eggs safely.

Moral and Psychological Issues in Egg Donation

For the infertile couple, most of the moral and psychological issues in egg donation are the same as those in donor insemination. If the sperm used is the husband's, the couple will face the asymmetry mentioned above—although, of course, in the opposite direction, for the husband will be biologically related to the offspring, whereas the wife will not be a provider of the child's gametes. Unlike the case of artificial insemination, though, a woman who carries a child, even if the egg came from another person, has the satisfaction of being the gestational mother, a source of meaning and connection to the child that a man can never experience.

If the husband cannot produce sperm with sufficient number or motility so that the couple must use both donated sperm and eggs, both social parents will lack a genetic link to the child. They then must face the problems encountered by adoptive parents.

No matter what the source of the gametes may be, the openness in communication required of all parties involved in donor insemination applies equally to cases of egg donation. Finally, the same demographic crisis and the same compassion for the infertile couple that should affect the moral evaluation of donor insemination should likewise make egg donation morally acceptable and even laudable when the couple cannot have a child in any other way.

Legally, in egg donation as in artificial insemination, contact of the genital organs and intent to have an adulterous relationship are both missing, and so the prohibition against adultery is not relevant. Furthermore, since egg donation costs much more than artificial insemination, it is even less plausibly construed as a form of licentiousness.

May a fertile brother donate sperm for the impregnation of his infertile brother's wife? That would have the advantage of carrying on the husband's family genes and the likelihood of producing a child who resembles the husband as much as any biological child of his would. Nevertheless, such donations are generally inadvisable, for while they are not technically incest, they *feel* very close to it and raise all kinds of boundary problems for the brothers and the child later on ("Is Uncle Barry really only my uncle, or is he my substitute father when I want him to be?").[65] Moreover, semen donations from others are easy and inexpensive to procure.

An egg donation from a fertile sister to an infertile one involves the same boundary issues for both the sisters and the child. Since donated eggs are relatively scarce and expensive, though, and since the lack of genital contact means that legally there is no taint of incest, a fertile sister may donate eggs to her infertile sibling, but only after appropriate counseling and careful consideration of how the sisters are going to handle these boundary questions as the child grows.

The Identity of the Mother

There is only one source in the Jewish tradition, to my knowledge, that even contemplates anything close to egg donation. Noting that the Torah specifically calls Dinah "the daughter of Leah" (Genesis 30:21) rather than following its more usual practice of identifying the child by her father's name, the Talmud tells a story to explain why the Torah did this. When Jacob already had ten sons, the story goes, Leah became pregnant. She knew through divine inspiration that Jacob was to father a total of twelve sons, and she did not want her sister, Rachel, to bear him less than the two sons that each of the maidservants, Bilhah and Zilpah, had already produced. Consequently, Leah prayed that the child she was carrying not be a boy, and ultimately Dinah was born to her. The most common understanding of that story is that in response to Leah's prayers, God changed the gender of the child in utero. (For some reason, the commentators never imagined that Leah could have been carrying a girl in the first place!) The *Targum Yonatan*, however, understands the story to mean that in response to Leah's prayers, God exchanged the female child (Dinah) in Rachel's womb with the male child (Joseph) in Leah's, thus effecting an embryo transfer so that Leah would give birth to a girl and Rachel to her first son. Rabbi Samuel Edels (the "Maharsha," 1555–1631) also claims that this is the correct interpretation of the talmudic story.

The question is whether this interpretation of the story, ultimately built on the Torah's identification of Dinah as Leah's daughter, should serve as a precedent for determining the identity of the mother of a child conceived through egg donation. Even if we assume that the story is indeed one of embryo transfer, and even if we ignore the fact that in the story it is God, rather than human beings, who effects the embryo transfer, there are real questions as to whether any story should be used for legal rulings, and all the more so one like this, which is really only one possible interpretation of a talmudic tale. Rabbi J. David Bleich, who called attention to the story, himself casts doubt on the use of it for this purpose.[66]

Still, one could argue on other grounds that the bearing mother should be identified as the mother of the child. Specifically, since Jewish law, for purposes of redemption of the firstborn son, defines that child as the one who "opens the womb,"[67] it may be that the bearing woman, rather than the egg donor, should be defined as the child's mother. On the other hand, one might argue that there should be a parallelism between the identity of the father and that of the mother, and since Jewish law defines the sperm donor as the father, the egg donor should likewise be seen as the mother.

Even though it is possible to argue in both directions, the Conservative movement's Committee on Jewish Law and Standards has determined that it is the Torah's phrase, *peter reḥem* ("opening the womb") that should be determinative.[68] In doing so, the committee, following the general trend in Jewish law, preferred explicit precedent *(gezerat ha-katuv)* to logical reasoning as the basis of the law. It is thus the bearing mother who determines the Jewish identity of the child; if she is Jewish, the child is Jewish, regardless of the source of the egg used in the child's conception; if she is not Jewish (as in many cases of surrogacy), the child is not Jewish by birth and must undergo the rites of conversion to become Jewish.

The Problem of Selective Abortions

As in IVF with the wife's own eggs, IVF with donated eggs produces the possibility that multiple embryos will implant themselves in the uterus; and since it is dangerous to both the mother and fetuses if she carries more than three, this results in the need to abort some of them to reduce the number left to a maximum of three.

While "reducing" the number of embryos to three is legitimate after the fact if more than three zygotes are introduced into the woman's uterus and more than three implant themselves into the uterine wall, it is better to avoid this situation in the first place so as to circumvent the need for such selective abortions. This is especially so since, as indicated in Chapter 3 above, the European practice of using only three eggs for each attempt has achieved the same success rate in producing children as the American practice of using five or six. Thus, with donated eggs, just as with the wife's own, Jews should permit the use of only two, or at most three.

The Obligation to Procreate

Couples who choose *not* to use egg donation as a means of overcoming their infertility need not feel guilty about their decision. As noted above,[69] even though men clearly cannot have children without women, the rabbis restricted the commandment to procreate to men. That does not accord with contemporary egalitarian values, and some may argue on that basis that the law should be changed. In traditional Jewish law, however, since women do not have the legal obligation to procreate, infertile women are not failing to fulfill any commandments relevant to them by refusing to be impregnated by donated eggs. Given the asymmetry involved in most cases of egg donation and the accompanying psychological problems, let alone the cost and stress involved, one can understand why some women would refuse to undergo the procedure, and such a decision must be respected.

This will mean, though, that the woman's husband will not be able to procreate with his wife (assuming that his sperm is fit to produce children in the first place), and the Mishnah rules that a man who cannot procreate with his wife after trying for ten years must divorce her and marry another in an attempt to make it possible for him to fulfill that commandment.[70] By the late Middle Ages, though, that rule had largely fallen into disuse, as Rabbi Moses Isserles ultimately codifies:

Today it is not the custom to force somebody on this issue. Similarly, anybody who has not fulfilled the commandment "be fruitful and multiply" and goes to marry a woman who is not capable of having children because of sterility, age, or youth, because he loves her or [even] for her wealth, even though by law we should prevent such a marriage, it has not been the practice for many generations for the court to interfere in the affairs of couples. Similarly, if a man marries a woman and waits ten years [without children], we do not force him to divorce her, although he has not fulfilled the commandment "be fruitful and multiply." And the same applies to other matters regarding couples.[71]

Infertile couples who choose not to pursue egg donation, then, need not feel that they are thereby violating traditional Jewish law. Again, they *may* use egg donation as a means to have children, but they *are not required* to do so. Those who opt not to use this method should consider adoption, for that will satisfy many of the same needs and enable the couple to fulfill many other commandments associated with children.

Donating One's Sperm or Eggs

Until now we have considered donor insemination and egg donation from the point of view of the couple seeking children. Jews, though, can be donors as well as recipients. Is it permissible in Jewish law for a Jewish man to donate his sperm for purposes of donor insemination? May a Jewish woman donate her eggs for the purpose of enabling another woman to become pregnant? If the answers to either or both of these questions are affirmative, are there any restrictions on that permission?

Donating Sperm

As we have noted earlier, in Jewish law donor insemination constitutes procreation by the donor. This introduces an appropriate note of seriousness to semen donation. It is not, and should not be construed as, simply another way for a college or medical student to earn some spare change. The (typically) young man involved should recognize that he is making it possible for a couple to have a child, with all the positive implications of that for the couple and, if Jews are the recipients, for the Jewish people. He should approach this whole process, in other words, with a sense of mitzvah, duly appreciative of the awesomeness of the human ability to procreate and of his role in helping an infertile couple make that happen.

He should also understand that, like it or not, he will have an important biological relationship to the offspring. He may want to keep his identity confidential so as not to incur any risk of personal or legal problems with the couple or with the child later on. Since the laws on this are not universal and not totally clear, his wish to retain confidentiality is understandable.

Since the child will inherit the donor's genes, however, the donor should supply the sperm bank and, through it, the child with as much information about his physical and personal characteristics as possible without compromising the confidentiality of his identity. Only then can the child eventually know enough about his or her medical history to take appropriate preventive and curative steps against genetically inherited diseases or susceptibilities to disease, and only then can the child avoid having sex with a genetic relative. Furthermore, as we have said above, the more the donor reveals about his personal characteristics and interests, the more the child can achieve a sense of self-identity. For all these reasons, the donor should be as forthcoming as possible, within the bounds of confidentiality, to the sperm bank and, through it, to the social parents and the child.

The donor should also be concerned about his own future children unwittingly marrying a genetic relative. This too argues for sharing information with the child born through artificial insemination so that both the child and the donor can guard against such an occurrence.

All of these problems disappear, of course, if the donor and the social parents decide to reveal their identities to each other and to the child, but that raises the legal problems we have mentioned and the psychological pitfalls of conflicts in raising the child between the donor and the social father. The donor, then, must carefully consider the implications of both openness and confidentiality, and he must seek to minimize the difficulties of whichever option he chooses.

There are, at least potentially, yet other people who have a stake in a man's decision to donate his sperm. As R. Snowden puts it, "Does a person have a right, independently of his existing or future family affiliations, to donate or sell his gametes? . . . Should the consent of a potential donor's partner be required? Should the donor inform his own children of his [present or past] activity?"[72]

Certainly the donor's present or future spouse and children are affected by his decision to donate. They should definitely be informed of the donation if it happened in the past, and if a married man is considering a sperm donation, he owes it to his wife to gain her consent.

To determine the nature and extent of this duty, it will be helpful to think of another case that is analogous in some ways even if not in others—specifically, that of a divorced man with children who marries a second time. Such a man has a clear duty to inform his new wife before the wedding of the existence of children from his first marriage. If the children are young, the duty is obvious, for she may find herself playing the role of their mother, at least during the times they are in his custody, and she has a right to know that such responsibilities will come with the marriage. Even if the children from his first marriage are grown and not dependent upon her care, however, she has a right to know of their existence because his close relatives will inevitably affect his life and therefore hers, to say nothing about the future disposition of his property after his death.

In DI, the duty of the man to inform his wife (and, in the case of a planned donation, gain her consent) does not depend on the obligations the man's previous children may impose on the woman, for children born through DI will probably never know the identity of their biological father, much less come to live with him and his wife. The duty of disclosure rather stems from a marital equivalent of "truth in advertising." Part of the essence of marriage is that it functions as the sole context of one's procreative activities. That expectation, in fact, is built into the very construct and meaning of marriage. If that has not been true, as in the case of a previous marriage or of a sperm or egg donation, or if that is not going to be true because of a planned sperm or egg donation, the spouse has a right to know that this common assumption of marriage will be, or has been, breached in these specific ways so that the bonds of marriage can nevertheless be assumed and maintained with full honesty, understanding, and trust.

None of these difficulties should make semen donation forbidden; the great good of enabling an infertile couple to have a child outweighs them all. Similarly, any objections to the masturbation through which the semen will be procured are also set aside, for the intent to produce a child removes any stigma of "wasting the seed." The donor, though, must at least understand the complications involved, as described above, and plan for how he will respond to them with seriousness, honesty, and wisdom.

Donating Eggs

The same concerns apply to egg donation, but that procedure incurs the additional risks involved in procuring the eggs. As indicated above, there is some evidence that hyperovulation increases the risk of ovarian cancer and other maladies. Jewish law does not permit one to endanger oneself unduly: "[The strictures against] endangering oneself are more stringent than [those against violating] a prohibition," says the Talmud.[73] One must not "stand idly by the blood of one's neighbor," according to the Torah, and so some risk is required or at least permitted to save the life of another.[74] In the case of egg donation, though, we are not talking about saving a life but rather enabling a couple to conceive a new life. Since no physical danger will ensue to the couple if they fail in that project, we cannot justify the danger to the egg donor on that basis.

The authors of the study on the linkage between egg donation and susceptibility to cancer concluded that "especially careful consideration should be given to counseling women who wish to donate eggs, particularly repeat donors, because they derive no reproductive benefit from their fertility drug exposure."[75] According to their findings, though, the increased risk is not so great as to warrant prohibiting egg donation altogether out of concern for the life or health of the donor, and that medical finding is crucial in making it permissible for Jewish women to donate their eggs.

In line with Jewish law's concern that we first preserve our own life and health, however, a Jewish woman who chooses to donate should do so only once or twice, and then only if she is assured by physicians after due examination that she personally can donate her eggs without much danger to her own life or health. Enabling an infertile couple to have children is a great good, but according to Jewish law, preserving one's own life and health clearly takes precedence over that.

Egg donors face some of the same issues of confidentiality as semen donors do, but one important factor is different. No state has yet enacted laws unequivocally declaring the social mother, and not the egg donor, to be the legal mother (perhaps because of the newness of the procedure), and so the legal risks of future obligations are substantially greater for egg donors than they are for semen donors. This situation, together with the added physical danger of egg donation over DI, means that ovum donors are far scarcer than semen donors. In light of this scarcity, it is important to minimize as far as possible the objections to a woman donating her eggs. Among other things, a greater measure of confidentiality should be tolerated in egg donation than we would be prepared to accept in semen donation. Nevertheless, the egg donor, no less than the semen donor, contributes substantially to the child's genetic structure, and so she too should reveal as much as possible of her medical history and personal characteristics for the good of the child.

Adoption

When a couple cannot have children, adoption is an available option. Several passages in the Bible suggest that adoption existed during biblical times,[76] but the evidence is equivocal, and no legal source in the Bible specifies a procedure for adoption or the legal rights and duties that accompany it.

In later Jewish law, adoption is not a defined institution as such, but rabbinic law provided for its approximate equivalent.

The rabbinic court, "the parent of all orphans,"[77] appoints guardians for orphans and children in need, and the guardians have the same responsibilities as biological parents do. They must care for the child's upbringing, education, and physical accommodations, and they must administer the child's property. If the guardian dies, his or her estate is responsible to continue providing for the child's care. The sense of guardianship in Jewish law is so strong that it was once invoked in a New York case to extend the obligations of the adoptive father beyond the demands of civil law.[78]

Contrary to modern American adoption practice, however, in Jewish law the adoptive parents do not become the legal parents but rather function as the agents of the biological parents.[79] Therefore, biological parents continue to have the usual parental obligations to the child, and the guardian fulfills those obligations on behalf of, but not in legal substitution for, the biological parents. Along the same lines, the personal status of the child in matters of Jewish identity, ritual, and marriage depends upon the status of the biological parents.[80] Thus when it is not known that the gestational mother was Jewish, the child must be formally converted; the status of priesthood can only be passed from a man to his biological sons; and the biblical prohibitions against incest are violated only by sexual intercourse between blood relatives.

At the same time, rabbinic sources express immense appreciation for the adoptive (or "social") parents. Taking a child who is, in essence, an orphan into one's home and raising that child is a ḥesed (an act of faithfulness, of lovingkindness) of the first order. Thus the Talmud says that one who does so "is as if he has given birth to him," and, in a source quoted earlier that bears repeating, the Talmud notes that the adoptive parents manage to act rightly at all times:

> "Happy are they that act justly, who do right at all times" (Psalms 106:3). Is it possible to do right at all times? . . . Rabbi Samuel bar Naḥmani said: This refers to a person who brings up an orphan boy or girl in his/her house and [ultimately] enables the orphan to marry.[81]

This appreciation has legal consequences. As we have noted above, the possessions, earnings, and findings of minor, adopted children go to their custodial rather than their biological parents. This provision of rabbinic law is probably a matter of equity in partial compensation for the expenses of raising children,[82] but it is also a recognition of the strength of the functioning, adoptive family. Similarly, according to Rabbi Moses Sofer, adopted children do not incur the obligations of mourning upon the death of their biological parents, but they do have such obligations when their adoptive parents die.[83] Moreover, in appreciation of the immensely significant role that adoptive parents have in their children's upbringing, and in recognition of the close bonds that adopted siblings create with each other, the Conservative rabbinate considers adopted children, like children born through donor insemination, to have the status of relatives of the second degree *(sheniyot)*, and therefore sex or marriage between them is prohibited.[84] Furthermore, the social parents' names may be invoked when the child is being identified by his or her Hebrew name, as, for example, when being called to the Torah, when being identified in a marriage contract *(ketubbah)*, or when having a prayer recited in the synagogue for his or her recovery from an illness.

Many infertile Jewish couples cannot find Jewish children to adopt because of the high rate of abortion among Jews. This argues for two things: first, Jews should understand that while Jewish law *requires* abortion when the life or physical or mental health of the mother is at stake and *permits* it when there is a risk to the mother's life or health above that of normal pregnancy, by and large the Jewish tradition *prohibits* abortion. They also should come to understand that even if they cannot or will not care for the child, an abundance of infertile couples would do so willingly and lovingly, which makes nontherapeutic abortions even less justifiable.

In addition, though, Jewish couples contemplating adoption need to widen their search to include non-Jewish children. If the bearing mother was not Jewish, conversion will be necessary, but in the case of children that is a relatively easy process. More-

over, couples should consider adopting children of a race different from their own. Race, of course, is not a factor in Jewish
identity—or in the joy (and troubles!) of raising children—except to the extent that parents will need to help children overcome racial prejudice.[85] Couples might also consider children
older than infancy and/or those with some disability; they, after
all, are also God's children, and many more of them are available for adoption. Indeed, Jews should consider the possibility
of adopting such children even when they have already had two
or more children through their own sexual intercourse and have
thereby fulfilled the demand of Jewish law to procreate.

At the same time, couples need to be aware of some of the
special legal and psychological issues that may arise in adoption. The highly publicized Baby Jessica case in August 1993,
where a two-and-a-half-year-old child was taken from the
adoptive parents who had raised her from birth and returned
to her biological parents, indicates the importance of attending to the legal details of adoption—and of changing the laws
in those states that make such a case possible.[86] Losing a child
in that way is undoubtedly among adoptive parents' worst
nightmares, and it probably is not in the child's best interests
either. Biological parents do have a right and an obligation to
care for their children, but if they give up both the rights and
obligations of parenthood in a formal, legal way, adoptive
parents and children have the right to be secure in their status
as a family.

More commonly, adoptive parents face psychological issues.
Family members may say insensitive things—or bend over back-
wards to avoid mentioning the adoption. Adopted children will
be reminded of their special status each time school forms ask
for their medical history. During adolescence, when all children
need to differentiate themselves from their parents and often feel
misunderstood in the process, adopted children may think that
their biological parents *would* understand them if they were
present. That may be the occasion for some angry and hurtful
remarks as the child attacks the adoptive parents where they are
most vulnerable.

Moreover, many adopted children feel that they have been fundamentally rejected by their biological parents, leading some adopted children, as adults, to seek the identity of, and a meeting with, one or both of their biological parents. That often produces less than desirable results for all parties concerned: the child may be deeply disappointed in the reality, as against the dream, of the kind of human beings the biological parents are; the biological parents may find being discovered by the child after all these years most unwelcome, making the child feel rejected yet again; and the social parents in turn may feel inadequate as parents, that they never succeeded in overcoming the lack of a biological relationship between them and the child despite years of love and effort.[87] To help adoptive parents understand that the child's search for his or her biological roots does not usually mean a rejection of them as parents, and to help them cope with the other issues involved in adoption, adoptive parents are well advised to get appropriate counseling even before the child comes into their home and to avail themselves of subsequent counseling as needed.

Along the same lines, Jewish men and women, whether they can have children or not, should seriously consider becoming Jewish Big Brothers or Jewish Big Sisters. That program enables children who have lost their father or mother through death or divorce to have a close adult male or female model to balance the gender of their single parent as they grow up. Both adoption and service as a Jewish Big Brother or Big Sister are significant acts of *ḥesed* whose beneficial effects often last throughout the child's life, and thus those who adopt or mentor a child should feel religiously as well as personally confirmed and appreciated.

Single Parenthood

Most single parents become so through the death of, or divorce from, their spouse. Donor insemination, though, makes it possible for single women or lesbian couples who want a child to be artificially inseminated for that purpose (and, in some cases, also implanted with the egg of another woman), while surrogacy makes it possible for single men, whether straight or gay, artificially to impregnate women who agree to be surrogate mothers. In addition, of course, single men or women, whether straight or gay, may adopt children. Becoming a single parent through DI or surrogacy is a very new phenomenon, and so the incidence of it is still small. In 1988 the Office of Technology Assessment of the United States Congress found that

> [f]ewer than 4 percent of the women accepted for artificial insem-
> ination in the past year stated that they sought insemination because
> of the lack of a male partner . . . . Overall, those currently seeking
> and obtaining artificial insemination, with a few exceptions, iden-
> tify themselves as married couples with a male reproductive prob-
> lem, primarily male infertility.[88]

The incidence of the use of the new technologies by singles will, however, undoubtedly increase with time. Indeed, one California sperm bank reports that 25 percent of its donor insemina- tions are done for single women.[89]

Jewish law clearly assumes that it is best for children to have parents of both genders, for it describes differing roles for moth- ers and fathers.[90] Furthermore, psychological studies reaffirm the importance of fathers in the raising of a child. So, for exam- ple, Lee Smith reports that

> Data on thousands of children collected for the Department of
> Health and Human Services show that:
> —Kids from single-parent families, whether through divorce or
> illegitimacy, are two to three times as likely to have emotional or
> behavioral problems, and half again as likely to have learning dis-
> abilities, as those who live with both parents.
> —Teenage girls who grow up without their fathers tend to have
> sex earlier. A 15-year-old who has lived with her mother only, for
> example, is three times as likely to lose her virginity before her 16th
> birthday as one who has lived with both parents.[91]

Smith also cites David Popenoe, a Rutgers University sociolo- gist, who says that while the social sciences can seldom prove anything in the strict sense of proof, there remains "a strong likelihood that the increase in the number of fatherless children over the past 30 years has been a prominent factor in the growth of violence and juvenile delinquency." Thus more than half of the fourteen thousand inmates surveyed by the Justice Department in 1991 had not lived with both parents while they were growing up.[92] The consensus of the experts Smith consulted indicates that

> a father shows a child, especially a boy, how to fit into the community. Dr. Frank Pittman, an Atlanta psychiatrist, says in his recent book, *Man Enough*, that a father's role is not to make his sons more aggressive or to show them how to take what is theirs. On the contrary, his function is to define the limits of manhood. A boy doesn't have to be John Wayne. Jimmy Stewart is man enough.[93]

These considerations recall Rabbi Jakobovits's characterization of all donor insemination as "stud farming." In cases where a couple use donor insemination because they cannot have a child with the husband's sperm, that execration, I contend, is completely unwarranted. Where DI consciously creates a single-family household, though, we must give more serious consideration to the problems children have in growing up without both parents, even if we do not go as far as he does in denouncing it.[94]

A *Newsweek* article summarized in a popular form both the psychological literature and the responses of single parents themselves to their situation:

> The greatest burden of single parenthood falls on the children. As research increasingly shows, children reared in one-parent families tend to have more educational, emotional, and financial difficulties than those who grow up with two parents. Since the problems are often economic, some of the effects may be eased for children of well-educated, middle-class women. Psychologist Anna Beth Benningfield argues that children can accept any situation as normal, as long as there's a strong sense of family. Though [single parent Jane] Saks would have preferred a more conventional setup, she believes it makes little difference in an era of sky-high divorce rates. . . . What is critical is how mother responds when her child asks: where's Dad?[95]

Current research indicates that children, on average, do indeed do worse with one parent rather than with two, but only when that single parent is isolated as the only caregiver for the child. If the parent has sufficient funds to hire help or if, in poor as well as rich families, there is a strong network of support from family and friends, children do no worse, on average, than they do with two parents. In making these comparisons, one must remember that the criteria for measuring adjustment and well-being are themselves sometimes at issue and that many contemporary families with two parents are themselves dysfunctional. Still, the findings remain a concern.[96]

Adoption by single people on the face of it poses fewer problems, since the child is already born and is, by hypothesis, an orphan. In contrast to cases of divorce or the death of a spouse, however, adoption by one adult, like DI of a single woman, consciously creates a single-parent home. Single parents often do a remarkable job of raising their children, and it is certainly better for a child to have one caring parent than temporary foster parents or no parents at all. Still, if the child could be adopted by two parents, that might well be better for the child's welfare.

There are also complications raised by American law. Protections of the semen donor built into the Uniform Parentage Act and similar legislation against the legal obligations of paternity have not been applied by recent court decisions to sperm donors to single women.[97] Moreover, some states do not recognize the right of lesbians or gay men to be parents, even if they are the biological parents.[98]

At bottom, we must acknowledge that these family configurations made possible by medical assistance and by increasing social acceptance of single parenthood are very new for all of us. The psychological and social implications of creating families in these new ways are still far from clear, and thus a formal ruling regarding them on behalf of the Jewish tradition is premature. The parameters of such a decision, though, are not in doubt: we Jews clearly need to have more children, and we want them to grow up in environments that offer them the psychological, educational, and economic support that will enable them to become well-adjusted and productive members of society as well as active Jews. The question is no longer whether single-parent families exist, for they already do; rather, the question is what Jewish law should say about procedures like DI of single women and single-parent adoption that knowingly create such families, and for that more experience with their results is required.

As medicine becomes ever more adept at helping infertile couples conceive on their own, the use of other people's genetic materials to have children, while necessary and permissible now, may no longer be required in the future. Just recently, for example, Belgian scientists "invented a new treatment for male infertility that they say may allow virtually any man, no matter how few or misshapen or immobile his sperm cells, to father a child" through the direct injection of a single human sperm cell into a human egg in a petri dish.[99] Hopefully, one day egg donation will not be necessary for infertile women either.[100] Then the emotional, moral, and legal problems these procedures raise may resolve themselves.

CHAPTER FIVE

Preventing Pregnancy

S INCE JUDAISM INVESTS MARRIAGE AND CHILDREN WITH SO
much significance, it is not surprising that traditional Jewish texts look askance at interruptions in the process of
conception and birth. Jews were supposed to marry and have
children. Masturbation, birth control, sterilization, and abortion were, both physically and ideologically, counterproductive.
Our task in this chapter, then, is to revisit those topics today to
see whether changes in contemporary circumstances, medical
knowledge, concepts, or values should affect our Jewish approach to these matters and decide in that light whether to re-
lax the tradition's prohibitions, rephrase them, or reinforce
them.

Masturbation

While women clearly can and do masturbate, and while some
recent studies track the relationship between female masturbation and sexual function in intercourse,[1] female masturbation
is a very new subject for public discussion. When Jewish and
general sources discuss masturbation, they are referring exclusively to males. Since female masturbation normally does not
involve emission of fluids, and since that is the focus of most of
the discussion in historical texts about male masturbation,

much of what follows will not mention or even be relevant to women. It is therefore up to us now to apply any of the precedents regarding males to females, if, in our judgment, they seem apt. That in turn will require an evaluation of the traditional stance on male masturbation.

Jews historically shared the abhorrence of male masturbation that characterized other societies.[2] Interestingly, although the prohibition was not debated, legal writers had difficulty locating a biblical base for it, and no less an authority than Maimonides claimed that it could not be punishable by the court because there was not an explicit negative commandment forbidding it.[3]

In the case of males, the prohibition undoubtedly stemmed in part from assumptions about the medical consequences of ejaculation. Maimonides articulates this:

> Semen constitutes the strength of the body, its life, and the light of the eyes. Its emission to excess causes physical decay, debility, and diminished vitality. Thus Solomon, in his wisdom, says: "Do not give your strength to women" (Proverbs 31:3). Whoever indulges in sexual dissipation becomes prematurely aged; his strength fails; his eyes become dim; a foul odor proceeds from his mouth and armpits; the hair of his head, eyebrows, and eyelashes drop out; the hair of his beard, armpits, and legs grow abnormally; his teeth fall out; and besides these, he becomes subject to numerous other diseases. Medical authorities have stated that for each one who dies of other maladies, a thousand are the victims of sexual excess.[4]

Maimonides here is speaking about ejaculation during sexual intercourse. Jewish sources on ejaculation in the specific context of masturbation, however, do not base the prohibition primarily on medical considerations, at least not in that language. They focus rather on concerns about self-pollution, the murder of unborn generations, and the creation of demons.

The first of these concerns accounts for the most common line of reasoning.[5] Exposed semen, in the view of those who take this approach, somehow contaminates the environment and taints its holiness. The sources do not go into great detail as to how or why this happens, but that is because they rely on earlier sources regarding purity.

In the Torah, impurity results whenever there is a loss of *elan vitale*, of life energy. The extreme case of impurity is therefore a dead body, the most potent source of spreading impurity as "the father of the fathers of impurity" *(avi avot ha-tumah)*. Impurity arises also, however, when bodies deviate in any way from their wholeness. This happens even when what is going on is perfectly normal and natural, such as a woman's menstrual flow—or a man's ejaculation. At that point, the woman or man becomes impure, which means that she or he is unfit to engage in public rituals until a prescribed time has passed and a ritual of ablution, later transformed into immersion in a natural body of water or a specially constructed pool (mikveh), has been fulfilled.[6] Even though, ironically, the public, ritual disqualifications of men after seminal emission fell into disuse,[7] the initial sense that ejaculation produced impurity persisted, and that undoubtedly undergirds much of the talmudic and medieval horror concerning masturbation.

What is the point behind the Torah's laws of impurity in the first place? One common scholarly theory is that impurity marks the loss of life energy.[8] If that is correct, the medieval concern with masturbation as polluting the man who masturbates (and possibly anyone else who comes into contact with the semen) is simply a ritual expression of the same medical theories expressed in Maimonides' medical language. That is, masturbation is objectionable because it saps the sexual energy of a man and thereby threatens his health and well-being.[9] That is why the exposed semen and the man himself become impure.

While this is the primary concern about masturbation expressed in the sources, the mystical tradition in Judaism gave particular emphasis to another objection. In the Bible, Onan is killed by God for "wasting the seed." The act to which this phrase refers is interrupted coitus, but the Jewish mystical tradition applied it to masturbation as well. Taking their cue from this biblical phrase, the mystics asserted that since a man who masturbates prevents the use of that semen for conceiving a child, he is guilty not only of murder but of the murder of his own (potential) children. He is therefore a criminal more reprehensible than any other.[10] On the other hand, ejaculation is prized in heterosexual relations, even in those that do not lead to procreation, and no "murder" is said to take place, nor are the forces of evil enhanced.[11]

The mystics also claimed that even involuntary emissions of semen created demons,[12] which were a danger not only to the man who masturbated but to the entire community. Such notions appear in folk literature as well as in rabbinic mystical texts. Thus the narrator in I. B. Singer's short story, "From the Diary of One Not Born," says: "I was not born. My father, a yeshivah student, sinned as did Onan, and from his seed I was created—half spirit, half-demon. . . . I am and I am not."[13]

In modern times, many Orthodox Jews retain these beliefs and prohibitions, but Conservative, Reform, and unaffiliated Jews largely do not. The grounds for this change are largely medical: neither physicians nor laypeople believe that masturbation has the medical consequences described by Maimonides.[14] Moreover, few believe the mystical tradition's depiction of the dire results of masturbation. To date, none of the three movements has taken an official position validating masturbation, but in practice the tradition's abhorrence of masturbation is largely ignored.

Part of that reaction, no doubt, stems from the realities of modern life. Large percentages of Jews today postpone marriage until after college or graduate school, long after they are physically mature. Although the sexual hormones are plenty strong in teenage women too, males in particular feel this hormonal pressure during their teenage years, for the largest number of ejaculations a male will experience per year during his lifetime occurs between ages sixteen and eighteen, whereas the largest number of physical climaxes a female will experience per year will occur between ages twenty-six and thirty. That means that realistically, the choices for teenagers and people in their twenties are either to masturbate or to engage in nonmarital sex.

Jewish concepts, values, and laws advance compelling reasons to oppose nonmarital sex. Because nonmarital sexual intercourse communicates commitments that the couple clearly are not ready to take on, it is effectively a lie. Even if the couple say explicitly to each other that their sexual act is only for pleasure and not part of any intended long-term relationship, the sexual act itself belies what they say they intend. The implications of that miscommunication, together with the inability or unwillingness of the couple to assume responsibility for each other and for any child that may result, are very important moral reasons to oppose nonmarital sex. In addition, the medical risks of transmitting venereal diseases or AIDS through nonmarital sexual intercourse add yet another important Jewish reason to oppose it, for Judaism puts great emphasis, as we have seen, in preserving life and health. The reasons to oppose masturbation, on the other hand, are at best questionable.

Consequently, even if contemporary Jewish authorities are not prepared to revise Jewish law's prohibition of masturbation entirely, they must surely agree that on the basis of Jewish moral values, if the choice is between masturbation and nonmarital sex, masturbation is preferable. One certainly should not spend an inordinate part of one's time masturbating, to the extent that it is the major focus of one's life, and masturbation should be done only in private. Masturbation in and of itself, though, should no longer carry the opprobrium it had for our ancestors, both because the original grounds for opposing it are no longer tenable and because it is at least preferable to nonmarital sex as a way of dealing with sexual energies before marriage.

If that conclusion is true for males, it is all the more true for females. Discussion of female masturbation does not appear in the sources, and it is therefore not explicitly prohibited in the first place. Moreover, the same considerations that would make us prefer that males masturbate rather than engage in nonmarital sexual intercourse would apply to females as well.

Contraception

Despite the command to have two children and the ideal of having more, contraception is permitted and even required under certain circumstances. Because the command to propagate is legally the obligation of the male and not the female in Jewish law, and because of the traditional prohibition against "wasting the seed," whatever its basis, male forms of contraception are treated less favorably in the sources than female ones.

Jewish sources from as early as the second century C.E. describe methods of contraception and prescribe when they may or should be used. Until the latter half of the twentieth century, though, Jews never contemplated using contraceptives for purposes of family planning. Judaism, after all, values large families. Moreover, if one wanted even two children to survive to adulthood, one had to try to have children continually, for many such attempts would be frustrated in miscarriages or in stillbirths, and many of the children who survived birth would die of childhood diseases or infections before being ready to propagate themselves. In addition, many Jews would find that they could not beget or bear children, as the stories of the difficulties endured by Abraham and Sarah and by Jacob and Rachel so poignantly describe.

In judging the permissibility of contraceptives, then, we must recognize that we are asking an entirely new question. Not only have the techniques of contraception improved considerably, but the very purpose for which Jewish couples use them has changed. Thus although the use of contraceptives in our time may bear some formal resemblance to their use in times past, these changes in method and purpose must be kept clearly in mind as we examine traditional sources on contraception.

Male Forms of Birth Control

The only nonpermanent male form of contraception currently available is the condom. The provision in Jewish law making the male legally responsible for propagation argues against his use of condoms, at least until he has fulfilled that duty.[15] Condoms, moreover, sometimes leak, split, or slip off,[16] and even if they remain intact and in place, they do not always work.

Nevertheless, condoms must be used if unprotected sexual intercourse poses a medical risk to either spouse, for condoms do offer some measure of protection against the spread of some diseases, and the duty to maintain health and life supersedes the positive duty of the male to propagate. So, for example, if the previous sexual or medical history of either partner suggests the possibility of HIV infection, the man must use a condom. In addition, both partners must have their blood tested for the HIV virus, and if either partner tests positive, the use of condoms is not enough: abstinence is necessary, for life must take precedence over the joys of sex.[17]

Female Forms of Birth Control

The specific conditions under which female contraception is permitted (and in some cases even required) depend upon one's interpretation of the following second-century rabbinic ruling:

> Rabbi Bebai recited before Rabbi Naḥman: There are three classes of women who employ an absorbent (for purposes of contraception): a minor, a pregnant woman, and a nursing mother; a minor lest she become pregnant and die, a pregnant woman lest miscarriage result, and a nursing mother lest she become pregnant and prematurely wean the child so that it dies. And what is a minor? From the age of eleven years and a day until the age of twelve years and a day. One who is under or over this age carries on her marital intercourse in the usual manner—so says Rabbi Meir. But the other Sages say: The one as well as the other carries on her marital intercourse in the usual manner, and mercy be vouchsafed from Heaven, for [as Scripture says in Psalms 116:6], "The Lord preserves the simple.[18]

As a matter of course, the law follows the majority opinion, in this case that of the Sages. But what are they saying? The Hebrew text uses a present indicative verb in the first clause, as the translation "employ" indicates. If that verb is taken to mean that there are three classes of women who *may* use a contraceptive device, the implication would be that other women may not, even according to Rabbi Meir. With that understanding, the Sages would not even permit the three classes of women to use contraception despite the fact that their health or that of their fetus or baby is at stake. Later rabbis who adopt this reasoning, however, permit contraception to preserve the woman's life or health; they then apply the prohibition of contraception embedded in this source exclusively to cases where the woman will incur only a minor elevation of risk beyond that of normal pregnancy if she becomes pregnant.[19]

If, on the other hand, the operative verb in the above quotation is interpreted to mean that there are three classes of women who *should* or *must* use an absorbent, the implication would be that those women are obligated to use a contraceptive device in order to protect their health or that of their fetus or baby, whereas other women *may* use contraceptive devices for other purposes as well. Those other purposes may then be strictly or leniently defined.[20]

As we shall see, Judaism restricts the legitimacy of abortion to cases where the life or health of the mother is at stake, and so those forms of contraception which prevent conception in the first place are to be preferred to aborting the fertilized egg cell (zygote) after the fact.

Thus from the point of view of Jewish law, the diaphragm is the most favored form of contraception, for it prevents conception and has little, if any, impact on the woman's health. If the contraceptive pill or implant is not contraindicated by the woman's age or body chemistry, those are usually the next most favored forms of contraception. Couples like these methods of birth control because they are easy to use and because they are quite reliable; Jewish authorities recommend them because their success rate minimizes the possibility that the couple will later consider an abortion as a form of retroactive birth control.

The Broader Context Affecting Decisions to Use Birth Control: Social, Religious, and Personal Matters

Since propagation is a commandment, it must be assumed that even the more liberal school among medieval and modern rabbis would limit the use of contraceptives to those couples who have already fulfilled the commandment by having a boy and a girl—except, of course, if the medical condition of the woman requires it.[21] In modern times, when couples frequently postpone marriage until after extended education and the initiation of a career for one or both of them, rabbis of the different Jewish denominations have varied widely in their response to the desirability and permissibility of family planning. Some allow contraception even before having children, and this has been the practice of the vast majority of Jews.

Several factors, though, have made Jewish religious leaders put increased stress on the need for Jews to procreate. One is social. We are, as a people, in deep demographic trouble. We lost one-third of our numbers during the Holocaust, bringing us down from eighteen million to twelve million worldwide. That situation is now exacerbated by the high rate of intermarriage and the extremely low birthrate among Jews. For a population simply to reproduce itself, it must have a reproductive rate of 2.3 — that is, statistically, 2.3 children for every two adults. (It is not 2.0 because some adults will never marry; some will marry and have no children, either by choice or through infertility; some will have only one child; and some will have two or more children, but these in turn will not all propagate.) The current Jewish reproductive rate among American Jews is between 1.6 and 1.7. That statistic means that we are killing ourselves off as a people. One must surely be educated to be a learned and practicing Jew, but one cannot educate people who do not exist. This social imperative has made propagation arguably the most important mitzvah in our time.

Religious factors complement this social concern. Judaism, after all, treasures children as one of God's chief blessings. To refuse to try to have them, or to plan to have only one or two, is to refuse to accept one of God's great gifts. It is also to renege on the duty we all have to create the next generation and to educate them in Torah so that the Jewish tradition may be passed down.

Personal factors also play an important role in this increased emphasis on procreation and the corresponding discomfort with birth control. Even with modern medical advances, the late teens and the twenties are biologically still the best time for both males and females to procreate.[22] Whether they wish to work outside the home or not, most women in our society find that they must earn money to support themselves and their families, just as their husbands do. Too many couples who wait long beyond their twenties, however, find that when they are ready to have children, they cannot. The frustration, anger, and agony over this is hard to watch and even harder to bear.

All these factors, then, have tempered an otherwise liberal approach to contraception on the part of many non-Orthodox rabbis and most Jews. As countercultural as this may seem at this stage in our history, Jews should think about finding a mate and beginning to have children before the end of their graduate studies; the pressures of graduate school are not necessarily greater than those of the first years of one's career. Even if young couples choose to use contraceptives for a time, they are well advised, both medically and Jewishly, not to wait too long to begin their efforts to have children. Moreover, couples who can have children should seriously consider having three or four children when the time comes. In the end, contemporary Jews must all be reminded of the way in which our tradition thinks of children and the way in which many people experience them, as a true blessing from God.

Sterilization

The same concerns govern the issue of sterilization, although here another issue arises, that is, the prohibition against a person mutilating his or her body in light of the fact that the body is really God's property. Although the procedures are rather new, vasectomies and tubal ligations are the subject of a few responsa.

Both traditional and liberal respondents forbid male sterilization on the basis of the rabbinic interpretation and extension of Deuteronomy 23:2 ("No one whose testes are crushed . . . shall be admitted into the congregation of the Lord"),[23] or Leviticus 22:24 ("That which is mauled or crushed or torn or cut you shall not offer unto the Lord; nor shall you do this in your land").[24] Even though vasectomies sterilize males without cutting off their testicles or crushing them, rabbinic rulings generally ban vasectomies under the same prohibition, since the function of the procedure is the same—namely, to incapacitate the male from reproducing—even if the form is different. Thus even when the man has already fulfilled the duty to procreate by fathering at least two children, so that frustration of that obligation is no longer a factor, vasectomies for the sake of preventing further conception are not permitted.

Rabbis have been somewhat more permissive in their rulings about female sterilization. A woman, after all, does not fall under the prohibition of castration, and she is not legally obligated to procreate.[25] Nevertheless, she may not be sterilized without the excuse of an elevated risk to her life and health over that of normal pregnancy, for she too falls under the prohibition of self-mutilation. But if, for example, a woman suffers from a form of diabetes that cannot be controlled sufficiently to make further pregnancy safe, so that any failure of normal contraceptives would require an abortion, sterilization would be preferable to subjecting her to the possibility of requiring recurrent abortions; and it would be justified, just as each of the abortions would be, as a measure to preserve her life and health.

Similarly, all sources agree that even male sterilization is permitted and perhaps even required if the man's life or health makes it necessary, as, for example, in cases of testicular cancer.[26] The obligation to preserve life and health takes precedence over the prohibition of castration. Moreover, the man who undergoes such a procedure for health reasons is certainly not excluded from the Jewish community under Deuteronomy's harsh stricture.

Furthermore, if a man's wife cannot safely bear children, and if, as is often the case, it is considerably safer for her husband to have a vasectomy than for her to undergo the more invasive surgery of tubal ligation, the man may, and perhaps should, have the vasectomy. This view does *not* constitute a general permission to have a vasectomy for purposes of birth control; it rather allows a specific measure in order to subject a particular couple to the least physical risk possible when pregnancy would be unsafe.

This ruling is justified by several factors. While vasectomies are generally prohibited as the functional equivalent of castration and as an act of self-injury, when the motive is to prevent a clear physical threat to the life or health of the man's wife greater than that of normal pregnancy, we can rely on the physical distinction between castration and vasectomy to circumvent the Torah's strictures against castration. Similarly, the vasectomy is transformed by that motive from self-mutilation to a procedure undergone to save a life, and for that reason it is permissible. The man's own physical health may not be threatened,[27] but he falls under the corollary obligation all Jews have of preserving life and health in others and under the special obligation men have to provide for the medical care of their wives.[28] Thus we can, and should, extend the overriding obligation to prevent danger to life and health to permit the man to undergo a vasectomy for the sake of preventing serious harm to his wife.

One other matter. The prohibition against vasectomies would certainly apply to young men who simply do not want to have children; Judaism does not support that plan of action altogether, let alone this particular way of achieving it. For men in their forties or fifties who have already had several children, though, the same surgical procedure takes on a very different moral hue. The wives of these men would generally be in their forties themselves, and pregnancy during those years, while still possible, is now much more risky for the woman than at an earlier stage in her life. Moreover, the contraceptive pill is no longer safe for most women by that time, and other forms of female contraception sometimes become problematic. Then, too, couples are aware that as the biological parents age, the risk of birth defects rises, and that can be the source of considerable anxiety, especially if there is a history of birth defects in the family. The particular facts of each case must be evaluated on their merits, of course, especially in a situation as serious as deciding not to have any more children. Nevertheless, in some cases at least, it does seem to me that for the reasons noted above, vasectomies even for purposes of birth control might be permissible for men in their forties or older who have already begotten children.

Abortion

There is a clear bias for life within the Jewish tradition. Indeed, it is considered sacred. Consequently, although abortion is permitted in some circumstances and actually required in others, it is not viewed as a morally neutral matter of individual desire or an acceptable form of post facto birth control. Contrary to what many contemporary Jews think, Jewish law restricts the legitimacy of abortion to a narrow range of cases; it does not give blanket permission to abort.

Judaism does not see all abortion as murder, as Catholicism does, because biblical and rabbinic sources understand the process of gestation developmentally. Thus the Torah stipulates that if a woman miscarries due to an assault, the assailant is not held liable for murder but rather must pay only for the lost capital value of the fetus.[29] That early law already indicates that the fetus is not to be viewed as a full-fledged human being but rather as part of one.

Based on this, the Talmud determines that within the first forty days after conception the zygote is "simply water."[30] Another talmudic source distinguishes the first trimester from the remainder of gestation.[31] These marking points are not based on a theory of ensoulment at a particular moment in the uterus; they are rather determined by the physical development of the fetus.

The effect of these demarcations is to make abortion during the early period permitted for more reasons than during the rest of pregnancy, when the fetus is legally categorized "like the thigh of its mother."[32] Because our bodies are God's property, neither men nor women are permitted to amputate their thigh except to preserve their life or health, and so, *by and large, abortion is forbidden.*[33]

It is for this reason that, as indicated above, if couples are going to engage in family planning, Jewish law prefers that they use forms of birth control that prevent conception in the first place rather than those that abort an already fertilized egg. Moreover, abortion may surely not be used as a post facto form of birth control.

Jews are often unaware of the fact that in most cases Judaism forbids abortion because they have heard, correctly, that Jewish law *requires* abortion in some cases and permits it in others. That fact leads them mistakenly to think that abortion is permitted at will, when in point of fact *Jewish law generally forbids abortion.*

Specifically, Jewish law *requires* abortion when the woman's life or health—physical or mental—is threatened by the pregnancy; Jewish law *permits* abortion when the risk to the woman's life or health (again, physical or mental) is greater than that of a normal pregnancy but not so great as to constitute a clear and present danger to her. The fetus does not attain the full rights and protections of a human being until birth, specifically when the forehead emerges or, if it is a breech birth, when most of the body emerges.[34] The mother, of course, has full human status. Consequently, if the fetus threatens the life or health of the mother, then it may, and in some cases must, be aborted, as the following Mishnah graphically stipulates:

> If a woman has [life-threatening] difficulty in childbirth, one dismembers the embryo in her, limb by limb, because her life takes precedence over its life. Once its head [or its "greater part"] has emerged, it may not be touched, for we do not set aside one life for another.[35]

With this mishnah as a basis, all Jewish sources would require abortion in order to preserve the life or organs of the mother,[36] but authorities differ widely concerning how much of a threat to a woman's health the fetus must pose to justify or require an abortion.

When a woman is impregnated with three or more fetuses, either naturally or artificially, an abortion of one or more of them may be indicated in order to preserve both the life of the mother and the viability and health of the remaining fetuses. Such abortions are therefore permitted (and, depending upon the circumstances, even required)—although, as indicated in Chapter 3, if the couple are using in vitro fertilization, it is best not to implant more than three zygotes in the first place so as to prevent the necessity of aborting those beyond the number the woman can safely carry. When it becomes possible to determine through genetic testing which of the fetuses have a greater chance to survive and be healthy, then it will be permissible selectively to abort those less likely to survive. This is the same criterion to be used for triage decisions made at the end of life. If all of the fetuses are equally viable, the abortions must be done on a random basis.

Based on a responsum by Rabbi Israel Meir Mizraḥi in the late seventeenth century,[37] many modern authorities also permit an abortion to preserve the mother's mental health, and this ruling has been variously construed both narrowly and leniently in modern times.[38] To the extent that Jewish law makes special provision for an unusually young or old mother, an unmarried mother, the victim of a rape, or the participant in an adulterous or incestuous union, abortion is permitted to preserve the mother's mental health.[39] As a ground for abortion, however, "mental health" has not been interpreted nearly as broadly in Jewish sources as it has been in American courts; the permission would not include, for example, the right to abort simply because the woman does not want to have another child.

There is no justification in the traditional sources for aborting a fetus for reasons having to do with the health of the fetus; only the mother's health is a consideration. As a result, some people object to performing an amniocentesis at all, even when the intent is to determine whether to abort a malformed fetus.[40] Others reason in precisely the opposite direction; they justify abortion of a defective fetus on the basis of preserving the mother's mental health where it is clear that the mother is not able to cope with the prospect of bearing or raising such a child.[41]

Many Conservative and Reform rabbis, and even a few contemporary Orthodox rabbis, have handled the matter in a completely different way. They reason that traditional sources recognize only threats to the mother's health as grounds for abortion because until recently it was impossible to know anything about the genetic or medical makeup of the fetus before birth. Our new medical knowledge, they say, ought to establish the fetus's health as an independent consideration.[42]

Although I personally agree with this last approach, there are problems with it. Aside from the fact that it would represent an innovation in the law, it raises the extremely difficult issue of determining what constitutes a sufficient defect to warrant abortion. The "easy" cases are those in which the fetus has minimal brain tissue (e.g., an encephaly) or a degenerative disease like Tay-Sachs that will lead to the baby's death within a few years of birth at most. What about Huntington's chorea, though, where the degeneration will not usually begin until age thirty-five or forty? I believe that abortion is not justified in that case, since the person will live an extended period of time without suffering from any of the disease's debilitating effects—indeed, enough time to have children of his or her own and even participate in much of their rearing—and since there is reasonable hope that a cure may be developed in that time. But then where do we draw the line? Twenty-five years? Fifteen years? Ten years? And what constitutes a defect justifying abortion in the first place? Mental retardation? If so, how much? Blindness or deafness? We quickly slide into the danger of defining qualifications for a master race, with the corollary depreciation of disabled people.

The difficulty of making these decisions does not mean that we can or should shrink from them. Human life requires decisions throughout. Unlike Christian Science, Judaism has taken the stand that we need not accept whatever nature serves us; we rather have the right, and indeed the duty, to intervene medically as partners or agents of God. The advances of modern medical science have created a whole new spectrum of decisions that we may prefer not to make, but there is no escaping our duty to confront these issues as responsibly as we can.

In the area of abortion, we will undoubtedly find that whereas in some cases abortion is clearly justifiable or unjustifiable, in others the matter is more clouded. In the latter group the traditional method of judging the issue on the basis of the mother's mental reaction to the defect may be the wisest. For some mothers, raising a mentally retarded child, while not pleasant, is manageable; for others it is beyond their psychological competence. This, of course, means that only the people who are psychologically strongest and most stable would have the responsibility for raising such children, and that is unfair. Moreover, if most families abort "defective" children, one wonders about the degree to which society in the long run will tolerate imperfections and provide for people who have them. Thus the very sensitivity of society to the sanctity of life is at stake. Even so, we must develop guidelines for making these decisions, at least in the relatively clear cases. We must also educate medical and religious professionals to help families face the excruciating decisions where no guidelines are possible.

In practice, much of this discussion is moot. Jews in North America and in Israel engage in abortion almost indiscriminately, to the extent that by 1975, as Rabbi Jakobovits notes, abortions

> deprived the Jewish State of over a million native-born citizens since its foundation, not to mention the even greater losses through the violation of the law on contraception—all this at a time when Israel is lavishing vastly superior resources, relatively, on boosting her precarious population figures, by inducing but a small fraction of this number among Western Jews to go on *Aliya*, with all the huge problems of finance and social adjustment involved in their absorption.[43]

The high rate of abortion among Jews is a particularly problematic phenomenon for the contemporary Jewish community because Jews are barely reproducing themselves in Israel and are falling far short of that in North America. As a result, the Conservative rabbinate, in its *Rabbinic Letter on Intimate Relations*, notes that "The contemporary demographic problem of the Jewish people . . . must also be a factor which figures into the thinking of Jews using contraception," that "abortion . . . may not be used as a *post facto* form of birth control," and that "couples should seriously consider having three or four children."[44] In other words, even those rabbis who are relatively liberal in their interpretation of Jewish law on contraception and abortion are simultaneously calling for Jews to marry and to have children so that the Jewish people and Judaism can continue for more than another generation or two.

CHAPTER SIX

The Social Context
of Generating Life

I T IS A BAD MISTAKE TO SEE MEDICAL QUESTIONS AS ISOLAT-
ed, almost mechanical, problems to be resolved by very specific solutions. That is the approach of most treatments of
Jewish medical ethics—and, indeed, of medical ethics as a
whole. It derives from the mechanistic view of life inherent in
American pragmatism, where each problem is simply a fault in
the larger machine of life that needs a specific and, hopefully,
quick and inexpensive fix.

That way of viewing life, however, is false: life is instead an
organic whole, with each part affecting every other part in some
way. Decisions we make in our individual and communal lives
that ostensibly have nothing to do with bioethics actually impinge on such questions, either directly or indirectly, and it is
only if we recognize that context and try to amend it as necessary that we can honestly and appropriately address the specific
questions of medical ethics.

In this chapter, then, we shall look at the larger social context
of some of the particular medical questions we have been considering in regard to generating and preventing conception. The
broad social context will have an equal effect on issues at the
end of life, the prevention of disease, and the allocation of medical resources, and we shall therefore consider its import for

each of those issues in later chapters. The interaction between what happens in the doctor's office or in the hospital and what happens in society at large, in other words, must provide the continual perspective of any adequate treatment of medical ethics and will be an ongoing theme of this book.

Education in Sexual Morals for Teenagers and Adults

Because the human being is understood within Judaism as an integrated whole of body, mind, emotions, and will, it is improper for us as Jews to think of the way we use our bodies as separate and apart from our conceptions and values. Living life as a Jew requires one's sexual activity, as well as the rest of life, to be governed by the concepts and values Judaism prescribes. The moral and religious purity of our souls cannot be saved, as it were, while we do whatever we wish with our bodies. Quite the contrary, the way we behave has a direct effect on our moral and spiritual status, and the converse is also true: our thoughts and feelings have a direct effect on how we use our bodies.

However obvious this linkage may seem to some people, contemporary American culture denies it. In advertising and movies, in particular, the body is portrayed as a pleasure-producing machine. Consequently, youth, the time when the body is typically most functional and least likely to be in pain, is idealized and idolized, and images of bodily pleasures are used to sell absolutely anything.

The sexual ethic that emerges from such a view is that people should use their bodies for as much pleasure as they can and they should not prevent others from deriving pleasure from their bodies. But even that restriction in American cultural values is of questionable status; tough movie heroes, for example, often could not care less about whose feelings they hurt in their sexual exploits.

For Judaism, the body is neither an absolute good, as it is in modern American portrayals, nor the source of sin, as it is among Christian writers like Paul, Augustine, Luther, and Calvin. It is rather part of who we are as human beings. God created us morally neutral, with tendencies to do both good and bad. God also gave us a book of instruction (the literal meaning of *torah*) to guide us in our choices. When we use our body, mind, emotions, or will for good purpose, as defined by the Torah, we please God; when we use them to violate the Torah's norms, we sin. The body is no different from our other faculties in this. From one perspective, in fact, the general aim of Judaism is to get us to channel our energies—whether physical, mental, emotional, or cognitive—to good purpose as defined by the Torah and the Jewish tradition.

As we have seen, the two roles Judaism assigns to sex are procreation and marital companionship. Sexual activity and procreation, of course, can take place outside the context of marriage, but classical Jewish texts do not see that as proper. Marriage *(kiddushin)* is holy precisely because a man and woman set each other apart from all others to live their lives together, taking responsibility for each other, caring for each other, and helping each other live through life's highs and lows. They also take responsibility for the children they bear. The willingness to assume these responsibilities is critical both for their own pleasure and growth and for the perpetuation of the Jewish community and the Jewish tradition. Marriage is also important in Judaism because it provides a structure for achieving core Jewish values in our intimate lives—values like honesty, modesty, love, health and safety, and holiness. Marriage is no guarantee that we will succeed in this, but it does help us attain those values. Thus Judaism is not being irrational, prudish, old-fashioned, unrealistic, or mean in demanding that we limit our sexual intercourse to the context of marriage; it is rather responding to concerns that are at least as real and important in the fragmented society of today as they were in the more stable society of times past.

Sometimes, though, people do not meet an appropriate mate despite a conscientious search, and sometimes marriages end in divorce. Moreover, because Jews commonly go to college and graduate school, they are often not ready to assume the responsibilities of marriage until well after they mature biologically. Some can nevertheless adhere to the Jewish tradition's ideal of restricting sex to marriage, but others fall short.

Although Judaism clearly would have Jews restrict sexual intercourse to marriage, singles in our society generally do not abide by that norm. Under such circumstances, it is important to understand that the violation of one Jewish norm does not entitle an individual to ignore all others; it is not an either-or situation, in which one either abides by all of what Judaism has to say about these matters or follows none of it. On the contrary, precisely those values that lead Judaism to advocate marriage—honesty, modesty, health and safety, love, and holiness—still apply to sexual relations outside marriage; they are just harder to achieve in that context. Indeed, precisely because unmarried couples cannot rely on the support of a marital bond to foster those values, it is all the more critical that if they engage in sexual intercourse, they must consciously strive to live by them. Even though their behavior will not be ideal by Jewish standards, to the extent that they can make those values real in their lives, they will be preserving their own humanity, their Jewishness, and their own mental and physical health, as well as that of their partner.[1]

Since sexual intercourse can lead to conception, sexual activity outside marriage raises questions not only in the realm of Jewish morals but also in the arena of medical ethics. Specifically, couples who conceive out of wedlock face the question of whether to abort the fetus, to carry it to term and give it up for adoption, or to raise it under the parentage of one or both members of the couple.

Jewish norms would, first of all, mandate sex education for preteens, teenagers, and adults. The topics should include not only the anatomy of sex and the mechanics of intercourse and contraception but also the overarching concepts and values that should inform a Jew's approach to sex. In addition, it should be emphasized to teenagers in particular that their sexual activity should not be determined by peer pressure and that there are forms of sexual activity short of intercourse that can be quite fulfilling but preclude the possibility of pregnancy and its complications.

Moreover, for all ages, an adequate curriculum in sex education from a Jewish perspective must pay considerable attention to the health and safety risks involved in sex with multiple partners. This is especially important these days, since a number of sexually transmitted diseases that could be cured by antibiotics until the early 1990s have now developed strains that are resistant to the drugs currently available. Moreover, AIDS, at least as of now, is both incurable and lethal. Because these medical developments pose increased danger to those involved in nonmarital sex, and because condoms offer some measure of protection against those diseases, an adequate sex education program must provide condoms and other contraceptive devices with clear instructions on how to use them.

Some fear that if rabbis and Jewish educators frankly discuss sex outside marriage and even make contraceptives available, people will conclude that Judaism is not serious in prohibiting nonmarital sex. There is undeniably some danger of such misunderstanding. If Judaism is to affect the world as it actually is, though, contemporary applications of its norms dare not ignore the widespread behavior of Jews and others within our society. According to the U.S. government's Centers for Disease Control and Prevention and other studies, fully 72 percent of high school seniors, and 90 percent of twenty-two year olds, have had sexual intercourse.[2] Therefore, failure to distribute condoms and other contraceptives invites abortion, AIDS, and the other medical risks of unprotected sex with multiple partners for many, many people.

The Jewish tradition mandates that sex be restricted to marriage for very good reasons, as briefly described above. Jewish law also requires, however, that we save lives and limit abortion. We must therefore earnestly engage in sex education, urging young adults to refrain from sexual intercourse before marriage for the many good reasons Judaism provides, but we must also deal realistically, supportively, and therapeutically with the many who fall short of that ideal to preserve their health and their very lives.

Homosexuality

> Do not lie with a male as one lies with a woman; it is an abhorrence." (Leviticus 18:22)

> If a man lies with a male as one lies with a woman, the two of them have done an abhorrent thing; they shall be put to death—their bloodguilt is upon them. (Leviticus 20:13)

Exactly what these verses in the Torah prohibit has recently been the cause of considerable debate. Some interpret them to refer only to homosexual relations within a cult, and since the context of these chapters, called "The Holiness Code," is an overarching demand that the Israelites separate themselves from Canaanite cultic practices and devote themselves solely to God, that interpretation has at least some plausibility. Others maintain that these verses intended to prohibit homosexual sex in any context, perhaps motivated by the need of Israelite society for procreation.[3] Still others maintain that they refer to noncultic sex as well as cultic sex, but only literally "as a man lies with a woman"—that is, face to face (at least in the paradigmatic forms of heterosexual sex); according to this interpretation, anal sex and oral sex between homosexuals would be permitted.

The only thing that is clear about these verses is that they speak only of male homosexual sex; no verse specifically bans sex between lesbians. The rabbis, though, understood that to be prohibited under the verse in the same holiness code that forbids following the practices of the Egyptians and Canaanites.[4] The rabbis also interpreted the verses cited above to impose a ban on all male homosexual sex, whatever its form or context.[5] That was not only the norm within Jewish law; it was apparently also the accepted practice within Jewish society over at least the last two thousand years, to the extent that the Talmud and medieval sources permit two Jewish bachelors to sleep under the same blanket together "because Jews are not suspected of engaging in homosexual relations."[6]

That, at least, has been the public Jewish stance until very recently. In our own time, however, a variety of historical, biological, and sociological studies have painted a very different picture of what happened in the past and what is the case now, and so even more controversial than the original meaning of the biblical verses is how we should respond to them in our own time.

One feature of this issue that plagues every treatment of it, including my own, is the paucity of firm knowledge we have about the etiology and malleability of human sexual orientation. Indeed, many who have written about this issue assume that we know much more about the relevant facts concerning homosexuality than we actually do. This is one manifestation of what John Dewey called a "quest for certainty"—although here for psychological and social rather than philosophical reasons. We like to have things neat and clean. It gives us a sense of security and order. It also confirms our sense of self. As Dewey noted, however, the world in which we live is neither static nor easily defined, and so that quest is not only misguided but potentially dangerous.

Law rooted in a quest for certainty when none can legitimately be had is almost always bad law. The same is true for ethics. As Aristotle said, "Our discussion will be adequate if its degree of clarity fits the subject-matter; for we should not seek the same degree of exactness in all sorts of arguments alike, any more than in the products of different crafts."[7] At the outset of this discussion, then, we must recognize that here, as in many places, we must make decisions with the information we have and be open to later revision as new information presents itself.

There have been four general approaches to homosexuality in recent writings, distinguished by the factor that is primarily determinative: the textual, the historical, the biological, and the moral. All may draw on other factors as well, but most find one of the four the most important in forming their particular view of homosexual sex.

Textualists maintain that the ban against homosexuality in Leviticus and in later Jewish texts must remain in force because the Torah as the word of God and as the fundamental document of Jewish law must trump any other factor. Others augment this literalist view with claims that in any case, other values reinforce the Torah's stance—values like procreation, family, and social stability. Even so, many who take this stance differentiate between the act of homosexual sex, which they condemn, and the person who engages in such acts, whom they see simply as another sinning Jew.[8]

All positions, of course, are open to question, but I draw attention to that fact particularly with regard to this one, because many of its proponents sound as if theirs is the only position that can preserve the authority of the Torah and the possibility of realizing its values. That is simply not true. Several understandings of the process of revelation exist that would not require adhering to a literal understanding of the Torah but would nevertheless preserve its divine authority.[9] Moreover, the rabbis of the Talmud and Midrash themselves often employed techniques that interpreted the text contrary to its plain meaning, narrowed its meaning, or interpreted it completely out of existence.[10] To insist on the literal meaning therefore demands justification. At bottom, Judaism is the religion of the Pharisees, not the more literalist Sadducees, and so simply quoting the text or even the later interpretations of it will not suffice; we must, as the Talmud says, subject the text in each generation to what the contemporary judges see with their own eyes.[11]

Furthermore, the values touted in support of this position, while indeed important values, do not warrant the negative conclusion of this group. Gays and lesbians are procreating through donor insemination and surrogate motherhood, and many are becoming parents through adoption. As a result, the failure to propagate can no longer plausibly be used as an argument against homosexuals (especially when the reproductive rate among Jewish heterosexuals is only 1.6 or 1.7 and we are in the throes of a demographic crisis). Similarly, the families created by gay and lesbian parents are clearly different in configuration from those run by heterosexual mates, but they are full-fledged families, providing the structure, discipline, and love that one would hope for in any family. Therefore, as one would expect, there is no evidence that children growing up with gay or lesbian parents are, as a group, any less well adjusted than children growing up with heterosexual parents. Homosexual families may have the special need to expose children to caring adults of the opposite gender, but single-parent families have the same need. Moreover, the percentage of children who themselves become homosexual adults does not seem to differ whether the households are headed by homosexual or heterosexual adults. The one difference that does seem to surface in the studies so far is that in general two parents, whatever their gender, are better than one, simply because they have double the time and energy to raise their children. These findings would argue for children to be placed, if possible, in homes with two parents, but not necessarily heterosexual ones. Thus to appeal to propagation and family as reasons to deny the legitimacy of homosexuality is to ignore the realities of contemporary homosexual families.

Those who take a more liberal approach to homosexuality generally do so on the basis of one of the other three approaches. The Conservative rabbi Bradley Shavit Artson is probably the most articulate in using a historical argument to accomplish that end. Basing himself largely on an extensive history of homosexuality by David Greenberg, Rabbi Artson maintains that the only forms of homosexuality practiced until recently were either cultic, oppressive (e.g., master-slave), or promiscuous. It was therefore those forms of homosexual relations that the Torah and classical rabbis forbade, he argues, and their rulings must be interpreted that way. They cannot be reasonably construed to have forbidden loving, monogamous homosexual sex, according to Rabbi Artson, for it was only in the nineteenth century that such relationships came into being. We should therefore in our day condemn cultic, oppressive, or promiscuous sex, whether heterosexual or homosexual, as an abomination, but we should sanctify loving, monogamous homosexual sex, just as we sanctify the same kind of heterosexual relationship in marriage.[12]

I appreciate the goal and cleverness of Rabbi Artson's approach, but I doubt the historical claim that serves as its foundation. Even in our own tradition, there are three passages that call his contention into question: The *Sifra* describes the marriages of men to each other or women to each other as one of the practices of the Egyptians and the Canaanites; the Talmud, at least as Rashi understands it, praises non-Jews for at least not writing marriage contracts for people of the same gender who were having sex together, presumably in an ongoing and stable relationship; and *Genesis Rabbah* says that the generation of the Flood was erased from the world only when people began writing marriage contracts for men with beasts and other men.[13] While admittedly, as Rabbi Artson argues, the words used in these sources for "marriage" and "marriage contracts" may be intended metaphorically to denote arrangements forced on the parties involved and not voluntary or loving at all, that interpretation is at least open to question. Moreover, even if Rabbi Artson is completely right, those of us who want to adopt a more liberal stance toward homosexuality are not doing so for his historical reasons but rather for a combination of biological and moral ones.

The approach I took in my responsum for the Committee on Jewish Law and Standards in March 1992 adopted instead a biological argument. Specifically, there is some evidence that a homosexual orientation is inborn as a product of a person's genes and neurological structure.[14] These, however, are only preliminary results, and the consensus of experts nowadays is that sexual orientation is a product of both nature and nurture. Moreover, even if we assume that there is a biological correlation between certain physical factors (such as the size of the hypothalamus gland) that commonly characterize homosexuals in contrast to heterosexuals, one can, at least at this point in the development of the research, raise "the chicken and the egg question"—that is, do these physical markers cause homosexuality, or is it homosexual behavior that engenders these physical features?

What was therefore more cogent for me in writing my opinion for the committee was the testimony of actual gays and lesbians, many of whom attest that being gay is not something they chose. In fact, because of the widespread discrimination against gays and lesbians in our society, such people usually denied their homosexual orientation for many years and actively tried to fight off their homosexual tendencies. The fact that society discriminates against homosexuals lends further credence to their testimony, for in light of that bigotry, nobody in his or her right mind would ever choose homosexuality over heterosexuality.

Jewish law takes such evidence very seriously. Although homosexuality is not an illness, according to all of the relevant professional organizations, it is a feature of a homosexual's being that he or she is likely to know better than anyone else. In that sense, it is akin (although not equivalent) to the case in which Jewish law recognizes a patient's need for food on Yom Kippur: "Wherever the person says, 'I need it,' even if a hundred [physicians] say that he does not need it, we listen to him, as Scripture says, 'The heart knows its own bitterness.'"[15]

Thus even if homosexual desires are culturally as well as biologically generated, and even if some people would then claim that the culture must be changed to deter homosexuality in some way, for the individual homosexual those desires are already a fact of his or her existence. Moreover, in line with this talmudic precedent, the homosexual himself or herself provides the most reliable evidence for his or her orientation, and on the best of medical and psychiatric authority, it cannot be altered. The 1973 stance of the American Psychiatric Association, reaffirmed and strengthened in December 1992, is that however a person's sexual orientation is fashioned, it is not a matter of choice. Moreover, "There is no evidence that any treatment can change a homosexual person's deep-seated sexual feelings for others of the same sex"; and furthermore, one should not try to do so, for "homosexuality *per se* implies no impairment in judgment, stability, reliability, or general social or vocational capabilities," and "gay men and lesbians who have accepted their sexual orientation positively are better adjusted than those who have not done so."[16]

The combination of these sources of evidence, it seems to me, necessitates a rethinking and recasting of the law, *for if anything is clear about the tradition, it is that it assumed that gay behav-*

ior is a matter of choice. Otherwise, a commandment forbidding it would logically make no sense—any more than would a commandment that prohibited breathing for any but the shortest periods of time.

Now of course it is logically possible to say to gays and lesbians, as some rabbis writing on the subject have said, that if they cannot change their homosexual orientation, they should remain celibate all their lives. That result, however, is downright cruel.

Moreover, I find such a position theologically untenable. I, for one, cannot believe that the God who created us all produced a certain percentage of us to have sexual drives that cannot be legally expressed under any circumstances. That is simply mind-boggling—and, frankly, un-Jewish. Jewish sources see human beings as having conflicting urges that can be controlled and directed by obedience to the wise laws of the Torah; it is Christian to see human beings as endowed with urges that should ideally be forever suppressed. To hold that God created homosexuals to be sexually frustrated all their lives makes of God a cruel playwright and director in this drama we call life, and our tradition knew better. It called God not only merciful but good.[17] God's law, then, must surely be interpreted to take those root beliefs of our tradition into account. Jewish theology and law are not two disparate realms; here, as always, they must be interpreted to reflect each other.[18]

Furthermore, it seems to me that to ask gays and lesbians to remain celibate all their lives is not halakhically required. If gays and lesbians are right in asserting that they have no choice in being homosexual—and, given the widespread discrimination in our society against them, I have no reason to doubt them in this claim, and indeed every reason to believe them—then they are as forced to be gay as straights are forced to be straight. That is, gay men can no more extirpate their sexual or emotional attractions to other men and cultivate sexual and emotional attractions of a romantic sort toward women than straight men can expunge their sexual or emotional attractions to women and redirect them toward men—and, of course, the same thing, *mutatis mutandis*, is true for lesbian and straight women. We are all equally "forced" *(anoosim)* in our sexual orientations.

What are the legal consequences if one is compelled to violate the law? Normally, Jewish law maintains that the person is exempted from any punishment even though the act itself remains forbidden *(patur aval assur)*.[19] Thus, if at some future time this person or any other adult Jew engages in the act *without* being compelled to do so, he or she would be totally liable at law for the infraction.

The category in Jewish law of *patur aval assur,* however, normally applies to cases where the compulsion is *temporary.* The classical case in the Mishnah is that of the person who vows to eat with his friend but is prevented from doing so because the friend or his child became ill or because a rising river prevented the one who took such a vow from reaching his friend's residence. As Rabbenu Nissim explains the passage, the Mishnah's cases are specifically cases where there is *not* full compulsion *and yet* the person is automatically freed of his vow without the need to go to a sage for release from it, for, as Rabbenu Nissim says, "it never occurred to the one exacting the vow that it would apply if something happened such that one could not fulfill it."[20] The word used to describe what happens to the vow in the first Mishnah of that chapter, in fact, is *"hittiru"* (they unfastened [released] it), the verb form of *"muttar"* (permitted), a considerably more accepting evaluation of the failure to fulfill the vow than *patur aval assur* (freed of liability but still prohibited). The Talmud, though, does not go that far. "When a person is compelled," explains Rava, even in these temporary ways, "the All Merciful One frees him [from any punishment] *(ones raḥmana patreih)*."[21] (Notice the theological language embedded in the law on this issue.)

What would happen, however, if the person could *never* fulfill the commandment because he or she is *always compelled?* The closest parallels to such a situation are those where our human bodies compel us to do something. That is true, for example, of our needs to eat, to eliminate waste, and to have sex. In each case, Jewish law assumes that we cannot, and indeed should not, refrain from these actions altogether. It instead regulates the ways we are to meet those needs. It says, for example, that we may eat only according to the dietary laws and with proper blessings before and after meals; that we must cover our feces; and that we must restrict sex to marriage.[22] This channeling of our natural energies into a specific path for their satisfaction is one way God makes us holy.

These analogues in Jewish law, then, suggest that *if* homosexuality proves to be an orientation beyond the person's control, then the proper reading of Jewish law should be that homosexual acts, like heterosexual ones, must be regulated such that some of them are sanctified and others delegitimated—or perhaps even vilified as abominations. Putting the matter theologically, as the texts on compulsion do, if human beings can never reasonably require a person to do what is impossible for him or her, one would surely expect that to be even more true of God, who presumably knows the nature of each of us and therefore commands only what is appropriate to the various groups of us.

This, then, leads us to the fourth, and last, moral approach to this whole question. The historical and biological approaches delineated above maintain that, for specific historical or biological reasons, the practice of homosexuality today (or our understanding of it) is sufficiently different from what existed in the past to warrant a change in the law. Presume now, though, that the evidence to demonstrate these differences is false, or at least questionable. Even so, this fourth approach would argue, we should reevaluate the traditional stance toward homosexuality on moral grounds.

That is, those who follow this line of reasoning maintain that the determining factor in our evaluation of homosexuality should not be textual, historical, or biological but rather moral. The appropriate deliberations should thus concentrate on what Jewish concepts and values would have us foster in the lives of individuals and of society as a whole. Considerable effort and ingenuity will then have to be exerted to integrate this moral deliberation into the corpus of Jewish law, but, the argument goes, our moral perception of homosexuality in our time is so vastly different from that of the past that we must begin with that and return to the law later, if necessary by amendment (takkanah).

Contemporary moral perception of homosexuality differs from that of times past because of several factors. Most homosexuals were tightly closeted until the last decade, and so most heterosexuals thought that homosexuals were perverts who chose to live a life of moral abomination and were thus surely not worth caring about. Now, with the closet doors increasingly being opened, many heterosexuals are discovering that they know and love a number of people who are homosexual, that indeed some are members of their own family or of families they consider close friends. They certainly do not all fit the usual negative stereotypes; quite the contrary, it appears that roughly the same percentage of homosexuals as heterosexuals live lives that are productive and morally exemplary. That newfound familiarity with actual homosexuals makes it much harder to hate and despise them as a group.

In addition, the new biological information we are discovering adds to our sense that homosexuality is not something worthy of moral blame. The possibilities now open to gays and lesbians to procreate and raise families eliminate objections to homosexuality based on that factor.

Finally, because of the high rate of nontraditional configurations of families in our day, we are learning to discern what makes family life so precious and the ways in which varying family configurations can achieve those aims. This makes homosexual families just another new type that needs to be understood and supported to make it as strong a family structure as possible. Indeed, a 1996 Newsweek poll found that 57 percent of the adults surveyed thought that homosexuals can be as good at parenting as heterosexuals; only 31 percent said that they did not think so. Moreover, in just the two years between 1994 and 1996 there was a dramatic decline in those who thought that homosexuals should be barred from adopting children.[23]

If one evaluates sexual behavior on moral grounds, then, forced, promiscuous, and cultic sexual acts, whether heterosexual or homosexual, would all be classified and treated as abominations. Forced sex violates the integrity of the individual; promiscuous sex violates the integrity of the family and undermines the community; and cultic sex violates the Jewish understanding of our proper relationship to God as well as to each other. On the other hand, the Jewish tradition sanctifies monogamous, loving sex among heterosexuals as marriage, and, the argument goes, we should do the same in our time for homosexuals.

This is increasingly the approach I myself advocate. As indicated above, the claims against sanctifying homosexual unions based on the goals of propagation and family life simply no longer hold. Conversely, there are two clusters of positive arguments for sanctifying homosexual unions, one moral and one medical.

Among heterosexuals, marriage enables couples to develop their human capacity to love and care for each other. It thus has both individual and communal benefits. On an individual level, living in a marital union is the primary way adults mature emotionally and psychologically. On a communal level, marriage provides a socially stable structure for people to satisfy their sexual needs. Marriage also provides the context for effectively nourishing children physically, educationally, morally, and psychologically—a major social goal. Since these moral goals apply to everyone, that analysis would argue for creating an institution parallel to marriage for homosexuals, so that they too can achieve these moral ends.

There is also a negative moral argument that supports sanctifying gay and lesbian unions. The institution of marriage is, among other things, society's way of telling heterosexuals that they are not to be licentious. Promiscuity undermines the strong relationships necessary for social order and the effective rearing of children. The public institution of marriage is thus a clear and powerful social vehicle announcing the ideals of monogamy and fidelity and reinforcing them emotionally and legally. It certainly does not prevent promiscuity among heterosexuals—

and those who complain about homosexual licentiousness usually ignore the degree of promiscuity among heterosexuals, both single and married—but without marriage there would be far fewer faithful, monogamous unions.

Heterosexuals often denounce homosexuals for being promiscuous, and the statistics bear this out, especially for males. The lack of a legal institution to lend legal sanction and support to homosexual unions, however, effectively communicates to gays and lesbians (and to straights too) that society does not care whether gays or lesbians are promiscuous because it places no value on homosexual monogamy. Then, unfairly and ironically, heterosexuals turn around and castigate homosexuals for being licentious. It seems to me that heterosexuals need to stop being duplicitous in this way.

If a social institution parallel to marriage existed for gays and lesbians, homosexual sexual morality could fairly be judged on the same basis as heterosexual morality is, for good or for bad. More important, such an institutional structure would announce moral expectations and encourage moral behavior in homosexual sex just as marriage does for heterosexuals.

Medically, the scourge of AIDS and other sexually transmitted diseases gives us very strong reasons to do what we can to encourage people to engage in safe sex. This is, in part, a humanitarian concern on our part to help people avoid the pain of illness. It is also a core Jewish concern, for the Jewish tradition puts strong emphasis on preserving people's health and saving people's lives, not only by curing them once they are sick but, even more humanely and effectively, by preventing illness in the first place. While using condoms and avoiding the most dangerous forms of sex can help to prevent the spread of sexual diseases, by far the most potent preventive measure an individual can take is to practice celibacy until one makes a firm, socially announced and supported commitment to one partner and then to restrict one's sexual activities to that person. The Jewish values of preserving health and saving lives, then, would argue for consecrating monogamous homosexual unions just as they argue for heterosexual marriage.

These moral and medical factors thoroughly convince me that commitment ceremonies should be allowed and encouraged. However, my position on homosexuality is definitely outside the mainstream of the Conservative movement, at least as of now. The Rabbinical Assembly's Commission on Human Sexuality, which met some ten or twelve times between 1992 and 1994 and produced the *Rabbinic Letter on Human Intimacy*, referred the issues surrounding homosexual sex back to the Committee on Jewish Law and Standards for further deliberations, with the recommendation that this time the committee interview many of the witnesses whom the commission heard on this topic. In the meantime, while only a few Conservative rabbis have performed commitment ceremonies for gay men or lesbians, the discussion and experimentation with a variety of forms of commitment ceremonies will no doubt continue.

Genetics

The Theological Underpinnings of Issues in Genetics

As explained in Chapter 2, the Jewish tradition assumes that God controls who lives and who dies, who is healthy and who sick; but God also commands us both to take preventive measures to ward off illness and to seek to cure illness when it occurs. These commands are part of our general obligation to protect our bodies, for they are God's property throughout our lives and even in death.

When applied to modern issues in genetics, these principles require us to take note of the distinct roles that God and human beings play in health care so that we carry out our divinely delegated tasks but stop short of playing God. As our ability genetically to alter people's lives increases, that balance is becoming harder and harder to strike. Indeed, the Tower of Babel story in the Bible figures more and more in discussions of these issues, warning us of the dangers of overstepping appropriate human bounds. That story clearly teaches us that we may not attempt to build a tower to heaven to dwell with God (assuming that that is where the Eternal lives), but applying that lesson to modern genetics is not easy. Are some of the procedures currently available to us (let alone some of the ones on the horizon) the theological equivalent of building that tower and, therefore, prohibited acts of human hubris; or are they simply expanded ways for humans to be God's honored partners in sacred, ongoing acts of creation and healing?

There is no simple criterion that we can invoke to distinguish one from the other; the proper line between them will have to be discerned over time on a case-by-case basis. We will undoubtedly stumble from time to time in the process, but the trick is to be constantly aware of the need to draw that line as we develop greater and greater ability to change God's plan for the very nature of human beings.

Genetic Screening and Counseling

For some time now, young Ashkenazic Jews have been warned to be tested for Tay-Sachs disease. That is appropriate, for although the disease affects only 3 percent of Jews of Eastern European origin, that percentage represents ten times the risk for the general population. Jews are even more prone to Gouche's disease. The latter, however, is not fatal, and so testing for it is not nearly as critical or as widespread. Ashkenazic Jews are more prone than the general population to some other genetic diseases as well, although not to the same degree as they are to Tay-Sachs.[24]

A few rabbis in the Orthodox community, such as Rabbi J. David Bleich, object to genetic testing altogether. They fear that discovery of a defective gene in a fetus will motivate the parents to abort, and they reject abortion for any reasons other than direct concern for the life or health of the mother. [25] (They also define her "mental health" for the purposes of abortion more narrowly than most Orthodox rabbis do.) Presumably, when it becomes possible to cure such diseases in utero, even such rabbis would permit genetic screening, for then a positive test would lead to cure rather than abortion.

Even Rabbi Bleich, though, countenances screening for Tay-Sachs through blood tests before marriage, preferably in the teenage years. He notes that a person found to be a carrier may suffer anxiety and depression as a result and that others may see such a person as a pariah, but both reactions would be unfounded and contrary to Jewish law. The Jewish community, in fact, would be duty-bound in such cases to make sure that carriers are *not* stigmatized in that way.

Carriers should, however, try to marry people who are not themselves carriers so as to avoid any possibility of producing a child with the disease. This is in conformity with "what is historically perhaps the oldest recorded item of genetic counseling," namely, that the Talmud advises a man not to marry into a family where leprosy or epilepsy has appeared in at least three people.[26] A person who is not a carrier need not fear marrying a carrier, as long as the couple's children are also tested and counseled, but a carrier should seek to marry a noncarrier. "It must be emphasized, however," Rabbi Bleich says, "that when Tay-Sachs screening is carried out before marriage and both prospective bride and groom have been identified as Tay-Sachs carriers, they must be counseled that Judaism does not sanction a sterile union."[27]

According to the vast majority of rabbis of all streams of Judaism, however, an abortion of a fetus afflicted with Tay-Sachs would be warranted.[28] The Jewish community has therefore mounted a concerted effort to have couples undergo genetic testing before marriage or shortly thereafter—or even as soon as they start dating—so that they know whether they need to have any future fetus of theirs tested for the disease.

With a genetic disease based on recessive genes, as Tay-Sachs is, there is a one-in-four chance that the child will be completely free of the disease, a two-in-four chance that the child will not suffer from the disease but will carry it as a recessive gene, and a one-in-four chance that the child will suffer from the disease. In the first and second of those possibilities, the child should later be informed whether or not he or she is a carrier, but abortion is not warranted.

In the last case, where the child will be afflicted with the disease, the parents, given that knowledge, may decide to abort the fetus if they so choose. If they allow the fetus to be born, however, no active measures may then be taken to hasten its death, and both the child and the parents must just wait out the ravages of the disease. Palliative care must be administered to make the child as comfortable as possible, but aggressively treating the child with medications, machines, or surgery to prolong life is neither necessary nor wise. One may even remove feeding tubes, for the child is like an adult with a terminal illness (that is, a *terefah*) who, as I shall explain below in Chapter 8, must be offered normal food and liquids but not artificial forms of nutrition and hydration.[29]

Moreover, as explained in Chapter 4, if both members of the couple are carriers of a particular genetic disease, they may engage in other approaches as well. According to my own rabbinic ruling, approved by the Conservative movement's Committee on Jewish Law and Standards, the couple may, with some restrictions, use donor semen or eggs as a way of avoiding the possibility that they will conceive a child who suffers from the disease and therefore wish to abort the fetus. They may also use birth control and adopt children.

Similarly, where there is concern that a fetus will suffer from other genetic diseases, screening may be done, and a decision may then be made as to whether to abort or not. So, for example, if the child has Down's syndrome, some couples may choose to abort it on the grounds that the couple (officially, the mother) cannot stand the thought of bearing such a child, let alone rearing it, whereas others may choose to carry the baby to term and then raise the child. The appropriate choice depends on the reaction of the parents (again, officially the mother) to the prospect of raising such a child. They should definitely confer with other couples who have raised Down's syndrome children and with professionals, so that their decision can be based on knowledge and not fear or unrealistic expectations. Ultimately, though, the decision is theirs, for the permissibility of abortion legally depends on the mother's mental reaction to the news.

Analyzing amniotic fluid for the presence of diseases, however, reveals many other things about the child, including gender, eye color, etc. It is generally *not* permissible, according to all interpreters of Jewish law, to screen specifically for gender just because one wants a boy or a girl or to screen for any characteristic other than disease (e.g., height or intelligence). Screening for gender is thus only acceptable when there is a family history of gender-related diseases linked to the chromosome for the child's gender. (Most such diseases affect males.)

The moral problems of genetic testing do not stop with fetuses. Tests now exist to determine susceptibility to a number of diseases. Huntington's disease, for example, is based on a dominant gene, and so if one parent has it, the child has a 50 percent chance of contracting it. While the onset of the disease can be as early as two years of age and as late as seventy, thirty-eight is the average age. That means that people who will be afflicted by the disease often marry and have children of their own before they know that they are destined to suffer and die of Huntington's. People who suffer from the disease often become depressed and violent toward themselves and others, sometimes killing themselves before they slip into the dementia and loss of bodily function that ultimately take their lives. On average, Huntington's patients live sixteen years after onset, most of which are spent in nursing homes.

Now, however, a test exists to reveal whether a particular person will contract the disease. The test is generally administered only to those with a family history of the disease. Should, then, someone whose near relatives have had the disease be tested? If such a person of age twenty, say, tests positive, how will that test result affect that person's life choices? Disclosure of the Huntington gene often leads to depression and even suicide. Moreover, employers, insurance companies, and even friends may shun those who test positive—and unfortunately, many have. On the other hand, if one knows that one is at risk, is it fair not to tell one's potential spouse? Employer? Insurance company? Is this any different from a predisposition toward cancer or heart disease, which testing can also detect? If one tests negative, survivor guilt becomes a burden, especially since members of one's own family are likely not to be so lucky. Perhaps one should not take the test in the first place, especially since the disease is not likely to manifest itself, if at all, for some twenty years.[30]

Similar issues arise with the BRCA1 mutation linked to breast cancer in Ashkenazi women. It is estimated that 10 percent of the women diagnosed each year with breast cancer have a family history of the disease, and BRCA1 mutations are estimated to account for about half of inherited breast cancer cases and over three-quarters of the cases of inherited breast and ovarian cancer combined. Samples originally taken to test for cystic fibrosis and Tay-Sachs in 858 Ashkenazi Jewish women in the United States and Israel revealed that the carrier frequency among them of the 185delAG mutation alone is approximately 1 percent. It is estimated that among Ashkenazi women, that mutation accounts for 16 percent of breast cancers and 39 percent of ovarian cancers diagnosed before age fifty. By contrast, in the non-Ashkenazi population the estimated contribution of *all* BRCA1 mutations is 4.1 percent of breast cancer cases (approximately one-fourth the rate of Ashkenazi Jewish women for the 185delAG mutation alone) and 12 percent of ovarian cancer cases (less than one-third the rate of Ashkenazi Jewish women for that one mutation). In families with a history of breast or ovarian cancer, the female inheritors of BRCA1 mutations have an 80 to 90 percent lifetime risk of breast cancer and a 40 to 50 percent risk of ovarian cancer, and so this finding of the link between this mutation and cancer is especially important to Ashkenazi Jews.[31] Although the results were not nearly as pronounced, the researchers also noted that males with BRCA1 mutations show an increased risk of contracting prostate and colon cancer.[32]

What should be done with these results? On the one hand, the researchers note that "the observed 0.9 percent prevalence of the 185delAG mutation is higher than the prevalence of many genetic diseases for which routine screening is conducted." They do not as yet recommend widespread genetic screening, however, because it is not clear that people being tested for being carriers of Tay-Sachs and cystic fibrosis are representative of all

Ashkenazi Jews. Therefore, more random testing of that population is necessary to determine whether all Ashkenazi Jews are part of the at-risk population identified in this study, or only a subset of them, namely, those also at risk for Tay-Sachs or cystic fibrosis. This further research should, in their view, also collect personal and family histories of cancer to determine the predictive value of a long family history of such cancers, and it should collect information on males as well as females in light of the "modestly elevated" levels of prostate and colon cancer among those who inherit this BRCA1 mutation.[33]

The Jewish tradition would certainly not object to such research; it would actually push us to do as much as we can to learn about this linkage so that hopefully one day soon we can help people avoid cancer or, failing that, cure it. This attitude follows from the fundamental Jewish approach to medicine, namely, that human medical research and practice are not violations of God's prerogatives but, on the contrary, constitute some of the ways in which we fulfill our obligations to be God's partners in the ongoing act of creation. We must, of course, ensure that respect for persons, honesty, disclosure of risks, balance of risks and benefits, and the other usual moral canons of medical research are upheld in the process of conducting this study; these would be required by Jewish norms no less than by general Western morals. Since we have initial evidence that this line of inquiry may be fruitful in attaining our medical goals of preventing or curing some kinds of cancer, however, from a Jewish perspective we have not only the right but the duty to pursue this investigation to the extent that we can, balanced against the time, money, and effort we need to expend on our other social needs.

Moral problems abound, though, when we turn from the desirability of further research to the arena of medical practice, both now and in the future. Should testing for this mutation be recommended to all Ashkenazi Jews, or only to those for whom other factors identify them as being at risk? If the tests show that a person has the mutation, what should be the course of medical treatment for that individual and his or her children and future concepti? Does that person's fiancé(e) have a right to know about the gene in his or her intended mate? Finally, in the future, if and when we develop the ability to affect this gene through genetic engineering, should we fix each fetus on a case-by-case basis, or should we attempt to affect the germ cells as well so as to protect future generations?

As difficult and as new as these questions are in the history of the Jewish tradition, the outlines of a Jewish approach to them can be drawn. As the researchers suggest, before testing every Ashkenazi Jew for the mutation, with the attendant financial and emotional costs involved, further research is needed to identify those at risk.

At the other end of the development in research on this gene, *once we have learned to cure the disease through techniques of genetic engineering or other methods*, there would be, in my view, a positive obligation for people in the group at risk to undergo the test and a second, positive obligation on the part of those found to have the mutation to undergo the procedures necessary to correct it so that they do not suffer from the forms of cancer associated with it. Jews have the duty to try to prevent illness if at all possible and to cure it when they can, and that duty applies to diseases caused by genes just as much as it does to diseases engendered by bacteria, viruses, or some other environmental factor.

The hard issues, of course, arise in the stage of research in which we find ourselves now and undoubtedly will find ourselves for some years—namely, when there is evidence of a genetic linkage to several forms of cancer but when we cannot alter the gene to avert the disease. This produces horrendous insurance and job implications for women who are known to have the gene. Moreover, the majority of incidences of breast and ovarian cancers are not genetic, and so a negative test result might produce a false sense of security in a woman, prompting her to forgo further breast self-inspections and visits to her gynecologist.

The first order of business, then, is not to test for the gene but rather to identify more accurately those who are at risk. A woman who has a family history of such cancers—still the most reliable indicator of risk—should be especially diligent in performing breast self-examinations and having regular medical check-ups. She should also engage in these diagnostic practices earlier in her life than would otherwise be recommended.

Second, even if the woman is tested and is found to have the gene, that finding does not in and of itself determine the proper course of action. Even if she undergoes a radical mastectomy in an effort to prevent breast cancer, the cancer linked to the gene may express itself at other sites in the woman's body. She should obviously consult her doctor to gain the most recent scientific information about how best to combat the disease. The one clear conclusion is that, unlike the case of Tay Sachs, genetic testing should *not* be used to justify aborting a fetus carrying the BRCA1 mutation. After all, the incidence of cancer among those who inherit the mutation is not 100 percent, and the age at which the disease begins to manifest itself in those who do contract the disease varies widely, with onset usually not until the thirties or forties.[34] By that time the woman will have lived a considerable portion of a normal life span and may even have children of her own. Moreover, by the time the woman is afflicted with the disease, a cure might be found. Furthermore, the fact that environmental factors clearly play a role in determining whether cancer will occur at all in inheritors of BRCA1 mutations, and if so, at what age,[35] suggests that some medical and environmental therapies available even now may be used by those who have the mutation to delay the onset of the cancer, perhaps for decades, or to cure it once it has begun to invade the body. All these factors make abortion of a fetus bearing the mutation unwarranted. (In this respect, the case of the BRCA1 mutation is closer to the case of carriers of Huntington's chorea than to victims of Tay Sachs.)

Our current information would not suggest that children should be tested, for at present nothing can be done in childhood to ward off the disease that could not be done just as effectively later. This would argue for girls to wait until they are older and can make decisions for themselves concerning the course of action to take.

Traditionally, Jews become adults in Jewish law at the age of twelve-and-a-half for girls and thirteen for boys; at those ages they become liable for all of the duties and prohibitions of Jewish law. The child's teenage years, then, are the time when it becomes a positive duty for girls at risk to begin breast self-examination and visits to the doctor about this. This coincides with good medical treatment, for while breast and ovarian cancer do not usually erupt until later in life, some women contract these diseases as early as their twenties. The objective of having at-risk teenagers follow these procedures would be to alert affected women to the need to test for any incidence of cancer much earlier and much more frequently than the general population is advised to do so that any cancer that does occur can be treated at the earliest sign of onset, thus providing the best chances of remission and cure. These duties to test and treat derive from the general Jewish obligation to preserve life and health.

Do women with a family history of these cancers have the duty to inform their prospective mates of their situation? I think they do, but the answer to this is not as obvious as one might suppose. The Jewish tradition places a premium on truth and honesty in speech, business practices, and in personal relations.[36] As we shall discuss in Chapter 12, though, Jewish sources recognize that there are some times in life when tact should take precedence over truth, specifically, when telling the truth will accomplish no important end and will make someone feel bad, diminish that person's hope, or cause strife.[37] Truth is thus a critical value, but not an absolute one.

In our case, the woman, by hypothesis, knows that her family has often suffered from these cancers. A potential mate has a need, and therefore a right, to know that for two reasons. First, this information may affect his decision whether to marry the woman or not. When we marry, we always know that situations we cannot predict will undoubtedly occur and that part of the marriage bond is the agreement to support each other if and when such occasions arise. When one partner knows ahead of time of a particular propensity to cancer or some other serious disease, though, it is only fair that his or her potential spouse be told so that the marriage is not created under false pretenses of normal, good health. (This is not, incidentally, only a female issue: the same requirement applies to a man who has a family history of a given disease and whose children would thus be at special risk of contracting it. He too would fall under this duty to inform his potential wife.)

Second, the man has the right to know of the woman's propensity to contract these diseases because the probability that she will do so would undoubtedly require the couple to have children early in their marriage, which in turn might well influence their professional and personal plans. There are, then, serious implications for the potential husband, and so in this case the woman would not be exempted from Jewish obligations to tell the truth.

Gene Therapy and Genetic Engineering

While gene therapy is very new and available only in limited areas, and while genetic engineering is still only a theoretical possibility, some principles have already emerged in Jewish discussions of this topic. Techniques of genetic engineering, for example, can already be used to cure such conditions as hydrocephalus while the fetus is still within the womb. Further research holds out the hope that other diseases will also be amenable to treatment in utero, with those caused by one gene exclusively—for example, sickle cell anemia and Tay-Sachs—being the most likely candidates.

There is already general agreement among rabbis that the legitimacy of human intervention to effect cure extends to procedures within the womb as well.[38] When used in this therapeutic way, genetic engineering is an unmitigated blessing.

The same techniques may potentially be used, however, to screen out and abort fetuses that have traits that are not manifestations of a disease at all but merely characteristics that are deemed undesirable by certain individuals or groups. In the future, such traits may be changeable through genetic engineering. Abortion or genetic engineering to eliminate clearly defective fetuses thus poses the danger of the "slippery slope," where the definition of "defective" is broadened to the point of allowing only "perfect" children to be born, thus creating a master race.

Once we have the capability of changing not only the genes of a particular fetus but even its germ line, this moral problem will become even more acute, for we will then be in a position to alter human descendance for all generations. That, of course, holds out the promise of rooting out genetic tendencies to heart disease, alcoholism, and a host of other medical problems, but it also will enable us to change the genetic traits of shortness, merely average intelligence, a particular skin color, and even perhaps homosexuality.

Some uses of genetic engineering are thus clearly legitimate or illegitimate, but there are many cases where it is, and will remain, difficult to tell. How do we determine when we are using genetic engineering appropriately to aid God in ongoing, divine acts of cure and creation and when, on the other hand, we are usurping the proper prerogatives of God to determine the nature of creation? More bluntly, when do we cease to act as the servants of God and pretend instead to be God?

While the material on these questions from a Jewish perspective is very sparse, an Orthodox rabbi finds grounds within the tradition to use genetic techniques even for enhancing the human being for nonmedical purposes. Specifically, Rabbi Azriel Rosenfeld uses the talmudic suggestions to prospective parents for having handsome and learned children as grounds for using genetic engineering techniques for accomplishing the same or similar ends but not for diminishing the status of the fetus:

> Our sages recognize, and perhaps even encourage, the use of prenatal (or better, pre-conceptual) influences to improve one's offspring:
>
> Rabbi Yoḥanan used to go and sit at the gates of the place of immersion [that is, the pool where women immersed themselves after their menstrual period so that they might resume sexual relations with their husbands], saying: "When the daughters of Israel come out from their required immersion, they look at me and may have sons who are as handsome as I and as accomplished in Torah as I."[39]

This concept might well be extended to allow the use of gene-surgical techniques to produce physically and mentally superior children. On the other hand, turning a person into a monster by surgical means would very likely be forbidden, unless it were necessary to save his life; and creating monsters through gene surgery might thus also be forbidden.[40]

On the other hand, Conservative Rabbi David Golinkin specifically restricts the Jewishly legitimate use of gene therapy to the prevention or cure of diseases, reasoning that the sources permitting Jews to get involved in medicine in the first place speak of using it only for therapeutic purposes. I would imagine that Rabbi Golinkin would respond to the talmudic source that Rabbi Rosenfeld adduces by maintaining either that that source does not intend to announce law in the first place but rather only to give advice (or to show how egotistical Rabbi Yoḥanan was!) or, if it is to be construed as a legal precedent, that it only permits people to look at images of, or imagine, the qualities they wish in their child, not to change nature to accomplish their end.

Certainly, the way in which Jews read such sources and the way in which they contemplate the eugenic possibilities of genetic engineering cannot but be colored in our day by the cruel Nazi experiments that were ostensibly conducted for the same goal. Those experiments make it frighteningly clear that although some changes in human genetics are undoubtedly therapeutic, others raise troubling questions about the criteria for judging what constitutes a good change.[41] If it were possible to treat or reverse the BRCA1 mutation linked to cancer, for example, every rabbi would construe that as Jewishly legitimate, but careful lines must be drawn and clear criteria formulated to define proper usages of this technique and avoid improper or even monstrous ones.

If we were to change not only this mutation but the germ line of all present inheritors of BRCA1, have we stepped over the bounds of our legitimate powers to cure and changed ourselves into virtual gods, or are we simply and legitimately preventing disease more effectively? If we are clearly talking about a *disease*, I would be inclined to permit stem cell change as well as somatic cell change, for I do not see any reason why it should be permissible to cure a given disease in one particular fetus and not in that fetus's future offspring as well. On the contrary, since sickness is degrading, it would be our *duty* to cure the disease at its root if we could, so that future generations will not be affected. But the more powerful our abilities to intervene in preventing genetic diseases, the more urgent it becomes to accomplish the philosophical and moral tasks of defining the line between therapeutic and nontherapeutic uses of this technology and, in so doing, the boundary between us and God.

As we learn more and more ways to change human genetics, some ancient theological images come increasingly to mind. Are we Prometheus trying to steal the fire from the gods, the people of Babel trying to build a tower to heaven, or God's covenanted partners who were entrusted with the world "to work it and guard it," as the Bible says in the Garden of Eden story?[42] Drawing these lines and reinterpreting these ancient stories will become more and more the surprising, but critical, subject of moral debate.

PART THREE

Matters at the End of Life

CHAPTER SEVEN

Preparing for Death

Our American culture is one that emphasizes youth and vigor. Most of its heroes are—or look—young; we regard old age as something to be delayed and denied with exercise and cosmetics. Because technology has brought far-reaching changes into our lives at a very rapid pace, the elderly are no longer respected for their worldly wisdom and experience; after all, their experience is so different from that of the younger generation. Moreover, because American pragmatism puts a premium on skills and achievement, the disabilities of old age are dreaded by the aging and seen as annoyances by young people who need to deal with them in their older relatives.

This context makes us Americans miserably unprepared to deal with our own old age or that of close relatives or friends, and it makes us even less prepared to deal with death. Even though Americans now statistically live almost twice as long as their great-grandparents did at the beginning of the twentieth century, and even though death is one of the few features of life that is guaranteed, we avoid all thought of old age and death, especially our own. Nobody, of course, likes to contemplate death; it reminds us that our own hold on life is not for long, and it raises the specter of frightful diseases or disabilities along the way. We would much prefer to focus on less morbid subjects so that we have the hope and enthusiasm to live life to its fullest.

While that may be understandable on one level, it is ultimately unwise and unhealthy. We need not and should not obsess about old age and death, but we do need to think about it enough to make some important decisions about our health care, possessions, and heritage.

Advance Directives for Health Care

In times past, most people died of acute illnesses. Nowadays, though, most of us die of chronic illnesses over long periods of time. Moreover, modern medical science has developed machinery and medications that can keep vital organs functioning almost indefinitely. The fact that we *can* do something, though, does not necessarily mean that we should. Whether we should depends, in part, on good medical information, but it depends at least as crucially on our own value system. After all, the issue is not only what *is* or *is likely to be* the case, which are factual questions; we also need to decide what *should be done* in response to such situations, and that is a moral question, requiring us to relate this specific question to our broader concepts and values.

In the last twenty years or so, American court decisions have established that individual patients have the legal right to make decisions about their own medical care. As a result, physicians, who in previous ages made difficult medical decisions on the basis of their own personal values and judgments, have now been trained to respect patient autonomy in these matters. The physician has the duty to diagnose the disease and to explain to the patient the available options for dealing with it in clear, nontechnical language. Ultimately, though, it is the patient who has the legal right and must take the moral responsibility to make the decision according to his or her own values. Health care personnel, of course, have the right to have their own values, and so if a given doctor or nurse cannot, in good conscience, help a patient execute his or her decision, the physician or nurse may withdraw from the case after transferring the patient's care to other medical personnel who will help the patient achieve his or her medical goals.

Because critical medical decisions now require a moral as well as a medical judgment, and because American law insists that it is the individual patient who has the right to determine the aims of his or her medical care, it is not surprising that secular and religious groups of all sorts have in recent years devised documents designed to help patients make those decisions. All four movements within American Judaism have published such documents, each in accordance with its own understanding of how the Jewish tradition should affect decisions at the end of life.

People should execute two types of documents. The Durable Power of Attorney for Health Care, or Health Care Proxy, allows a person to designate someone to make health care decisions when and if the patient cannot do that on her or his own. In many such forms, the patient also designates a second and even a third alternative in case the person named primary proxy is unavailable or unwilling to serve in this capacity at the time it becomes necessary. After the document is signed, witnessed, and notarized, copies are given to the patient's primary care physician, lawyer, and designees.

The second document, the Advance Directive for Health Care, or "Living Will," is longer. It lists a variety of medical decisions that commonly confront patients at the end of life and asks the person filling out the directive to indicate what she or he would like to have done under such circumstances. In the directives published by the four movements in Judaism, the options indicated are those that patients may elect according to the particular movement's interpretation of Jewish law and tradition; those considered illegitimate are omitted. For example, the Conservative movement's form indicates that the movement's Committee on Jewish Law and Standards has approved two rabbinic responsa on end-of-life issues that differ on some issues; after explaining the theoretical and practical variations between the two responsa, it lists options approved by one but not the other in italics. It does not, however, provide for the option of assisted suicide, because according to both responsa, that would violate Jewish law.[1]

The point of an advance directive is not primarily to determine exactly what the designated proxy will decide, for in actual practice many situations occur that the document did not describe and that the proxy therefore cannot use for specific instructions. The point is rather to serve as a means of education and communication: it teaches the person filling out the form about the most common kinds of decisions people are called upon to make, so that individuals can think about them in light of their own perceptions and values; and it helps those designated as proxies to know the particular person's health care aims so that they can make decisions in line with his or her general philosophy even if there was no specific decision about a particular matter. Moreover, the advance directive gives a patient the opportunity to express his or her wishes with regard to organ and tissue donations after death.

It is *very* important that Jews fill out such forms. American society encourages this in order to maximize the patient's autonomy. Jewish sources also appreciate the importance of a patient's role in determining his or her health care, but other factors come to the fore as well. First, if the patient does not fill out such a form, relatives will have to make the necessary decisions about whether to withhold or withdraw life support, for example, and the relatives often do not agree with one another. That sets the stage for family arguments, and since the issue at hand is often the life or death of a parent or sibling, such disputes are often extremely bitter, leaving lasting scars in their relationships. By filling out such a form, therefore, a person saves near and dear ones from the moral responsibility of making such decisions and from the arguments that may otherwise occur.

Second, whoever thinks that life support should be removed will often feel guilt in "abandoning" Mom or Dad, even if that is the only reasonable and the most beneficial thing to do in light of the medical diagnosis. Often, in fact, it is precisely the adult child who had the least good relationship with Mom or Dad who now wants to use every possible means to keep the parent alive, even when there is no chance of recovery and when continuing to use life support machines just prolongs the dying process. Relatives do that not because they are looking out for the best interests of the patient but rather so that they can tell themselves later on that they did every possible thing to keep Mom or Dad alive and therefore need not subsequently feel any guilt about his or her demise. An advance directive can save the patient from such battering in the misplaced name of love.

Finally, filling out such a form is important in order to arrange for organ donation. As we shall discuss in Chapter 9, the Conservative movement's Committee on Jewish Law and Standards has ruled that it is not only an act of ḥesed (loyalty, kindness) to provide for the donation of one's organs after death to someone who needs them or to an organ bank but that there is a positive obligation to do so. Representatives of all of the movements in Judaism have at least permitted cadaveric organ donation, and most encourage it. Filling out an advance directive enables one to carry out this mitzvah (in its senses of both duty and beneficence).

At what age should one prepare these documents? Normally, we think of them as for people fairly advanced in years to execute, for they, we reason, are facing death in the not too distant future and therefore need to confront such matters. That is certainly the pattern that has emerged: people fill out these documents, if at all, when they are in their sixties or beyond, or when they enter a hospital for a serious procedure.

All of the hard cases in the law, though—cases like those of Karen Ann Quinlan and Nancy Cruzan—have centered on people in their twenties. They were hard cases precisely because people in their teens and twenties, who are statistically the most likely to be involved in fatal traffic accidents or violence, nevertheless think of themselves as being invincible. They therefore almost never communicate to relatives or others how they would want to be treated in the context of critical care. They also seldom think of indicating that, in case of death, they would want to have their organs used for transplantation. Nobody, of course, wants young people to give up their lives so that others may live, but when young people are involved in tragedies that take their lives, it is often impossible, and always uncomfortable, to get their families to think of organ donation at such a time.

It is therefore important for people to complete a durable power of attorney and an advance directive for health care as soon as they get their driver's license. This admittedly will seem strange, counterintuitive, and even eerie to young people just beginning their adult lives and to their parents; but it is well worth the discomfort involved to assure that both their critical care and the disposition of their bodily parts in the case of death can be directed by their own wishes.

Material and Ethical Wills

So as not to undermine a patient's hope for recovery, Jewish law demands that we not dwell on death in the patient's presence but rather engage the person in discussions of important issues of ongoing life in the family and community. Indeed, one is not supposed to give a dying person any inkling that you, a relative or visitor, have given up on his or her ability to continue living.[2] This concern is so strong that it leads a minority of rabbis to oppose hospice care, which after all is based on the premise that the person acknowledges the inevitability and imminence of death and acquiesces in it.[3] A much stronger strain within the tradition cites the need to bolster the patient's hope as overriding the requirement to tell the whole truth about his or her medical condition.[4]

These provisions of Jewish law help both those who visit the patient and the patient in question to think in terms of recovery and of rejoining normal activities. When recovery is possible, that kind of expectation in both the patient and his or her visitors is often a self-fulfilling prophecy, giving the patient the will to fight the disease. Sometimes that is exactly what makes the difference between life and death, as the patient absorbs the message, "If others think that I can beat this disease, maybe I can!"

This general demand of Jewish law to avoid discussions of death in an attempt to bolster the patient's hope and drive for life is subject, however, to three exceptions. If the patient has not hitherto prepared a will to dispose of his or her material objects, that must be done before death if at all possible. It is obviously best to do this years in advance so that people in the last stages of life need not be burdened with these decisions. People should do this, in fact, as soon as they have children and/or accumulate some wealth, and they should then periodically update the will when changes become necessary. If they have not done so, however, then they may, and indeed should, take care of this duty in the last stages of life, and a relative or friend should remind and help them to do so.

The second exception is the prayer *tzidduk ha-din*. Before Jews die, they are supposed to confess whatever sins they have committed, whether consciously or not. They are also supposed to ask for God's forgiveness. Jewish law and liturgy would have us confess our sins and ask for God's forgiveness, of course, throughout our lives, but the prayer *tzidduk ha-din* is recited only in contemplation of death. We recite it to settle accounts with our Maker to the extent that we can. Those who suggest that a dying person say the prayer, though, must tell him or her that it is only *in case* their hopes for his or her recovery do not materialize.[5]

The third exception to the ban against mentioning death is the permission to suggest writing an ethical will. Just as executing a will and asking God for forgiveness are not restricted to the days or weeks before one anticipates death, so too creating an ethical will need not be delayed until then. In fact, like the other two activities, writing an ethical will is better done well before that time.

An ethical will is nothing but a letter that a person leaves for relatives and friends. There is no particular form for such a letter; nowadays, in fact, it often is not a letter at all but rather an audiotape or videotape. The point of such a communication is to leave in one's own words some of one's memories, hopes and dreams, beliefs and values (hence the name "ethical will"). Jews have written ethical wills since the Middle Ages,[6] and in our times Jews have written them during many stages in their lives. Rabbi Richard Israel, for example, wrote one at the age of thirty-two to the child his wife was soon to bear.[7] More commonly, Jews create them in their fifties or thereafter as a way of leaving an important part of themselves to their children and grandchildren.

Those visiting a sick person suffering from a chronic disease can help the patient find meaning in his or her life by suggesting that the person create such a will. Visitors can then help sick people do that with leading questions. This makes visiting the ill easier, for now the visitor has an agenda of items to discuss with the patient. It also gives the patient an important reason to get up in the morning, to address the significant task of creating and preserving memories for loved ones. Thus ethical wills can be an important format for helping people in sickness and for facing one's own death.

While ethical wills can contain anything the creator wants to communicate, they typically address subjects such as these: (1) memories of your parents, grandparents, and other relatives; (2) your own life story, describing not only the objective facts of your life but how you felt while experiencing some of the events of your childhood, teenage years, and adulthood; (3) some people or texts that have had special meaning for you at specific points in your life and/or have such significance to you today; (4) your relationship to Judaism and to the Jewish community throughout your life and the reasons it took the shape that it did and now does; (5) things you did that you are proud of, and things you wish you had done differently; (6) a recollection of the experiences and feelings that were most important to you in your relationships with the people who are to receive your ethical will; (7) your concerns and hopes for your loved ones after you die; (8) your specific desires for things to happen after you die, for example, how you want to be buried, that your children marry Jews, that they care for each other, that a surviving spouse remarry; (9) your passions—things that you love and hate, and why you react as you do—and your values; (10)

expressions of love for your spouse, children, other relatives, and friends.

Some people worry that since they are not very articulate, an ethical will that they would write or tape will fail to say what they want to communicate and will furthermore leave behind an unflattering record of them. People need to understand, though, that ethical wills are not public documents; they are designed to be read, heard, or seen only by those who are near and dear to the person creating the will. Those people will read the ethical will with all of their memories of the person in mind, and so the extent to which it is articulate will not be relevant in judging its merit. Those for whom it is intended will cherish it instead for the concrete reminder of the loved one that it affords and for the memories it invokes. Grandchildren, in particular, will prize it as a way to connect with the people and stories of their roots. The point in creating an ethical will is not to impress or entertain people who never knew you; it is rather to let those who did, or wish they had, get a glimpse into you personally and into that part of their family history that you describe. As such, all the family members who receive it will consider it a great gift.

CHAPTER EIGHT

The Process of Dying

Suicide, Assisted Suicide, and Active Euthanasia

The Medical and Legal Context of These Questions in Our Day

A FEW DEFINITIONS WILL SET THE STAGE FOR OUR DISCUSSION of medical issues at the end of life:

- "Murder" is the malicious taking of another's life without a legal excuse (such as self-defense or war).
- "Suicide" is the murder of oneself.
- "Active euthanasia" is acting with the intention of taking another's life, but for a benign purpose—typically to relieve the person from agonizing and incurable pain or from the degradation of mental incompetence due to diseases such as Alzheimer's. Since the motive is benign, active euthanasia is sometimes called "mercy killing." Some such cases involve "substituted judgment," where someone other than the patient (usually a family member or a designated surrogate) makes the decision for the patient's benefit, while others are in response to the express wish of the person who wants to die, stated either now or in the past through a living will. In pure cases of active euthanasia, though, the patient does not bring about his or her death except by expressing that wish.
- "Assisted suicide" combines active euthanasia with suicide, in that both the person who wants to die and his or her assistant contribute to executing the death.

- "Passive euthanasia" is a refusal to intervene in the process of a person's natural demise.

In what follows, we shall examine and reevaluate the classical Jewish stance on these forms of ending life at some length, but it will be helpful at the outset to state that traditional position succinctly: whereas Judaism justifies homicides in cases of self-defense and war, it prohibits murder, including one's own (suicide). Moreover, even though the motive in cases of active euthanasia or assisted suicide is benign, in sharp contrast to the malicious intentions of a murderer, Jewish sources view all forms of active euthanasia and assisted suicide as forbidden acts of murder.[1] That is true even if, as in the case of assisted suicide, the patient explicitly asks to be killed.

New medical and legal realities, however, make these positions far less than obvious to contemporary Jews. On the one hand, while people in the past had no choice but to endure the pain of dying, with minimal medication available to ease their suffering, now we have sophisticated ways to diagnose levels of pain and calibrate pain medication to an individual's need. We have also developed hospice care, a system whereby the patient is supported physically, psychologically, and socially by a whole team of people, including family and friends. These factors should diminish the number of people who seek to take their lives.

On the other hand, though, we can now sustain bodily functions almost indefinitely, and so dying people may live through a long period of disability. Moreover, the drive to save money in health care has limited medical services for the dying, and in the future even less money will be spent on the care of each dying person as more and more baby boomers call upon whatever resources exist and as the need to contain health care costs becomes even more critical. This limitation of resources is especially problematic in our age of protracted life spans, where people generally die of chronic rather than acute illnesses. Moreover, since we can now predict the course of a disease with greater accuracy, people have less room for unrealistic hope. We now also have the means to bring about a quick, virtually painless death.

These latter factors have prompted some people faced with an incurable disease to take their own lives, sometimes asking others to assist them. Assisted suicide has in fact been practiced quietly in North American hospitals for many decades, although it is only since Dr. Jack Kevorkian's highly publicized and controversial efforts to help people die that the practice has become a matter of public knowledge and concern.

Those who commit suicide and those who aid others in doing so act out of a plethora of motives. Some of them are less than noble, for example, children's desires for Mom or Dad to die with dispatch so as not to squander their inheritance on "futile" health care, or the desire of insurance companies to spend as little money as possible on the terminally ill.[2] The morally hard cases, though, are those where the primary intention is the benign desire to stop the pain of a dying patient. Indeed, some have claimed that mercy killing is the only moral path, that keeping a person alive under excruciating and/or hopeless circumstances is itself immoral.

Developments in American law have added to these medical factors in prompting a new discussion of these issues. The Ninth Circuit Court of Appeals and the Second Circuit Court of Appeals have both affirmed that under the Fourteenth Amendment it is an American's right to commit suicide and to request others to assist in that process. The Ninth Circuit based its argument on the amendment's clause that forbids states from depriving any person of liberty without due process of law. The Second Circuit, noting that people with terminal illnesses can legally request to be disconnected from life support systems but that other people are denied aid in dying, based its argument on the amendment's clause forbidding states from denying any person the equal protection of the laws. The United States Supreme Court, however, rejected these attempts to protect assisted suicide as a constitutional right, returning the matter to the discretion of each state.[3]

The entire discussion of suicide and assisted suicide in American courts calls into play two of the sharpest differences between American secular perspectives and Jewish views. America's ideology, as expressed in its economic system, its philosophy (especially the distinctly American school of pragmatism), its media (where it is almost always the young and the able-bodied who are pictured), and even its recent welfare legislation reforms, would have us Americans think of ourselves in utilitarian terms, with our worth being a function of what we can do for ourselves and others. American attitudes and laws thus permit suicide, especially when a person can no longer do anything useful for either herself or himself or for others. Judaism, in contrast, requires us to evaluate our lives in light of the ultimate value inherent in us because we were created in God's image, as explained in Chapter 2 above. Jewish ideology and law therefore strongly oppose committing suicide or assisting others in doing so, for life is sacred regardless of its quality or usefulness.

Second, in American law and ideology, as expressed in the Declaration of Independence and reinforced by American constitutional law and court rulings, we each own our own bodies and, short of harming someone else, we all inherit the liberty to do with our bodies what we will. This tenet, according to the interpretation of the Ninth Circuit Court of Appeals, has made it every American's right to determine the course of his or her medical care, even to the point of committing suicide and asking others for assistance in doing so. Suicide itself is a legal act in all fifty states.[4] In sharp contrast, as also described in Chapter 2 above, according to Judaism God created and therefore owns the entire universe,[5] including each person's body, and we therefore do not have the right unnecessarily to destroy or damage God's property, including even God's vegetation and inanimate property.[6] On the contrary, we each have a fiduciary responsibility to God to preserve our life and health. This obligation makes suicide an act of theft from God, a violation of God's prerogatives, and indeed a trespass of the proper boundaries between God and human beings.

Rabbi Yeḥiel M. Tuchinsky, in his restatement of the laws of death and mourning entitled *Gesher ha-Ḥayyim (Bridge of Life),* puts these points starkly:

The sin of one who murders himself is greater than that of one who murders someone else for several reasons: First, through this murder he has left no possibility for any remorse and repentance. Second, death (according to B. Yoma 86, etc.) is the greatest form of repentance, but he, on the contrary, has committed through his death the greatest sin, namely, murder. Third, through his act he has made clear his repudiation of his Creator's ownership of his life, his body, and his soul; he has denied the simple idea that he did not participate in his creation at all, but rather [maintains that] his entire identity is exclusively [within] his power to sustain, to reproduce his existence, or to destroy it. He is like one who actively [and intentionally] burns a scroll of the Torah, for our Sages, may their memory be blessed, compared the creation of the soul to a scroll of the Torah that [now] has been burned and he must therefore face judgment in the future for this as well.

He is also among the unequivocal deniers of the continued existence of the soul and of the existence of the Creator, may His name be blessed, and of the future judgment after the departure of the soul [from the body]. . . .[7]

Contemporary Jews may not share all of Tuchinsky's traditional beliefs about life after death enumerated here, but even a comparatively liberal view of Judaism must, in order to remain recognizably Jewish, begin with the tenet that the body belongs to God.[8]

The American and Jewish traditions, then, begin with radically dissimilar assumptions about the worth and ownership of our bodies. These disparities frequently lead the two traditions to different prescriptions for the care of the dying. Even when the two traditions agree on a given course of action, they often arrive at their respective positions using different arguments with different burdens of proof.

Suicide

Although the body is God's possession, God has granted us the normal use of our bodies during our lifetimes, and that inevitably involves some dangers and risks. As Owner, however, God has the right to impose specific requirements and prohibitions intended to preserve our life and health as much as possible, and, as delineated in Chapter 2 above, God does so.[9] One such

provision relevant to our topic is that Jews may not injure themselves, let alone kill themselves.[10] Either of those actions is
viewed as harming or destroying what belongs to God, and thus
a violation of our conditional use permit, as it were. The only
three occasions on which a Jew is supposed to prefer death at
the hands of others or even suicide to violating the law—namely, where the alternative is being forced to commit murder, idolatry, or adultery/incest[11]—are all choices of death for the sake
of God, not for oneself.

Thus when the Romans burned Rabbi Ḥananyah ben Teradiyon at the stake for teaching Torah, he refused to inhale the
flames to bring about his death more quickly, saying, "Better
that God who gave life should take it; a person should not injure himself." The Romans, though, had attached tufts of wool
soaked with water to his chest to make his dying slower and
more painful, and Rabbi Ḥananyah allowed his students to
bribe the executioner to detach them. From this and other sources, later Jewish authorities deduce that one may remove impediments to the natural process of dying but not actively cause
one's own death, much less someone else's.[12] Indeed, based on
the biblical story of Aḥitofel's suicide, medieval sources maintain that "he who commits suicide while of sound mind has no
share in the world to come" and is to be buried outside the Jewish cemetery or at its edge.[13]

Saul's suicide (I Samuel 31:3–5), though, is recorded in the
Bible without objection, and the Talmud, apparently approvingly, records the case of children who take their lives to avoid
being sexually violated.[14] These cases undoubtedly served as the
backdrop for the later justification of suicide in Jewish law when
committed as an act of martyrdom in defense of Judaism[15] or
as a way of avoiding the temptation to convert under torture.[16]
Moreover, by narrowing the definition of a suicide to those who
took their lives with competence of mind and freedom of will,
modern authorities have maintained that those who suffered,
or could be presumed to have suffered, from temporary insanity do not fall into the category of willful suicides and are therefore permitted a normal Jewish burial.[17]

This distinction between the status of suicide itself and what one does with the body of a suicide post facto has important implications for assisted suicide. One must distinguish justification from excuse.[18] If suicide is permissible, as it is in American law, a person who committed suicide would be justified in doing so, and an accomplice might or might not share in that justification. Hence the current debate over assisted suicide in the American courts and in state referendums. In Jewish law, though, suicide is a criminal act except in the specific situations mentioned above; in all other circumstances the principal at best has an excuse that does not render the act permissible but may mitigate punishment. The accomplice may suffer too. The aide's duress, however, is separate and apart from the principal's suffering, and so the aide's excuse in mitigation of punishment must be judged independently. Indeed, although that excuse may sometimes be compelling, as when the aide acted at the patient's express request to end his or her own suffering despite the advantages of full medical and social support, in cases at the other end of the spectrum the aide may have acted to put an end to the medical bills and the need to care for the patient, perhaps quite contrary to the desires of the patient. In no case, though, does the accomplice have a justification for assisting in the suicide. Even if the principal had a valid justification for committing suicide, the aide does not share in that justification and is therefore fully liable for the violations committed by assisting the suicide.

Suicide itself, then, remains forbidden by Jewish law except in the dire circumstances of martyrdom. Even then, a poignant ruling from the Holocaust indicates the extent to which suicide is to be avoided if at all possible. A man knew that he was to be tortured by the Nazis to force him to identify the whereabouts of other Jews. Rabbi Ephraim Oshry permitted him to commit suicide lest he betray those other Jews, but Rabbi Oshry did not permit this ruling to be published, for fear that it would undermine the commitment to life of the other Jews of the Kovno ghetto; and other authors, both during and after the Holocaust, have taken pride in the small number of eastern European Jews who committed suicide in the midst of the Nazi terror.[19] Moreover, Rabbi Oshry was ruling in a case where the person, were he not to commit suicide, faced the prospect of endangering the lives of others; those are not the circumstances in the vast majority of cases in which the contemporary question is being raised.[20]

In sum, then, Jewish tradition prohibits suicide except as an act of martyrdom. Contemporary medical cases that raise the question anew clearly do not fit into that exception: the people involved ask to die in response to the excruciating pain and hopelessness of their illness, not in fear of being tortured by interrogators or forced to convert to another religion. Their suicide, then, cannot be justified, even if it would be retroactively excused for purposes of burial.

Assisted Suicide

Since suicide itself is prohibited, aiding a suicide is also forbidden. The grounds for that prohibition depend upon how the assistance is administered.

Sometimes the aide provides the means for the patient to commit suicide but is not involved in any other way. In some typical cases, the assistant hands an overdose of pills to the patient or sets up a machine so that the patient can administer a lethal substance intravenously. Once supplied the means to commit suicide, the patient acts completely on his or her own.

In such cases, the helper minimally violates Leviticus 19:14, "Do not put a stumbling block before the blind," for the rabbis interpreted that verse to prohibit moral stumbling blocks as well as physical ones.[21] The aide is guilty at least of misleading the patient to think that a forbidden act is permissible, of placing a stumbling block before a patient who is morally blinded by his or her medical condition and thus unable to see the authority and importance of the Jewish norm prohibiting suicide.[22]

Worse, the aide in such circumstances makes it possible for the patient to do what is forbidden. In talmudic terminology, the aide is "strengthening those who commit a sin" or "aiding those who commit a sin," both of which are forbidden.[23] Such a person is even more culpable than the one who simply misleads a person into thinking that the act is permissible, because the culprit in this case actively makes it possible for another person to commit the sin.

The aide in such cases might also be construed to be liable for injuring the patient indirectly *(grama)*. One who does that is retroactively free of monetary liability for any harm done, but *ab initio* nobody may deliberately cause harm to another, even indirectly.[24] Furthermore, one who harms another indirectly, while free of liability in human courts, is culpable in the judgment of Heaven. In fact, one specific case that the Talmud includes in this category concerns a person who placed deadly poison before the animal of a neighbor; if divine retribution is to be meted out to a person who threatens the life of an animal, God would undoubtedly be even more upset with someone who puts the life of a human being at risk in that way.[25]

If the assistant not only provides the patient with the means to end his or her life but also participates in the process, the assistant's liability depends upon how the help is given. If the aide directly causes the wound that eventuates in the patient's death, then she or he violates Jewish laws prohibiting the deliberate injury of another. Even if the victim asks to be injured, others may not do that, and they are fully liable for the injury.[26] This would be true even if the patient willingly participated. So, for example, if a physician compromises the life of a patient by administering a given dose of medication or poison intravenously but leaves it to the patient to push a lever to insert the rest of the dose necessary to bring about death, the physician is liable both for misleading the patient morally and for causing injury.

Finally, some forms of assisted suicide amount to murder. So, for example, if the aide shoots the victim with a gun or knowingly administers a lethal dose of a medication or poison with intent to bring about the person's death, that clearly constitutes murder, even though the motive was, by hypothesis, benign.[27]

Note that these Jewish arguments against suicide and assisted suicide differ radically from the reasons invoked by many Christian opponents of euthanasia. Some Christians base their opposition on the redemptive character of suffering. Euthanasia is unwarranted, the argument goes, because pain is itself salvational, symbolized most graphically by the crucifixion of Jesus. Other Christian voices oppose any medical interventions, including those intended to reduce pain, as an improper human intrusion into God's prerogatives of deciding when to inflict illness and when to bring healing.[28]

Judaism's opposition to euthanasia cannot be grounded in either of these lines of argument. For Judaism, the pain of disease is not in and of itself a good thing to be sustained for its own sake. Retroactively, when trying to explain how God could be just and yet allow innocent people to suffer, the rabbis suggested, among other approaches, that their pain might be "afflictions of love" *(yissurim shel ahavah)* designed by God either to teach the person virtues of patience and faith or to punish the person in this life for a small number of sins so as to make his or her reward in the next life pure and all the greater,[29] but that doctrine was never used before the fact to justify withholding pain medication from the suffering. On the contrary, the Talmud records that Rabbi Hiyya bar Abba, Rabbi Yoḥanan, and Rabbi Eliezer all say that neither their sufferings nor the reward promised in the world to come for enduring them are welcome—that is, they would rather live without both the suffering and the anticipated reward.[30] Moreover, from its earliest sources, Judaism has both permitted and required us to act as God's agents in bringing healing or, failing that, in reducing pain.

I sympathize enormously with patients going through an agonizing process of dying. As described later in this chapter, in cases of irreversible, terminal illness I take a very liberal stance on withholding or withdrawing life support systems, including artificial nutrition and hydration, to enable nature to take its course. I would also permit the use of any amount of medication necessary to relieve pain, even if that is the same amount that will hasten a person's death, as long as the intention is to alleviate pain.[31] The Conservative movement's Committee on Jewish Law and Standards has validated both my stance and that of Rabbi Avram Reisner, who permits withdrawing machines and medications from the patient—but not withholding or withdrawing artificial nutrition and hydration—and using large doses of morphine to relieve pain up to, but not including, the amount that poses a risk to the patient's life.[32]

As discussed in Chapter 11 below, the Jewish tradition takes mental illness seriously as illness,[33] and so some might ask: What is the difference between administering a large dose of morphine for reducing physical pain and using that same dosage in response to a person saying, "I want to end this"? In other words, why is it the case that physical pain counts as sufficient ground to justify doses of morphine that may risk death, whereas mental distress does not?

The answer is that, by hypothesis, in these cases physical pain occurs against the will of the patient, and the morphine is therefore a therapeutic response sanctioned by Jewish law and theology. The statement, "I want to end this," however, is an expression of the individual's will, a desire that, according to Jewish law and theology, it is illegitimate to fulfill. We do indeed need to respond to the patient's mental distress, but our response must be in the form of supplying sufficient pain medication; treating clinical depression if that is present; and, most important, providing the personal and social support that patients in these circumstances so desperately need.

Even though Jewish law, then, goes quite far in permitting terminally ill patients to die with whatever palliative care they need and without any further medical interference, it does not permit suicide or assisted suicide. The tradition bids us instead to maintain a firm line between legitimately withholding and withdrawing medical efforts on the one hand and illegitimately helping a person actively to take his or her own life on the other. To fail to maintain that distinction would violate Jewish law and destroy creatures belonging to God.

The Contemporary Circumstances That Sully Arguments for Euthanasia

We have expounded explicit Jewish law on the issues involved in assisted suicide. Now sometimes contemporary circumstances or values argue for changing the stated law as it has come down to us. In this case, though, several aspects of today's context bring additional arguments to bear in favor of the traditional position prohibiting assisted suicide. These aspects are not simply general concerns but Jewish ones, and hence they are part of what should be our understanding and articulation of Jewish law on this issue.

THEOLOGICAL. First and foremost, as indicated above, theological concerns underlie the Jewish legal position forbidding assisted suicide, in sharp contrast to the American secular view. Specifically, since the American tradition of pragmatism and hedonism leads us, as Americans, to value life only if we can do things and enjoy life, a physically or mentally compromised life is not considered worth living. Moreover, each person has the right to determine the fate of his or her body. It is this perspective that undergirds requests for suicide in America, the legal grounding for those requests as expressions of autonomy and liberty, and the sense of compassion that those who assist in a suicide feel.

The Jewish tradition, in contrast, calls upon us to evaluate life from God's perspective. That means that the value of life does not depend on the level of one's abilities; it derives from the image of God embedded in us. The tradition thus strongly affirms the divine quality of the life of disabled people, even though everyone would undoubtedly prefer not to be disabled. Indeed, our tradition demands that, upon seeing a disabled person, we bless God for making people different, thus boldly reasserting the divine quality of such lives.[34] We certainly must do everything in our power to dissuade anyone thinking of committing suicide because of disability from doing so. Embedded in the arguments in favor of assisted suicide, though, is an assumption frighteningly close to an assertion of the worthlessness of disabled people, for the terminally ill are also disabled. In line with its view of the disabled, then, the Jewish tradition requires that we recognize the divine aspect of people in the last stages of life, regardless of the quality of their lives. Moreover, even when life is not ideal and we question its divine dignity and its character as a gift, we lack the authority to destroy it because our bodies belong to God, who alone has the right to terminate life. Arguments for permitting assisted suicide on the basis of autonomy have been taken very seriously in the American context, and in their worst forms these arguments are based on a culture of selfishness that diminishes human life by valuing only those who can be productive and fully enjoy it. The clear stance of Judaism, in contrast, strictly limits our autonomy in this arena, given that we are God's creatures and agents, and strongly affirms the value of human life regardless of its usefulness or quality.

We might ask why a compassionate God would deny us the authority to take our lives when we can no longer function. Moreover, according to Maimonides, we must keep our bodies in good health so that we may serve God,[35] and if we cannot do that any longer, it would seem that God should allow us to curtail our lives. Although we can certainly challenge God with either of these views, the tradition is unanimous in asserting that God does not give us that authority, that even when people are incapacitated by, say, a stroke, God forbids them to commit suicide or others to assist in one.[36]

From Judaism's perspective, then, it is not a compassionate act at all to assist a person in taking his or her own life, because doing so makes both the principal and the aide violators of some of the most fundamental values and laws of Judaism—namely, those insisting that we not murder and that, on the contrary, we set aside virtually all of Jewish law in order to save a life.[37] We all sin, of course, but these are the most serious sorts of sin, the kind that it is anything but compassionate to help someone commit.

SOCIAL/ECONOMIC. Several aspects of the current social and economic context make the prospect of permitting assisted suicide even more troubling than it inherently is. One element lurking in the background of this discussion is the history of condoned assisted suicide in Holland, where a wide range of rationales have prompted physicians to help people end their lives. In the United States, Dr. Jack Kevorkian has similarly assisted people in all sorts of physical conditions—even chronic fatigue syndrome—to commit suicide. He has admittedly sensationalized the whole subject, and it is not wise or fair to judge the issue on the basis of his actions alone. Moreover, I am not usually convinced by slippery slope arguments, for the essence of moral discernment is learning to distinguish cases.[38] Nevertheless, both the experience in Holland and Dr. Kevorkian's cases have clearly demonstrated just how slippery this particular slope is. Even though there are undoubtedly some situations in which the case for assisting a suicide may seem compelling, we must prohibit assisted suicide altogether in order to prevent diminishing the value of life in the public eye and in public policy.

Another current factor that makes any move to permit assisted suicide dangerous is the push to save money in health care. Motivated largely by how that economic agenda will affect care at the end of life, the American Medical Association, in briefs to the Supreme Court, strongly opposed legalizing assisted suicide. The association was justifiably worried about what such action would do to both the patient and the physician, for especially under conditions of managed care, permission to take one's own life and to enlist the aid of others in doing so could quickly become all but an obligation to end the lives of those who have no reasonable hope of being cured. Doctors, in the worst scenario, might be pressured by hospitals or health insurance companies to convince their patients that suicide is the best option, not only because it will end their pain and thus serve their best interests but also (and maybe primarily) because it will save the hospital or insurer money. The role of the physician as the patient's advocate thus threatens to become severely compromised.

The same considerations apply to the patient's family members. If assisted suicide becomes permissible in American law, patients will feel all the more pressed by their families to end their lives rather than drain the family's finances by prolonging the dying process. If Jewish law is also interpreted to permit assisted suicide, both the legal and the religious setting in which American Jews will be making these decisions will argue for the legitimacy of such pressure, to the point where patients or family members who resist the suicide option will eventually feel that they are being unreasonably obstinate, that "normal" people would just agree to end their life once they know they cannot be cured. Indeed, in the context of such changed social expectations, even when family members do not want the patient to commit suicide and express that view as clearly as they can, patients may feel that their families actually want them to do so; my relatives, the patient may think, are just trying to be nice, but they really want me to end my own agony and theirs. Legitimating assisted suicide thus dangerously shifts the burden of proof: currently, it is those who want to take a life who must justify that course of action, but if assisted suicide becomes legal, the onus will be on those who refuse the option to justify their resistance.

The economic arguments in support of assisted suicide are not completely frivolous. In the United States people spend more on their health care in the last six months of life than they do throughout the rest of their lives. About 2.5 million Americans die each year, and more than 50 percent of those deaths occur in acute care hospitals.[39] Surely the money could be better spent, the argument goes, if people were given the choice and aid to die.

Although the economic factor is real, assisted suicide is not the appropriate response. Hospice care is. In hospice care, all concerned recognize that the patient's disease is incurable, and the course of medical care is therefore directed not toward aggressively and invasively trying to prolong life but rather toward providing comfort and relieving pain. In hospice care, patients spend most of their last months of life at home, with some outpatient visits to hospitals along the way. That form of care is not only more medically realistic and inexpensive but also much more humane. Along with hospice care for the patient, respite care can and should be provided for family caregivers. The bill for hospice and respite care combined will pale by comparison with what we are spending for people's last weeks and months now, and the patient will gain in dignity and comfort in the bargain.

MEDICAL.   Possibly the most common and compelling ground suggested for justifying assisted suicide is to relieve a patient of racking, unrelenting pain. This argument would be both understandable and compassionate if there were no other alternative, but doctors today have ample means for controlling any amount of physical pain. Some dosages will make the patient unconscious, and patients may have to choose between some amount of pain with consciousness or loss of consciousness as all pain is quelled. That is a legitimate choice that should be offered to patients.

American physicians, though, often do not offer or employ sufficient pain medication. Reasons for this vary. Sometimes doctors honestly do not know how much morphine to administer, for people differ not only in weight but also in their thresholds of pain. That is an understandable reason for failing to employ enough pain medication at the beginning of treatment, when these variables may make the correct dosage hard to calibrate. As time passes, though, doctors have the duty to adjust the amount of pain medication to the needs of the patient.

Some doctors say they minimize pain medication for fear of inducing drug addiction. That is a proper concern in general, but a truly bizarre one in the case of terminally ill patients. Others have a "John Wayne attitude" toward pain, claiming that good, morally worthy patients grin and bear their pain rather than complaining about it and requesting medication to quell it. Even worse, some aspects of this problem are socioeconomic: centers that treat primarily white patients provide more adequate pain relief than do those treating minority patients; consequently, on a percentage basis, many more requests for assisted suicide are made among the latter.

Perhaps the most pervasive aspect of this phenomenon is the culture of American medicine itself. American medicine, far more than medicine in other Western countries, is based on technological cures,[40] and when those do not work, doctors consciously or subconsciously give up on the patient who symbolizes the failure of their methods. They therefore do not bother to administer pain relief, for that is either not part of their goals in the first place (the "John Wayne attitude") or a secondary goal to be invoked only when they have failed to cure. Whatever the basis for this pattern of supplying insufficient pain medication, physicians should seek to control pain rather than acquiesce in a request to die.[41]

Another medical phenomenon prompts other patients to appeal for aid in committing suicide: far too many people with irreversible, terminal illnesses are subjected to futile, aggressive treatment. If, as indicated earlier, 50 percent of those who die in the United States each year spend their last days in an acute care hospital, that suggests that too few terminally ill patients are taking advantage of hospice care.

Moreover, as an editorial in the Annals of Internal Medicine maintained, far too many people are finding that their express desire for withholding or withdrawing life support, as stated in their advance directives, is being ignored by "physicians who are so preoccupied with the preservation of life that they can no longer see the broader human context of their work." Similarly, the largest study to address the human context of dying, known by the acronym SUPPORT, involves more than ten thousand seriously ill people at medical centers in five cities. A chief finding of that study was that about half of all patients spent their last days in what the researchers termed "an undesirable state," including a week or so in an intensive care unit; having a physician who was unaware of wishes not to be resuscitated; or being in serious, insufficiently treated pain. "I believe the enthusiasm for physician-assisted suicide is driven, in part, by the fear that we will receive overly aggressive care at the end of life and that our suffering may be prolonged," said Dr. William Knaus, an internal medicine specialist at the University of Virginia Medical School and a coordinator of SUPPORT.[42] Clearly, if that is what is prompting requests for assistance in suicide, the appropriate response is for physicians conscientiously to make themselves aware of their patients' advance directives and then to adhere to their expressed desires to remove impediments to the natural process of dying.

PSYCHOLOGICAL. While some requests for assistance in dying are prompted by the patient's excruciating pain, others are rooted in the hopelessness of his or her situation. We are, after all, mortal, and some diseases cannot be cured. Patients afflicted with such diseases cannot realistically hope to return to the life they knew. They instead face the prospect of continued suffering and debilitation until death, and some would prefer to end things quickly so as to avoid the suffering and degradation of the last stages of their illness.

Such cases are precisely the ones that have produced the term "mercy killing" to describe active euthanasia, and indeed the hopelessness embedded in the medical situation of such people often makes their requests for assistance in dying emotionally compelling. Nevertheless, we should respond to such cases by taking constructive steps other than acceding to their requests.

Physicians or others asked to assist people in dying should recognize that those contemplating suicide are often alone, without anyone who takes an interest in their continued living. Rather than assist such a patient in dying, though, the proper response is to create a group of people who clearly and often reaffirm their interest in the patient's continued life.

My mother once had a roommate in a nursing home whom literally nobody visited. She had one son who lived on the other side of the country and who called from time to time, but she had no other family or friends. Worse, some clothes her son sent her as a birthday gift were stolen by the night staff. Under such conditions of abandonment (and, in this case, violation), one can understand why people would wonder why they should continue to fight to live—indeed, why they should get up in the morning at all.

Requests to die, then, must be evaluated in terms of the degree of social support the patient has; often such requests are withdrawn as soon as someone shows an interest in the patient staying alive. In this age of individualism and broken and scattered families, and in the antiseptic environment of hospitals where dying people usually find themselves, the mitzvah of visiting the sick *(bikkur ḥolim)* becomes all the more crucial in sustaining the will to live.

As discussed above, hospice care recommends itself for economic and medical reasons. Perhaps it works best, though, as a response to the psychological pressures that prompt people to ask for help in committing suicide. Much of the loneliness inherent in being confined to a hospital is eliminated when the patient is cared for at home instead. Family members cannot be expected to shoulder all of this burden; *bikkur ḥolim* remains an important imperative for friends, even when the patient is living at home. The very familiarity of the home setting, though, together with its increased chances of providing the companionship of family and friends, makes hospice care clearly preferable to hospitalization when doctors cannot realistically expect to cure the patient.

The medical hopelessness of these situations by hypothesis remains, however, and it violates our duty to tell the truth to try to deceive patients into believing otherwise. Although some sources in our tradition justify such behavior in the name of buoying up a patient's spirits,[43] deception is generally not the way to do that. Patients usually have a sense of their medical prognosis, and so they do not believe those who tell them otherwise and instead come to distrust them. Moreover, lies are bound to lead to anger and feelings of disrespect and abandonment in the patient. Infantilization in this situation should be avoided at all costs. Patients already feel reduced in stature by their illness, and deception makes them feel further diminished, as if they were being treated as children (who, by the way, should also not be misled). Family and friends should clearly not appear at the bedside with sullen faces, dwelling on the patient's terrible prognosis. At the same time, they should not pretend that the medical situation is other than what it is. The patient's spirits can be lifted substantially and appropriately, though, if family and friends concentrate on those elements that can make the remainder of the patient's life meaningful. Some topics that should be raised are practical in nature. Specifically, as explained in Chapter 7 above, if patients have not previously filled out a will or a living will, they should be asked to specify their wishes about the distribution of their property and their preferred course of medical treatment, respectively. They should also be helped to create an ethical will. Beyond these practical projects, visitors will buoy patients' spirits by treating them as adults, respecting them enough to engage in conversation about the same adult topics that previously interested them—and even some that they had not previously explored.

In addition to general topics of conversation, some families can heal troubling relationships in a hospice setting that they were not able to resolve earlier in their lives. The limited term of life becomes very clear in such a setting, and that often motivates all concerned to be more forthcoming in their relationships with family and friends than they were previously. Moreover, in positive relationships, the time spent together in a beloved's last days can be the last gift children give their parents or that spouses give each other. Thus, even though life at this stage may be physically painful, emotionally these may be some of the most significant days the person has lived.[44]

Indeed, the American courts that dealt with assisted suicide addressed what is, in many ways, the wrong question in the first place. We should not be asking whether one may aid another in dying; we should rather explore what prompts people to seek to die in the first place, and then we should remove those motivations through proper pain medication and through attentive care. Those are the most appropriate responses to requests for assisted death.

Medical hopelessness, then, need not and should not amount to psychological hopelessness. People asking for help in dying to overcome the loneliness and the futility of their lives should not be offered aid in dying but should rather be given assistance in making the remainder of life meaningful.

MORAL. In refusing to allow people to "shuffle off this mortal coil"[45] when and how they wish, we are taking upon ourselves the moral responsibility of imposing our will on them, and why should a society based on individual liberty do that? This last argument, in fact, is precisely the basis of the Ninth Circuit's decision affirming the legality of assisted suicide. This argument, however, is not nearly as cogent in Jewish thought as it is in American ideology and law, for Jews are born with duties rather than rights. Even in the American context, though, the government must protect the most vulnerable populations, and the dying are surely among them. Similarly, the Torah's demand, "Do not stand idly by the blood of your brother," was interpreted by the rabbis as a duty to come to the aid of those at risk.[46]

As indicated above, permitting assisted suicide may at first look like an affirmation of the patient's liberty, but it soon transforms into a duty to die. Protecting individuals' liberty, then, is more effectively achieved by making assisted suicide a socially unacceptable option so that individuals need not defend their desire to continue living. The current ban on assisted suicide inevitably infringes on the liberty to gain assistance in dying, but that is a reasonable price to pay in order to preserve the liberty of a far greater number of people to continue living without having to justify their choice.

Moreover, until now we have assumed the morally pure situation, where the patient is in pain or in an increasing state of degradation (as in Alzheimer's patients) with prospects for only further deterioration, and where the aide's sole motive is to help the patient fulfill his or her wishes (stated now or previously) to end life under such circumstances. Real situations, however, are almost never that simple, and they prompt some hard questions. With regard to the patient, is the request to die a response to lack of social support, as we have discussed? Does it reflect a state of psychological depression that can be treated medically? Or does it indicate the patient's worry that further medical care will seriously deplete the estate to be left to the heirs? With regard to the aide, does he or she stand to benefit from the end of the person's life, either monetarily or simply by being freed from taking care of this person any longer? Assisted suicide, in other words, rarely occurs in the morally pure atmosphere usually assumed in arguments about its moral appropriateness, and as soon as one exposes the less noble motives involved, it often seems considerably less honorable.

Another moral issue arises in these cases. As the Ninth and Second Appellate Courts maintained, modern medical advances have made the line between active and passive euthanasia increasingly hard to define. That does not mean, however, that it has completely disappeared. The distinction between them constitutes the very real moral difference between, on the one hand, helping someone live and die in a natural way and, on the other, homicide. Moral sensitivity is precisely the ability to make distinctions, including some hard ones.[47] We have, then, an important moral interest in discerning that line, however difficult it may be to see at times, because nothing less than our moral character is at stake.

All of these theological, social, economic, medical, psychological, and moral factors, then, reinforce the ban embedded in Jewish law on suicide and on assisting a suicide. They also demand that we take a much more active role in ensuring that the dying are not abandoned to physical pain or to social ostracism, that instead we make the mitzvah of *bikkur ḥolim* (visiting the sick) a critical part of our mission as Jews. This is especially important as the Jewish population, along with North Americans in general, ages, for in the years to come more and more of us will need such care. In attending to the sick, we must assure that their physical needs are met and that their ending time in life is as psychologically, emotionally, and religiously meaningful as possible. Our compassion, in other words, must be expressed in these demanding ways rather than by merely acquiescing in a request for assistance in dying, for ultimately the Jewish tradition calls upon us to recognize God's rights of ownership of our bodies and God's exclusive right to decide when to take our lives.

Although neither the patient nor others may induce a person's death, they may pray to God to permit death to come, for God, unlike human beings, has the right to destroy His own property. One of the small number of classic stories on the dying process, in fact, describes just such an instance. Rabbi Judah, president of the Sanhedrin and editor of the Mishnah, is dying, and his students are keeping him alive through their prayers. Seeing what a difficult time he has in eliminating bodily waste, his handmaid prays that he be allowed to die and then crashes a jug so that the noise will interrupt the students' prayers. In that instant, Rabbi Judah dies. The talmudic story records no objection to what the handmaid did; quite the contrary, one gets the distinct impression that the students themselves were at fault. They should have paid more attention to Rabbi Judah's condition and stopped their prayers of their own accord so that he could be relieved of his pain in death. The later codes go even further: they not only allow one to desist from praying for a person's recovery but explicitly permit one to pray that God speedily take the life of a dying person in pain. (Incidentally, notice that this story attributes considerable healing power to prayer, a subject to which we shall return in Chapter 12). While we may not assist a person in committing suicide, then, we may pray that God intervenes soon.[48]

Letting One Die: Passive Euthanasia

Although Judaism forbids suicide and active euthanasia, it does permit passive euthanasia in specific circumstances. Our increased abilities to keep people's bodies functioning through machines and medications make it critical to determine when life support may be withheld or withdrawn.

Unfortunately, the sources on this subject are sparse. That should not be surprising. Until the discovery of penicillin in 1938, physicians could do very little to impede the process of dying. Even when a gangrenous leg could be amputated, the patient stood a very good chance of dying from the surgery itself or from infections associated with it. Modern hygienic procedures, antibiotics, new machines, and microsurgery have changed that picture dramatically. Since physicians can now do a great deal for the dying, Jews seeking moral guidance from our tradition on these matters must place a heavy legal burden on the few sources that describe people who thought that they had an effective choice of whether or not to delay death.[49]

One source is the account of the martyrdom of Rabbi Ḥananyah ben Teradiyon, described above. In this story Rabbi Ḥananyah permitted the removal of an agency he knew to be beneficial in maintaining his life (the tufts of wool soaked in water), and his decision had the approval of God Himself.[50]

Another source on this issue is the comment of Rabbi Moses Isserles on an authoritative code, the *Shulḥan Arukh*:

> It is forbidden to do anything to hasten the death of one who is in a dying condition. . . . If, however, there is something that causes a delay in the exit of the soul, as, for example, if near to this house there is a sound of pounding as one who is chopping wood, or there is salt on his tongue, and these delay the soul's leaving the body, it is permitted to remove these because there is no direct act involved here, only the removal of an obstacle.[51]

Here again, impediments to dying may be removed. *Sefer Ḥasidim,* the thirteenth-century source of Isserles's ruling, actually prohibits any action that may lengthen the patient's agony by preventing his quick death, and it forbids those attending at the moment of death to cry, lest the noise restore the soul to the deceased.[52] According to some authorities, even medicines must not be used to "delay the departure of the soul."[53]

In former ages these precedents caused little difficulty because human ability to prevent death was extremely limited. Nowadays that is not true, and so the following crucial question arises: When does our obligation to cure end, and when does our permission (or, according to some, our obligation) to let nature take its course begin?

Authorities differ. All agree that one may desist from all medical efforts to save the patient (but not those to relieve pain) once the patient becomes a *goses,* a moribund person. But when does that state begin? Definitions vary. Rabbi J. David Bleich restricts it to situations when all possible medical means are being used in an effort to save the patient and nevertheless the physicians assume that he or she will die within seventy-two hours.[54] Because medicine can now sustain and even cure people who formerly would have died within three days, however, other contemporary rabbis have defined the state of *gesisah* more flexibly to include all those who suffer from an incurable, terminal illness, even if it will be a year or more before the person dies.[55]

In a rabbinic ruling approved by the Conservative movement's Committee on Jewish Law and Standards,[56] I noted that Jewish sources describe a *goses* as "a flickering candle," who may not even be moved for fear of snuffing out the candle of life. That description and that medical therapy apply only to people within the last hours of life (not even the last three days). Consequently, I argued, the appropriate Jewish legal category to describe people who have incurable diseases but who may live for months and even years is, instead, *terefah* (an imperiled life), that is, a person diagnosed as having a terminal illness. Permission to withhold or withdraw medications and machines would then apply to people as soon as they are in this state.

This makes Judaism's conception of the end of life exactly parallel to its understanding of the beginning of life. As we have seen, Jewish sources depict the inception of life in stages, ranging from the "mere water" of the zygote through the fetus of forty or more days of gestation being "like the thigh of its mother" to the full human life of an infant once its head emerges from the vaginal cavity and the "confirmed existence" of the child who attains the age of thirty days. Similarly, at the end of life, while some people die of a sudden accident or heart attack, those who die of chronic diseases go through stages. A person who has been diagnosed with an irreversible, terminal illness is no longer a healthy human being but a *terefah;* in the last minutes or hours of life the person becomes a *goses,* like a flickering candle, unable to be moved for fear of extinguishing life; when the person ceases to have heartbeat and breath, death has officially taken place according to the criteria of traditional Jewish law; even then, according to the Midrash, the soul does not fully depart from the body until three days after death.[57]

Jewish law's depiction of progressing by stages both into and out of life is biologically accurate. Life does not begin or end at one distinct moment but rather emerges in stages and, more often than not, ends that way too. Moreover, conceiving of birth and death in stages has practical consequences. We have already seen the implications of this way of viewing life with regard to issues like abortion and contraception, and the process of dying produces similar, staggered results.

Specifically, there is general agreement among rabbis who have written on these matters that a Jew need not use heroic measures to maintain his or her life but only those medicines and procedures commonly available in the person's time and place. We are, after all, commanded to cure based on the verse in Exodus 21:19, "and he shall surely cure him"; we are not commanded to sustain life per se.[58] Moreover, since Jewish law does not presume that human beings are omniscient or omnipotent, it is only the best judgment of the attending physicians about what they can and cannot do in the given situation that counts in determining a plausible response to the illness. Even if some cure is just around the corner, we are not responsible for knowing that.

Thus a person who is currently incurable *(terefah)* may choose to undergo experimental therapies in an attempt to overcome the illness. Even if the therapy brings with it the risk of advancing the time of dying, use of it is permissible if the intent is not to bring about death but rather to prolong life.

On the other hand, a person with an incurable illness may also choose to have machines and medications withheld or withdrawn and to engage in hospice care, where only palliative treatment will be administered. We are not omnipotent or omniscient, as God is, and therefore neither patients nor physicians can appropriately expect to be able to cure every illness. Indeed, to presume that we could would be to engage in a form of idolatry, making idols of ourselves and our abilities. (The parallel psychological description of this religious language is megalomania.) Withdrawing or withholding life support from terminally ill patients is justified in Jewish law by its mandate that we not prolong the process of dying.

On both theological and legal grounds, however, we can and definitely should administer to the needs of the dying through pain medication and through our presence and loving care. Our legal duty to care for the sick definitely extends to those situations when all that we can do medically is to relieve pain. Even (or, perhaps, especially) in treating the dying, Jews are required theologically to imitate God, who, according to the tradition, visits the sick.[59]

Effective Versus Beneficial Therapies: Rules Versus Policies

The line drawn by the tradition between sustaining a person's life and prolonging his or her death also bespeaks another of its concerns. In times past, choosing an appropriate course of care with this distinction in mind was relatively straightforward, since nothing much could be done to keep the patient alive anyway. In our time, though, this is no longer true. We can now keep people alive long past their natural life spans. In some cases—as, for example, in the prescription of antibiotics to cure pneumonia in an otherwise healthy patient—there is no question that we should use the medical means available to us to restore a person's health. Even when most other functions of the body have shut down, though, we have effective means to prolong the functioning of vital organs, and this poses the independent issue of whether a given therapy is not only effective but also beneficial to the patient.

To apply Jewish sources intelligently and authentically to such cases, it will be helpful to invoke legal philosopher Ronald Dworkin's distinction, described in more detail in the Appendix to this volume—namely, the difference between rules, on the one hand, and principles and policies, on the other. Some standards invoked by judges are rules, "applicable in an all-or-nothing fashion." If the rule fits the facts of a given case, then either the rule is "valid" (that is, we have agreed that it governs this situation) or it is not valid, in which case the rule contributes nothing to the decision.

In contrast, principles and policies do not automatically determine consequences when the conditions stipulated are met; they rather describe what we generally do, either because that fulfills what we construe to be morally demanded (our "principles") or because it helps us to achieve our social goals (our "policies"). In any given instance or set of instances, however, the usual patterns of action embodied in principles or policies are open to change if such alteration would better achieve the aims of society or meet its moral demands. While rules, then, are by their very nature inviolable, principles and policies may or may not be followed, depending upon our judgment as to how they should be balanced against each other and applied.[60]

Distinguishing rules from principles and policies differentiates Conservative approaches to issues at the end of life from most Orthodox views. Orthodox responsa have closed off all discrimination between effective versus beneficial therapies on the grounds that, according to their interpretation, Jewish law establishes an inviolable rule that all life is sacred and must be preserved in any amount and under all circumstances. That, I maintain, is a mistaken reading of the tradition, for there are cases where Jewish law expressly requires that we take a life (for example, when execution is mandated by law, or when killing another is required to defend oneself) or even give up our own life (specifically, when the alternative is that we ourselves must commit murder, idolatry, or incest).[61] Jewish law does embody a strong push for life as a consistent policy (or, perhaps, principle), but not as an unbreakable rule. So, for example, the later tradition's distinction between sustaining life and prolonging the dying process establishes the minimization of pain as one factor that, under specific circumstances, can be used to set aside the general policy of preserving life.

Several sources in the tradition substantiate my interpretation of it in this way, for they argue that we should use the benefit to the patient as the primary criterion for determining a course of action rather than our ability to accomplish a limited, medical goal (like keeping one or more organs functioning). Thus the Talmud specifically states that one need not be concerned for "the life of the hour" *(ḥayyei sha'ah)*. The context is a discussion of an opinion by Rabbi Yoḥanan that "where it is doubtful whether [a patient] will live or die, we must not allow them [gentiles] to heal, but if he will certainly die, we may allow them to heal."[62] It is clear, then, that the Talmud defines "the life of the hour" as the time a person lives after being diagnosed as having a terminal illness. After that time, we need not try to cure a person who, as far as we know, cannot be cured, and therefore we may employ the services of a nearby gentile doctor rather than go to the trouble of hunting for a Jewish one. (This is probably not because the rabbis assumed that Jewish doctors are more skilled than gentile ones; it is rather because they were worried that gentile doctors might not do their best in healing Jews and might even do things that would hasten a Jewish patient's death.)

In our setting, this means that if the patient is dying of a terminal disease, we may relinquish aggressive medical treatment, even if it is effective in prolonging vital organs. We then may, and probably should, concentrate instead on relieving pain.

The Tosafists, rabbis primarily from the twelfth century whose questions and deliberations appear on the standard talmudic page, point out that while the Talmud says in this case of hiring a gentile physician that we need not be concerned about "the life of the hour," in another case the Talmud apparently holds that we should try to save even small amounts of life. Specifically, if a building collapses on a person on the Sabbath, the Talmud says that we should violate the Sabbath rules and remove the debris in an attempt to try to save the person. The Talmud specifies, though, that if, after exposing the nostrils and heart, we find that the person is dead, we must wait until after the Sabbath to uncover the rest of the body and bury it, since we can no longer justify violating the Sabbath rules in the name of saving the life of a person. The Talmud's permission to violate the Sabbath to begin digging in the first place, though, is specifically for the sake of preserving what may well be only the brief time that one who suffered such trauma would be likely to live. The two talmudic sources therefore seem to conflict with each other over whether we must strive to preserve the lives of people who have only a short time to live, and the Tosafists try to reconcile them in this way:

There are grounds to say that in both sources we should act for his benefit, for there [in the case of the person under the debris] if you do not care [about "the life of the hour"], he will die, and here [in the question of using a gentile physician], if you do care [about "the life of the hour" and therefore prohibit the gentile physician from treating him], he will not be healed by the gentile and will certainly die. So here and there we abandon the certain [course of action] to do that which is doubt [fully appropriate so that in both cases we can act for his benefit].[63]

Jewish vitalists—if I may call them that—seize upon the specific therapy that the Tosafists prescribe here to claim that we should always act to sustain life, for that is always "for his good." Such an interpretation, however, confuses examples with rules. It in fact uses the examples to create a rule in direct contradiction to the principle the Tosafists were here enunciating. In these two cases, acting for the victims' good amounts to trying to preserve their lives, despite the grounds in each instance for thinking that we should not do so; however, that does not mean that such a goal would be appropriate in every case. On the contrary, the Tosafists specifically announce that the proper objective of the medical care of a patient is to act for *his or her benefit*. When we apply that standard to some contemporary cases, we may have to abandon the attempt to save a life in the name of acting in the patient's general best interests.[64]

It is legally and morally much easier, of course, to ignore all such considerations. One can then take what appears to be the moral high ground by insisting on expending every effort to save any human life, no matter how tenuous or painful. With the ongoing development of more and more means to sustain vital organs, however, what may once have been the high moral position has ceased to be that, for aggressive medical treatment comes at considerable cost in pain to the patient. Like it or not, we can no longer rely solely on what can be done to sustain a patient but must rather face the difficult decisions concerning what will benefit him or her.

Taking into account the benefits of alternative therapies for the patient will inevitably involve decisions about quality-of-life issues, and such an approach always poses the danger of embarking on a slippery slope. Moreover, the patient, physician, nurses, and insurance companies may disagree as to what constitutes the most beneficial course of action for a patient. The risks of such controversy or of sliding down the slippery slope to active euthanasia should not be exaggerated, however, for we certainly can discern at least some cases in which aggressive treatment is clearly in the patient's interest and others in which it is not. Moreover, the essence of moral sensitivity is not the evasion of life's complexities but rather the ability to make distinctions among them.

We can now apply these considerations to some specific cases. Even when a patient can be cured, it is not always clear that he or she should be treated. For reasons of scarcity and cost, the government or insurance plans may decide that people of a certain age or condition should not be treated for a given disease because the chances of recovery are not good and/or because the money required for the treatment would be better spent on preventive care; more effective curative care; or, in the case of government, on other social needs entirely. We shall address such triage questions in Chapter 12.

When the therapy involved is readily available and not very expensive, we might nevertheless question whether we should use it. For example, a person suffering from multiple, incurable illnesses, one of which is bound to cause death soon, often develops pneumonia. Doctors are then in a quandary. A generally healthy person who contracts pneumonia would be treated with antibiotics, which frequently would cure the disease. According to Jewish law, in those situations both the physician and the patient would be required to use antibiotics, and few would need Jewish law to persuade them to apply that therapy. But what should happen in the case of the incurable patient described above? The physician can probably cure the pneumonia, but that would only restore the patient to the pain and suffering caused by his or her other terminal maladies. The alternative would be to let the patient die of the pneumonia so that death would come more quickly.

From the perspective of Jewish law, the question is whether our inability totally to cure the person gives us the right to refrain from curing what we can. Normally we do not have this right. So, for example, we must try to cure the pneumonia of a child who has Down's syndrome, even though we cannot cure the Down's syndrome. If a person has an irreversible, terminal illness, however, we do not need to intervene; we may rather let nature take its course. We must view the person as a whole rather than consider each individual disease separately. Thus even though we could probably cure the pneumonia, and even though the means for doing so are not unusual or expensive, nevertheless the person is a *terefah* and cannot be cured, and therefore we may refrain from treating the pneumonia if that will enable the patient to die less painfully.

This decision would be in line with the strain in Jewish law that we have been describing, namely, one that does not automatically and mechanically assume that preservation of life trumps all other considerations but rather judges according to the best interests of the patient. That principle does not extend so far as to permit mercy killing, but it does make it permissible to refrain in this case from administering the antibiotic so that the patient can die of his or her other diseases.

Along similar lines, once an individual has contracted an irreversible, terminal illness, that person may ask his or her doctor—either personally, through an advance directive for health care, or through a designated surrogate—to withhold or withdraw machines or medications that maintain vital bodily functions but do not offer any reasonable chance of cure. Such a request is justified on two grounds: it serves the interests of the patient, and it avoids prolonging the dying process. The physician therefore need not have any moral compunctions in withholding or withdrawing machines or medications, for doctors can never be plausibly required by our interpretation of Jewish law to persevere in using a procedure that does not effect cure or an amelioration of a patient's condition. Moreover, it is the patient's disease, not the lack of a machine or medication, that ultimately brings about his or her demise.

If a physician feels queasy about assuming the full moral responsibility of turning off the machine or medication drip, however, she or he may put the procedure on a timer and then return shortly before the timer would discontinue the procedure. At that time, the physician can decide whether the patient's condition warrants resetting the timer to continue use of the machine or rather suggests that the timer should continue running to turn off the machine automatically. Doctors, though, need not feel any guilt whatsoever in personally removing life support systems from patients who cannot recover from their underlying illness.[65]

Removal of Artificial Nutrition and Hydration from the Terminally Ill

People who cannot eat and drink in the usual way for either physical or mental reasons are fed through tubes. This group includes, for example, those in the last stages of throat cancer or Alzheimer's disease.

Under such circumstances, physicians first use the least invasive way to provide tubal feeding, that is, the naso-gastric tube, which is inserted into the nose and down the throat. Because of the instinct to cough, however, patients sometimes try to cough up the naso-gastric tube or pull it out; and since coughing is a reflex reaction controlled by the brain stem rather than the upper cortex of the brain, this may happen even when the patient is comatose. When it does, caregivers must either tie the patient's hands to the bed or proceed to the next most invasive form of intubation, intravenous feeding. Veins, however, are not designed to carry the load of intravenous nutrition and hydration. They therefore collapse after a certain amount of time or develop infections at the point of the tube's entry. As a result, veins in various parts of the body must be successively tapped.

Finally, when all else fails, physicians use a gastrointestinal tube, which must be surgically inserted directly into the stomach. Because the point of the tube's entry is an open wound, the danger of infection is considerable. Indeed, all of these available forms of intubation are uncomfortable and pose some risk of infection, but doctors take that risk to give terminally ill patients the fluids and nutrients they need.

While most rabbis would agree that, at least at some stage, withdrawing or withholding machines and medications from the terminally ill is halakhically justifiable, there is considerably more debate concerning artificial nutrition and hydration. Every person must be afforded normal food and liquids. This is an obligation of the community with regard to the poor,[66] and if a sick person cannot afford normal food and liquids, it becomes part of the duty of the community and its agent, the physician, to provide them as part of the individual's medical care.

When the person cannot or will not ingest food and liquids through the mouth, however, may the community — or must it — feed the patient through tubes? In the *Cruzan* case, the United States Supreme Court ruled that if there were a sufficiently clear expression of Ms. Cruzan's will that she would not want to be kept alive through artificial nutrition and hydration, her will would govern, for in medical care a person's right to liberty takes precedence over a state's right and duty to assure the welfare of its citizens.[67]

Because Judaism begins with a duty to maintain life and health rather than an individual's right to control his or her health care, in the Jewish context this question is formulated quite differently. Specifically, in light of the individual's duty to take care of God's property, may an individual who can no longer orally ingest nutrition and/or hydration refuse to receive it intravenously or enterally (that is, through the intestines), or may a person acting on his or her behalf refuse to provide it?

Most rabbis who have written on this issue have answered negatively, even if the patient is terminally ill. They draw a distinction between medications on the one hand and nutrition and hydration on the other, permitting the withdrawal or withholding of the former but not the latter. They reason that medications are by definition an unusual substance introduced into the person's system to cure an illness, and therefore they may be removed or withheld if they have little chance of functioning in that way. Nutrition and hydration, however, are needed by everyone. Therefore, the burden of proof shifts: one needs to justify the use of medications, but one needs to justify the failure to provide nutrition and hydration.

I accept this reasoning, but I think that the more stringent burden of proof can be met in one of four ways.

1. First, one should note that what we are calling "nutrition and hydration" fulfills the function of normal food and water, but in form and administration it is much closer to medication. We are, after all, talking about inserting tubes into a patient and running liquids through them into the body—just as we introduce medications when the patient cannot swallow. This would argue for viewing intravenously or enterally administered nutrition and hydration as medication rather than as normal food and water.

Furthermore, there are halakhic grounds for such an analogy. The Torah, after all, expressly forbids us several times from eating blood (e.g., Genesis 9:4; Deuteronomy 12:16), but we are nevertheless permitted to accept blood transfusions because from talmudic times on, Jews, in contrast to Jehovah's Witnesses, have not considered the insertion of blood through tubes to be a case of "eating" interdicted by the law.[68] (Even if it were, of course, Jewish law would permit eating blood to save a life, for that takes precedence over the dietary laws, but we do not need to use that justification because our tradition has already restricted "eating" to what we swallow orally.)

Similarly, I would argue, intravenous or enteral administration of nutrition and hydration is not providing food and water in the usual sense, which we must do. If the patient cannot swallow normal food and water, we may, but may also choose not to, administer such nutrition and hydration intravenously. The decision is a medical one, based upon the likelihood of the patient's being cured or at least benefiting from this course of therapy—just as it is with all other medications.

2. A related line of reasoning points out that in intubating a dying person with artificial nutrition and hydration, we are effectively prolonging the person's dying process. As indicated above, we are not required and, according to some sources, are

not even allowed to do that. We are, of course, required to give dying patients normal food and water, but if, for the reasons described above, artificial nutrition and hydration are to be construed as medicine instead, it would become not only permissible but perhaps mandatory to remove them so as to enable the dying to gain the relief of death.

3. Both lines of reasoning just described depend on defining artificial nutrition and hydration as medicine. Even those who demur from doing so could still argue for withholding or withdrawing artificial nutrition and hydration from a terminally ill patient on the grounds of the elevated risks of infection to the patient. Starvation, of course, is a much more certain and severe risk than the aspiration and infections that gastrointestinal and other tubes may cause. Normal food and liquids, though, would still be offered to the patient on the regular schedule (even though, by hypothesis, the patient is not in a state to ingest them), and so we would not be derelict in our duty to provide them.

The question, then, is only whether we must also offer a form of nutrition and hydration that by its very nature exposes the patient to elevated risks of life-threatening illness. When thought of in this way, the issue reduces to the risk-benefit calculus that exists in many critical-care medical decisions, where the crucial question is whether it makes sense to expose the patient to the elevated risk. All such decisions, including this one, are properly and justifiably left to those involved, who alone can know the patient's threshold of pain and exposure to danger, can accurately assess all other relevant aspects of the particular situation, and can then apply the patient's understanding of "reasonable risk" and "benefit" under such circumstances to the situation at hand. Such people would include, first and foremost, the patient (possibly by a previous expression of his or her will in some form) or designated surrogate, but hopefully the physician, family, rabbi, and other relevant parties would also be consulted.

Some forms of injecting nutrition and hydration bear greater risks than others. As a result, this argument will vary in its strength depending on the degree of risk the patient must assume in order to be fed in a particular way.

4. We are, of course, being more than a little disingenuous in offering the patient food and liquids that we know cannot be ingested and then treating artificial nutrition and hydration as a strictly medical decision to be determined by a risk-benefit calculus. It would be logically and morally more elegant if the physician's decision could be straightforwardly based on the criterion of what is in the patient's best interests *(le'tovato)*. The Jewish sources that support using that standard, together with its problems and advantages, are discussed above.

Patients whose medical condition makes it reasonable to ask whether artificial nutrition and hydration should be removed usually can no longer make decisions on their own, and therefore determining the patient's best interests in such cases is especially difficult. We must rely on previous expressions of the patient's will or on the interpretations of his or her will by surrogates or family. Provisions can be made to guard against abuses in making this judgment, but even so, this remains a major worry.

On the other hand, this approach does not require, as the previous ones did, that one be sly in applying categories of the legal theory to the case at hand. Moreover, it empowers us to make decisions even in cases where there is no shortage of medical facilities and where the patient feels no pain—Alzheimer's patients or unconscious patients in the last stage of life, for example. All such cases will clearly involve decisions and dangers of utmost gravity, but medical care of the terminally ill often requires such decisions, and we can at least make some relatively confident moral judgments in many such cases.

If all of the above arguments are unacceptable for some reason, physicians, to fulfill their role of saving life, would be required by Jewish law to prescribe artificial nutrition and hydration when the patient can no longer swallow. As Rabbi Reisner has pointed out, however, ultimately all Jews must decide whether or not they will follow the law.[69] Under the hypothesis that none of the above arguments justifies withholding or removing artificial feeding tubes, obeying Jewish law in this case amounts to following the physician's directions to use them. Patients for whom this procedure is prescribed, however, are often already unconscious, and therefore the surrogate or family member would have to refuse the therapy on the patient's behalf. If the patient had been sufficiently clear while conscious about his or her wish to refuse artificial feeding, such a third party might properly make this decision as the patient's representative. It would be for the delegate, however, as it would be for the patient himself or herself if conscious, a decision that the decisor had the power, but not the legal sanction, to make—again, based on the assumption that none of the above arguments is persuasive enough to alter the substance of the law. I, for one, think that one or more of them—in particular numbers one, two, and four—should be accepted as grounds to permit removal or withholding of artificial nutrition and hydration when it is in the best interests of the patient to do so, thereby making such disobedience unnecessary.

Removal of Nutrition and Hydration from Those in a Persistent Vegetative State

All of the above discussion relates to a person with a terminal, irreversible illness. A much harder case is the person in a persistent, vegetative state (PVS).

A patient who has no brain wave activity, indicating neurological death in both the brain and the brain stem, can on good authority be considered dead within the terms of Jewish law. There is by no means unified opinion accepting the neurological standard for death, but no less than the Chief Rabbinate of Israel has approved heart transplants on this basis, and many others agree, including the Conservative rabbis who have written on this issue.[70]

In many cases, however—especially after accidents or strokes—some brain wave activity persists, but little else. The patient in these instances does not have a terminal illness, and so we cannot justify withholding or withdrawing treatment on the grounds that we need not, or should not, delay the process of dying. A PVS patient may be sustained through the use of heart and lung machines, but many, like Karen Ann Quinlan and Nancy Cruzan, manage to survive even when such machines are removed. Since these patients clearly cannot ingest food and liquids orally, the question quickly turns to whether we must administer artificial nutrition and hydration, and if so, for how long.

Such cases are complicated in Jewish law by virtue of our strong stance against making judgments on the basis of the quality of a given life. Every life is precious in God's eyes, we aptly say, and so we may not decide to remove or withhold treatment from people just because we would prefer not to continue living under such circumstances. This principle serves the crucial role of reminding us that people who are handicapped in some way must be treated with the full respect warranted by the divine image embedded within them, that indeed we must bless God for such variations among creatures, even if (or especially if) we would much prefer not to be like them.[71]

When it comes to the PVS patient, however, this principle is tested in the extreme. Arguments based upon minimizing pain to the patient become less plausible, since the patient has lost all neocortical function and is thus by definition incapable of experiencing pain. Similarly, it would be hard to make the case that feeding a nonterminal person artificially prolongs the dying process; the patient, after all, is not in the process of imminently dying, and so one cannot plausibly talk of hastening his or her death. Triage considerations would apply to heart and lung machines and other advanced technology, but the tubes necessary for nutrition and hydration per se are generally not in short supply.

There are, then, only two arguments that might justify removal of nutrition and hydration from such patients. One is a version of the first argument presented above: if nutrition and hydration are categorized as medicine, and if they are not curing the patient, they may be removed, even though we know the patient cannot ingest the normal food and liquids we bring to the bedside.

While the slyness involved in this approach may make us squirm, we should recognize that in all cases of PVS, it is the underlying disease that causes the death rather than the withholding or removal of treatment—even though the latter action would, of course, be the proximate cause of death. The same is true for people with advanced Alzheimer's disease. In such patients the inability to swallow may be seen as a system failure that the feeding tube seeks to circumvent. Thus, even though neither PVS nor Alzheimer's disease is inherently terminal, the person who has lost the ability to swallow as a result of these diseases is in the process of dying, and when there is no reasonable prospect of recovery, we should not delay that process. Treatment of such a person, then, including artificial nutrition and hydration, should be considered optional and perhaps even contraindicated.

The other possibility is to follow those in the medical community who would define brain death as the irreversible cessation of the functions of the neocortex (the upper brain) rather than of the whole brain. Permanently unconscious people would then be classified as dead, and nutrition and hydration tubes could be removed.[72] Maimonides may provide a basis for this line of reasoning through his concept of ensoulment. Maimonides writes:

> The vital principle of all flesh is the form that God has given it. The superior intelligence in the human soul is the specific form of the mentally normal human being. To this form the Torah refers in the text, "Let us make a human being in Our image, after Our likeness" (Genesis 1:26). This means that the human being should have a form that knows. . . . Nor does (this) refer to the vital principle in every animal by which it eats, drinks, reproduces, feels, and broods. It is the intellect that is the human soul's specific form. And to this specific form of the soul, the Scriptural phrase "in Our image, after Our likeness" alludes.[73]

In his article on end-of-life issues, Rabbi Avram Reisner argues against this line of reasoning, asserting that defining death in terms of the absence of intelligence would impugn the sanctity of the vessel that carried God's image. Moreover, he points out the risk inherent in this theology of medicine, as it were, for if followed, one could easily argue that one should discontinue treatment of the mentally ill, who also, after all, do not exhibit the rational soul described by Maimonides. I agree with Rabbi Reisner's objections to this approach.

I do think, however, that the first analysis of this situation — namely, that tubes are medication and therefore may be removed as an inappropriate medical intervention when patients lose the ability to swallow — should make it unnecessary to use nutrition and hydration tubes to treat PVS and advanced Alzheimer's patients for long periods of time. One would presumably intubate such patients for some time to test whether there is any reasonable chance of recovery, but once it becomes clear that there is not, one should extubate the patient so as not to prolong the process of dying.

I also think that the slippery slope can be contained; indeed, as I have stated previously, the essence of developing moral sensitivity is to recognize that moral principles cannot be applied indiscriminately, that acute moral judgment must be used in deciding when and how to apply and balance our moral concerns. In this case, it is, minimally, highly unaesthetic to remove feeding tubes from such patients. After all, since their brain stems are intact, they are, by hypothesis, still breathing on their own. This should help us guard against rash judgments about such patients.

In line with current practice, then, PVS patients should be maintained on nutrition and hydration for at least some time — especially if they need no scarce resources — to guard against the possibility that they were misdiagnosed as being PVS patients and are instead in a reversible coma. This also will give family members time to get used to the reality of their loved one's impending death before removing the tubes. Similarly, advanced Alzheimer's patients who have lost the ability to swallow should be given nutrients and liquids artificially during the time that there is any reasonable hope that they will regain that function. Triage considerations do apply to the other machinery necessary to sustain such patients, and the withdrawal of such machines may permit their disease to cause their death even before artificial nutrition and hydration are removed. Like many physicians, though, I would give up on such patients only reluctantly and only after trying to restore them to health for some time.

The Use of Animal or Artificial Organs and Other Hazardous, Experimental Therapies

Even though physicians, patients, and families who are making critical-care decisions are not duty-bound by Jewish law to invoke heroic measures and untested drugs, such therapies may be employed if they offer some hope of cure. Typically, such experimental drugs or procedures involve an elevated level of risk, but the patient may elect to take that risk as long as the goal is not to hasten death but rather to sustain life.

One such therapy is the use of artificial or animal organs in transplantation. Because donated human organs are in short supply, physicians have recently tried to use these alternatives. If the procedure is perfected, the use of such organs would afford a reliable, relatively inexpensive supply for transplants, and it would also obviate the need to make precise determinations of the moment of a person's death to enable transplantation of a vital organ. From a Jewish perspective, these are certainly great advantages.

Although some have raised questions about the use of animal parts for direct transplant or for making artificial organs, it is not a problem in Jewish law or ethics. Judaism, after all, does not demand vegetarianism, and if we may eat the flesh of animals under Judaism's dietary rules *(kashrut)* when life is not at stake, then we may certainly use animal parts for saving a life. Indeed, Jewish sources go further: if the use of animal parts can save a human life, we have a moral and religious obligation to use them. The animal parts we use do not even have to come from a kosher animal, for saving a human life takes precedence over the dietary laws. Consequently, those Jews who choose to be vegetarians (and there is support for this within the tradition[74]) would nevertheless be obliged to use animal parts for medical purposes if that was the method that held the greatest promise for curing a person or saving a life. So, for example, if a porcine valve is more likely to work effectively in a person undergoing heart surgery than a mechanical one would, Jews should instruct their physician to use the nonkosher animal's valve.

At present the use of animal or artificial organs is in an early, experimental stage. Patients who have undergone such operations have not been cured, and in the process they have given up what could have been several days or weeks of life. Jews may not employ such therapies with the intent of hastening death, but they may use them in an attempt to preserve life when no known cure is available. The same would hold true for hazardous therapies of other sorts.[75]

Hospice Care

The fact that Jewish law does not require the use of heroic measures means that a Jew may enroll in a hospice program in good conscience. There are some buildings actually called hospices, but "hospice care" typically does not take place in a special facility, at least until the very last hours or days of life (and not necessarily even then); instead the patient lives at home as long as possible, doing whatever he or she can do. The word hospice thus designates not so much a building but rather a form of care.

In hospice care, the goal is not to cure the disease, for the patient has been diagnosed as incurable, a diagnosis usually confirmed by tests and by a second opinion. It is rather to make the patient as comfortable as possible. The patient still seeks medical help, as Jewish law demands, but the object of the medication has now shifted from cure to comfort.

This goal is accomplished, in part, through pain medication, administered as needed. Because hospice care involves the active participation of family and friends, patients in these circumstances are likely to get the pain medication they need. As indicated earlier, even in the last stages of life, when the dosage of morphine needed to control pain may actually hasten the patient's death, it is permissible to use that dosage as long as the intent is not to kill the person but rather to alleviate his or her pain.[76]

Crucially, though, hospice care also addresses all the nonmedical ways in which people require support during crises. Most important are the forms of care provided by family and friends who keep the patient company and make the patient feel still part of their world and not simply a locus of illness and pain. Nurses, social workers, and rabbis may also be involved in the patient's care at various points.

Since most hospice care takes place at home, it is often the most comfortable, meaningful, and humane way for people to live their last days or months. Hospital care, after all, puts the patient in a strange, antiseptic setting where she or he is subjected to the hospital schedule, to repeated and possibly painful medical procedures, and to the loneliness of having the company of only occasional visitors. Hospice care, by contrast, puts the patient at home amidst family and friends, where pain medication can be administered when and how the patient feels most comfortable and where the company of family and good friends is constantly available.

Hospice care should therefore be suggested to most people afflicted with terminal, irreversible illnesses. Moreover, contrary to current practice, patients should not first have to endure initial stays in intensive care units where improbably successful or knowingly futile aggressive care is attempted; rather, they should be provided with hospice care as soon as it becomes clear that the odds of curing the patient are slim to nil.

Along these lines, Jews may sign an advance directive for health care indicating their desire to choose hospice care over aggressive attempts to save them when such efforts are clearly futile. Patients and the physicians can never be plausibly required to do what is humanly impossible. Thus the advance directives published by all four movements in American Judaism permit hospice care.

For American medical personnel, hospice care is often perceived as a new and strange phenomenon. Trained to fight disease as one would fight a war—and using much of the same, military terminology—American doctors find hospice care a counterintuitive approach at best and a weak acquiescence to disease at worst. They also dislike their loss of control; for now other people provide much of the patient's care, making many of the decisions along the way; and much of that care takes place off hospital grounds.

Hospice care, though, is actually the oldest form of care in existence. After all, through most of human history hospitals did not exist, and people died at home. Hospitals provide access to experts and technology unavailable in other settings, and so when there is a reasonable chance of cure, hospitals serve a very important purpose. When cure is unrealistic, though, hospitals become unfriendly, expensive places all too prone to subject patients to futile tests and procedures. In such circumstances, we are now learning, the familiar, home environment where our ancestors met their Maker amidst family and friends may well be the place where we should too.

CHAPTER NINE

After Death: Cremation, Autopsy, and Organ Donation

PPROPRIATE TREATMENT OF THE BODY AFTER DEATH IS defined in Jewish law by three primary principles. One is *kavod ha-met,* "honor of the dead": we should honor the deceased's memory and, as part of that, take appropriate care of his or her body. Treating the body with respect is demanded also by the theological tenet that the body, even in death, remains God's property. Honor of the corpse, then, underlies Jewish burial customs such as closing the eyes of the deceased, preserving modesty even in death by having women prepare a female body for burial and men a male body, washing the body before burial and clothing it in burial shrouds, burying the body as soon after death as possible in a closed coffin so that onlookers will not notice its disintegration, and convening family and friends to say memorial prayers and eulogize the deceased.

The second Jewish principle relevant to how Jews should treat the body after death is *ḥesed.* Judaism includes a highly developed set of laws requiring Jews to help those in need. When the help offered is financial—either donating money or helping people find ways to support themselves—the term used is *tzedakah* (literally, "justice"). When one aids people in other ways, the term describing the value and attitude grounding such assistance is *ḥesed*. *Ḥesed*, meaning originally an act done out of loyalty to one's fellow, came to mean also acts of kindness, care, and concern. Thus while acts of *tzedakah* are legally mandatory, acts of *ḥesed* are not, but they have a degree of obligation to them beyond that connoted by the English word "charity," as the following makes clear:

> "To walk in all His ways" (Deuteronomy 11:22). These are the ways of the Holy One: "gracious and compassionate, patient, abounding in kindness and faithfulness, assuring love for a thousand generations, forgiving iniquity, transgression, and sin, and granting pardon . . ." (Exodus 34:6). This means that just as God is gracious and compassionate, you too must be gracious and compassionate. "The Lord is righteous in all His ways and loving in all His deeds" (Psalm 145:17). As the Holy One is righteous, you too must be righteous. As the Holy One is loving, you too must be loving.
>
> "Follow the Lord your God" (Deuteronomy 13:5). What does this mean? Is it possible for a mortal to follow God's Presence? The verse means to teach us that we should follow the attributes of the Holy One, praised be He. As He clothes the naked, . . . you should clothe the naked. The Bible teaches that the Holy One visited the sick . . . ; you too should visit the sick. The Holy One comforted those who mourned . . . ; you too should comfort those who mourn. The Holy One buried the dead . . . ; you too should bury the dead.[1]

The concepts underlying the obligation to help those in need in acts of *ḥesed* are among the most central and powerful in the Jewish tradition. They include the meaning, privileges, and responsibilities of membership in a community; compassion for fellow human beings; obedience of God's commandment to care for others and to act to help them; the need to preserve the dignity of God's creatures; the obligation to live up to the Covenant with God, including the promises and expectations inherent in that relationship; and the mandate to aspire to holiness and imitation of God.[2] No wonder, then, that this concept and its derivative obligations occupy a central place in the minds of Jews at all connected to the tradition, and no wonder that they are one important factor—as the psychological background, even if not as the legal basis—in the attitudes of Jews and Judaism toward burial of the dead and organ transplantation.

The third principle that plays a major role in the topics of this chapter is *pikuah nefesh*, the obligation to save people's lives. As we have seen, this tenet is so deeply embedded in Jewish law that, according to the rabbis, it takes precedence over all other commandments except murder, idolatry, and incestuous or adulterous sexual intercourse. Jews are commanded not only to do virtually anything necessary to save their own lives; they are also bound by the positive obligation to take steps to save the lives of others.[3] This principle has informed much of our discussion to this point with regard to other stages of life, and as we shall see, it threads through Judaism's responses to death and thereafter as well.

Cremation

Jewish law prohibits cremation as the ultimate form of dishonor to the dead. Cremation also represents the active destruction of God's property, and it is improper for that reason as well. Moreover, in the generations after Hitler's gas chambers, it is hard to understand how we would do to our own beloved what Hitler did to our people. Even though the intent of those who cremate their dead is clearly different from Hitler's, the backdrop of the gas chambers cannot but affect the meaning conveyed by disposing of the dead in that way. The symbolism is all wrong, communicating disdain for the dead instead of the love and respect we want to express as we depart from them.

Cremation is, of course, less expensive than burial, and that, more than anything else, motivates some to cremate their dead. The factors delineated in the paragraph above, however, make cremation an inappropriate response to the need to make burial affordable. The proper approach is to educate Jews to avoid expensive caskets and to use, instead, the plain wooden box mandated by Jewish law in any case to express modesty and equality in death. Moreover, each synagogue should set up its own "holy society" *(hevrah kaddishah)* to deal with the dead, primarily for the merit of doing what community members ought to do for each other but also to help to reduce the cost of a traditional funeral. Finally, in those cases of hardship where burial is truly unaffordable, the Jewish community must make sure that the family concerned can bury their dead for little or no cost; a number of Jewish funeral directors already perform this service for such families. Money, then, is honestly and legitimately a concern for families who must deal with the remains of their dead, but the Jewish community must not allow it to be the determinative factor in preferring cremation over burial.

Autopsies

Autopsies were known in the ancient world, but Jewish sources largely looked askance at them as a violation of human dignity. In the nineteenth and especially the twentieth centuries, however, as the prospects of gaining medical knowledge from autopsies improved considerably, many rabbis have become more sanguine about them. One even suggested a popular campaign to persuade people to grant their written consent to an autopsy as a service to medicine.[4]

A definitive position was enunciated by Israeli Chief Rabbi Isaac Herzog in his 1949 agreement with Hadassah Hospital in Jerusalem. Under that agreement, autopsies would be sanctioned only when one of the following conditions obtained:

1. The autopsy is legally required.
2. In the opinion of three physicians, the cause of death cannot otherwise be ascertained.
3. Three physicians attest that the autopsy might help save the lives of others suffering from an illness similar to the one that caused the death of the patient.
4. Where a hereditary illness was involved, performing the autopsy might safeguard surviving relatives.

In each case, those who perform the autopsy must do so with due reverence for the dead, and upon completion of the autopsy, they must deliver the corpse and all of its parts to the burial society for interment. This agreement was incorporated into Israeli law four years later.

When an autopsy is justified, whether for legal or medical reasons, it is construed not as a dishonor to the dead but, on the contrary, as an honorable use of the body to help the living. Indeed, it is assumed that the dead person himself or herself would, if asked, want the autopsy to take place if it could accomplish the legal or medical end for which it is intended. That is, the issue is not so much a preference of the principle of saving a life *(pikuah nefesh)* over that of the honor due to the dead *(kavod ha-met)*, but rather a different form of preserving the honor of the deceased in contexts where saving other people's lives is possible.

In recent years there has been considerable controversy over autopsies in Israel because they have become routine, and so the government changed the law in 1980 to make autopsies more difficult to justify, to the consternation of Israeli medical researchers.[5] New procedures, such as a needle biopsy of a palpable mass, or a peritoneoscopy with biopsy, may soon accomplish most of the same medical objectives as autopsies do without invading the corpse to the same degree, and that would clearly be preferable from a Jewish point of view;[6] but in the meantime, autopsies continue to be permissible if there is a specific legal or medical reason to warrant one in a particular case.

Organ Donation

The other procedure that may interrupt the usual process of burial is organ transplantation. Here too the overriding principles of *kavod ha-met, hesed,* and *pikuah nefesh* work in tandem: saving a person's life and acting faithfully and kindly to others are values so sacred in Judaism that if a person's organ can be used to preserve someone else's life, it is actually an honor to the deceased person to use the organ in that way. Enabling a person to live through donation of an organ is also a supreme act of *hesed*— and the fact that the organ is a gift freely given is an important part of how both the donor and the recipient perceive it.[7]

That is certainly the case if the person completed an advance directive, either orally or in writing, indicating willingness to have portions of his or her body transplanted; but even if not, the default assumption is that a person would be honored to help another live.

Living donors

Because preserving your own life takes precedence over helping someone else live, you should provide whatever medical care you can for others, short of endangering your own life. In line with this principle, since every organ donation from a living person involves surgery and therefore at least some risk, contemporary rabbis have not understood donating an organ, even to a relative in need, to be legally required. At the same time, rabbis have generally permitted such donations when they can be accomplished without a major risk to the donor's life or health. So, for example, Rabbi Immanuel Jakobovits, former chief rabbi of the British Commonwealth and author of the first comprehensive book on Jewish medical ethics, says, "Since the mortality risk to kidney donors is estimated to be only 0.24 percent and no greater than is involved in any amputation, the generally prevailing view is to permit such donations as acts of supreme charity but not as an obligation." Conservative and Reform rabbis have taken the same stance.[8]

Cadaveric Donors: The Permissibility of Using the Body for Donation

While it is generally prohibited to delay burial or to gain benefit from a dead body, these prohibitions are superseded when, as in the case of autopsies or organ donation, the goal is to save another person's life or health.[9] Moreover, just as it is not considered a desecration of the dead to extract organs for saving another person, so, too, delaying burial for that purpose does not diminish respect for the dead but, on the contrary, enhances it.

Despite this predominant opinion, some rabbis have limited organ transplantation to varying degrees. The most restrictive opinion would permit donations only when there is a specific patient before us *(lefaneinu)* who stands to lose his or her life or an entire physical faculty. According to this opinion, for example, if the person can see out of one eye, a cornea may not be removed from a dead person to restore vision in the other eye. Only if both eyes are failing, such that the potential recipient would lose all vision and therefore incur serious danger to life and limb, may a transplant be performed. Moreover, according to this view, the patient for whom the organ is intended must be known and present; donation to organ banks is not permitted.[10]

That is definitely an extreme position. Most rabbis, including Orthodox ones, would expand both the eligibility of potential recipients and the reasons justifying an organ transplant. For reasons delineated below, all authorities would insist that the family agree to the use of their loved one's body for this purpose. Assuming such agreement, most rabbis would, in our example, permit the transplantation of a cornea into a person with vision in only one eye on the grounds that impaired vision poses enough of a risk to the potential recipient to justify the surgical intrusion of the corpse to provide the cornea.

Some rabbis would require that a specific person for whom the organ is appropriate be identified before a transplantation may take place, even if that person is not nearby and ready for transplantation. In these days of organ banks, however, most rabbis would be satisfied that there is sufficient demand for the organ that it is known that it will eventually, but definitely, be used for purposes of transplantation. Thus the Rabbinical Assembly, the organization of Conservative rabbis, approved a resolution in 1990 to "encourage all Jews to become enrolled as organ and tissue donors by signing and carrying cards or driver's licenses attesting to their commitment of such organs and tissues upon their deaths to those in need."[11]

Subsequently, the Conservative movement went even further when its Committee on Jewish Law and Standards adopted the rabbinic ruling of Rabbi Joseph Prouser in 1995. Rabbi Prouser pointed out that in light of the organ shortage, failure to arrange to donate organs after death fails to come to the rescue of those who need a transplant, thus violating the commandment, "Do not stand idly by the blood of your neighbor." Moreover, refusing to be an organ donor endangers the lives of those people who might be called upon to be living donors for family or friends, for while donation of a kidney from an otherwise healthy person (the usual example) is reasonably safe, such donations always incur at least the risks involved in any surgery. As a result, providing for the donation of one's organs upon one's demise is, according to the official policy of the Conservative movement as articulated in Rabbi Prouser's ruling, not simply a voluntary act of beneficence but a commanded obligation.[12]

Cadaveric Donors: Defining the Moment of Death

Transplanting vital organs, however, introduces another consideration, namely, the moment of death. We must, after all, guard against the possibility that the physician will murder the donor while trying to save the life of the recipient through the transplant of the vital organ. The recipient's life does not take precedence over the donor's. Consequently, defining the criteria to identify when the potential donor has died becomes crucial in matters of organ donation.

Classical Jewish sources use two criteria for death. One is the breath test: a feather is placed beneath the patient's nostrils, and movement of the feather indicates life, whereas lack of movement signifies death. The exegetical bases for this test are the verses in Genesis according to which "God breathes life into Adam" (2:6) and the Flood kills "all in whose nostrils is the breath of the spirit of life" (7:22),[13] but there is clearly also a cogent, practical reason for using the breath test, namely, that it is easy to administer. A minority view in the Talmud maintains that cessation of heartbeat is also required to determine death.[14]

Later codifiers, though, insisted on both respiratory and cardiac manifestations of death. Some even held that the breath test is sanctioned by the Talmud only because it is normally a good indication of the existence of heartbeat, but that it is actually the cessation of heartbeat that forms the core of the Jewish definition of death.[15] Moreover, in the sixteenth century Rabbi

Moses Isserles ruled that "nowadays" we do not know how to distinguish death with accuracy from a fainting spell, and consequently even after the cessation of breath and heartbeat we should wait a period of time before assuming that the person is dead. Some rabbis today claim that we should still wait twenty or thirty minutes after observing these signs, but others claim that the availability of the sphygmomanometer and electrocardiogram permit us to revert to the traditional mode of defining death as cessation of breath and heartbeat.[16]

Waiting even a short amount of time, however, would generally be too long if doctors are to be able to use the dying person's heart. Consequently Conservative rabbis Daniel C. Goldfarb and Seymour Siegel suggested in 1976 that a flat electroencephalogram, indicating cessation of spontaneous brain activity, be sufficient to determine death, on the grounds that this test conforms to the medical practice of our time just as our ancestors determined Jewish law in light of the medical practice of their time.[17] In 1988 the Chief Rabbinate of Israel approved heart transplantation, effectively accepting that a flat electroencephalogram guarantees that the patient can no longer independently breathe or produce a heartbeat, and that has become the accepted opinion of virtually all modern Jewish authorities, with the exception of a few Orthodox rabbis.[18]

The same concern applies to transplanting any other organ from a dying person, namely, the need to ensure that the doctor is not causing the death of the donor by removing the organ. The same definition of death, though, also applies: if a flat electroencephalogram is confirmed, the donor is officially dead within the terms of Jewish law as now interpreted, and the transplantation is permissible.

Cadaveric Donors: The Issue of Ḥillul ha-Shem

As discussed in Chapter 2, Jews are commanded to sanctify God's name *(kiddush ha-Shem)*. During ancient and medieval times, Jews often died a martyr's death "to sanctify God's name"—that is, to preserve Judaism—but the concept has a much broader application than that. It requires that Jews behave in such a way that non-Jews (and other Jews, for that matter) will see their actions as a blessing. Conversely, desecrating God's reputation *(ḥillul ha-Shem)* by acting in such a way that Jews and Judaism are defamed is to be avoided.

Since there is definitely a shortage of organs for transplantation, the willingness of Jews to donate their organs in proportion to their numbers in the population is a clear litmus test in the eyes of non-Jews as to the character of Jews and Judaism. Unfortunately, not nearly as many Jews have donated organs as have benefited from them, and this imbalance has already caused considerable *ḥillul ha-Shem.* In the United States, when asked to be donors, about 60 percent of the general population and their families consent, but only about 5 percent of Orthodox Jews do so, and the record of Conservative and Reform Jews is not much better. Israelis have also had major problems in this area. In 1994, fifty Israeli patients needed heart transplants, but only twelve hearts became available; seven hundred people were on the list for kidneys, but only twelve received transplants from people who died in Israel. This reluctance to donate has meant that Israelis, who are part of Europe's organ transplant network, Eurotransplant, have already been barred from having transplants done in most European hospitals because Israel has not done its share in providing organs while drawing on the supply.[19] Our obligation to avoid a *ḥillul ha-Shem,* then, constitutes yet another reason for Jews to donate their organs for transplantation.

Cadaveric Donors: Factors Impeding Jews' Willingness to Donate

Few Jews donate their organs for transplantation after death. This refusal is clearly *not* in consonance with official Jewish belief and practice, for as we have seen, principles strongly embedded in Jewish law and theology should motivate Jews expressly to arrange to be organ donors after death. Unfortunately, Jews are impeded from donating their own organs or those of a deceased family member because of both deeply rooted misconceptions about the whole process and psychological, legal, and theological concerns.

COMMON MISCONCEPTIONS ABOUT THE PROCESS AND COST OF ORGAN DONATION. Two common misconceptions impede donation. One is the fear that the donor's body will be mutilated as a result of the organ extraction. Unlike dissection, where the body is indeed dismembered, after organs are extracted the body is then sewn up for burial. This can be, and usually is, done quickly, even when multiple organs are donated, and burial therefore need not be substantially delayed. Since Jews in any case traditionally bury their dead in closed caskets so as to preserve the dignity of the body despite its disintegration after death, any surgical markings on the body as a result of the transplant are invisible to everyone at the funeral. The family, in the meantime, can rest assured that the transplantation did not disfigure the body or degrade it.

The other common misconception is that the donor or his or her family will have to pay for the procedure. That is never the case. It is the recipient's family or, more commonly in this country, his or her insurance company that pays for the transplantation. The rules governing transplantation in the United States prohibit payment to the donor or his or her estate for any organ, and that keeps the donation on the high moral level of a gift of life.[20] While the donor thus does not gain monetarily from the donation, she or he does not lose anything either; no costs whatsoever are charged to the donor. This is true for living as well as cadaveric donors.

PSYCHOLOGICAL FACTORS. The misconceptions just described can be easily corrected by supplying the patient or family with the necessary information—preferably long before they experience the grief and, depending upon the mode of death, possibly the shock of losing a loved one. The psychological factors that impede donation, however, are not as easily remedied.

Like everyone else, Jews find it difficult to contemplate their death, let alone the prospect of donating one or more organs after it. As a result, some Jews fail to enroll as donors simply because their aversion to thinking about death has prevented them from expressly planning to do so. That failure unfortunately deprives someone of a much-needed organ—and possibly of life itself.

Others who do consider donating organs have found it hard to think of having their bodies invaded for any purpose, even one as noble as transplantation. People have difficulty imagining the state of death, and so they think about enduring the surgery necessary to remove the organ and the subsequent state of their body as if they were still alive and conscious throughout the whole procedure and thereafter. They should remind themselves, though, that those who have died are not aware of any part of the process of donation.

Finally, people often worry that if they agree to donate their organs after death, physicians and other health care personnel who care for them will not fight as hard to keep them alive. Precisely to avoid such a danger, the protocols for organ donation require that the teams of physicians who deal with the recipient patient's transplantation be totally separate from those who care for the donor patient.

SLIDING INTO DEATH. Legally, part of the resistance of Jews to organ donation may come from the Jewish tradition's view that death does not come at a clear, definable moment but rather happens in stages over time. As we have seen, that process begins when a person is diagnosed with a terminal, irreversible illness, thus becoming a *terefah*. The individual then advances to the stage of being moribund *(goses)*, when he or she can no longer swallow saliva and when life is like "a flickering candle." Next comes the moment of death, defined traditionally as the cessation of breath and heartbeat and, more recently, as the termination of all brain wave activity.

Even then, though, the story is not over. Early rabbinic sources speak of death as "the going out of the soul," but rabbinic lore maintains that the association between body and soul is not altogether severed until three days after death. During that time, according to the classical rabbis, the soul hovers over the grave, hoping to be restored to the body. It departs only when the body begins to decompose and the face changes in character. This, it was believed, was why mourners' grief often reaches its emotional climax on the third day after a loved one's death.[21] Traditionally, it is believed that the soul begins its journey in the person's life after death only after this three-day period.

This belief did not alter Judaism's insistence on immediate burial of the body, but it did serve to disallow evidence concerning the identity of a person when the body was viewed more than three days after death.[22] It also motivated the permission, notwithstanding the ban on heathen practices, to watch graves for three days in case the interred body was still alive, "for once it happened that they watched one who thereupon continued to live for twenty-five years and another who still had five children before dying."[23]

The story does not even end there. At least according to some rabbinic sources, for the first twelve months after death the soul retains a temporary relationship to the body, coming and going until the body has disintegrated. This explains, for the rabbis, why the prophet Samuel could be raised from the dead within the first year of his demise in the story of the witch of En-dor. During this year, people's souls—or, according to another view, only the souls of the wicked—are in a kind of purgatory, after which the righteous go to paradise *(Gan Eden)* and the wicked to hell *(Gehinnom)*. The actual condition of the soul during that time is unclear. Some sources see it as being quiescent, but most seem to ascribe it full consciousness, with one even saying, "The only difference between the living and the dead is the power of speech." There is also a series of disputes about how much the dead know of the world they leave behind.[24]

During the Middle Ages, these beliefs in continuing life after physical death were amplified considerably, especially in folklore and superstition. According to such sources, people's ghosts live a very full life. They gather nightly by the light of the moon, converse with one another or pursue their studies (the Jewish emphasis on education persists even in ghost stories!), adjudge disputes between the latest arrivals and older members of the spirit community, and pray. According to *Sefer Ḥasidim*, a thirteenth-century book of ethics written in the German pietist Jewish community *(ḥasidei Ashkenaz)*, the ghosts can also be met during the day as they carry out their punishments on earth or tell their survivors of their good fortune in the world to come.[25]

The spirits' concern with the state of their bodies on earth, though, is not only a residual expression of interest in their earthly existence; according to many legends, the spirits of people who have died retain their bodily forms. Consequently, spirits also torment the living when the clothes in which they were buried are inadequate for their spiritual existence.

The living have an effect on the dead, just as the dead have an effect on the living. Thus, during the Middle Ages some rabbis loudly decried the practice of eating a meal—and especially drinking water—between the Sabbath afternoon prayers and the close of the Sabbath after sunset (both very common practices today). This prohibition was due to the belief that there was a large courtyard for the dead, in front of which was a brook that flowed out of the Garden of Eden, and beyond which was a field. Every Sabbath afternoon, between the afternoon prayers and the evening prayers at the close of the Sabbath, God would let the spirits of the dead out of their storage place and give them food from that field and water from that brook. Any Jew who drank water at that time, it was believed, was effectively stealing the water of the dead. Note that this story assumes that ghosts still have bodily needs for food and liquids.

The Jewish tradition, then, depicts dying as a process that extends over several phases; it has a basic diffidence in our ability to define the moment of death exactly; and it has official and popular beliefs in spirits who live on after death in bodily form. Given these beliefs, one can understand how it is that at least some Jews are wary of agreeing to donate their organs. The medical community, and indeed Jewish law, may define you as dead, but there are elements within the tradition that might prompt you to be less than certain about these scientific and legal pronouncements.

RESURRECTION. The remaining objection centers on the issue of resurrection: A surprising number of Jews think that they need to be buried complete so that they can be resurrected whole, and that giving up an organ for transplantation would thus leave them without it when they are resurrected. In speaking about organ transplantation with Jewish audiences across the country, I have found that this matter is almost always raised in the question-and-answer period if I have not addressed it earlier, and if I have already spoken about it, people nevertheless ask about it again. One might expect this objection from the Orthodox, but my own experience in hearing this concern in many Conservative congregations is borne out also by Judith Abrams, a Reform rabbi in Missouri, Texas, who has spoken about this subject to Reform audiences.[26] This belief, then, is deeply ingrained in the folk religion; indeed, it is often expressed by Jews who are otherwise totally secular in their thought and actions. Modern rationalism goes only so far! Similarly, in Israel, when the Labor Party in 1977 failed to form a coalition with the religious parties in part because of Orthodox objections to autopsies, a reporter for the *Jerusalem Post*, interviewing an Orthodox rabbi in Tel Aviv, began his questions with this one: "Is it true that the Orthodox are against post mortems because at the 'resurrection of the dead,' *(teḥiyat ha-metim)* those who lack parts (or organs) from their bodies cannot rise from the grave?" The rabbi denied this in the strongest possible terms: "There is no truth in all this. It is some sort of mysticism to which we do not subscribe. When the dead arise, nobody will be excluded, even if parts or all of his body are missing." He then explained that Orthodox objections to autopsies were based instead on fears of unnecessary desecration of the body.[27]

A historical note on the Jewish belief in resurrection may be helpful in understanding both the popular belief that impedes donation and the rabbinic disgust with this belief. In most biblical literature, people after death go down to the dark realm of the dead, where they presumably no longer have an independent existence as persons. "The dead cannot praise You, nor any who go down into silence," the Psalmist reminds God. Job and Ecclesiastes know of the doctrine of the resurrection of the dead but deny it; it is only the Book of Daniel, chronologically the last book of the Hebrew Bible (c. 165 B.C.E.), that affirms this tenet.[28]

In the last two centuries before the common era and the first five centuries of the common era, ideas about what happens after death were hotly debated. Members of some Jewish groups, especially the Sadducees, continued to deny any particular existence of individuals after death. Some Jewish groups supported the idea of the immortality of the soul, whereas others affirmed resurrection of the dead in bodily form.

The Pharisees—that is, the rabbis who shaped the Jewish tradition—affirm both the resurrection of the body and the immortality of the soul. On this theological tenet as on all others, the rabbis never drew their thoughts together in a clear, consistent doctrine; instead, as was their wont, they made a number of individual comments, some of which frankly do not sit well with others. They apparently believed, however, that after death the soul continues on with God until messianic times, when it is rejoined with the dust of the earth in resurrection. However resurrection occurs, the Pharisees believed in it so strongly that they claimed that a Jew must not only believe the doctrine but aver that it is rooted in the Torah—where, as we have said, the idea of resurrection never occurs.[29]

Medieval Jewish philosophers continued to believe strongly in the doctrine of resurrection. Of course they did not address organ donation per se, but in the course of discussing resurrection they provided some important arguments to counteract the popular claim that one must be buried with all one's parts in order to have them at the time of resurrection. Saadiah Gaon (892–942 C.E.), for example, pointed out that if one believes that God created the world from nothing, one should certainly believe that God can refashion and revive the dead, for that only involves the comparatively easy task of creating something out of something that has existed already but has disintegrated:

> We know of no Jew who opposes this doctrine, or finds it difficult from the point of view of his Reason that God should revive the dead, since it has already become clear to him that God created the

world *ex nihilo*. He can find no difficulty therefore in believing that God should, by a second act, create something from something disintegrated and dissolved.[30]

Note that this view would also answer the question of what happens to those who die in an accident in which their body is badly maimed. For that matter, all of us die of some bodily malfunction, and so God would certainly have to replace some of our parts, for in the end they did not serve us very well!

Maimonides (1135–1204 C.E.) takes a different tack. Like many of the neo-Platonists and neo-Aristotelians of his time, he denigrates the body. As a result, he actually mocks his coreligionists who look forward to a bodily resurrection:

> Concerning this strange world to come, you will rarely find anyone to whom it occurs to think about it seriously or to adopt it as a fundamental doctrine of our faith, or to inquire what it really means, whether the world to come is the ultimate good or whether some other possibility. Nor does one often find persons who distinguish between the ultimate good itself and the means which lead to the ultimate good. What everybody wants to know, both the masses and the learned, is how the dead will arise. They want to know whether they will be naked or clothed, whether they will rise in the same shrouds with which they were buried, with the same embroidery, style, and beauty of sewing, or in a plain garment which just covers their bodies. Or they ask whether, when the Messiah comes, there will still be rich men and poor men, weak men and strong men, and other similar questions.[31]

According to Maimonides, such literal understandings of bodily resurrection are childish, taught by the Sages to encourage the masses to obey God's commandments in hopes of a future physical reward or in fear of future physical punishment. The truth is rather that after death the soul continues on without the body, and its pleasures are the vastly more enduring and important pleasures of the spirit. In support of this view, he quotes a talmudic passage: "In the world to come there is no eating, drinking, washing, anointing, or sexual intercourse; but the righteous sit with their crowns on their heads enjoying the radiance of the Divine Presence."[32]

Such philosophic views, however, have not penetrated to the beliefs of most of those Jews who believe in resurrection. For them, bodily resurrection continues to be a living element of their faith, and Saadiah's argument, which most do not know in any case, has not relieved their anxiety over what will happen to them at the time of resurrection if they give up some parts of their bodies for organ donation.

Perhaps the clearest indication of this ongoing concern for keeping the body intact after death has been Jews' response to autopsies. According to a survey carried out in New York City, Jews, even if they are not religiously observant, are much less likely than others to give consent for an autopsy to be performed on a deceased family member.[33] In Israel demonstrations, street riots, and cabinet crises have periodically occurred over this issue.[34] Although the religious protesters are motivated by concern for Jewish law, both they and the secularists are undoubtedly moved as well by subconscious feelings of the need to preserve bodily integrity after death and by worries about the possibility of a future resurrection of their body without all its parts.

This factor may also be relevant when interpreting how Jews respond to polls on this issue. A *Los Angeles Times* poll taken in December 1991, for example, found that 67 percent of Christians and 45 percent of those with no religious identity believed in life after death, but that only 30 percent of Jews said that they did.[35] The fact that so many Jews object to autopsies and to organ donation on the grounds of their incompatibility with a belief in resurrection means, however, that far higher percentages of Jews believe in a bodily life after death than are willing to admit that they do. This discrepancy is borne out even more by the extent of Jewish belief in reincarnation: 23 percent of the Jews surveyed believed in the birth of the soul in a new body after death, compared with 20 percent of Christians and 33 percent of the nonreligious. This finding is especially remarkable because it is only the mystical forms of Judaism that profess belief in reincarnation.[36] The fact that as many as 23 percent of Jews asserted such a belief thus clearly indicates that afterlife beliefs lie just beneath the skin of many avowed secularists.

Rationally, of course, those who believe in reincarnation certainly should not object to organ donation. After all, they are going to inhabit a new body anyway! Similarly, those who believe in resurrection should also not object to organ donation. If resurrection is the blessing that most who believe in it hold it to be, God should surely be trusted to resurrect us in a better body than the one in which we died.

However one conceives of life after death, the important thing to note is that for all branches of Judaism, *saving life in the here and now clearly and indubitably takes precedence over whatever one believes about future resurrection.* If there is to be bodily resurrection, God must surely, as Saadiah says, create the individual anew, and the Eternal can be trusted to have ample ability to restore all organs and bodily tissues, which, given that the person died in his or her old body, God will need to do at that time anyway. In the meantime, we live under the divine imperative to save the lives we can, and organ donation is one important way to do that.

Cadaveric Donors: Donating One's Body to Science

May one donate one's entire body to science for purposes of dissection by a medical student as part of his or her medical education? Objections to this center on the desecration of the body involved in tearing it apart and the delay in its burial until after the dissection. Rabbi Bleich and others take a very hard line on this, claiming that any invasion of the corpse for purposes of autopsy or transplant is warranted only if there is a *ḥoleh lefaneinu,* a patient who will benefit immediately thereby.[37] In contrast, Israeli Chief Rabbi Herzog issued the following statement in 1949:

> The Plenary Council of the Chief Rabbinate of Israel . . . do not object to the use of bodies of persons who gave their consent in writ-

ing of their own free will during their lifetime for anatomical dissections as required for medical studies, provided the dissected parts are carefully preserved so as to be eventually buried with due respect according to Jewish law.[38]

This seems to me to be a much more sensible reading of the sources and the process of medical research than that of Rabbi Bleich. Dissection is crucial to the training of physicians. Consequently, participating in medical education in this way is an honor to the deceased and a real kindness in that it helps the living. The levity that sometimes accompanies dissection occurs not because medical students find dissection funny; rather, it is a way for them to dissipate their discomfort in handling a corpse. No disrespect is intended, and therefore dissection is not objectionable on that ground.

Rabbi Isaac Klein cites yet another argument to permit the donation of one's body to science:

> In a country where the Jews enjoy freedom, if the rabbis should refuse to allow the Jewish dead to be used for medical study, their action will result in Ḥillul ha-Shem, for it will be said that the Jews are not interested in saving lives; there is (therefore) reason to permit it.[39]

This view would not apply, however, if there were ample bodies available for dissection. Then there would be no special gift being given by the donor to future physicians and their patients, and there would be no particular taint involved if Jews did not generally donate their bodies to science. Since medical schools currently have more than enough bodies from county morgues, largely bodies of unknown people who have been abandoned, Jews need not and therefore should not offer to have their bodies dissected, for there is no medical necessity to set aside the honor due a corpse according to the Jewish concept of *kavod ha-met*.

Moreover, if Jews donate the body of a loved one to medical science for purposes of education or research, there are two restrictions that must be observed. First, after dissection, the remains must be buried in a timely fashion according to Jewish law and custom. Second, this decision must accord with the wishes not only of the deceased but of his or her family as well.[40] After all, after a person's death, relatives and friends must separate themselves psychologically from the deceased if they are to be able to resume their normal lives. By graphically indicating that the person has died, burial helps people gain the emotional catharsis and closure that they need. Therefore, the permission of the family is necessary not only to accord with American law but also to assure that even without immediate burial, relatives of the deceased in the particular case at hand can effectively carry out the mourning process so that they can have psychological closure and return to their lives in full.

Families, then, may refuse to give permission for dissection if they cannot be assured that their relative's organs will ultimately be buried or if they will not be able to mourn properly with a funeral but no burial. Under either of those circumstances, families should not be made to feel guilty for refusing to allow donation of their deceased relative's body for dissection.

This matter of dissection, however, should not be confused with the Jewish attitude toward organ donation, where there is a critical shortage. Consequently, as we have seen, most Jewish authorities would not only permit organ donation but encourage or even require it. Thus while Jews should refrain from donating their bodies for purposes of dissection as long as there is a plentiful supply, they should definitely arrange to have their organs donated for transplant purposes, for in doing so they are doing nothing less than saving lives.

PART FOUR

The Communal Context of Medical Care

CHAPTER TEN

Preventing Illness

Personal Measures to Prevent Illness

Prevention in Preference to Cure

I LLNESS IS DEBILITATING. IN ADDITION TO ANY PHYSICAL pain involved, sickness brings us the frustration of not being able to pursue our normal tasks in life. It shakes our sense of physical and psychological integrity, our sense of safety and security, and, indeed, our sense of ourselves.

Illness is also degrading. When sick, we feel diminished as human beings. As much as we need to divorce ourselves from the American evaluation of people in terms of their skills and accomplishments, recognizing instead the inherent value in every human being, when sick we inevitably feel that the divine aspect of power has been reduced in us. It is also humiliating to have to be dependent on others for help in doing the everyday tasks of living. One feels like an infant.

These characteristics of illness make it preferable to prevent it in the first place rather than cure it once it strikes. There are, of course, pragmatic considerations as well. It is still true today that "an ounce of prevention is worth a pound of cure," and sometimes, as is currently the case with regard to AIDS, we cannot cure a disease at all but we can prevent it. Historically, that was true for most diseases; for doctors were not able to cure very much, but their knowledge of preventive techniques was, in some ways, quite sophisticated. The fact that in practice we can prevent disease more easily than we can cure it, though, is not the whole story; we must prefer prevention to cure also in order to ward off the debilitating and degrading aspects of disease.

Personal Measures to Preserve Health

Some of the ways to prevent illness are the responsibility of individuals, whereas others fall to the community. In both cases, prevention is achieved through both positive and negative steps.

On the personal level, one has the positive duty to take care of oneself. As indicated in Chapter 2, in classical Jewish sources proper hygiene, diet, exercise, and sleep are not just a recipe for feeling good and living a long life but rather legal obligations to God, for our bodies belong to God and we thus have a fiduciary responsibility to care for them. So, for example, the following story was told about Hillel, one of the most important Jewish leaders of the first century C.E.:

> When he had finished the lesson with his students, he accompanied them part of the way. They said to him, "Master, where are you going?" "To perform a religious duty." "Which religious duty?" He answered them, "If somebody appointed to scrape and clean the statues of the king in the theaters and circuses is paid to do the work and furthermore is considered noble for doing so, how much more so should I, created in the divine image and likeness, take care of my body!"[1]

Similarly, Maimonides, both a rabbi and a physician, devoted several chapters of his code of Jewish law to the obligations of proper diet, exercise, hygiene, and sleep, thereby indicating that these measures are not simply practical advice but rather positive legal obligations. They are just as incumbent upon us, in fact, as other positive legal duties, such as educating ourselves and our children and caring for the poor.[2] Moreover, as we have noted in Chapter 2, Maimonides explicitly articulated the theological motivations for preventive rules of health:

> He who regulates his life in accordance with the laws of medicine with the sole motive of maintaining a sound and vigorous physique

and begetting children to do his work and labor for his benefit is not following the right course. A man should aim to maintain physical health and vigor in order that his soul may be upright, in a condition to know God. . . . Whoever throughout his life follows this course will be continually serving God, even while engaged in business and even during cohabitation, because his purpose in all that he does will be to satisfy his needs so as to have a sound body with which to serve God. Even when he sleeps and seeks repose to calm his mind and rest his body so as not to fall sick and be incapacitated from serving God, his sleep is service of the Almighty.[3]

Many Jews and non-Jews have assumed that Jewish dietary laws were designed to maintain health. Some modern Jews even use that explanation in order to justify their abandonment of those rules, reasoning that the work of government agencies now makes the health reasons for observing the Jewish dietary laws superfluous.

The truth of the matter is that health was never given as the principal rationale for the dietary rules. Maimonides came closest. He thought that observing the dietary rules would benefit one's health by prohibiting dangerous and dirty foods and, more important, by curbing one's lust for food so that one did not regard the desire for food as an ultimate end. For Maimonides, however, God is a good and beneficent Being who gave us all the commandments for the welfare of our bodies and souls, both individually and collectively; ultimately, therefore, one should obey the dietary rules and all the other commandments because God commanded them.[4]

Part of the confusion may well have resulted from the Torah's terminology in describing the dietary rules, for its Hebrew words *tahor* and *tameh* are often rendered "clean" and "unclean." They have nothing to do with sanitation, however, and they are more properly translated "pure" and "impure." That is, the categories refer to the ritual fitness or lack thereof of specific foods or acts or people. The dietary restrictions in particular probably began as a method to mark off the priests as a special people; they were later extended to all Israelites to make them "a kingdom of priests and a holy nation" (Exodus 19:6), "a people consecrated to the Lord" (Deuteronomy 14:21).

Similar remarks apply to hygiene. Thus the Talmud, commenting on the biblical verse, "Sanctify yourselves and be holy," (Leviticus 11:44) says, "'Sanctify yourselves'—that is, wash your hands before the meal, 'and be holy'—that is, wash after the meal."⁵ Until the advent of indoor plumbing in the twentieth century, it was also forbidden to live in a town that lacked public bathing facilities because "physical cleanliness is conducive to spiritual purity."⁶

In addition to diet and hygiene, physical exercise is important for preserving health. This has not been a clear mandate in codes of Jewish law, however, for a variety of reasons. Most people before this century exercised considerably just in the process of carrying out their work, and so special attention to getting enough physical activity was not needed. Moreover, ever since the revolt of the Maccabees against the Syrian Greeks in 165 B.C.E., athletics have symbolized the essence of the pagan values that Jews should shun. The rabbis built that sentiment into the prayer said when leaving the academy and as part of a *siyyum* ceremony celebrating the completion of study of a book of the Mishnah or Talmud:

> On leaving [the academy] what does he say? "I give thanks to You, O Lord my God, that You have set my portion with those who sit in the House of Study and You have not set my portion with those who sit on [street] corners [alternate reading: in circuses and theaters], for I rise early and they rise early, but I rise early for words of Torah and they rise early for frivolous talk; I labor and they labor, but I labor and receive a reward and they labor and do not receive a reward; I run and they run, but I run to the life of the future world and they run to the pit of destruction.⁷

If a sport involved cruelty to either humans or animals, it was opposed for that reason as well.

While athletics were never valorized in Jewish culture as they were among the Greeks, rabbis have not objected to sports for purposes of physical exercise or as part of military training, for in both of those settings physical activity contributes directly to preserving life and health. Moreover, during the last century, a number of rabbis have gone from not objecting to sports for reasons of health to actively endorsing physical exercise. This new acceptance of athletics stems in part from the new appreciation of the importance of exercise in maintaining health given the largely sedentary lifestyle of many in the modern world. In addition, for some rabbis and lay Jews, the new interest in sports is an expression of the self-assertiveness built into the Zionist movement.

Even now, though, rabbis warn that sports must not become the focus of one's life; ample time must be set aside for study, work, family, and community. Moreover, the purpose for engaging in athletics should not be self-aggrandizement but rather the physical and mental health, the camaraderie, and the good clean fun that comes from sports.

Personal Measures to Avoid Hazards to Health

The positive steps we are commanded to take to preserve life and health are accompanied by the demand that we avoid danger and injury.[8] As discussed in Chapter 8 above, we certainly may not injure ourselves intentionally, let alone kill ourselves. Jewish law goes further, though, prohibiting us also from endangering our health unnecessarily, and viewing such an act as worse than violating a ritual prohibition.[9]

The tradition's demand that we avoid hazards to health should influence individuals' behavior in a variety of areas.

ACCESS TO LIFE'S NECESSITIES AND TO HEALTH CARE. As discussed in Chapter 2 above, anyone who cannot subsist except by taking charity but refuses to do so out of pride is, according to the tradition, shedding his or her own blood and is thus guilty of a mortal offense.[10] We also must not live in a community lacking a physician lest that put us out of striking distance from the help we need when we are sick.

SMOKING. In light of what we now know about the hazards of smoking to smokers, their progeny, and those around them, Conservative, Reform, and some Orthodox authorities in our day have prohibited smoking as an unacceptable risk to our

God-owned bodies. Since by far the largest number of new smokers are middle and high school students, parents have a special responsibility to talk to their children well in advance of those years and frequently during them about the importance of avoiding smoking as an important measure to preserve health. It is best, of course, that parents themselves model that behavior, but even if they smoke and cannot quit, they should make very clear to their children the importance of not starting to smoke in the first place.

The dangers of secondhand smoke have, in addition, led the Rabbinical Assembly, the association of Conservative rabbis, to ban smoking in its public meetings and to call on government officials to ban smoking in all public places.[11] Similarly, anyone who does smoke should at least restrict smoking to outdoor areas, where it is possible for people to avoid harm from secondhand smoke. The last place a person should smoke is at home, where the effects of secondhand smoke will inevitably injure those nearest and dearest to the smoker.

ALCOHOL.   While the Jewish tradition never forbade the consumption of alcohol in and of itself—indeed, the Book of Psalms recognizes that "wine will gladden a person's heart"[12]—it looks down upon drunkenness, and one is not freed from responsibility for one's actions while drunk.[13] Here again, the inability of drunken people to control their actions and the harm repeated drunkenness can cause to their health (especially the liver) are reasons to avoid intoxication, to say nothing of the negative impact of continual drunkenness on other aspects of life, like family relationships, friendships, and work.

Drunkenness all too often poses risks to others as well. Since drugs or alcohol are involved in well over half of fatal car accidents, those who plan on drinking, especially those who know that they have a propensity to get drunk, need to enlist the aid of family and friends ahead of time in preventing them from driving while drunk.

Recent studies have suggested that some people are born with a genetic propensity toward alcoholism, a theory supported as well by its frequency within specific families. A genetic base for alcoholism, though, does not justify drunkenness in people born with that proclivity; on the contrary, people who know from their family history that they have that predisposition must take extra steps to ensure their sobriety by, for example, enrolling in a program to help them avoid alcohol. Jewish twelve-step programs are often offered by synagogues or by the local Jewish Family Service.

Although Jewish alcoholics and drug abusers have a duty to seek help in recovering from their addictions, the Jewish tradition should not be interpreted harshly to add to their problems. While drunkenness has traditionally been disdained for its potential to cause poverty, quarrels, strange visions, errors in judgment, injury, and even death, it is not seen as a sin per se. Consequently, current medical thinking that conceives of it more as an illness than a moral failing is very much in keeping with Jewish tradition, and since that therapeutic approach is much more likely than moral condemnation to bring recovery, it should be used.

DRUGS.   Jews may not use hallucinatory drugs for at least three reasons. First, their use is prohibited by civil law, and in Judaism "the law of the land is the law."[14] Second, since people under the influence of drugs cannot act responsibly, they thereby endanger themselves and others. Third, such drugs have lasting, deleterious effects on the user's own life and health.

Consequently, all of the preventive steps mentioned above with regard to alcohol are incumbent as well on those addicted to drugs: Drug abusers must take steps to ensure that when they are tempted to use drugs, they first alert others to make sure that while under the influence they do nothing to harm others through activities like driving. Moreover, like alcoholics, drug addicts have a Jewish duty to enroll in detoxification and avoidance therapy such as a Jewish twelve-step program.

SEX.   Those who are sexually active must employ proper safeguards, especially outside the relative safety of marriage. Although antibiotics cured several sexually transmitted diseases in the recent past, those diseases have now developed strains resistant to these drugs. In some cases the implications are only embarrassment and discomfort, but in others the end result is death.

AIDS is still, as of this writing, one such disease; even though promising new combinations of drugs can delay or reduce its symptoms, the illness is still lethal. In the 1980s, after the virus was identified, the gay community did a remarkable job of educating its members with regard to the need for, and methods of, safe sex, but the rate of infection in the new generation of gays now in their teens and twenties indicates that renewed efforts must be made. Moreover, the disease has spread in large numbers to the heterosexual community, where in recent years the largest increase of infection, in both numbers and percentages, has occurred.

The safest policy among unmarried people with regard to all sexually transmitted diseases is, of course, abstinence. Jewish sexual norms would have us restrict sexual intercourse to marriage, and those abiding by that moral norm thereby ensure their safety as well. For those who cannot attain that ideal, though, Jewish norms of health and safety require that unmarried people engaging in sex take appropriate precautions to avoid being infected with sexually transmitted diseases.[15]

Communal Measures to Prevent Illness

Social Steps to Preserve Health

Public health measures have undoubtedly been the most important factor in raising the age of life expectancy in the United States from the mid-forties in 1900 to the mid-seventies now. These developments include health education; sex education; governmental health regulations to govern food distribution, drugs, and building codes; the establishment of agencies like the Centers for Disease Control and Prevention to monitor diseases and implement social responses to them; and, in our day, inoculations to prevent many diseases. Advances in technology that have brought us indoor plumbing, rapid communication with emergency and routine health services, and new drugs and machines have contributed significantly to the length and quality of our lives as well.

With its strong sense of community and duty, the Jewish tradition would have us use communal measures to preserve our lives and health as much as possible. It would be a violation of Jewish law, for example, for a Jew to refuse to be inoculated against a disease, at least where the inoculation has a proven track record of effectiveness. Jews, on the contrary, have a positive duty to have themselves and their children inoculated against all diseases where that preventive measure is effective and available.

In addition to using currently available public means to maintain and ensure health, Jews should support government funding for new medical research, especially when it is directed to producing new preventive measures that can be used widely and inexpensively. If public health measures have been the most important factor in improving and lengthening our lives in the past, there is every reason to believe that such measures will be immensely significant in achieving those ends in the future as well.

Furthermore, the Jewish value of saving health and life requires Jews to lobby for government measures to preserve or restore the conditions for good health. So, for example, legislation to ensure clean water and air deserves Jewish endorsement for many reasons, including the adverse effects of pollution on our health.

In some cases these effects are direct and clear, for example, the implications of air pollution on the incidence and severity of asthma. In other cases the relationship of our activities to medical problems is suspected but not yet fully documented. One guess as to why sperm counts in human males have diminished 50 percent in the last fifty years, for example, is that female hormones given to cows to increase the yield of their milk have caused the reproductive organs in boys and men who drink it to malfunction. Whether that theory will prove to be true is not clear, but the need to test the effects of additives repeatedly is beyond all doubt. In general, we must take steps to avoid introducing pollutants into the environment in the first place and eliminate them when they occur so as to preserve a context for human living conducive to health.

Social Measures to Avoid Health Hazards

Along with taking positive steps to establish and maintain a natural and social environment conducive to life and health, the community must also use its best efforts to eliminate hazards to health. So, for example, effective education concerning the risks involved in smoking, including advertisements to that effect in the media, should accompany government regulation of smoking in an effort to reduce its incidence, especially among the young. Moreover, governmental bans on smoking in public places to protect people against the hazards of secondhand smoke should be universally enacted and enforced. Similarly, Jews should back new, creative efforts on the part of government and the private sector to diminish, if not root out, the use of narcotics.

Although people are often conscious of the need to eliminate health risks in the ways just described, they frequently neglect one other important way to accomplish that end. For a variety of political reasons, the number of the homeless and the hungry in American society has skyrocketed since the 1980s. To a large extent this phenomenon is a consequence of the closure of public mental health facilities. Few things can cause disease in people more quickly and effectively than depriving them of adequate food, clothing, and shelter. That compounds the shame of homelessness with the degradation of disease. Social efforts to prevent disease, then, must begin with ensuring that everyone in our society has adequate food, clothing, and shelter. Compared to that, all other issues in health care must take second place.

CHAPTER ELEVEN

Linking Mind and Body

Visiting the Sick

T HE COMMUNAL MEASURES NECESSARY TO PRESERVE OR restore health are not limited to physical factors alone, for sick people are not simply physical organisms afflicted with a virus or bacterium; they are whole human beings. Thus even if medicine cannot cure a person, Jews have a collective duty to attend to his or her emotional, psychological, and social well-being. As the Zohar, a thirteenth-century work of Jewish mysticism, says, "If a physician cannot give his patient medicine for his body, he should [at least] make sure that medicine is given him for his soul."[1] Visiting the sick *(bikkur ḥolim)* is a requirement of every Jew (not just the rabbi, doctor, or nurse); and so at least as early as the fourteenth century and continuing today in many congregations of all denominations, synagogues have established Bikkur Ḥolim societies consisting of members who have taken it upon themselves to make sure that the sick people in their community are visited, whether they have family doing that or not.[2]

Visiting the sick is important not only to give emotional and social support to the ailing but for physical reasons as well. As some of the talmudic and medieval sources we will consider below point out, often physical illness is affected significantly by the state of the other parts of a person's being. Certainly, those who are visited often have much more motivation to fight to overcome their disease, for it is clear that others want them to survive. This makes the social setting in which people cope with their illness absolutely critical in their prognosis for recovery.

We meet most people in the active course of our working lives. Recreation with friends commonly involves going out somewhere to play ball, watch a movie, listen to a concert, or enjoy a meal together. Good friends and some family members visit each other at home, but everyone is aware that that is only one setting in which their relationship is played out, that they could choose at any time to leave home to do something somewhere else.

Illness changes all of that. The sick person must stay at home or in the hospital; she or he cannot leave to engage in normal work routines or to do something enjoyable with friends. This requires colleagues, family members, and friends to make time in their schedules to go to the sick person's home or hospital room and to interact with the person in strange circumstances. Visiting the sick is therefore both inconvenient and alien.

The encounter, in fact, is uncomfortable for both the sick person and the visitors. The ill feel not only the physical pains of their illness but also the loss of self-esteem associated with diminished capacity. They do not know how to handle themselves in these new, strange circumstances. This awkwardness is compounded by the additional embarrassment of having friends see them dressed in pajamas. Moreover, the ill often feel as if they are intruding on their friends' time and making them do something they really would prefer not to do.

Their suspicions are frequently accurate. Friends and family feel annoyed and put upon by this new duty. They may also feel ill at ease because they are not used to interacting with people in this diminished state and do not know what to say or do. This uneasiness is compounded by general discomfort with illness: seeing a sick person starkly reminds them of their own vulnerability.

For all these reasons, people commonly avoid visiting the sick as much as they can, thus isolating the ill and making their recovery all the harder. After all, if you were bedridden by illness, especially by a long-term one, and were seldom visited, you might well feel that nobody cared about you. This would diminish your motivation to combat your illness or, when it could not be cured, to learn how to live life as fully as possible with it. In extreme cases, you might even think seriously about taking your life.

Conversely, if you were visited often, it would be hard to wallow in self-pity. After all, you would reason, one or more people care enough about me to see me often, and I cannot let them down. This would reinforce your will to live.

The Jewish tradition was keenly aware that recovery from illness involves the patients' minds and spirits as well as their bodies. The Talmud says this:

> Rabbi Abba son of Rabbi Ḥanina said: He who visits an invalid takes away a sixtieth of his pain [or, in another version, a sixtieth of his illness]. . . .
> When Rabbi Dimi came [from Palestine], he said: He who visits the sick causes him to live, while he who does not causes him to die. How does he cause this? . . . He who visits the sick prays that he may live, . . . [while] he who does not visit the sick prays neither that he may live nor die.[3]

The Talmud here is asserting two aspects of the spiritual elements of recovery. On a social plane, those who visit the sick help to shift the patient's focus from the pain and degradation of the illness to the joy of the company of friends and family. They thus take away a sixtieth of the pain of the illness. Visitors also reassure the patient that family and friends are keenly interested in their recovery, and they remind the patient of life outside the sickroom. They thereby reinforce the patient's determination to overcome the illness altogether, or at least as many of its effects as possible. Visitors are thus instrumental in motivating the patient to follow a medical regimen of healing, however tedious or painful it may be, and so, in the Talmud's alternative reading, they effectively take away a sixtieth of the patient's illness itself.

Visitors affect the patient on a more religious plane as well. By praying for the patient, and by indicating that prayers are being offered in the synagogue on his or her behalf, visitors invoke the aid of God, the ultimate Healer. Jewish prayer is traditionally done in community, in part because Jewish sources maintain that communal prayer persuades God to grant a request more effectively than private prayer does.[4] Visitors' prayers and those recited in the synagogue on behalf of the patient thus throw the weight of the entire community behind the patient's own plea to God for recovery.

The tradition links sickness with sin, and so the Talmud records this remark by Rabbi Alexandri in the name of Rabbi Hiyya bar Abba: "A sick person does not recover from illness until all his or her sins are forgiven, as [the juxtaposition in the following verse shows, for] it is written, 'God forgives all your sins, God heals all your diseases' (Psalms 103:3)."[5] Jewish confessional prayers, though, are expressed in the first person plural, for Jewish sources maintain that requests for forgiveness are most effective when *we* recite them as part of a community rather than when *I* recite them by myself.[6] Praying for the sick may thus alleviate feelings of guilt connected with the disease, for now the entire community is asking for both forgiveness and healing.

Visitors must also pay attention to the physical needs of the sick. Thus the Talmud tells the following story:

> Rabbi Ḥelbo fell ill. Rabbi Kahana then went [to the house of study] and proclaimed, "Rabbi Ḥelbo is ill." Nobody, however, visited him. Rabbi Kahana rebuked them [the disciples], saying, "Did it ever happen that one of Rabbi Akiba's students fell ill, and the [rest of the] disciples did not visit him?" So Rabbi Akiba himself entered [Rabbi Ḥelbo's house] to visit him, and because they swept and sprinkled the ground before him [that is, cleaned the house and put it in order], Rabbi Ḥelbo recovered. Rabbi Akiba then went forth and lectured: He who does not visit the sick is like one who sheds blood.[7]

Taking physical care of the sick can include not only cleaning house but shopping for groceries, doing laundry, taking over carpool duties, and seeing to the other needs of the patient's family. Depending upon the circumstances, it can also include more direct physical interventions like taking the patient for a ride in a wheel-chair (if medically permitted), feeding the patient (if necessary), and attending to the patient's other physical needs.

Mostly, though, visiting the sick involves talking with the patient, and that is often what causes the greatest degree of discomfort for the visitor. People often do not know what to say or do. Some would rather not hear about the patient's aches and pains, much less about a painful or dangerous procedure the patient has just endured or is facing, because such talk makes them sad and engenders thoughts about their own vulnerability. The food served at the facility and the weather quickly pall as topics of conversation. Since few of us are trained in effective visiting techniques, visitors soon feel frustrated in their desires to help and support the patient. All of these feelings deter people from visiting the sick any more than they feel they absolutely must.

The Jewish tradition has some practical advice for making such visits more pleasant and effective:[8]

1. *Identifying who should visit the sick.* The duty of visiting the sick is not confined to friends and family—or, for that matter, to rabbis; rather, everyone is obligated to visit the sick, regardless of the relative social station of the patient and the potential visitor.[9] Jews are obligated to visit not only ill Jews but non-Jews as well, as part of our duty to promote peace between Jews and non-Jews.[10] "Anyone who visits the sick has, as it were, taken away a part of the illness and made it easier to bear," says Maimonides, "and anyone who neglects to visit the sick has, as it were, shed blood."[11]

2. *Ensuring that a visit is welcome.* Through consultation with the patient's family or friends, potential visitors should make sure that a visit would be neither embarrassing nor physically detrimental to the patient.[12]

3. *Timing the day of one's visit.* "As a matter of good manners," according to the Jerusalem Talmud,[13] only family and close friends should visit during the first two days of an illness, and others should wait until the third day. That restriction does

not apply, however, to patients with acute, life-threatening illnesses.

4. *Timing the hours of one's visit.* The hours of visitation must not interfere with the patient's medical treatment or unduly tax the patient's strength.[14] Hospitals have the right to restrict visiting hours to assure this. If the patient is helped by visits, though, they need not be limited to one per day.[15]

5. *Positioning oneself to make the patient feel comfortable.* Visitors who stand or sit higher than the patient's head accentuate the patient's incapacity in contrast to the visitor's able-bodied state. They also make the patient look up to them, thus further symbolizing a gap in status. To avoid these feelings, visitors should sit down to communicate equality and support.[16]

6. *Attending to the patient's needs.* As discussed above, part of the point of visiting the sick is to learn how one can help the patient or the family cope with the illness. Since patients and their close family members are often reticent in asking for help, visitors need to offer it. They should make one or two specific suggestions so that the patient or family members understand that the offer is serious and get a sense of the scope of what the visitor is willing to do.

7. *Praying for and with the patient.* Jewish sources state that one fulfills the commandment of visiting the sick only if one prays with and for the patient for healing.[17] Many Jews—patients as well as visitors—are unaccustomed to prayer, but illness is often an occasion for a felt need to pray. One can use the short, standard formula stated in the Talmud and codes—*hamakom ye'raḥem 'aleikha be-tokh ḥolei yisrael* (May the All-Present have mercy on you among the sick of Israel)[18]—and then add whatever one thinks appropriate and meaningful, whether in Hebrew or in English.[19] Many prayer books include suggested texts, often from the Book of Psalms.

8. *Speaking with the patient.* Aside from praying for and with the patient, how do you fill the time? What do you talk about? Conversations normally flow out of joint activities, but patients cannot engage in the work or recreation that usually brings people together and gets them talking. Moreover, the illness it-

self and the strange setting of a sickbed, especially in a hospital, make visitors feel uncomfortable. How, then, can they overcome these obstacles to meaningful and helpful conversation?

Some topics that should be raised are practical in nature. Specifically, as discussed in Chapter 7, if the patient has a life-threatening illness and has not previously filled out a will or a living will for health care, visitors can help the patient specify his or her desired disposition of property and preferred course of medical treatment.

Regardless of the seriousness of the illness, visitors can also help a patient complete an ethical will. As stated in Chapter 7, ethical wills are often read and reread (or heard and reheard) by descendants of their author. They can be a treasure trove of information about the author and the extended family, the kind of information we all want to know as part of learning about ourselves.

Ethical wills, though, are just as valuable to their authors, especially if they are bedridden for a long time. Patients who know that they have a task to accomplish in order to leave their children and (especially) grandchildren a record of their experiences, values, thoughts, dreams, and hopes will redouble their efforts to live as long as they can so that they can complete this important project.

Ethical wills are also a boon for visitors. In providing a program and goal for visits, helping a patient complete an ethical will can transform visits from boring and uncomfortable encounters to be avoided as much as possible to interesting and meaningful exchanges for all concerned.

Most time spent with the patient, though, does lend itself to discussion of specific decisions or projects. How, then, should visitors fill the time of their visit?

Jewish legal sources are silent about this, but Jewish theological concepts provide important clues. Every human being, according to the Torah, bears the dignity of being created in the image of God. The key to speaking with sick people, then, is to bolster that sense of worth.

Illness is inherently degrading: the person is not capable of engaging in normal activities. Visitors must be especially on guard, then, to avoid infantilizing the patient, for doing so reinforces his or her sense of loss of power and honor. Visitors should rather engage the patient in conversations on the level and subjects of the patient's normal interests.

Sometimes ill people can even stretch beyond the topics that normally occupy them. One of the most enlightening experiences of my early rabbinic career was giving a series of lectures on Jewish theology to residents of a Jewish nursing home. The group included former doctors, lawyers, teachers, and entrepreneurs. The residents themselves, all college graduates, had specifically asked for these classes, even though none of them had ever studied Jewish theology before, because they were sick of playing Bingo. They had been intellectually active at earlier stages of their lives, and their physical illnesses now had not significantly changed their intellectual interests or even their mental capacity—except that I had to speak just a little more slowly and loudly than I usually do. The social workers who arranged these lessons had also warned me not to be deterred by the fact that sometimes the students' eyes would close, for in older people closed eyes do not necessarily signal sleep. As the social workers predicted, some of the people who had their eyes closed through most of the class later asked me pointed questions about what I had said; they clearly were awake and listening. The students even read assignments in preparation for the class from specially prepared sheets with enlarged print. I wish my younger students were always as well prepared!

Visitors do not normally discuss Jewish theology, but this example will, I hope, make clear that conversations with patients should be challenging and should cover a wide variety of topics. The very normalcy of such discussions communicates that the illness has not diminished the visitor's respect for the patient's intelligence and humanity and that the remainder of even a very limited life can still be filled with meaningful conversation.

Finally, in the spirit of Nel Noddings's book *On Caring*,[20] I would like to pose some questions. Do male and female patients need different kinds of emotional caring? Do male and female visitors, as a rule, offer different forms of caring to patients, whether male or female? Put more broadly, are gender issues relevant to emotional caring?

Apart from the contemporary work of Noddings, Carol Gilligan, Deborah Tannen, and many others,[21] there is one hint in the Jewish tradition that gender does affect one's mode of caring and one's need for specific types of care. Traditionally, a Hebrew name comprises the person's given name(s) and then "son of," or "daughter of," that person's *father's* name, for it is the man who represented the family in the community. When a blessing is invoked in the synagogue to heal an ill person, however, that person is usually referred to as son or daughter of his or her *mother*. One common explanation for this custom in the folklore is that when one is ill, one needs the kind of caring that mothers are known to give.[22] In recognition of changing gender roles, and in greater fulfillment of the command to honor one's father *and mother*, contemporary Conservative and Reform congregations now often call people to the Torah using both their father's and mother's name; and blessings for those who are ill increasingly name both parents as well. Fathers, after all, can and should be involved in caring for their sick children just as much as mothers are. Nevertheless, it may be the case that in illness, as in other areas of life, fathers care for their children somewhat differently than mothers do, and sons may need somewhat different kinds of care than daughters do. The traditional practice at least hints in that direction, and it is a direction, I think, worth considering.

Talking with a patient about a will, a living will, and an ethical will, coupled with the other forms of conversation and physical ministration mentioned above, makes visits to the sick a critical part of the person's chances for speedy recovery. No wonder, then, that in a source we met before in discussing burial of the dead, the rabbis understood visiting the sick, too, as an activity we do in imitation of God:

> "Follow the Lord your God" (Deuteronomy 13:5). What does this mean? Is it possible for a mortal to follow God's Presence? The verse means to teach us that we should follow the attributes of the

Holy One, praised be He. As He clothed the naked, for it is written, "And the Lord God made for Adam and for his wife coats of skin and clothed them" (Genesis 3:21), so you should clothe the naked. The Holy One, blessed be He, visited the sick, for it is written [after the description of Abraham's circumcision], "And the Lord appeared to him near the oaks of Mamre" (Genesis 18:1), so you should visit the sick. The Holy One, blessed be He, comforted those who mourned . . . and so should you comfort mourners. The Holy One, blessed be He, buried the dead . . . and so should you bury the dead.[23]

Moreover, visiting the sick, as an act of both loyalty and kindness *(ḥesed)*, is, according to the rabbis, one of a small list of commandments that have no limit and that "yield immediate fruit [to both the visitor and the patient] while the principle redounds to the benefit of those who do them in God's ultimate judgment in the World to Come."[24]

Mental Health

If it was difficult to discover effective medications for the body before the twentieth century, it was all the more difficult to treat illnesses of the mind. The Bible describes in detail the paranoid psychopathia and perhaps the epilepsy of King Saul, and others in the Bible and Talmud suffer from visual and auditory hallucinations, insanity, and "possession by demons or spirits."[25] Biblical prophets experienced trances and ecstasies. In antiquity, Jews interpreted such phenomena positively, as proof of divine contact. The later tradition, though, treated reports of such experiences negatively, as signs of illness, and it sought to exorcise the ghosts *(shedim)* or furies *(dybbuks)* that caused them. Music was used often in an attempt to seduce demons to leave the minds of the insane and thereby calm and cure them.

Because insanity had legal implications, the rabbis tried to define it as specifically as possible:

Our rabbis taught: Who is deemed insane? He who goes out alone at night, and he who spends the night in a cemetery, and he who tears his garments. It was taught: Rabbi Huna said: he must do all of them [to be considered insane]. Rabbi Johanan said: Even if [he does only] one of them. It was taught: Who is deemed insane? One who destroys everything given to him.[26]

Maimonides notes, however, that these behaviors are to be construed as symptoms, not as an exhaustive definition of insanity.[27] In line with this, Moshe Halevi Spero, a modern Orthodox psychologist, suggests specific criteria for determining mental disorders for purposes of legal excuse in Jewish law. "Generally speaking," he says, *shtus* [or, in the Sephardic pronunciation more often used today, *shtut*, meaning mental incompetence or insanity] might denote one who has lost the ability to reason or make reality-based judgments. *Shtus* may also signify the loss of emotional control."[28] In addition to the chronic mental diseases normally classified as insanity, then, this would include developmental forms of mental incompetence such as advanced cases of Alzheimer's.

A diagnosis of insanity had many legal implications in Jewish law. When the degree of mental incompetence warranted it, the rabbis of the Mishnah and Talmud exempted the insane from responsibility in both ritual and civil law. At the same time, they made the insane ineligible for certain legal roles (for example, serving as another person's legal agent).[29] They also sought to define the exact degree and scope of legal responsibility of someone who did not have full free will as a result of his or her own decisions, as, for example, those under the influence of alcohol or drugs.[30]

The general approach in Jewish sources was to disenfranchise the mentally ill as little as possible. So, for example, after the bands of prophets during biblical times,[31] we do not hear of Jewish communities isolating the mentally ill. Moreover, the rabbis distinguished between those times when a person was apparently sane and therefore legally capable and those times in which she or he was not.[32] Modern rabbinic authorities are therefore interested in the progress of psychology as a science for its legal as well as for its therapeutic ramifications.

Probably the most important legal step in the history of Jewish law with regard to mental illness has been its classification as an illness rather than a moral fault. The Talmud permitted lighting a candle in violation of the Sabbath rules for a woman in labor in order to spare her psychic anguish.[33] Citing that precedent, Nahmanides (thirteenth century) specifically included mental illness in the category of "saving a life" *(pikuah nefesh)* so that almost all obligations and prohibitions could be laid aside in order to save a person's mental as well as physical health.[34]

Especially because mental illness was often incurable, the Jewish tradition sought to prevent it by offering advice for maintaining mental health, often suggesting the cultivation of specific personal characteristics and values. The Book of Proverbs provides an early instance of such advice. Perhaps the most famous example in rabbinic literature is Ethics of the Fathers *(Pirkei Avot)*, a tractate of the Mishnah (edited c. 200 C.E.) that is read every Sabbath afternoon during the weeks between Pesah and Shavuot. A thousand years later Maimonides wrote a book on personality traits in which he embraced the Aristotelian golden mean as the proper guideline. He suggested that one who was very calm, for example, should try to go to the other extreme in order to maintain a balance of spirit.[35] Jews in medieval Spain also produced important psychological-ethical handbooks, including *Hovot ha-Levavot (Duties of the Heart)* by Bahya ibn Pakuda (eleventh century); *Sefer ha-Hinnukh (Book of Education)* by Aaron ha-Levi of Barcelona (thirteenth century); and *Kad ha-Kemah (Measure of Flour)* by Bahya ben Asher (thirteenth century). In the eighteenth century, the Italian Kabbalist Moses Hayyim Luzzato wrote the ethical tract, *Mesillat Yesharim (The Path of the Upright)*.[36] In the nineteenth and twentieth centuries, the Musar movement spread through some Orthodox communities of eastern Europe, seeking to balance the heavy emphasis on study of texts and intellectual analysis common in traditional seminaries with materials and sessions devoted to moral and spiritual development.

In such ways, Jews sought to prevent or cure mental illness. However primitive their understanding of it was, Jews saw it *not* as something for which one should repent or be punished but rather as an illness we must seek to prevent or cure as part of our general obligation to heal. This attitude prepared the way for Sigmund Freud and many other Jews in the field of psychiatry to develop and practice the modern medical forms of psychological care in addition to the many other nonmedical forms of treatment of mental illness.

Tattooing and Body Piercing

Since time immemorial, people have sought to make themselves look and feel good not only through the things they accomplish and the people they help but also through the clothes they wear and, sometimes, through the ways in which they change their bodies. The Bible itself provides evidence of women piercing their ears and noses to adorn themselves with earrings and nose rings.[37] Biblical verses also describe tattooing, but in each case it is for a religious purpose, whether prohibited or permitted, rather than for the aesthetic reasons that motivate most tattooing today.

People may certainly seek to make themselves look beautiful as a way of contributing to their own self-image, for they thereby contribute to their mental health. Moreover, although this usually is not their conscious purpose, people honor God by beautifying their bodies, for everyone's body is, after all, God's creation and property. The Talmud recognizes this with regard to clothes when it points out that Rabbi Yoḥanan called his clothes "my honorers," for even though we are created in God's image, our clothes dignify us yet further.[38] Just as adorning ourselves through clothes must respect the Jewish value of modesty, though, so too efforts to enhance one's appearance through tattoos or body piercing must be balanced against other Jewish laws and values.

Tattoos

The Torah prohibits tattooing oneself: "You shall not make gashes in your flesh for the dead, or incise any marks on yourselves: I am the Lord."[39] The Mishnah records a dispute about this, but both opinions narrow the scope of the proscription. The unnamed (and therefore presumably the majority) position maintains that the Torah's ban applies only to permanent marks, while Rabbi Simeon bar Judah asserts that the penalty of lashes applies only to those tattoos that include a divine name. The Talmud then debates further whether Rabbi Simeon bar Judah meant to penalize people who had a tattoo that contains God's name or that of a pagan deity.[40]

It does seem that the Torah's prohibition was intended to cover only those tattoos that were part of a pagan cultic rite. The ban, after all, appears in the Holiness Code of Leviticus, which is centrally concerned with distancing Israelites from the pagans and their idolatrous practices. Moreover, there are some instances in the Bible itself of permitted tattooing—for example, "One shall say, 'I am the Lord's,' another shall use the name of 'Jacob,' another shall mark his arm 'of the Lord' and adopt the name of 'Israel.'"[41] The rabbis, though, extended the prohibition to include all permanent tattooing, disagreeing only as to which tattoos subject a person to the penalty of lashes for violating a negative commandment. Even if the tattoo is not idolatrous in intention or design, they reason, tattooing itself is a pagan practice, to be prohibited as such. Many in our own day, of course, and presumably many in talmudic and medieval times as well, tattooed themselves not to participate in idolatrous cults or even to imitate non-Jewish customs, but for the sake of adornment. The rabbis, though, saw tattooing as an inappropriate way to improve one's appearance, both because it came too close to what idolaters did and because they felt, one suspects, that putting permanent marks on one's skin violated the divine image in which we were all created.

Several caveats to this overall prohibition, though, must be stated. First, only permanent marks on the body are forbidden; hand stamps, children's decorations that mimic tattoos, and any painting of the skin in a nonpermanent manner (including cosmetics) do not fall under this prohibition.

Second, even permanent tattoos may clearly be used if necessary, for example, in medical procedures such as cancer radiation therapy. Here, as usual, saving a life takes precedence over the prohibition of tattooing.

Third, those who were tattooed against their will, such as Holocaust victims, are free of any culpability for violating this law. Indeed, long before the Holocaust, Jewish law stipulated this exemption from liability as long as the Jew did not aid in the process of being tattooed—presumably in reaction to Jews being taken captive and tattooed as a mark of enslavement or shame.

Finally, while the Torah itself, as interpreted by the rabbis, broadly prohibits Jews from following pagan practices, the rabbis did not directly classify tattooing as a violation of that verse, which would invoke a penalty of lashes for violating one of the Torah's negative commandments. Only tattooing using pagan symbols or intended for cultic purposes incurred that punishment—but then as a violation of the Torah's specific ban against tattooing. Tattooing without idolatrous symbols or purposes was instead forbidden as a pagan practice, but its violation did not carry any specified penalty. That is, Jews were not supposed to tattoo themselves, but if they did, no legal sanction would be imposed.[42]

The sources thus do not support what many Jews believe to be clear law. Jews with nonidolatrous tattoos are *not* barred from participating in the ritual life of the Jewish community, even in positions of honor, and they are *not* to be excluded from burial in a Jewish cemetery. That such restrictions apply is a remarkably common belief among Jews and a good example of the power of folklore—but in this case, mistaken folklore.

Body Piercing

While the Bible knew of piercing the ears and nose, today people pierce virtually every part of the body, including the genitals. In some biblical instances, the body piercing had legal meaning, most notably in the case of piercing a Hebrew slave's ear if he refused to be emancipated after the maximum six-year enslavement. That piercing symbolized his permanent status as a slave and may also have indicated disdain for his refusal to accept the responsibilities of freedom.[43] In the talmudic and medieval periods, men pierced their ears to hang tokens identifying their profession,[44] but in most cases it was women who pierced their noses and ears, for the purpose of beautification.

While the new forms of body piercing may offend some people, that could equally be said for much older forms of body piercing like nose rings. In any case, such aesthetic judgments cannot be a legal or moral basis for objecting to the practice.

The only two concerns that do affect the new forms of body piercing are modesty and health. In general, Jewish law prohibits injuring ourselves or others. Body piercing escapes that prohibition because it is done in the name of adorning, rather than injuring, oneself.[45] If the point of piercing the body is to add to one's beauty, though, one cannot but wonder how many people besides the person so adorned are supposed to see the pierced genital areas and thus appreciate them as a mark of beauty. If it is only the person whose body is pierced and that person's spouse, well and good. The Jewish value of modesty, though, demands that others should not be shown those areas of the body or the piercing or rings attached to them.

The other concern is health. Infections occur in pierced ears, and piercing can just as surely provide the site for infection in other parts of the body. Indeed, in piercing of the genitalia, one needs to worry about infections not only of the surrounding skin but of the entire urinary tract. The risk is not so great or life-threatening as to prohibit the practice altogether, but those who pierce their bodies have the duty to guard against infection through regular inspection and cleaning of the pierced areas.

Cosmetic Surgery

Cosmetic surgery is done for both therapeutic and aesthetic reasons. Some forms of cosmetic surgery (for example, that performed on burn victims) are done to diminish a threat to one's health or life. That is just another form of healing permitted and even mandated by the tradition.

Whereas therapeutic surgery seeks to reestablish what existed before and was damaged, cosmetic surgery done for aesthetic reasons seeks instead to improve the body a person inherited. Since surgery always involves risks, people contemplating such procedures should first determine whether alternative courses of action can make them feel better about themselves. Cosmetic surgery, for example, is not a good way to respond to problems in one's personal life or job. It is also not a good antidote to psychological depression.

The most pervasive motivation for cosmetic surgery done for aesthetic reasons, though, is to become more like the "ideal" people projected by the movies and television. The media even describe such people as "the beautiful people." The proper response to such pressure, however, is not to undergo the risks of cosmetic surgery to resemble others but rather to take nonsurgical steps to gain a better estimation of oneself. That, in part, can be done by realizing what the Bible said long ago in its ode to a capable wife—namely, "Grace is deceptive, beauty is illusory; it is for her fear of the Lord that a woman is to be praised."[46] Resisting the immense pressure exerted by the media in these matters is, of course, not easy for either men or women, but it is part of what the Jewish tradition would have us do in recognizing that we all, regardless of our physical shape, have ultimate value as people created in the image of God.

In line with this view, one might think that cosmetic surgery for aesthetic reasons alone should be prohibited on theological, if not legal, grounds, for it is effectively saying that what God gave us is not good enough. As such, it is an act of ingratitude toward God, a lack of appropriate appreciation of the body God gave us. The Jewish tradition does not, however, take that position with regard to illnesses; it says instead that we have God's permission to aid in the healing process. We are not, in other words, required to accept whatever physical lot we have been given in life. Theologically, then, one could justify cosmetic surgery for purely aesthetic reasons as another form of aiding God in the healing process, this time to aid a person to feel good about himself or herself.

In sum, from a medical point of view, the risks of cosmetic surgery are not so great as to prohibit its use for aesthetic reasons altogether on the grounds of avoiding harm to one's life or health. Theologically, cosmetic surgery can be understood as just another form of beautifying oneself, which is permitted, rather than an affront to God. Therefore, even though people contemplating cosmetic surgery for aesthetic reasons should think several times over about why it is warranted, searching all the while for more appropriate and less dangerous alternatives, in the end such procedures are permitted in the name of augmenting a person's own sense of self-worth and, hence, mental health.

The Disabled

Psychological issues heavily influence the disabled as well. The way in which both the disabled person and those around him or her respond to the disability often spells the difference between a life filled with significance and feelings of self-worth as against one crippled by a sense of oddity and even shame.

Although Judaism places strong emphasis on the community, it has gone a long way to protect individuals and minorities, especially those most vulnerable. This tradition is in large measure based on the Torah's depiction of each individual as the creature of God, to be valued and protected as such. It requires Jews to think of people not merely as means for some social or theological goal but also as ends in themselves with their own inherent, divine worth.[47]

The Jewish tradition insists on this perspective even with respect to non-Jews, who, by hypothesis, deny the essence of Jewish faith. Thus in thirty-six passages, by the rabbis' count, the Bible boldly proclaims equality in law between Jew and alien; for instance, "There shall be one law for you and for the resident stranger; it shall be a law for all time throughout the ages. You and the stranger shall be alike before the Lord; the same ritual and the same rule of law shall apply to you and to the stranger who resides among you."[48] Rabbinic Judaism even reserves a place for righteous gentiles in the world to come.[49]

Jewish law also protects the rights of individual Jews and of minorities within the Jewish community. So, for example, Jewish law, like American law, safeguards an individual's right to express his or her own opinion, however unpopular. Although Judaism does not recognize the right of Jews to adopt another religion, it does preserve the other First Amendment rights — and, for that matter, many of the privileges embodied in the other sections of the Bill of Rights.[50]

These rights were not only theoretical; they were broadly used. Thus those from other cultures who read the Talmud are often amazed at the high degree of tolerance in the Jewish tradition for questioning and disagreement. Ultimately, a rule of law had to be established, but individuals were free to question it and argue against it, and "all are the words of the living God."[51] If Judaism, to a remarkable degree, tolerated and protected those who voiced dissent, it certainly sought to shield and support those who were different from the majority through circumstances beyond their control. So, for example, treatment of the poor in Jewish law and in actual practice was truly remarkable in its level of service and humanity.[52]

It is in this broad context that it makes most sense to explore Judaism's stance vis-à-vis the disabled. Its view of each person as created in the image of God affects what it prescribes at every stage of life, from neonates to the elderly.

Disabled Newborn Infants

Once a child is born, the child is a full-fledged human being and is to be treated in its health care like all other human beings. That is true for disabled newborns just as much as it is for those fully abled. The image of God in each one of us does not depend upon ability or skill; as discussed in Chapter 2 above, in asserting this principle the Jewish way of evaluating life is distinctly at odds with the utilitarian approach embedded in American secular culture.

If a child is born with severe disabilities that threaten his or her life, however, heroic measures need not be employed to keep the infant alive. Here the same rules that govern the withholding and removal of life support systems from any human being apply to newborns, with all of the diversity of opinion among rabbis noted in Chapter 8. Some rabbis, however, are more lenient with respect to the treatment of newborns than they are regarding people dying later on in life because of the possibility, noted in Jewish law, that the child was born prematurely. Specifically, until the child is thirty days old, she or he is not considered to be a person whose life is confirmed (bar kayyama). Therefore, while we certainly may not do anything actively to hasten death, we may, according to these authorities, do less to sustain the child's life than we would be called upon to do with regard to people who had lived beyond thirty days. Thus some who would insist on artificial nutrition and hydration for most dying people would not require it for life-imperiled infants less than thirty days old—except, of course, if the intervention holds out significant promise of curing the disease or condition. Some would require incubators, but most would not require surgery or medications beyond those necessary to relieve the infant of pain.[53]

Children and Adults with Disabilities

The Torah forbids tormenting the handicapped by, for example, insulting the deaf or placing a stumbling block in front of the blind.[54] The rabbis enhanced these negative measures with a number of positive provisions on behalf of the disabled. Thus with the exception of a few functions that specific handicaps make it impossible to perform, the disabled were treated in Jewish law like everyone else.

In addition to these practical measures affecting action, the rabbis sought to change abled people's emotional reaction to disabilities. Abled people who see the disabled often recoil in a combination of disgust, horror, and fear. Many abled people do not often see disabled people, and so part of this reaction flows from their sheer newness and oddity. A much larger part of what makes abled people shrink from the disabled, though, is the fear that they too will suffer disability. Seeing the disabled removes the comfortable psychological cover assuring abled people of their own bodily integrity and safety; the disabled starkly remind the able-bodied that they too are vulnerable to disability, and that their confidence in their own health and capabilities rests on a shaky foundation that can be undermined at any moment. That is unsettling, to say the least.

It is precisely in that emotional context that the rabbis require anyone seeing a disabled person not to shrink away in horror but to *say a blessing!* One must say: "Praised are You, Sovereign of the universe, who has made people different *(meshaneh ha-briyyot)."* Just when I am horrified by the sight of the disability, wonder why God would inflict such a thing on anyone, and contemplate thanking God that I do not suffer from the same disability—all expressions of how I am tempted to diminish the disabled person—I must instead utter a blessing praising and thanking God for making people different. The rabbis thus powerfully force me to get beyond my negative feelings about the disability so that I recognize and appreciate the divine quality in each and every human being, regardless of the person's capacities or lack thereof.

That new reaction, of course, must then be translated into action. Not only may I not ridicule or taunt the disabled; I must take positive measures to make it possible for them to live honorably and productively among the rest of us—the people the disabled community aptly calls "the temporarily abled." That means minimally making sure that the disabled have access to all means of transportation and buildings, including the raised platform in synagogues.

More substantially, blessing God for making us all different requires us to make it possible for people of all sorts, including the disabled, to compete on an equal plane for schools and jobs whose qualifications are irrelevant to their gender, race, religion—or disability. Sometimes that means being willing to alter the physical environment in which the work is to take place so that the disabled can do the work. At other times it may require schools to provide an interpreter for the deaf. More pervasively, it means overcoming any prejudice that the school authorities or employer might have about the disabled and refusing to bow to any such prejudice in potential customers or clients. There are certainly some economic costs and risks in this, but Jewish religious concepts and values demand that we pay those costs and take those risks.

Disabilities Late in Life

As we grow older, many of us become disabled in one way or another. Since the body is older and less flexible then, it is often harder to develop other parts of the body to compensate. Psychologically, too, adjustment is often even harder than it is for young people who are disabled, for older people are used to full maneuverability and now find that they are suddenly limited in what they can do. Their days become filled with frequent visits to doctors and physical therapists.

Boredom and loneliness also accompany old age. In times past, the elderly were at least honored and consulted for the life of experience and wisdom they had accrued. Since the conditions of life change so rapidly in this technological age, however, many of the young now think of the old as living in a vastly different era, whose lessons simply do not apply to the current world. Whether that is true or not is open to question, but they often do not even bother to find out. The old, then, are left to their own devices. The plaintive plea to God in the High Holy Day liturgy becomes ever more poignant: "Cast us not off to old age, do not abandon us when our powers fail."

One of the most bitter and resentful depictions of the disabilities of old age occurs in the last chapter of the Book of Kohelet (Ecclesiastes):

> When the guards of the house [the arms] become shaky,
> And the men of valor [the legs] are bent,
> And the maids that grind [the teeth], grown few, are idle,
> And the ladies that peer through the windows [the eyes]
>   grow dim,
> And the doors to the street [the ears] are shut—
> With the noise of the hand mill growing fainter,
> And the song of the bird growing feebler,
> And all the strains of music dying down;
> When one is afraid of heights
> And there is terror on the road.

For the almond tree [thought apparently dead in winter]
  may blossom [again],
The squill resume its burden [i.e., its blossom-stalk
  and leaves],
And the caper bush may bud again;
But man sets out for his eternal abode,
With mourners all around in the street . . . .
And the dust returns to the ground as it was,
And the lifebreath returns to God
Who bestowed it.
Utter futility—said Kohelet—
All is futile![55]

Kohelet's dismay is rooted, in part, in his conviction that for human beings there is no life after death, contrary to the plants he mentions that go into hibernation in winter only to revive in spring. The Pharisees' (rabbis') belief in a life after death may, for those who accept it, soften his frustration with life as a whole and its last stages in particular. Even so, the familiar physical waning that he describes in the opening lines cannot but engender anger and fear.

It is precisely in such a state that a person's Jewish grounding in the covenantal relationship with God and in the ultimate value God implants in us by creating us in the divine image must come to the fore. Disability is obviously not pleasant, and it may take considerable adjustment. Ultimately we all die, and according to the rabbis, at some point even death is good.[56] Until that time, though, we owe it to ourselves and to God to derive as much meaning from each day as possible.

That may require getting used to new, diminished physical circumstances. It may also require learning new skills to be able to negotiate life's simplest tasks. That can be frustrating and demeaning. A Jewish perspective on life, though, would urge us to do what we need to do in order to find ever new ways to add to the significance of our lives and of those around us.

This can take the form of learning new things or developing new interests. Some of the most meaningful activities involve others. If you are an elderly disabled person, you might volunteer to do a task for a charity or school, such as teaching someone to read. One increasingly popular activity you might undertake is to serve as a substitute grandparent for children with few adult role models, reading and telling them stories and responding with a willing ear and an open heart to their problems and joys. Depending upon your condition, you might even help others worse off than you are. You might also create an ethical will for your family and friends. This anonymous poem bespeaks a truth for the end of life just as much as it does for its earlier stages:

> I sought my God;
> My God I could not see.
> I sought my self;
> My self eluded me.
> I sought my brother,
> And I found all three.

The disabilities of old age can be disconcerting and even painful. Those who make up their minds, however, that they will live life to its fullest at each of its stages, helping others along the way, generally find that they can cope with their disabilities much more successfully than if they just resign themselves to them. They also find that they honor both themselves and God in the process.

CHAPTER TWELVE

Nonmedical Aspects
of Medical Care

S OME OF THE ISSUES THAT HAVE ARISEN IN MEDICAL ETHICS
in recent years are not strictly medical; they involve serious social considerations. Some, such as the availability
and cost of medical care, have gained the attention of policy experts and national and state politicians, whereas others, such
as the treatment of the disabled and the nonmedical treatment
of the sick—though less prominent in the national consciousness—affect our lives in ever more pervasive and important
ways.

Although these matters are not "medical" in the narrow
meaning of the word because they do not directly concern a
doctor's physical treatment of a patient, they are definitely medical in the broader understanding well known by ancient and
medieval physicians and now being relearned by modern medicine, namely, that a person's health is at least as much affected
by the availability of health care and by the spiritual support
provided to that person as by the direct application of medical
techniques. Because of the extremely high cost of much end-
stage medical care, contemporary doctors and hospitals have
turned to hospice care as an alternative to surgery and pills. The
exorbitant costs of other medical treatments have now reinforced that lesson with regard to other stages of human devel-

opment as well. Moreover, physicians are becoming increasingly aware that as important as their ministrations are—and nothing said here is intended to minimize that—health is also a function of the morale of the patient, and that is not likely to be boosted by a lonely, antiseptic hospital setting. Consequently, the nonmedical aspects of health care treated in this chapter are not really nonmedical; they rather fill out the larger picture of illness and health.

The Distribution of Health Care

Until the discovery of penicillin in 1938, physicians could do little to cure disease. From the time of the Greeks, doctors would try bloodletting, but that worked only for a small number of diseases, like polycythemia. In desperation, they would also operate in an attempt to cut a problem out of a patient, and so we have ample records of, for example, surgical removals of gangrenous legs and attempted Caesarian sections when a woman could not deliver her fetus vaginally. Surgery, though, was done without the benefit of modern anesthesia (although often the patient was made drunk to ease the pain); and through lack of either knowledge or ability, it was often done without making the surgical theater sanitary. As a result, many surgeries done before 1865, when Joseph Lister demonstrated the effectiveness of antiseptics, were lethal, for if the patient did not die of the trauma of the surgery itself, he or she would often die of ensuing infections. Preventive medicine was much better developed, although not uniformly practiced.

When physicians could not do much to heal a sick patient, their services were easily attainable, relatively cheap, and frankly not much sought after. "The best of physicians should go to hell," the Mishnah says,[1] reflecting people's frustration with doctors' inability to cure.

With the advent of antibiotics, other new drug therapies, and especially new diagnostic and surgical techniques, however, there has been an immense increase in the demand for medical care—precisely as it has become much more expensive. This raises not only the "micro" questions of how physicians and patients should treat a given person's disease but also the "macro" questions of how society should arrange for medical care to be distributed.

On both levels, the ultimate question is the one first posed by Immanuel Kant: nobody has a duty to do what humanly cannot be done, but once we gain the ability to do x, the moral question arises as to whether we should. On the micro level, that translates into the questions we considered in Chapter 8—namely, whether a person who has an irreversible, incurable illness must expend all of his or her resources (or those of the state or insurance company) in an effort to do what is, by all estimates, futile, or whether that person may engage in hospice care instead. On the macro level, this becomes the question of how much medical care should be provided to everyone as part of our collective duty to care for one another, and how that social obligation should be balanced against the community's other duties to provide benefits like education, defense, and roads and bridges.

As explained in Chapter 2, we do have the clear duty to try to heal, and this duty devolves upon both the physician and society. Because medical care before this century was largely ineffective and inexpensive, however, Jewish sources on distributing and paying for health care are understandably sparse. The classical sources that describe distribution of scarce resources and apportionment of the financial burden for communal services deal instead with questions like providing for the needy or rescuing someone from captivity. Still, the moral problems and their suggested solutions are often similar to those associated with scarcity and cost in modern medical care. We shall discuss the availability of medical care under conditions of scarcity in this section of this chapter and the cost of medical care in the next part.

As we noted in Chapter 2, Talmud describes ten prerequisites a city must have to make it fit for a Jewish scholar to live there, and a physician is one of the ten. Since each Jewish community needed a rabbi to interpret Jewish law and to teach the tradition, this list of requirements effectively makes it every Jewish community's responsibility to provide medical services:

A scholar [of Torah] should not reside in a city where [any of] the following ten things is missing: (1) a court of justice that [has the power to] impose flagellation and decree monetary penalties; (2) a charity fund collected by [at least] two people and distributed by [at least] three; (3) a synagogue; (4) public baths; (5) a privy; (6) a circumciser *(mohel)*; (7) a physician; (8) a scribe [who also functions as a notary]; (9) a [kosher] butcher; (10) and a school-master. Rabbi Akiba is quoted as including also several kinds of fruit [in the list] because they are beneficial to one's eyesight.[2]

If particular forms of medical treatment are scarce or expensive, though, who should get them? While this question of triage is most dramatic when the decision is one of life or death, it affects the quality of people's lives in less threatening situations as well. Who, for example, should get a hip replacement when society cannot afford to provide one for everyone who would benefit from one? Who should be granted a heart bypass operation or transplant, and who should be denied that? Which AIDS patients should get the regimen of drugs now available to lengthen their lives, if not cure the disease, and for whom are those drugs just too expensive? In many ways, in times past when we could do much less, making moral decisions about health care was easier: since the state of medical science gave us no other choice, we could let nature take its course, with a little help from physicians in relieving pain, in full confidence that that was the moral high road. In the High Holy Day liturgy, "who shall live and who shall die" is God's decision; now we find ourselves all too often in the uncomfortable position of having the responsibility to decide that ourselves.

Five Classical Criteria for Triage

The rabbinic passages that might give us some guidance about triage go in five different directions. They all deal with saving lives, although generally not in a medical context, since medical intervention to save a life was usually impossible. The analogous cases in the literature therefore occur instead in contexts like saving a drowning person or rescuing someone from captivity.

One passage in the Mishnah makes the decision a matter of the victim's hierarchy in society—with knowledge of Torah trumping all other social stations:

> A man takes precedence over a woman when it comes to saving a life or restoring something lost, but a woman takes precedence with regard to the provision of clothes and redemption from captivity. A priest *(kohen)* takes precedence over a Levite, a Levite over an Israelite, an Israelite over a bastard, a bastard over a Nathin,[3] a Nathin over a proselyte, and a proselyte over an emancipated slave. This order of precedence applies only when all these were equal in other respects, but if the bastard was a scholar and the High Priest an ignoramus, the learned bastard takes precedence over the ignorant High Priest.[4]

As the Talmud and codes note,[5] a person must first save himself or herself; subsequently, the order of this Mishnaic passage holds. A man takes precedence over a woman, according to traditional commentaries, because a man has more religious obligations to fulfill and therefore more opportunities to carry out God's will. The rest of the hierarchy is built on social status, first within the Jewish community and then outside it. When the *Shulhan Arukh,* an important sixteenth-century code, repeats this ruling, it adds one other familial element to the hierarchy:

> Whoever is greater in wisdom takes precedence over anyone else. But if one of them was his teacher or his father, then even though there is someone greater than they in wisdom, his teacher or his father who is also learned [a scholar, *talmid hakham*] takes precedence over the one who knows more than he.[6]

Contemporary Jews would undoubtedly find morally repugnant not only some of the criteria embodied in these attempts to articulate a social order of preference but also the very notion of creating such a hierarchy in the first place. Even though the list of priorities appears in an anonymous mishnah, a style usually taken to mean that the ruling represents the position of the majority of the rabbis, and even though this ruling does have some echoes in the later codes, there is also evidence that the rabbis themselves did not like making decisions in this way and that they would never use this method in actual cases. Specifically, in talmudic cases where one would have expected this mishnah to be invoked, it is strikingly ignored. That is especially true in the famous case where two men in a desert discover that they have only enough water for one of them to survive. Rabbi Akiba and Ben Betairah disagree about what the men should do, but neither suggests that the two men should ascertain whether one is a *kohen* or whether one knows more Torah than the other.[7] Since each of us inherits inestimable worth from being created in the divine image, deciding difficult triage cases on the basis of social hierarchy or even on the basis of learning was simply unthinkable.

However objectionable it may be to invoke a social hierarchy to decide whose life to save, the order of preference in these sources remarkably does not consider the utilitarian benefits the various groups could offer society, and therefore factors like age and skill do not count.[8] The criteria are instead based on the obligations and abilities of the individuals involved to know and do the will of God and, in the *Shulḥan Arukh,* on the duty to honor one's parents and teachers.

Jewish laws on charity provide a second reservoir of precedents that may guide the provision of health care. In general, individuals are most responsible for those closest in relationship to them. For example, while it is a legal duty to support one's children while young, to do so after they have attained the age of majority (age thirteen) is an act of charity. Similarly, as a corollary of the duty to honor one's parents, it is obligatory to ensure that they have enough on which to live, but anything beyond that is an act of charity. Thus these gifts to parents and adult children need to be classified in the hierarchy of other potential recipients of one's donations, and the *Shulḥan Arukh* does it this way:

> One who gives [money] to his grown sons and daughters, for whom he is no longer legally liable for their sustenance, to teach the sons Torah and to guide the daughters in the right path, and similarly

one who gives gifts to his father [and mother] when they need them is in the category of one who gives *tzedakah* [required charity]. Moreover, he must prefer them to others, and even if [we are not talking about] his child or parent but his relative, he must prefer him [his relative] to every other person . . . . And the poor of his own household take precedence over the poor of his city, and the poor of his city take precedence over the poor of another city.[9]

Similarly, according to the Tosefta, a second-century rabbinic source, in providing what we would now call welfare, communal authorities were to prefer the poor of their own town over other poor people:

> The soup-kitchen [provides enough food] for a full day, but the communal fund gives [sufficient food to last] from one week to the next. The soup-kitchen [provides food] for anybody, but the communal fund [gives support only] to the poor of that locale. [A poor person] living there for thirty days attains the status of being a resident of the locale for [purposes of receiving assistance]from the communal fund. But [to receive] shelter [he must have lived there] for six months, and to be liable to the town tax [he must have been a resident] for twelve months.[10]

If health care is to be seen as a benefit to be provided by individual donors and by the community as a whole, like other forms of economic support, then these sources would argue that whether the party making the decision is an individual or a community, health care should be provided to one's own first.

One could object to this line of reasoning directly, claiming on some ground that individuals and their relatives have no prior right to their own attention and care, that people must care for others just as much as they care for themselves. That, though, would most likely be an uphill fight within both Jewish and secular systems of ethics, both of which assert the duty to care for oneself first.

One might also object to this criterion on the narrower grounds, however, that health care is significantly different from property and that decisions regarding health care should therefore not be based on principles that govern the distribution of property. There are, after all, some clear dissimilarities between health care and other forms of economic support. One might assert, for example, that health care is different from food and shelter because, however displeasing it may be, people can beg and live on the streets for quite some time without imperiling their lives, whereas health care is a basic human need that often has lethal consequences if not met immediately. While one might prefer one's relatives in matters of food, clothing, and shelter, then, one must ignore that claim in deciding who gets health care. (According to this line of reasoning, one would provide even food and shelter only when the results of not doing so would be lethal, unless the society could afford more.)

On the other hand, one could also argue that providing health care is exactly like supplying food, clothing, and shelter on both pragmatic and humanitarian grounds. Specifically, since an ounce of prevention is still worth a pound of cure, the very duty to provide health care requires us first to supply food, clothing, and shelter wherever necessary in order to ward off disease. Furthermore, since sickness is inherently degrading, preventing it through the provision of food, clothing, shelter, vaccines, and health education is much more humane than seeking to cure a person once sick. If one supports this line of reasoning, then, one might employ the same criteria that govern the distribution of these goods to the provision of health care—namely, oneself first, one's relatives next, then one's townsfolk and fellow citizens, and finally all other people in need.

A third set of sources we might use as the basis for a Jewish ethic for the distribution of health care concerns the prioritizing of the community's duties to fund specific needs. The *Shulḥan Arukh* specifies the order of preferences as follows:

> There are those who say that the commandment to [build and support] a synagogue takes precedence [over] the commandment to give charity [*tzedakah*, to the poor], but the commandment to give money to the youth to learn Torah or to the sick among the poor takes precedence over the commandment to build and support a synagogue.[11]

One must feed the hungry before one clothes the naked [since starvation is taken to be a more direct threat to the person's life than exposure]. If a man and a woman came to ask for food, we put the woman before the man [because the man can beg with less danger to himself]; similarly, if a man and woman came to ask for clothing, and similarly, if a male orphan and a female orphan came to ask for funds to be married, we put the woman before the man.[12]

Redeeming captives takes precedence over sustaining the poor and clothing them [since the captive's life is always in direct and immediate danger], and there is no commandment more important than redeeming captives. Therefore, the community may change the usage of any money it collected for communal needs for the sake of redeeming captives. Even if they collected it for the sake of building a synagogue, and even if they bought the wood and stones and designated them for building the synagogue, such that it is forbidden to sell them for another commanded purpose, it is nevertheless permitted to sell them for the sake of redeeming captives. But if they built it already, they should not sell it . . . .

Every moment that one delays redeeming captives where it is possible to do so quickly, one is like a person who sheds blood.[13]

The list of communal priorities today may be the same or different from what it was in the sixteenth century, when these paragraphs were written, but these sources would argue for identifying a list of communal needs and ranking them according to some clear and justifiable measure, presumably on the basis of broader Jewish values. The criterion embedded in the *Shulḥan Arukh's* list is that the saving of the life most threatened must come first, the saving of lives in danger but not as much at risk comes second, followed by the education of the youth and the curing of the sick among the poor, and then either the provision of food and (then) clothing to the poor (with women coming first) or the building and maintaining of synagogues so that Jewish life and the Jewish tradition can be carried on.

The *Shulḥan Arukh's* prioritization is a combination, and hence a recognition, of the varying needs of the community — physical, educational, religious, and social. If the Jewish community of that time, rather than the state, additionally had been responsible for the society's economic infrastructure, undoubtedly issues like building and maintaining roads and bridges and providing for the common defense would also have found a place on the list. Each of these items can be easily justified in terms of broader Jewish commitments to life, human dignity, worship and other religious expression, education, economic solvency, and close social ties. Consequently, if one were to create a contemporary list based on these Jewish values for funding communal projects in the United States, it might well differ somewhat in order and in the scope of application from that of the *Shulḥan Arukh,* but its substance would probably not be all that different. Saving lives that are threatened by human attackers would clearly come first, followed, I think, by providing food and clothing to prevent disease, followed by some order of curative health care, defense, education, culture, and economic infrastructure.

Yet a fourth criterion one could read out of Jewish sources is that health care should be provided to the ones who need it most. Thus the *Shulḥan Arukh* includes the following paragraph:

> We redeem a woman before a man. If, however, the captors are used to engaging in sodomy, we redeem a man before a woman.[14]

This ruling is clearly based on the author's judgment of the relative needs of women and men in captivity. Since male captors would be more likely to rape women captives than to sodomize males, we must redeem women first, for they need to be saved not only from slave labor but also from sexual violation. If, on the other hand, the captors are known to sodomize male captives, we must redeem men first, for sodomy is, in this author's estimation at any rate, an even greater threat to the captive's life and dignity than rape is. Whether one agrees with that assessment or not, it is clear that the attempt of this ruling is to base the priority of recipients on whose needs are greatest.

This hierarchy of need takes precedence over the hierarchy of social position and personal duty, as the next ruling in the *Shulḥan Arukh* makes clear:

If he, his father, and his teacher are in captivity, he takes precedence over his teacher [because saving one's own life comes first], and his teacher takes precedence over his father [because his father brought him into this world, but his teacher prepares him for the World to Come]; but his mother takes precedence over all of them.[15]

Even though the man has a duty to honor his father and his teacher, and even though saving them from captivity is included in those duties, saving himself from that life-threatening situation takes precedence over those duties.[16] However, saving his mother from captivity takes precedence over all the other males, even himself, because she is in peril not only of being killed, as they are, but of being sexually violated as well. Because her need is therefore greater than theirs, she comes first on the list. According to these sources, then, one would award the expensive operation or the organ transplant to the one who needs it most, and that, in turn, presumably depends upon an assessment of who can benefit from it most.

Even if the criterion is to be need, though, correct needs calculus is often unclear. So, for example, normally the person who will die soonest without a given procedure would be saved first because the short-term need is greatest. If, however, that person needs not only this procedure but several others, and if even then the prognosis is not good, the scarce or expensive procedure might instead be awarded to someone else who could wait a bit but must have the procedure soon in order to live and will in all probability live a long and productive life thereafter.

Finally, a fifth strain in Jewish thought and law objects to any hierarchy—whether governed by social position, family ties, communal duties, or even the relative needs of the specific individuals involved in the choice—emphasizing instead the equality of everyone. This approach is most dramatically illustrated in a mishnah that has influenced our discussion on many matters. It describes the warning given to the witnesses in a case where there is a possibility of capital punishment. The person whose value is being stressed is thus someone accused of a major crime, and one would expect at least as much value to accrue to all those who had not committed such crimes. Moreover, there are two manuscript versions of this mishnah, one saying that all Israelites (Jews) are to be considered equal in the worth of their lives, and one omitting that social reference and thus declaring the divine worth of every human being:

> For this reason Adam was created as a single person, to teach you that anyone who destroys one (Israelite) soul is described in Scripture as if he or she destroyed an entire world, and anyone who sustains one (Israelite) soul is described in Scripture as if he or she sustained an entire world. . . . Therefore each and every person must say: "For me the world was created."[17]

The Creation story also undergirds this expression of the same egalitarian ethic:

> Ben Azzai said, The most important verse in the Torah is this (Genesis 5:1): "This is the record of Adam's line. When God created the human being, God made the human in the likeness of God."[18]

A somewhat different expression of this focus on the equality of everyone's worth is embodied in this talmudic watchword:

> A favorite saying of the Rabbis of Yavneh was: I am God's creature, and my fellow [i.e., the *am ha-aretz*, or nonstudent] is God's creature. My work is in the town, and his work is in the country. I rise early for my work, and he rises early for his work. Just as he does not presume to do my work, so I do not presume to do his work. Will you say, I do much [in the way of Torah] and he does little? [No, for] we have learned, "One may do much or one may do little; it is all one, so long as each directs his/her heart to heaven."[19]

Unlike the hierarchy of the first mishnah cited in this section, this talmudic text refuses to see even knowledge of Torah as grounds for measuring a person's worth. Instead, all are equal as long as they are trying to do God's will. This is a somewhat narrower group than all human beings, for after all, some people—criminals, for example—are presumably not doing God's will, at least in the act that brought them to prison. This talmudic text, though, still argues in the direction of equalizing everyone in terms of lives valued and, ultimately, saved.

Although this guideline for the distribution of health care evokes warm, universalistic feelings in us, as well as deep theological roots in our common humanity and our common origins as the creations of God, it falls victim to the hard, pragmatic realities that prevent us from giving all things to all people. These egalitarian principles, however, must have a call on us if we are to take our Jewish roots seriously.

Applying These Principles: A Specific Case

One rabbinic text represents the struggle between these principles more graphically than any other. Not only does it include differing opinions, which themselves are open to differing interpretations, but the story also appears in two differing forms. All of this indicates the extent to which the tradition struggled with defining what constitutes just distribution.

The first opinion in the first version is this:

> Caravans of men are walking down a road, and they are accosted by non-Jews who say to them: "Give us one from among you that we may kill him; otherwise we shall kill you all." Though all may be killed, they may not hand over a single soul of Israel. However, if the demand is for a specified individual like Sheva, son of Bikhri, they should surrender him rather than all be killed.[20]

The first clause, rooted in some of the texts we saw in the fifth line of reasoning above, asserts the ultimate divine value of each human being. The inhabitants of the besieged city may not become accessories to murder by singling out any one of them, even though refusing to pick one of their number will mean the death of them all. The second clause asserts, however, that if *the enemy* singles out a person in the city who is himself liable for the death penalty anyway (as Sheva, son of Bikhri, was in the biblical story in II Samuel 20), then the inhabitants should surrender him rather than all be killed. Handing him over may itself be construed as complicity in the crime, but it is a lesser degree of involvement because it was the enemy, and not they, who chose who should die, and in any case he was independently liable for the death penalty. Even so, handing him over to the enemy rather than executing him according to legal procedures is justified only by the need to save everyone else.

In the second section of this source, however, Rabbi Judah maintains that the citizens of the city may save themselves even if the designated person is not liable for the death penalty:

> Rabbi Judah said: When do these words apply [that they may hand over to the enemy only someone who is named and also liable for the death penalty like Sheva ben Bikhri]?[21] When he [the individual in question] is inside [the city walls] and they [the enemy] are outside. But if he is inside and they [the enemy] are inside, since he would be slain and they [the other city dwellers] would be slain, let them surrender him [that is, someone named by the enemy but not liable for the death penalty] so that not all of them will be slain.

Here Rabbi Judah is saying that if the enemy is still outside the city walls and, therefore, there is a chance that all the city dwellers will be able to outlast the siege and survive, they should not hand over any innocent party, even if the enemy names a specific person. In that situation, Rabbi Judah agrees with the first opinion above. But if the enemy has already broken inside the walls, such that everyone is in immediate danger of being slain, the city dwellers may hand over the named person, even if she or he is not liable for the death penalty. In so doing, they are, of course, indirectly involved in causing the innocent person's death, but Rabbi Judah permits that degree of complicity when the objective situation makes it clear that the city dwellers would otherwise all die and when it is the enemy, and not they, who choose the one to die.

Is it plausible to use this source as a basis for health care decisions? There is a clear disparity between the situation in this source and health care: although some strains of the tradition maintain that sickness is the result of sin,[22] most, and certainly most Jews today, would deny that nexus, at least in the majority of cases.[23] This source, though, speaks of being guilty of a crime for which the penalty is death, whereas today, at least, we would say that the vast majority of terminally ill people are not dying due to any misdeeds on their part. As a result, the criteria for resolving the dilemma of the siege may not coincide with those appropriate for distributing health care.

On the other hand, though, this source is directly parallel to the dilemmas we face in health care if we see death or illness as an enemy besieging us. Since our frailty and mortality make us continually susceptible to illness and, ultimately, death, I do not think it is stretching credulity unduly to think of ourselves in that way. It certainly is the case that there are sick and dying people within any human population at all times and that some of them are more immediately threatened than others. It is, then, as if the enemy is singling out those people who are especially sick or actually dying.

According to this interpretation, the first clause of this source on siege would demand that we seek to protect everyone's life, even if that means that all will die. That is, we may not single out some to get a cure while others do not; either all must get what they need or none must, even if that means that many will die.

The second clause qualifies this, however, asserting that if given individuals are not only sick or dying but directly responsible for their illness or impending death through habits like smoking or alcoholism, they are at least somewhat to blame for their situation, especially if they were repeatedly warned. The medical care for such people can be forgone (they may be given up to the enemy) in favor of providing medical care for those whose patterns of living did not contribute to their illness. Since this position invokes moral criteria to make one ineligible for communal protection, one might also argue that, according to this opinion, prisoners would not be eligible for organ transplants or other scarce or expensive medical care until and unless every law-abiding citizen who needed such care received it. These, though, would be the only exceptions to universal care tolerated.

One would imagine, however, that, consistent with the fourth principle enunciated above, if a given therapy is in short supply, even those who hold this position would permit physicians to identify those who can most benefit from it and apply the principle of equality only among them. In line with this, Rabbi

Menaḥem Meiri (1249–1316), an important medieval rabbi, says that if the person designated by the enemy is a *terefah*, that is, one suffering from a terminal illness that doctors presume will kill the person in a year or less,[24] he or she may be handed over to the enemy:

> It goes without saying that in the case of a group of travelers, if one of them was a *terefah*, he may be surrendered in order to save the lives of the rest, since the killer of a *terefah* is exempt from the death penalty.[25]

After this first opinion is stated in our source, Rabbi Judah qualifies the principle of equality further. Applying his position on siege to health care, he holds that if supplies are short, we may and should stop aggressively treating those singled out by the Angel of Death even if they did not directly contribute to their illness so that those who *can* be saved do not die. Presumably, though, we would continue to treat even the terminally ill with palliative care. Similarly, since Rabbi Judah says that those under siege should give up the person destined by the enemy to die, regardless of guilt, if a convicted felon could benefit from a kidney transplant more than a free person could, the felon should get it. In general, for Rabbi Judah the moral quality of the individual is irrelevant in deciding who should get health care; only the relative potential for healing counts.

Normally, when a rabbinic source records an unnamed opinion and then a named one on the same issue, the former is understood to be the opinion of the majority and therefore the law. As a result, in the source we have been discussing, the law would be according to the first, anonymous opinion and not Rabbi Judah. The Jerusalem Talmud, however, adds two further sections that complicate matters further. The first is this:

> Resh Lakish stated: [He may be surrendered] only if he is deserving of death as Sheva, son of Bikhri. Rabbi Yoḥanan said: Even if he is not deserving of death as Sheva, son of Bikhri.[26]

Resh Lakish is ruling in accordance with the unnamed opinion discussed above and Rabbi Yoḥanan is ruling in accordance with Rabbi Judah. This is surprising on two grounds. First, it is Rabbi Yohanan himself who established the rule that the law is according to an anonymous mishnah,[27] and here he is disagreeing with it. Second, Rabbi Yohanan (c. 180–c. 279 C.E.) was the founder of the rabbinical academy in Tiberias and arguably the most important rabbi of his generation, and in his many disagreements with his brother-in-law, Resh Lakish, it was his (Rabbi Yohanan's) opinion that was generally followed.[28] In other words, if the general rules of authority are followed, within one generation there was a shift in the accepted opinion on this issue, such that the person was no longer required to be culpable in order for his or her surrender to the enemy to be justified, as long as the enemy had singled him or her out.

Up to this point in our analysis of this source, it seems that there are some categories of people, however narrowly or broadly defined, to whom medical care may be denied. The fourth section of this source, however, dispels any sense of an emerging consensus:

> Ulla, son of Qoseb, was wanted by the [non-Jewish] government. He arose and fled to Rabbi Joshua ben Levi at Lydda. They [troops] came, surrounded the city, and said: "If you do not hand him over to us, we will destroy the city." Rabbi Joshua ben Levi went up to him, persuaded him to submit and gave him up [to them]. Now Elijah [the prophet], of blessed memory, had been in the habit of visiting him [Rabbi Joshua], but he [now] ceased visiting him. He [Rabbi Joshua] fasted several fasts and Elijah appeared and said to him: "Shall I reveal myself to informers [betrayers]?" He [Rabbi Joshua] said: "Have I not carried out a *mishnah* [a rabbinic ruling]?" Said he [Elijah]: "Is this a ruling for the pious *[mishnat hasidim]*?" [Another version: "This should have been done through others and not by yourself."]

Since Ulla, son of Qoseb, apparently stood indicted by the government, all of the opinions discussed above would have instructed Rabbi Joshua to do what he did; that is not denied in this last section. He is nevertheless castigated because while ruling that way may fulfill the demands of justice, it is not exemplary. Instead, Elijah claims, he should have been more pious in defending Ulla's life. That course of action, of course, would have endangered all the other inhabitants of Lydda, but this last source seems to demand such a risk; even if it seems quite certain that the troops would kill them all, Rabbi Joshua was obliged to try to save them all, including Ulla. He gave in much too easily.

According to this version of this last source, medical care should never be denied. It may be pragmatically sound to deny expensive operations or scarce drugs to those who are unlikely to benefit from them, and doing so may even fulfill the demands of justice, but that is not the kind of social policy appropriate to pious Jews. Instead, everyone who has the least chance to benefit from a drug or procedure should receive it. Piety would make it unthinkable to deny any human, created in the image of God, any help we can give; and piety would also have us trust that despite our current calculations of cost or shortage, when the need arises, God will provide. (These last two understandings of the role of piety in this decision are not in the text; they are my own interpretation of what it might mean by naming piety to be the characteristic that Rabbi Joshua failed to demonstrate.)

This position takes human equality to its logical extreme. Contrary to the fourth principle enunciated above, Elijah, based on this reading, would not allow differentiation among potential recipients of a therapy even by degree of medical need. He would presumably be willing to exclude those who do not need a given therapy at all, but that would be the only group to be denied medical care. Even felons convicted of a capital offense must get the care they need. Later Jewish authorities, presumably on the basis of such a reading of Elijah's words, rule just this way.[29] Under conditions of scarcity, both Elijah, if interpreted this way, and these later Jewish authorities would, I imagine, support a lottery system among all those who need a given form of medical care, much as some authorities in France first proposed in the early months of 1996 when a new American anti-AIDS drug was first delivered to that country but in short supply.

Another possible reading of Elijah's first response to Rabbi Joshua understands Elijah to be complaining not about Rabbi Joshua's actions but rather about his failure to be bothered by the tragedy of the situation. It is possible, that is, that Elijah is simply demanding that Rabbi Joshua acknowledge that the choice is morally distressing and emotionally heartbreaking and that no matter what one does, rough moral and emotional edges will remain.

If applied to contemporary medicine, this interpretation would argue that we should make necessary triage decisions, but both in doing so and after having done so, we must demonstrate sufficient moral and emotional sensitivity to be bothered by our inability to respond fully to all the moral and human needs present. We should also seek to alleviate the human suffering involved, even if the decision to deprive expensive therapy to some people is both necessary and morally correct.

The other version of Elijah's response, "This should have been done through others and not by yourself," would lead to yet a different conclusion. Rabbi Joshua's decision was the correct one, according to this reading, and it should be carried out. However, since it appears to lack piety, someone else should have made it. If we then ask who and why, the source is silent. It seems like a classic case of avoiding the responsibility a community leader has and should exercise. We can only guess that if someone else, presumably someone in a position of authority but less well known than Rabbi Joshua, had made the decision, then the community could still retain its sense of its own piety and that of its most visible leaders, even as it did what was just and what it had to do.

The application of this last version to contemporary medical care is not straightforward. I do think, though, that it has something to teach us. It is not fair to ask physicians to decide who shall get scarce or expensive medical treatments and who not; society as a whole must assume the moral burden of that decision. It is also against society's best interests to place the burden of such decisions on physicians, for the doctor must be seen by the patient as his or her advocate with only the patient's well-being in mind. Part of the physician's ability to gain the respect of the patient, so that the patient will obey the doctor's instructions, in fact, depends on the patient's trust in the physician as someone genuinely trying to promote his or her own welfare. This view would therefore argue against "gag rules" in medicine, according to which physicians may not tell patients that forms of treatment not covered by their health plan are better for them; physicians must be free to advise the patient according to the best medical information they know.

Although doctors should not be the ones to make the decisions that would limit medical care in the face of cost or scarcity, someone must do that; we do not, after all, live in a world where every good can be provided to everyone without limit. As the words of Elijah to Rabbi Judah demonstrate, decisions about the extent of health care offered must be made, but they should be made by others. According to one model, that of socialized medicine, government authorities who can speak for the people as a whole make these decisions. In a modification of this, the Oregon model, those insured by the government choose as a group what they want for the amount of money the government is willing and able to provide for health care.

At the opposite end of the spectrum from these models of group decisions are systems that maximize individual choice. Capitalism, when applied to health care, would argue for private insurance companies, each competing in a market in which individuals can buy whatever they want. The problem with this, of course, is that what people want depends critically on what they can afford, and some are unable to afford anything; one wonders whether we should tolerate a society in which some people do not have even minimal medical coverage (however that is defined). Moreover, except for the wealthiest segment of society, it is the employer who chooses the health plan, not the individual employee. Thus the high degree of individual autonomy that capitalism promises is, except for the rich, a myth. We will explore this issue further in the next section on the cost of medical care. Suffice it to say here, though, that, in accordance with Elijah's instructions to

Rabbi Judah, decisions regarding the scope of health care should not be made by physicians alone and maybe should not even be communicated by them.

The Cost of Medical Care

Lessons from the Sources and Jewish Historical Practice

Who is responsible for paying for medical care? The Jewish tradition divides that responsibility among the physician, the individual, family members, and the community.

Normally, Jewish law permits physicians to charge a fee for their services. Indeed, the Talmud opines that "a physician who charges nothing is worth nothing"![30] At the same time, there is great concern that the poor should have access to medical services. The Talmud thus approvingly sets forth the example of Abba, the bleeder, who

> placed a box outside his office where his fees were to be deposited. Whoever had money put it in, but those who had none could come in without feeling embarrassed. When he saw a person who was in no position to pay, he would offer him some money, saying to him, "Go, strengthen yourself [after the bleeding operation]."[31]

There are similar examples among medieval Jewish physicians; the ethic must have been quite powerful, because it was not until the nineteenth century that a rabbi ruled that the communal court should force physicians to give free services to the poor if they did not do so voluntarily.[32]

In our own day the cost of medical care no longer puts it out of reach of the poor alone. Most people simply cannot pay for some of the new procedures, no matter how much money they have or can borrow. The size of the problem makes even conscientious and morally sensitive physicians think that any individual effort on their part to resolve this issue is useless. Moreover, the costs they themselves assumed in gaining a modern medical education must somehow be repaid—to say nothing of malpractice insurance, overhead for their offices and for the hospitals in which they practice, staff, and the like. Paying for medical care in American society therefore becomes a critical issue, and its burden cannot fall to physicians alone.

Indeed, like other people, doctors have a right to earn a living, and Jewish law imposes a limit on them no less than on other Jews as to the percentage of their income that they may donate to charity:

> If a poor person comes and requests enough for his needs and the one asked does not have enough to supply him, then he gives him what he can. How much is that? Up to a fifth of his assets is an elegant way of fulfilling the commandment; a tenth is the intermediate amount; and less than that is stingy. In any case, one should not give less than a third of a *shekel* per year, for anyone who does that has not fulfilled the commandment [to give charity]. Even the poor person who is himself sustained by charity must give charity to another.[33]

Individuals also bear some of the responsibility for paying for their own medical care. Thus the *Shulḥan Arukh* rules as follows:

> If someone is taken captive and he has property but does not want to redeem himself, we redeem him [with the money his property will bring] against his will.[34]

While this source speaks of redemption from captivity and not health care, the duty to redeem captives is based on the danger to their lives in captivity. This rule about financing a person's freedom is thus a reasonable source for determining whether an individual has a financial responsibility for his or her own health care as well, and the ruling makes it clear that one has.

Moreover, one must pay for one's own health care before one pays for anyone else's, for saving one's own life takes precedence over saving anyone else's. The Talmud makes this clear in discussing the case referred to earlier of two men in a desert, one of whom is carrying a flask of water when they discover that they have only enough water for one of them to make it back to civilization and survive. There is a dispute as to what to do, but the law is ultimately according to Rabbi Akiba, who says that whoever has possession of the flask of water should drink it. He justifies that ruling exegetically on the basis of the law in Leviticus that one must give to the poor "so that the poor will live *with you*," but that can only happen, as Rabbi Akiba notes, if you are alive first.[35] On a moral plane, Rabbi Akiba is saying that since suicide and murder are both equally prohibited, one should remain as passive as possible in a tragic situation such as this and let the bad outcome result from nature taking its course rather than from your conscious action. Despite contemporary opinions about euthanasia to the contrary, Jewish law draws a clear line between the moral culpability of consciously acting in a prohibited way versus remaining passive in a situation. In any case, this precedent establishes that a person must first pay for his or her own health care and then worry about others.

In addition to paying for his own health care, a man assumes an explicit obligation in marriage, according to Jewish law, to pay for the medical care of his wife.[36] If both spouses are taken captive, both of their lives may be threatened, in which case the man's obligation to care for himself first overrides his duty to his wife. Since the captors want ransom money, though, it would be counterproductive for them to kill the couple. Therefore, because the wife was more at risk of being raped than the husband was of being sodomized, the *Shulḥan Arukh* rules that the husband's resources must be used to pay for preserving her health before his:

> If a man and his wife are in captivity, his wife takes precedence over him. The court invades his property to redeem her. Even if he stands and shouts, "Do not redeem her from my property!" we do not listen to him.[37]

Thus a man has a clear duty to provide medical care for his wife—especially, but not exclusively, when her life is threatened in captivity or, presumably, in some other way.

A man has the same duty vis-à-vis his children and other relatives if they cannot care for themselves. Once again, the precedent for this comes from the laws of redemption from captivity:

> A father must redeem his son if the father has money but the son does not. Gloss [by Rabbi Moses Isserles]: And the same is true for one relative redeeming another, the closer relative comes first, for all of them may not enrich themselves and thrust the [redemption of] their relatives on the community.[38]

In our own more egalitarian society today, this would presumably mean that spouses of either gender have responsibility for the health care of each other and of their children.

The immediate implication of these teachings is that one may not preserve the family fortune and make the Jewish community or government pay for one's health care, except to the extent that the government itself makes provision for all sick elderly citizens in programs like Medicare without restrictions based on the recipient's income or estate. Absent such provisions in the law, one must provide for one's own health care and for that of one's relatives. One might do that by using one's own assets or through buying a health insurance policy, either privately or through one's employer. According to these sources, one may call on public aid only when and if one qualifies for aid to the poor through programs like Medicaid.

The individual also has a duty to contribute to the medical care of others besides one's family. Although this is never spelled out in just those words, the rabbis, as we have seen, see the absence of providing health care as shedding blood. Since the physician alone cannot be expected to bear the costs of health care for those who cannot afford it, this duty devolves upon the community, and the costs of health care for the poor become part of the charity one must give. According to Maimonides:

> If a person wants to give no charity at all or less than is fitting for him, the court compels him and flogs him for disobedience until he gives as much as the court estimates is proper. The court may even seize his property in his presence and take from him what it is proper for that person to give. It may pawn possessions for purposes of charity, even on the eve of the Sabbath.[39]

With donations from, or taxes on, its members, the community as a whole has the duty to pay for the health care of those who cannot afford it themselves. Therefore, the sick enjoy priority over other indigent persons in their claim to private or public assistance. As we have seen, Joseph Caro, author of the *Shulḥan Arukh,* records the view that while contributions to erect a synagogue take precedence over ordinary forms of charity, even the synagogue's needs must give way to the requirements of the indigent sick. The sick, in turn, may not refuse such aid if they require it to get well.[40]

Reliance on the generosity and ethical sensitivity of physicians for the care of the poor was the norm, but there were cases where Jewish communities organized medical care in a form of socialized medicine. In medieval Spain, for example, Jews played a prominent role in the state's program of socialized medicine, and in other places Jewish communities on their own hired surgeons, physicians, nurses, and midwives among their staff of salaried servants.[41] Whatever the arrangement, both the community and individual doctors were under the obligation to heal, and that was taken very seriously.

The community in turn must use its resources wisely, a demand that can serve as the moral basis within the Jewish tradition for some system of managed care. The community must balance its commitment to afford health care against the need to provide other services. As we have seen, the Talmud lists ten such services, but it assumes others that the non-Jewish government in talmudic and medieval times took care of. However we identify vital communal services in our own day, since no community's resources are limitless, each one must ensure that those who receive public assistance for health care deserve it.

Thus if a person repeatedly endangers his or her health through practices—such as smoking, drug or alcohol abuse, or overeating—known to constitute major risks, the community may decide to impose a limit on the public resources that such a person can call upon to finance the curative procedures she or he needs as a consequence of these unhealthy habits. The legitimacy of the community in enforcing such limits is established in Jewish sources with regard to captivity, the case that has served as the paradigm for many of the rules of assessment of cost described above:

> He who sold himself to a non-Jew or borrowed money from them, and they took him captive for his debt, if it happens once or twice, we redeem him, but the third time we do not redeem him. . . . But if they sought to kill him, we redeem him even if it is after many times.[42]

Here, as in the other instances of establishing policies for distributing and paying for health care, extending the rules of rescue from captivity to preserving life and health in other ways is, I think, not only reasonable but compelling. In this instance, it would mean that everyone is helped in overcoming the consequences of the first and perhaps even the second indiscretion that endangers the person's life, but beyond that the community no longer has the duty to act.

Even when the person will definitely die unless something drastic is done, the community has the right to assess the chances of success before deciding to expend the resources. The precedents on captivity generally serve as good models for many of our contemporary medical decisions, but here they may not, for whereas the *Shulḥan Arukh* assumes that a high enough ransom will surely redeem the captive, even after many times, medical procedures do not carry that certainty. So, for example, smokers cannot rightfully expect the community to pay for repeated lung transplants, and alcoholics may not call upon the community to pay for repeated liver transplants. Indeed, in light of the shortage of organs for transplantation, the cost of the procedure, and the improbability that smokers and alcoholics will benefit significantly from such transplants, current medical practice denies them even one transplant. This policy is also warranted from the standpoint of Jewish law: individuals must take responsibility for the consequences of their behavior, especially after being duly warned through captivity or sickness.

Those, of course, who have no resources to pay for health care may accept public assistance to procure it. In fact, they must do so, for to refuse needed care is to endanger their lives, which in Jewish law is tantamount to committing suicide. Still, the *Shulḥan Arukh* strongly condemns those who use public funds for their health care when they do not need to do so, and it appreciates those who postpone calling upon the public purse for as long as possible:

> Anyone who does not need to take from the charity fund and deceives the community and takes will not die until he does indeed need charity from others. And whoever cannot live unless he takes charity—for example, an elderly person or a sick person or a suffering person—but he forces himself not to take [communal funds] is like one who sheds blood [namely, his own] and he is liable for his own life, and his pain is only the product of sin and transgression. But anyone who needs to take [charity] but puts himself instead into a position of pain and pushes off the time [when he takes charity] and lives a life of pain so that he will not burden the community will not die until he sustains others, and about him Scripture says, "Blessed is the man who trusts in God."[43]

Conversely, unless a given drug or medical procedure is so scarce that the government has put limits on who may obtain it even with their own money, individual patients who have the money to afford something that the government or their private plan does not provide may decide to pay for the drug or procedure privately. Thus, the *Shulḥan Arukh*, following earlier formulations of Jewish law, limits the amount of money a community may spend on redeeming any given captive in order to depress the market in captives and, ultimately, to deter kidnapping altogether. Even though that is a distinct social good, individuals are free to spend as much of their own funds as they wish to redeem themselves or their relatives:

> We do not redeem captives for more than their worth out of considerations of fixing the world, so that the enemies will not dedicate themselves to take them captive. An individual, however, may redeem himself for as much as he would like. . . .[44]

This is unfair in one sense, but it is only the unfairness built into any capitalistic system, and Jewish sources do not require that Jews use socialism as their form of government or their rule for distributing and charging goods.

A Contemporary Jewish Synthesis on Managed Care

In what follows, I shall suggest what I take to be a reasonable, contemporary synthesis of at least some of the principles the tradition enunciates in the precedents we have discussed above and apply them to the context of contemporary health care delivery systems of managed care. What I will say is directly rooted in the sources we have examined, but because those sources conflict with one another, my synthesis will necessarily choose among them in formulating a Jewish approach to distributing and paying for health care.

Over the long history of Jewish law, rabbis have often applied precedents from other areas of life or other historical contexts to new situations and problems. That practice sometimes permits one to play fast and loose with the law or to pretend that there are legal grounds for a decision when there are none. More often, though, rabbis search for precedents that, while not exactly on point, bear a significant resemblance to the case at hand. Legal systems depend for their relevance on such a process, and they in turn provide a sense of authority, coherence, and continuity to those who follow them. The norms that are announced on a new issue are, then, not totally new and made out of whole cloth; they are rather plausible extensions of traditional precedents and values to the new case, and as such they share in the authority of the tradition and add to its story.[45] Thus what I am about to do is no different methodologically from what rabbis have done for centuries. Other rabbis, or other Jews for that matter, may evaluate these sources differently, and in that case they will articulate the thrust of Jewish law for health care in a way different from mine. The ultimate test of which formulation is best will depend upon two things: the degree to which any given proposal is rooted in Jewish sources and Jewish concepts and morals (its Jewish authenticity), and the extent to which it gives wise guidance to contemporary conditions (its practicality).

An individual must worry about providing for his or her own health needs first, then those of near relatives, then more distant relatives, then the people of the local community, then the nation, and then the rest of humanity. The individual's financial contributions to health care, then, should be distributed on that basis.

Jewish sources make it clear, though, that health care is not only an individual and familial responsibility but also a communal one. This social aspect of health care manifests itself in Jewish law in two ways: first, no community is complete until it has the personnel (and, one assumes, the facilities) to provide health care; second, the community must pay for the health care of those who cannot afford it as part of its provision for the poor.

As health care has become more effective and also more expensive, it is no longer the poor alone who need communal assistance; it is most members of society. It is as if all of us today are poor vis-à-vis health care, and the community therefore, on the basis of these Jewish sources, has a responsibility to ensure that all of us receive the health care we need. This does not mean that everyone should get every possible treatment, no matter how remote its possibility of benefit or how high its cost; the community has both the right and the duty to make considered decisions about how it will allocate its resources among its various responsibilities.

For any given society, those who can benefit most from the procedure must come first; after that the distribution should be on a first-come, first-served basis, regardless of social position, wealth, or relationships to the health care personnel involved. The one restriction here is that Jewish principles could justify concern for the people of one's own nation first in, for example, the supply of organs for transplantation and rare new drugs. Such a limitation would not be justified, however, and would, in fact, be counterproductive to possible international agreements providing medical services, for example, to the citizens of any nation visiting another or in the organ transplant supply based on need, not nationality. It is only absent such agreements that concern for one's own can legitimately come first.

The Jewish demand that everyone have access to health care does not necessarily mandate a particular form of delivery, such as socialized medicine: any delivery system that does the job will meet these Jewish standards. So, for example, the current combination in the United States of employer-related insurance plans, individual payments, and government programs like Medicaid would suffice *if* that blend were effective in providing health care for everyone within our borders. However, the fact, that more than forty million Americans have no health insurance whatsoever is, from a Jewish point of view, an intolerable dereliction of society's moral duty. And the fact that some of those people will ultimately get health care in the most expensive way possible—in the emergency room, usually when they are sickest—means that as a society we are also currently neglecting our fiduciary responsibility to one another to spend our communal resources wisely.

The enlarged demand for health care in our day and its increased cost do not merely impose a new level of burden on the community to ensure that everyone has access to it; these factors also require the public to become much more directly involved in decisions about what services to provide. Under current conditions, our disarray on this issue has produced, if I may borrow a term from football, an ironic double-reverse: in the 1980s and early 1990s, physicians saw malpractice lawyers as their enemy, forcing them to engage in a brand of defensive medicine that often made little or no medical sense; now those very physicians seek out those same lawyers to sue health maintenance organizations for forcing them to provide what they consider to be inadequate care. Both reactions, I submit, stem from our failure to come to a social consensus as to what constitutes good medical care—and, even worse, our inability to decide how we are going to arrive at a definition in the first place. In both cases, the community is guilty of negligence by its failure to assume and fulfill its rightful moral responsibilities.

Physicians as a group should, of course, have input into such decisions, but they should not collectively, and certainly not individually, be charged with the responsibility of making them alone. Placing that responsibility in the hands of physicians alone would undermine the patient-physician relationship so much that patients could no longer trust that their doctors were committed to their care. Patients also should have a say in formulating the policy of health care distribution, but they certainly may not demand whatever they want and expect the community to pay for it. Even if a patient desires a test or treatment that is medically warranted, medical costs preclude the provision of all available services, since the community must pay for other important things as well. Health care managers interested in making a profit should not be given free rein either. Judaism imposes a duty to provide good medical care, even if it would be cheaper not to do so. While all three parties—physicians, patients, and health care managers—cannot by themselves determine the community's triage policy, they must all be involved in formulating an appropriate policy for deciding who shall receive specific drugs and procedures.

Since health care is ultimately the responsibility of the community as a whole, the public in some way must also be involved in deciding the scope of the health care that each person has a right to expect. Some countries and states have done this, at least in part, through direct government involvement. Systems of socialized medicine, of course, are one example of that approach, and the Oregon plan is another. In others, like the current system almost everywhere else in the United States, the government acts as an insurer of last resort through Medicaid, with all others— except the elderly covered by Medicare—fending for themselves.

While the specific form of health care system may vary, Jewish ethics definitely demands that American Jews work to ensure that the United States, as a society, provides health care to everyone in some way. Recent legislation guaranteeing the transfer of health care from one job to another, regardless of preexisting conditions, is one step in fulfilling that social duty. Moreover, recent court cases forbidding "gag rules" on doctors and making for-profit health maintenance organizations liable for inadequate care have served as a healthy communal check on their original, unbridled concern for the bottom line.[46]

In sum, then, the Jewish principles enunciated above—namely, that each of us individually and collectively has a responsibility to cure and, conversely, that society has the duty to balance this obligation with the other services it must provide—are important guidelines for the ongoing discussion in the United States on the cost of medical care.

Medical Research: The Case of Cloning

The amazing advances in contemporary medicine's ability to prevent and treat illness stem partly from luck (as in the accidental discovery of penicillin) but mostly from protean efforts on the part of those engaged in medical research. Since the function of medicine, as construed in Jewish sources, is to aid God in the process of healing, research into further ways to accomplish that end finds enthusiastic endorsement within Jewish ideology and law. It is thus not surprising that historically, Jews have been deeply involved not only in delivering health care but also in ongoing medical experimentation.[47]

In recent times, though, as researchers experiment with ever more potent ways to avoid or cure disease, moral questions have been raised about the path of medical research itself. Are we acting morally, for example, in using animals for our research? If so, should they be protected from unnecessary pain? May we use human beings for advancing medical science? If so, under what conditions? What limits should we impose on those forms of research that threaten the environment—or should such research be banned entirely?

While these issues have been aired in the public media from time to time, nothing has focused public attention on them up to now as much as Dolly, the sheep cloned from the udder of an adult ewe in Scotland in 1996. Cloning—that is, copying the DNA (the chemical code that programs each cell of the body) from one organism to produce another—has already been used commercially to produce tomatoes, and scientists have been able to clone animal embryos for some time. Until the advent of Dolly, though, scientists presumed that adults could not be cloned because of two characteristics of DNA. Specifically, in the early stages of an embryo's development, the undifferentiated character of DNA enables some cells produced with it to become, say, liver cells and others to become heart cells. Once that has happened, though, the parts of the DNA that could have become another organ become dormant, and so the DNA loses its ability to reproduce an entire organism. Moreover, because DNA mutates with aging, scientists believed that DNA cloned from an adult would show all the wear and tear of the organism furnishing it, and that the diminished malleability and purity of DNA in adult cells thus made cloning from an adult animal impossible.

Then came Dolly. We still do not know whether she will live a sheep's normal life or begin life as if she were as old as the adult sheep from which she was cloned; that is, we do not know how the latter factor of cell mutation over time will affect the aging process and life expectancy of a clone. Dolly's birth proved, though, that scientists were wrong about the former factor, for DNA taken from an adult ewe clearly did mutate to form all of Dolly's new organs. Dolly's creation most immediately affects agriculture.

When cloning embryos, a scientist never knows the quality of the animal being cloned, for there is no way to predict how the embryo itself will develop. Farmers, however, want to reproduce the sheep that grow the most wool and the cows that give the most milk. Currently, they must live with the odds of natural reproduction or the improved odds of breeding to procure productive animals; but if adult animals can be cloned, farmers can choose the most productive animals for cloning, thereby guaranteeing maximum yield.

This, though, raises environmental issues. If the only species of sheep bred in the future is the one that produces the most wool, all other species of sheep will eventually die out. What happens, then, if a particular virus or bacterium attacks that specific variety of sheep? The whole sheep population could disappear.

This problem illustrates just one aspect of the issue of *biodiversity*, the need to protect multiple forms of vegetable and animal life. Biodiversity helps to ensure that a given disease will not wipe out a whole species of plants or animals. Biodiversity also helps to assure our own survival by providing abundant sources for medications. The wider the range of living things, the more likely it is that some of them will contain elements that can be used medicinally to overcome a specific disease in humans. As more and more cloning of specific species takes place, however, fewer and fewer varieties remain available in the environment for such purposes, and the more vulnerable we and every other species become.

Furthermore, new forms of life created by scientific manipulation may be lethal for currently existing forms of life, including humans. Genetic engineering endangers the environment much more acutely than cloning does, for the parent of a cloned plant or animal already exists, whereas a genetically engineered plant or animal is, by hypothesis, totally new. That our own creativity may turn on us, to the point of imperiling our very existence, is the fear that underlies some versions of the Jewish legend of the golem—a humanlike creature created by the talmudic sage Rava (fourth century) and by later rabbis, especially the frightening golem created by Rabbi Judah Loeb of Prague (sixteenth century)[48]—and this same fear makes some science fiction books and films both menacing and terrifying.

The creation of Dolly suggests that cloning human beings may not be far behind. People are interested in that possibility for a number of good reasons. Scientists could learn much about the etiology and cures of diseases like cancer and Parkinson's, and the technique could be used to overcome infertility.

Even when used to accomplish those good ends, though, human cloning poses what are undoubtedly the most intriguing and the most complex moral problems of scientific research. Some of these problems have already arisen in some form in relation to the new methods of assisted reproduction—especially those using donor gametes or surrogate mothers—and in experiments currently being conducted on human subjects. The prospect of human cloning, though, puts these problems in new relief and gives them added urgency. Moreover, human cloning presents not only moral but also theological problems, challenging as it does our very sense of who we are as human beings, both individually and collectively, and requiring us to reaffirm or redefine our role in God's universe.

Since human cloning presents such a clear and dramatic instance of the moral and theological problems involved in medical research, we shall examine it below in some detail, not only for its own sake but also as a paradigm of the issues that arise in other forms of medical research. Similarly, the public policy recommendations for structuring further research on human cloning that follow the moral and theological analysis below are intended to serve as models for regulating other forms of medical research.

Moral Issues

THE SUBJECTS OF CLONING: WHO WOULD BE CLONED?   If cloning is left to the economic forces of the marketplace, presumably it is the rich and the famous, but not necessarily the good, who would be cloned. This outcome would exacerbate the socioeconomic divisions in society, but that, one might say, is just a result of the capitalistic economic system that the United States has chosen. Still, one would hope to relieve tensions of inequality rather than heighten them, and this would add to them in the most personal way possible: so-and-so is worthy to be cloned, but I am not. That certainly could make those unable to afford this procedure feel bad.

Human cloning may also be open to economic exploitation. A sports agent, for example, might seek to clone a star basketball player to earn fees from many copies of him (assuming that human clones would have the original's athletic abilities). Indeed, since DNA can be copied from even a hair, clones of the player might even be made without his knowledge and against his will. While such an act would undoubtedly violate American laws against theft and American values of autonomy and freedom, from a Jewish perspective it would also constitute economic oppression *(ona'ah)* and personal violation akin to rape.

If the United States as a society were to legislate that the decision as to who is to be cloned is not to be determined by who can afford it but rather by some social process, what would that process be? Who would be entitled to have a vote in selecting those to be cloned? What would be the criteria for the decision?

If we Americans settled on the pragmatic considerations so common to American ideology and practice, we would have trouble implementing those standards, for those most useful to society today will not necessarily be the most useful to society tomorrow. Moreover, should we be making such decisions on utilitarian grounds in the first place? If we do, we surely commodify human beings—that is, treat them like commodities on the market—even more than capitalist economics does; for whereas the labor market commodifies people's skills, cloning commodifies their very being. This certainly denies the inherently sacred character of human life affirmed by the Jewish tradition, transforming people instead into fungible commodities to be judged by a given person's worth to others.

Even if we find less demeaning criteria to decide who is to be cloned, we would nevertheless be establishing a social hierarchy in the most personal of ways, such that some people are deemed intrinsically better than others. The equal protection of the laws mandated in the Fourteenth Amendment certainly does not guarantee that every person will have equal status socially, educationally, or economically; but any social mechanism for deciding who shall be entitled to be reproduced through cloning and who shall not does seem to be elitist in the extreme. It certainly flies in the face of the Jewish principle that we all have inalienable worth as creatures created in the image of God.

These issues have arisen in other areas of medical research as well. The cost of new AIDS treatments, for example, is often not covered by health insurance and is thus prohibitive for many AIDS patients. Pharmaceutical companies have made some ad hoc pricing concessions, but they rightly point out that they must cover their own costs of research, testing, and development—and that they have a right to make a profit. Who, then, is entitled to benefit from expensive research, and who pays for it? The Jewish considerations and guidelines discussed in the first two sections of this chapter on the distribution and cost of ongoing health care become critical in light of new research.

THE RESULTS OF CLONING.   What would determine good results? How would bad results be disposed of? How would the environment be protected from the effects of bad results?

Even if we set aside the issue of who would be cloned, the very process of cloning commodifies human life. After all, good results would presumably be measured by the degree to which the clone matches the original; thus the standards of pre-dict-ability and quality control—the standards of industrial de-sign—would be applied to human beings, thereby cheapening life and making human beings like inanimate objects on an assembly line.

What may be even worse, at least in the short term, is the prospect of bad results. After all, Dolly the sheep represents only one success out of 277 attempts. Even with regard to animals, then, the process is, as of now, extremely inefficient. Since human beings are considerably more complex organisms, we have every reason to believe that the technology needed to clone humans will be every bit as inefficient, if not more so. What, then, will we do with the mistakes? Abort them? Kill them once born? Let them live in whatever way they turn out and then pay for their medical bills?

Jewish law regulating abortion, extended in recent times to permit aborting badly malformed or terminally ill fetuses, is stretched to new limits by the prospect of mistakes in cloning. Nature spontaneously aborts many fetuses that cannot survive, and that spares us the responsibility for many decisions concerning who should live and who should die. Presumably a woman's womb would also eject the most egregious cloning mistakes, but even then, cloning would subject a woman to the prospect of many miscarriages. Those fetuses the woman's body did not spontaneously abort could only be aborted, according to Jewish law, if the mother's physical or mental health required it or, according to some rabbis, if the child itself was grossly malformed or terminally ill. Abortion could never be justified simply because the clone was not an exact copy of the original— that is, for the quality control standards common in industrial production. Jewish law would certainly prohibit killing the clone once born, requiring us instead to bear what might be the substantial costs of the child's medical care.

Cloning also raises ecological concerns. Genetic engineering poses the real possibility of introducing into the environment organisms harmful to current life forms, including human ones. Cloning presumably avoids that risk because it simply reproduces an already existing organism. But the possibility—indeed, the likelihood—of mistakes in the cloning process makes cloning also a potential source of threats to the environment and to us humans.

That is more than a general moral concern; it is a distinctly Jewish one. Adam's charge in the Garden of Eden was "to work it *and to preserve it*" (Genesis 2:15), and ever since then ecological concerns have carried both theological and legal authority within Judaism.[49] The threat to the environment posed by cloning mistakes, then, requires that if we do permit human cloning under certain conditions because of its promise in advancing research and in overcoming infertility, as described below, we must take conscientious steps to prevent environmental catastrophe.

THE USES OF CLONING.   To what uses will cloning be put? Until now we have assumed that cloning would be used for the morally good purposes of overcoming infertility and advancing human ability to understand and cure disease. Even those good uses, though, would have to be regulated to avoid moral pitfalls. Specifically, human clones would have to assured the protections afforded any other human subjects used in scientific research, and the children born through cloning would have to be given all the same rights and protections as children born through sexual intercourse.

Once the technology for cloning human beings is developed, though, it is open to abuses as well. Although it would be legitimate from a moral and a Jewish point of view to produce a clone with the intent of transplanting bone marrow to an existing person with leukemia as long as the intention of those involved was to raise the clone as they would raise any other child, it would definitely be illegitimate morally and Jewishly to produce the clone, perform the transplant, and then destroy the clone, whether in utero or after birth. Such organ harvesting must be prohibited if human cloning is to be allowed.

Similarly, cloning must not be used in an effort to create "model" human beings. Just as the Nazis' cruel medical experimentation on human beings lurks in the background of any discussion about using human subjects in medical experiments today,[50] so too the Nazis' eugenics efforts inevitably color consideration of human cloning in the public mind, and certainly in Jewish minds. Any use of cloning to create "ideal" people must clearly be forbidden.

Again, genetic engineering poses more of a risk here than does cloning, for the ability to change genes immediately raises the question of which genes to change. Few would object to rooting out genetic diseases like Tay-Sachs, but does homosexuality (assuming it is genetic) constitute a "disease"?[51] Does being short? Once we are able to change the genetic structure of gametes, these questions will loom large, but they also affect the choice of whom to clone. After all, in agriculture the farmer's interest is to reproduce sheep and cows that fit certain specifications, and cloning might be used in the same way in human beings. But which humans? Why? Who decides?

Fears of eugenics are not unfounded in human cloning or, for that matter, in much of medical research, where the line between unwanted disease and precious diversity in human beings will become ever harder to identify. We need to be constantly reminded in these discussions of the Jewish tradition's demand that when we see someone who is disabled, we must bless God for making people different. Cloning and, even more so, genetic engineering raise the question of whether in the future we will still appreciate God's creativity in making people different or whether we will instead try to make everyone the same—presumably like the majority of us.

Cloning, like all other technologies, is in and of itself morally neutral. Its moral valence depends upon how we use it. Its enormous potential to affect us both negatively and positively requires that we be especially alert to the uses we plan for it.

THE RIGHTS AND SPECIAL PROBLEMS OF THE CLONE.   Special attention must be paid to the fate of the clone. No clone may legitimately be denied any of the rights and protections extended to any other child. Images of clones in literature and film as slaves of their creator make us instinctively fearful that clones may not be treated as full human beings. If cloning human beings ever becomes possible, it will produce independent people with histories and influences all their own and with their own free will. That independence must be fully recognized by all parties concerned.

Even when everyone does everything possible to acknowledge the individuality of the clone, though, some of the psychological problems children and parents normally have in relation to each other will undoubtedly be exacerbated by the way the child came into the world. Because of the parent and child's identical genetic structure, the parent of a clone will be even more sorely tempted than many parents now are to say things like, "I got A's in school; you should too!" More generally, the identical genetic structure that clones share with their parent will make it very hard for clones to establish their own identity and for their creators to acknowledge and respect it. These problems do not speak to the permissibility of cloning in the first place, but they do warn us of the need for counseling for the parent and the clone if cloning is to proceed.

Theological Issues

THE PLACE OF HUMAN BEINGS IN THE UNIVERSE.   Cloning brings us back to the principles in the opening chapters of Genesis, defining our relationship to God and to God's universe. As noted above, Adam and Eve are put into the Garden of Eden "to work it and to preserve it" (Genesis 2:15). As long as we preserve nature, then, we have both the right and the duty to work with it to fulfill human needs. In a parallel talmudic phrase, we are God's "partners in the ongoing act of creation" when we improve the human lot in life.

At the same time, we are not God. The Tower of Babel story (Genesis 11:1–9) reminds us that there is a boundary between what we do and what God does, that God refuses to allow a situation in which "nothing that people may propose to do will be out of their reach" (Genesis 11:6). Moreover, even when we accomplish things within our proper bounds as human beings, we must take due note of God's role in our achievements, for the essence of human hubris is to boast that "my strength and the power of my hand accomplished these things" (Deuteronomy 8:11–20).

We must strike a balance, then, between our actions and God's. In the medical arena, the Jewish tradition has been very explicit as to how this balance is to be struck. As discussed in Chapter 2, the Torah maintains that God imposes illness as punishment for sin and that God is our healer. That, however, does not lead the Jewish tradition to conclude that medicine is an improper human intervention in God's decision to inflict illness, an act of human hubris. Quite the contrary, in the rabbinic interpretation of the Torah, we have not only the right but the duty to try to heal. God is still our ultimate healer, and hence Jewish liturgy has us pray to God for healing of body and soul three times each day; but the physician, in Jewish theology, is God's agent in accomplishing that task, and so use of the medical arts is not only permissible but required. In fact, as we have mentioned several times throughout this book, Jews may not live in a city lacking a physician.

This mode of balancing the divine and human roles in medical care has made the Jewish tradition very aggressive in trying to promote health both preventively and curatively. Human cloning certainly pushes this envelope very far, but ultimately it must be understood within these parameters.

Cloning plants or animals for medical cures, or cloning tomatoes and milk cows to provide food, would thus fall under the human mandate to provide food and medical care, thereby improving the world—assuming that we pay due attention to the risks to the environment involved and take precautions to avoid them. The same would be true for human cloning: if used to cure disease or overcome infertility, it is a permissible activity for us as God's partners, on condition that we take due regard of the moral issues discussed above. We cannot foresee every possible result, of course, and we must therefore be especially cautious if we are manipulating the genetic structure of the environment through genetic engineering or, when mistakes occur, through cloning. While the possibility of mistakes argues for precautions, it does not automatically preclude cloning, for we are not expected to be omnisicent as God is. Moreover, we are, after all, commanded to seek to feed the hungry and to cure the ill, and cloning and genetic engineering may provide us with new effective ways to accomplish those ends.

THE FACTORS THAT CONSTITUTE OUR INDIVIDUAL IDENTITIES. One of the ways the Mishnah highlights the difference between human and divine creation is that when people make a mold, every object formed by it is the same, but God creates each of us in the divine image and yet each of us is also unique.[52] Cloning holds out the danger that some people will think that they can literally reproduce themselves through this process. If that were so, the rabbis' differentiation of God's creation from ours would become all the more poignant and threatening, for then cloning would produce people who are the exact equivalents of those already existing, with no individuality whatsoever. I would become nothing more than the sum of my genes, and tough questions would need to be raised about whether I have any modicum of free will separate and apart from that of my creator.

Fortunately, human cloning does not hold out that prospect, for the clone would be a new person, shaped by new experiences. Ironically, then, cloning is theologically very healthy, for it refocuses our attention on the rabbinic doctrine that we are not equivalent to our bodies—nor, for that matter, to our minds or souls. We are instead integrated wholes, as discussed above in Chapter 2, and cloning provides a dramatic proof that we are not just our bodies alone. Moreover, cloning draws our attention to the fact that our identity stems also from the *experiences* that shape our life. This fact is already apparent to those who are, or who know, identical twins, but it will become even more evident if cloned individuals begin to walk this earth. In other words, exactly contrary to the hopes of some people and the fears of others, the reality that even duplicating a person's genes does not make for the same person underscores the interacting roles of nature and nurture in our identity and the uniqueness of each one of us.

THE DANGER OF SELF-IDOLIZATION.   Human cloning threatens to undermine our humility and our sense of being limited in two important ways: it makes it possible to reproduce asexually, and it seems to promise immortality.

Children, by their very nature, represent a piece of our hold on eternity. Biblical and rabbinic sources affirm that individuals live on after death in one form or another[53] and that the influence we have had on others during our lifetime continues after death, but according to these sources, we also live on through our children.

While children give us a sense of our own personal eternity, sexual reproduction of children forces both partners to get out of themselves, to participate with another in the creation of the child. Both the man and the woman become highly conscious of this through courting and foreplay, in which they persuade each other to engage in sexual activity in the first place, as well as through the mutuality of sexual intercourse itself; the very word *intercourse*, in fact, denotes an interaction between two distinct people. One partner's distinctiveness from the other is further highlighted by the fact that their respective genders must be different. Moreover, genetically, the child produced is a combination of the genes of the two partners—a condition that remains true even if the child is produced through in vitro fertilization. These aspects of sexual reproduction help to curb human pretense: one is not able to reproduce alone but must participate with another in creating a child.

Human cloning, on the other hand, permits me to produce my filial link to eternity myself. I may have to engage a physician or others to make it happen, but ultimately they are just assisting me in what is essentially my act. Moreover, the genes of the child are exclusively my genes. These factors potentially contribute to, rather than curb, human self-idolization.

Another aspect of cloning makes this danger even worse. Adam and Eve were not permitted to eat of the Tree of Life lest they be like gods in living forever (Genesis 3:22). Even though, as we have said, the cloned person is made different from the original by the experiences she or he has, the fact that the child comes from one person's genes alone makes it all too easy for that person to forget that the child is nevertheless a different, independent human being. Some people will be motivated to try cloning in an effort to make themselves immortal.

Our mortality, though, is beneficial for us. It curbs our arrogance, for it forces us to recognize that we are limited in time as well as power. Moreover, our mortality forces us to focus on what is important in life; as the Psalmist said, "Teach us to number our days so that we may attain a heart of wisdom" (Psalms 90:12). Cloning done to overcome immortality conversely panders to human self-idolization and grandiosity by making us think that we can live forever, and it lets us think that we have an eternity to accomplish our ends, thus contributing to our tendency to procrastinate.

Recommendations for Morally Guiding Research

Given these considerations from the Jewish moral, legal, and theological heritage, I would recommend the following:

1. Human cloning should be regulated, not banned. The Jewish demand that we do our best to provide healing makes it important that we take advantage of the promise of cloning to aid us in finding cures for a variety of diseases and in overcoming infertility.

The dangers of cloning, though, require that it be supervised and restricted. Specifically, cloning should be allowed only for medical research or therapy; clones must be recognized as having full and equal status with other fetuses or human beings, with the equivalent protections; and careful policies must be devised to determine how cloning mistakes will be identified and handled.

Moreover, to pretend that human cloning will not take place if it is banned in experiments funded with government money is simply unrealistic; it will happen with private funds in the United States and/or abroad. The dangers of cloning, some of which were listed above, therefore make it imperative that its practice be kept out in the open, supervised, and regulated.

2. Regulation should be accomplished in part through legislation, but that will work only to a limited degree. Ethics committees and institutional review boards must also be called upon to ensure that the moral concerns described above guide research into human cloning.

As a member of three hospital ethics committees and an institutional review board in a hospital that specializes in treating AIDS patients, I have been immensely impressed by the seriousness with which members of these boards discharge their responsibilities. There is, if my experience is any indication, every reason to trust such committees to establish a high moral plane for research into human cloning. Moreover, government regulation cannot possibly anticipate new developments in cloning as they happen, whereas hospital committees can take such developments into account virtually as soon as they occur. Most important, whereas government legislation imposes rules from the outside and makes medical personnel feel that they are morally suspect, self-regulation through hospital committees appeals to the best motives in the same medical personnel and is thus more likely to be effective. Some laws must be established to ban the most egregiously immoral practices, but most supervision of this process should come from self-regulation akin to what we already have in place for experiments on human subjects.

3. Since the first successful cloning of an adult animal took place in Scotland, cloning is clearly not a technology restricted to the United States. The restrictions on it must therefore be negotiated worldwide. Given the even greater danger to the environment posed by genetic engineering, future international

agreements on cloning can also serve as a good basis for similar accords on genetic engineering. Only through such cooperation can we human beings carry out the mandate in Genesis to Adam and Eve, the paradigmatic universal people, "to work [the world] and to preserve it."

Although I have phrased these recommendations specifically with regard to cloning, I would suggest similar measures for other forms of medical research. Only if we openly confront the new medical frontiers that are opening each day; regulate that research responsibly through legislation and through committees including community representatives as well as medical personnel; and wage our ethical efforts, like our scientific ones, worldwide will we be able to reap the fruit of these new medical advances without endangering ourselves and our environment in the process.

Epilogue:
An Imperative to Choose Life

THE POWER AND POTENTIAL OF CONTEMPORARY MEDICINE
is truly amazing; each of us has already benefited from
its advances. The need to continue medical research and
to assure the availability of modern medical therapies to as
many people as possible clearly constitutes both a Jewish and a
social imperative. At the same time, however, we must deal sensitively with the many moral issues that our new medical capabilities raise. In that process, even though the Jewish tradition
may not be able to answer all of the questions, it has much to
teach us. Its respect for life and for medicine is tempered with a
keen appreciation for moral and religious values and for the
other needs of a community.

Jewish perspectives are often different from those of the fun-
damentalists who go under the banner of "the right to life," but
the Jewish tradition is no less respectful of God's gift of life to
us. On the contrary, Jewish directives on matters of medical ethics incorporate careful consideration of the best ways to preserve good health and to act as God's partners in restoring it to
the sick. Therefore, in our own day, when medicine is at once
so promising and so morally perplexing, these famous words
from the Torah have new and deep significance:

I call heaven and earth to witness against you this day: I have put before you life and death, blessing and curse. Choose life—if you and your offspring would live—by loving the Lord your God, heeding His commands, and holding fast to Him. (Deuteronomy 30:19–20)

Notes

KEY TO NOTES

The following abbreviations are used in the notes throughout this book:

M. = Mishnah (edited by Rabbi Judah ha-Nasi, president of the Sanhedrin ["Judah the Prince"] c. 200 c.e.)

T. = Tosefta (edited by Rabbi Hiyya and Rabbi Oshaiya c. 200 c.e.)

J. = Jerusalem (Palestinian) Talmud (editor unknown, but edited c. 400 c.e.)

B. = Babylonian Talmud (edited by Ravina and Rav Ashi c. 500 c.e.)

M.T. = Maimonides' *Mishneh Torah* (completed 1177 c.e.)

S.A. = *Shulḥan Arukh,* completed in 1565 c.e. by Joseph Caro, a Spanish (Sephardic) Jew, with glosses by Moses Isserles indicating differences in German and eastern European (Ashkenazic) Jewish practice

All modern books and articles are referred to in the notes solely by their author(s) or editor(s) and date. They are listed with full bibliographical information in the Bibliography.

NOTES TO CHAPTER ONE

1. The value of quarantine: Leviticus 13–15; Numbers 5:1–4; see also B. Bava Kamma 60b. Physical cleanliness is conducive to spiritual purity: B. *Avodah Zarah* 20b; J. *Shabbat* 1:3. Wash hands and feet: B. *Shabbat* 108b. Precautions with regard to water: B. *Avodah Zarah* 27b, 30b; cf. B. *Sanhedrin* 70a. Maimonides on not eating too much and on the need for exercise: M.T. *Laws of Ethics (De'ot)* 4:1–2, 14–15; on the selection and mixing of foods: ibid. 4:6–13. Some talmudic cures and preventive measures: B. *Avodah Zarah* 11a, 28b–29a.

2. Karl Llewellyn (1950) and (1960), Appendix C. Excerpts from these are reprinted in Elliot N. Dorff and Arthur Rosett (1988), pp. 204–213. Ronald Dwor-

kin (1985), pp. 159–177. For a good exposition of the deconstructionist position, cf. Stanley Fish (1980). For a critical review of the Fish/Dworkin controversy, see R. V. Young (1987), pp. 49–60.

3. Louis E. Newman (1990).

4. For example, Eliezer Berkovits (1983), pp. 82–84; Shubert Spero (1983), esp. pp. 166–200; David Hartman (1985), esp. pp. 89–108.

5. For example, Robert Gordis (1990), esp. pp. 50–68; Simon Greenberg (1977), esp. pp. 157–218; and Seymour Siegel (1971) and (1980).

6. I think, though, that conflicts between rituals and ethics, however those terms are defined, are far fewer and therefore far less important than they are often touted to be. Moreover, I would claim that both rituals and ethics are authoritative within Judaism, neither necessarily always taking precedence over the other. Cf. my *Mitzvah Means Commandment* (1989), pp. 7–9, 223–229.

NOTES TO CHAPTER TWO

1. See, for example, Exodus 19:5; Deuteronomy 10:14; Psalms 24:1. See also Genesis 14:19, 22 (where the Hebrew word for "Creator" *[koneh]* also means "possessor," and where "heaven and earth" is a merism for those and everything in between); and Psalms 104:24, where the same word is used with the same meaning. The following verses, although not quite as explicit or as expansive, have the same theme: Exodus 20:11; Leviticus 25:23, 42, 55; Deuteronomy 4:35, 39; 32:6.

2. Bathing, for example, is a commandment according to Hillel: *Leviticus Rabbah* 34:3. Maimonides summarized and codified the rules requiring proper care of the body in M.T. *Laws of Ethics (De'ot)*, chaps. 3–5. He spells out there in remarkable clarity that the purpose of these positive duties to maintain health is not to feel good and live a long life but rather to have a healthy body so that one can then serve God.

3. The requirement of saving one's own life *(pikuaḥ nefesh)*: B. *Yoma* 85a–b (with Rashi there); B. *Sanhedrin* 74a–b; *Mekhilta* on Exodus 31:13; and, for a general discussion of this topic, see Immanuel Jakobovits (1959, 1972), pp. 45–98. That no civil or theological culpability attaches to violating other Jewish laws in the effort to save a life: S.A. *Hoshen Mishpat* 359:4; 380:3; cf. Jakobovits (1959, 1972), pp. 95–96.

Since the principle of *pikuaḥ nefesh* derives from the Torah's command to live by the commandments, there is some question in Jewish law as to whether a Jew may violate Jewish law to save the life of a non-Jew, who, after all, is not commanded to obey Jewish law in the first place. See B. *Yoma* 84b; M.T. *Laws of the Sabbath* 2:20–21. The Talmud (B. *Yoma* 85a) already specifically includes non-Jews within the bounds of *pikuaḥ nefesh*, and later rabbis generally concur, either for the sake of intercommunal peace and goodwill, or because the non-Jews of our time, in contrast to the times of the Mishnah and Talmud, are not to be construed as idolators. See B. *Avodah Zarah* 26b, Rashi and Tosafot there, s.v., *la'apukei*; B. *Avodah Zarah* 65a; B. *Gittin* 61; M.T. *Laws of Idolatry* 10:2; Menaḥem Meiri on B. *Avodah Zarah*, p. 62; and see Katz (1961) pp. 114–128; S.A. *Yoreh De'ah* 158:1; and see the commentary of the Gaon of Vilna there; *Be'er*

Ha-Golah, comment no. 300 *(shin)* on S.A. *Hoshen Mishpat* 425:5; *She'arim Met-zuyanim B'Halakhah* to the *Kitzur Shulḥan Arukh* 92:1.

4. B. *Sanhedrin* 73a. The imperative to save other people's lives is derived from the biblical command, "Do not stand idly by the blood of your neighbor" (Leviticus 19:16). This means, for example, that if you see someone drowning, you may not ignore him or her but must do what you can to save that person's life. In an interesting contrast to American law, most American states do not impose such an obligation. Until recently, in fact, in many American states one could actually be sued if, in the process of trying to help someone, that person suffered injury, but now a number of states have enacted "Good Samaritan" laws to prevent such an outcome. In those states, saving a person in trouble (e.g., who is drowning) still remains an option and not a positive obligation, but now the person who attempts rescue is at least protected from suit. See, for example, Samuel Freeman (1994) and Mitchell McInnes (1994).

Only Vermont and Wisconsin have created a legal requirement to save those in dire straits. In Wisconsin the law requires that "anyone who knows that a crime is being committed and that a victim is exposed to bodily harm shall summon law enforcement officers or other assistance or provide assistance to the victim," unless compliance would put the potential rescuer in danger or would interfere with duties the person owes to others or assistance has already been summoned or provided by others (Wisconsin Criminal Statutes 940.34, "Duty to Aid Victim or Report Crime"). In Vermont, the law states that "a person who knows that another is exposed to grave physical harm shall, to the extent that the same can be rendered without danger or peril to himself or without interference with important duties owed to others, give reasonable assistance to the exposed person unless that assistance or care is being provided by others" (Vermont Statutes, Title 12, par. 519). Even in those two states, though, failing to save someone's life is a misdemeanor, punishable by a small fine (in Vermont the fine cannot be more than $100). Typical for American legal theory, this positive obligation, limited as it is, is justified as a protection against an abuse of the rights of the person in distress (since s/he has a right to life), not a moral duty that now also has legal consequences. See Lon T. McClintock (1982).

On this duty in Jewish law generally, together with some comparisons with Western law, see Anne Cucchiara Besser and Kalman J. Kaplan (1994); Ben Zion Eliash (1994); and Aaron Kirschenbaum (1980). I would like to thank Professors Martin Golding and Arthur Rosett for these references.

5. B. *Bava Metzia* 62a.

6. B. *Shabbat* 32a; B. *Bava Kamma* 15b, 80a, 91b; M.T. *Laws of Murder* 11:4–5; S.A. *Yoreh De'ah* 116:5 gloss; S.A. *Hoshen Mishpat* 427:8–10.

7. B. *Hullin* 10a; S.A. *Oraḥ Ḥayyim* 173:2; S.A. *Yoreh De'ah* 116:5 gloss.

8. S.A. *Yoreh De'ah* 255:2.

9. J. David Bleich (1977); Solomon Freehof (1977), chap. 2; *Proceedings of the Rabbinical Assembly*, 44 (1983), p. 182. All of the above are reprinted in Elliot N. Dorff and Arthur Rosett (1988), pp. 337–362.

10. Genesis 9:5; M. *Semahot* 2:2; B. *Bava Kamma* 91b; *Genesis Rabbah* 34:19 states that the ban against suicide includes not only cases where blood was shed but also self-inflicted death through strangulation and the like; M.T. *Laws of Mur-*

der 2:3; M.T. *Laws of Injury and Damage* 5:1; S.A. *Yoreh De'ah* 345:1–3. Cf. J. David Bleich (1981), chap. 26.

11. Specifically, forty-four states currently have made aiding a person to commit suicide a felony. See David G. Savage, "Supreme Court to Decide Issue of Right to Die," *Los Angeles Times*, October 2, 1996, p. A-16.

12. *Compassion in Dying v. State of Washington* 79 F.3d 790 (9th Cir. 1996); *Quill v. Vacco* 80 F.3d 716 (2d Cir. 1996). (A subsequent petition for the Ninth Circuit to rehear the case *en banc* was denied: 85 F.3d 1440 [9th Cir. 1996]). The cited language—which presumably includes nurses, pharmacists, and even family members serving as caregivers—comes from the Ninth Circuit's opinion, written by Judge Stephen Reinhardt. The argument is based largely on the liberty guaranteed by the due-process clause of the Fourteenth Amendment, and on the Supreme Court's past decisions on abortion interpreting that clause to protect a person's right to make his or her own health care decisions. Thus Judge Stephen Reinhardt, writing for an 8–3 majority, stated, "By permitting the individual to exercise the right to choose, we are following the constitutional mandate to take such decisions out of the hands of government, both state and federal, and to put them where they rightly belong, in the hands of the people." The Second Circuit, in a 2–1 vote, arrived at the same conclusion through a different path, arguing that because doctors can now end people's lives by withdrawing life support systems, to forbid them to help people not on life support to commit suicide illegally discriminates against the latter group of patients, violating the Constitution's guarantee of equal protection of the laws. See also "Assisted Deaths Ruled Legal: 9th Circuit Lifts Ban on Doctor-Assisted Suicide," *Los Angeles Times*, March 7, 1996, pp. A-1, A-16; and "Supreme Court to Decide Issue of Right to Die," *Los Angeles Times*, October 2, 1996, pp. A-1, A-16. The U.S. Supreme Court refused to locate these rights in the Constitution: *Washington v. Glucksberg* 117 S.Ct. 2258 (1997); *Quill v. Vacco* 117 S.Ct. 2293 (1997).

13. This extends to inanimate property as well: we may use what we need, but we may not destroy any more of God's world than we need to in order to accomplish our purposes in life. This is the prohibition of *ba'al tashḥit*, "Do not destroy," based on Deuteronomy 20:19–20 and amplified in the tradition to prohibit any unnecessary destruction: B. *Bava Kamma* 8:6, 7; B. *Bava Kamma* 92a, 93a; M.T. *Laws of Murder* 1:4, where Maimonides specifically invokes this theological basis for the law against suicide; M.T. *Laws of Injury and Damage* 5:5; *Sefer ha-Ḥinnukh*, commandment 529; S.A. *Hoshen Mishpat* 420:1, 31. See Schwartz and Cytron (1993).

14. Genesis 1:27; see also Genesis 5:1.

15. See Genesis 1:26–27; 3:1–7, 22–24.

16. See Genesis 2:18–24; Numbers 12:1–16; Deuteronomy 22:13–19. Note also that *"ha-middaber,"* "the speaker," is a synonym for the human being (in contrast to animals) in medieval Jewish philosophy.

17. Maimonides, *Guide for the Perplexed*, part I, chap. 1.

18. See Deuteronomy 6:5; Leviticus 19:18, 33–4, and note that the traditional prayer book juxtaposes the paragraph just before the *Shema*, which speaks of God's love for us, with the first paragraph of the *Shema*, which commands us to love God.

19. Consider the prayer in the traditional, early morning weekday service, *"Elohai neshamah she–natata bi,"* "My God, the soul (or life-breath) which you have imparted to me is pure. You created it, You formed it, You breathed it into me; You guard it within me . . ." Harlow (1985), pp. 8–11. Similarly, the rabbis describe the human being as part divine and part animal, the latter consisting of the material aspects of the human being and the former consisting of that which we share with God; see *Sifre Deuteronomy,* para. 306; 132a. Or consider this rabbinic statement in *Genesis Rabbah* 8:11: "In four respects man resembles the creatures above, and in four respects the creatures below. Like the animals he eats and drinks, propagates his species, relieves himself, and dies. Like the ministering angels he stands erect, speaks, possesses intellect, and sees [in front of him and not on the side like an animal]."

20. *Genesis Rabbah* 24:7.

21. M. *Sanhedrin* 4:5. Some manuscripts are less universalistic; they read "Anyone who destroys one *Israelite* soul is described in Scripture as if he destroyed an entire world, and anyone who sustains one *Israelite* soul is described in Scripture as if he sustained an entire world." A Ḥasidic *bon mot* (from Martin Buber [1948, 1961], vol. 2, pp. 249–50) reminds us that we must balance this recognition of our divine worth with a proper dose of humility:

Rabbi Bunam said: A person should always have two pieces of paper, one in each pocket. On one should be written, "For me the world was created." On the other should be written, "I am but dust and ashes" (Genesis 18:27).

22. For a thorough discussion of this blessing and concept in the Jewish tradition, see Carl Astor (1985).

23. Romans 6–8, especially 6:12; 7:14–24; 8:3, 10, 12–13; Galatians 5:16–24; see also I Corinthians 7:2, 9, 36–38.

24. Corinthians 6:19.

25. Romans 7:23.

26. The Greek side of Maimonides is most in evidence in his *Guide for the Perplexed*, where he states flatly:

It is also the object of the perfect Law to make man reject, despise, and reduce his desires as much as is in his power. He should only give way to them when absolutely necessary. It is well known that it is intemperance in eating, drinking, and sexual intercourse that people mostly rave and indulge in; and these very things counteract the ulterior perfection of man, impede at the same time the development of his first perfection [i.e., bodily health], and generally disturb the social order of the country and the economy of the family. For by following entirely the guidance of lust, in the manner of fools, man loses his intellectual energy, injures his body, and perishes before his natural time; sighs and cares multiply; and there is an increase of envy, hatred, and warfare for the purpose of taking what another possesses. The cause of all this is the circumstance that the ignorant considers physical enjoyment as an object to be sought for its own sake. God in His wisdom has therefore given us such commandments as would counteract that object, and prevent us altogether from directing our attention to it. . . [f]or the chief object of the Law is to [teach man to] diminish his desires. . . ." (part 3, chap. 33).

Philo's views can be found, in part, in the selections from his writings in Hans Lewy (1960), part I, esp. pp. 42–51, 54–55, and 71–75. He calls the body a "prison house" on p. 72.

27. Genesis 2:7; B. *Ta'anit* 22b; *Genesis Rabbah* 14:9. The different parts that the mother, father, and God contribute to the newborn: B. *Niddah* 31a. See also B. *Sanhedrin* 90b–91a. The departure of the soul and its return upon waking is articulated in the first words one is supposed to say as one regains consciousness: "I am grateful to You, living, enduring Sovereign, for restoring my soul (life-breath, *nishmati*) to me in compassion. You are faithful (trustworthy) beyond measure" (see, for example, Jules Harlow [1985], pp. 2–3).

28. This prayer appears toward the very beginning of the daily liturgy. See, for example, Jules Harlow (1985), pp. 8–11. See *Leviticus Rabbah* 18:1 (toward the end); and *Midrash Shahar Tov*, chap. 25, for the roots of this prayer. The latter interpretation (namely, that the blessing refers not to resurrection after death but to the return of consciousness after sleep) is also supported by the language of the first sentence a Jew is supposed to utter upon waking, cited in the previous note, which also speaks of God restoring the soul to the body at that time.

29. The predominant view seems to be that it can (cf. B. *Berakhot* 18b–19a; B. *Hagigah* 12b; B. *Ketubbot* 77b), but even such sources depict the soul in terms of physical imagery, thereby enabling it to perform many of the functions of the body. Some sources, in the meantime, assert that the soul cannot exist without the body, nor the body without the soul (e.g., *Tanhuma*,Vayikra 11).

30. *Leviticus Rabbah* 34:3.

31. B. *Sanhedrin* 91a–91b. See also *Mekhilta*, Beshalah, Shirah, chap. 2 (ed. Horowitz-Rabin, 1960, p. 125); *Leviticus Rabbah* 4:5; *Yalkut Shimoni* on Leviticus 4:2 (464); *Tanhuma*, Vayikra 6. The very development of the meaning of the term *neshamah* from physical breath to one's inner being bespeaks Judaism's view that the physical and the spiritual are integrated.

32. M. *Pe'ah* 1:1; B. *Kiddushin* 40b.

33. M. *Avot* 2:1. See B. *Berakhot* 35b, especially the comment of Abayae there in responding to the earlier theories of Rabbi Ishmael and Rabbi Simeon bar Yohai.

34. B. *Berakhot* 17a; the earlier rabbinic teaching cited at the end as what we have learned appears in B. *Menahot* 110a. While a few of the classical rabbis belonged to wealthy families, most were menial laborers and studied when they could. Hillel, for example, was so poor that he became the symbol of the poor man who nevertheless found the time and money to study Torah (B. *Yoma* 35b); Akiba had been a shepherd before he devoted himself to study at age forty, subsisting on the price he received for the bundle of wood he collected each day (*Avot d'Rabbi Natan*, chap. 6); Joshua was a charcoal burner (B. *Berakhot* 28a); Yose bar Halafta worked in leather (B. *Shabbat* 49a-b); Yohanan was a sandal maker (M. *Avot* 4:14); Judah was a baker (J. *Hagigah* 77b); and Abba Saul kneaded dough (B. *Pesahim* 34a) and had been a grave digger (B. *Niddah* 24b).

35. Cf. Leviticus 23:32; M. *Yoma*, chap. 8, and later rabbinic commentaries and codes based on that. Similarly, while there is a rabbinic doctrine of *yissurim shel ahavah*, "afflictions of love," this is always used to explain post facto why the good suffer. It is *not* a directive to experience pain. See chap. 8, n. 31 below.

36. Cf. M.T. *Laws of the Sabbath*, chap. 30.

37. This is based on Exodus 21:10. Cf. M. *Ketubbot* 5:6–7 and the later commentaries and codes based on those passages. This topic will be treated in a more expanded way below.

38. The law of the Nazirite appears in Numbers 6:11; and cf. the rabbinic derivation from that law that abstinence is prohibited, which appears first in B. *Ta'anit* 11a. Cf. also M.T. *Laws of Ethics (De'ot)* 3:1.

39. M.T. *Laws of Ethics (De'ot)* 3:3.

40. *Sifra* on Leviticus 19:16; B. *Sanhedrin* 73a; M.T. *Laws of Murder* 1:14; S.A. *Hoshen Mishpat* 426.

41. That God inflicts illness as punishment: Leviticus 26:14–16; Deuteronomy 28:22, 27, 58–61. That God cures: e.g., Exodus 15:26; Deuteronomy 32:39; Isaiah 19:22; 57:18–19; Jeremiah 30:17; 33:6; Hosea 6:1; Psalms 103:2–3; 107:20; Job 5:18.

42. B. *Bava Kamma* 85a (on the permission to heal based on Exodus 21:19). B. *Sanhedrin* 84b (with Rashi's commentary there, s.v. *ve'ahavta* (on the premission to inflict a wound for purpose of healing based on Leviticus 19:18). B. *Bava Kamma* 81b (on the permission to heal based on Deuteronomy 22:2). B. *Sanhedrin* 73a (on the use of Leviticus 19:16 both to ground the obligation to save a life [e.g., a drowning person] and to extend the obligation to heal from applying only to what one can personally do to spending money to hire others to help one do so). B. *Yoma* 85b: "It was taught: How do we know that saving a life supersedes the laws of the Sabbath? Rabbi Judah said in the name of Samuel: 'For it is written, "And you shall observe My statutes and judgments which a person should do and live by them" (Leviticus 18:6), [meaning] that he should not die by them.'" B. *Sanhedrin* 74a: "With regard to all transgressions in the Torah except for idolatry, sexual licentiousness, and murder, if enemies say to a person, 'Transgress and then you will not be killed,' the person must transgress and not be killed. What is the reason? 'And you shall live by them [my commandments]' (Leviticus 18:5) and not that he should die by them." See also *Sifrei Deuteronomy* on Deuteronomy 22:2 and *Leviticus Rabbah* 34:3.

43. The best of physicians deserves to go to hell: B. *Kiddushin* 82a. Abraham ibn Ezra, Bahya ibn Pakuda, and Jonathan Eybeschuetz all restricted the physician's mandate to external injuries: see ibn Ezra's commentary on Exodus 21:19; and cf. his comments on Exodus 15:26 and 23:25, where he cites Job 5:18 and II Chronicles 16:12 in support of his view; Bahya's commentary on Exodus 21:19; and Eybeschuetz, *Kereti u'Pleti* on S.A. *Yoreh De'ah* 188:5. See Immanuel Jakobovits (1959, 1975), pp. 5–6. That a Jew may not live in a city without a physician: J. *Kiddushin* 66d; see also B. Sanhedrin 17b, where this requirement is applied only to "the students of the Sages."

44. S.A. , *Yoreh De'ah* 336:1.

45. *Midrash Temurrah* as cited in *Otzar Midrashim*, J. D. Eisenstein, ed. (New York, 1915) II, 580–581. Cf. also B. *Avodah Zarah* 40b, a story in which Rabbi Judah ha-Nasi expresses appreciation for foods that can cure. Although circumcision is not justified in the Jewish tradition in medical terms, it is instructive that the rabbis maintained that Jewish boys were not born circumcised specifically because God created the world such that it would need human fixing, a similar idea to the one articulated here on behalf of physicians' activity despite God's rule; see *Genesis Rabbah* 11:6; *Pesikta Rabbati* 22:4.

46. B. *Shabbat* 10a, 119b. In the first of those passages, it is the judge who judges justly who is called God's partner; in the second, it is anyone who recites Genesis 2:1–3 (about God resting on the seventh day) on Friday night who thereby

participates in God's ongoing act of creation. The Talmud in B. *Sanhedrin* 38a specifically wanted the Sadducees *not* to be able to say that angels or any being other than humans participated with God in creation.

47. B. *Sanhedrin* 73a (on the use of Leviticus 19:16 to extend the obligation to heal from applying only to what one can personally do to spending money to hire others to help one do so). Nahmanides, *Kitvei Haramban*, Bernard Chavel, ed. (Jerusalem: Mosad ha-Rav Kook, 1963 [Hebrew]), vol. 2, p. 43; this passage comes from Nahmanides' *Torat ha-Adam* (The Instruction of Man), *Sha'ar Sakkanah* (Section on Danger) on B. *Bava Kamma*, chap. 8, and is cited by Joseph Caro in his commentary to the *Tur, Bet Yosef, Yoreh De'ah* 336. Nahmanides bases himself on similar reasoning in B. Sanhedrin 84b.

48. B. *Sanhedrin* 17b.

49. The biblical command to sanctify God's Name publicly: Leviticus 22:32. The biblical command to live by the laws: Leviticus 18:5. The talmudic rules governing martyrdom: B. *Sanhedrin* 74a–74b. Cf. M.T. *Laws of the Foundations of the Torah*, chap. 5; S.A. *Yoreh De'ah* 157:1.

50. For example, Tosafot on B. *Avodah Zarah* 18a, s.v. *v'al y'habel 'tzmo*; Tosafot on B. *Gittin* 57b, s.v., *v'kaftzu*.

51. The Mishnah even warns that "Whoever desecrates the name of Heaven in private will ultimately be punished in public; whether the desecration was committed unintentionally or intentionally, it is all the same when God's name is profaned." M. *Avot (Ethics of the Fathers)* 4:5; see also 3:15.

NOTES TO CHAPTER THREE

1. That these are independent commandments is made clear by the mishnah in which the rabbis, based on Exodus 21:10, deduced that a man is obligated to offer to have sex with his wife even when there is no possibility of propagation. See M. *Ketubbot* 5:6. See also nn. 17 and 18 below.

2. I want to thank Rabbi Mark Loeb for suggesting this interpretation.

3. That the couple may have conjugal relations any way they want: S.A. *Even ha-Ezer* 25:2, gloss. Isserles there says that "he may do what he wants with his wife," but this is a comment on the same paragraph of the *Shulhan Arukh* that says, "He may not have intercourse with her except with her consent" (literally, "desire"), and so the upshot is that both members of the couple must agree to the way they are having sex, presumably for the mutual satisfaction of both.

4. The wife's rights to sex within marriage: M. *Ketubbot* 5:6; M.T. *Laws of Marriage* 14:4–7, 15; S.A. *Yoreh De'ah* 235:1, *Even ha-Ezer* 76; 77:1. The husband's rights to sex within marriage: M. *Ketubbot* 5:7; M.T. *Laws of Marriage* 14:8–14; S.A. *Even ha-Ezer* 77:2–3.

5. That the man may not force himself upon his wife: M.T. *Laws of Marriage* 14:15; S.A. *Even ha-Ezer* 25:2, gloss.

6. M. *Ketubbot* 5:7 ("*Ha-moredet al ba'alah,*" i.e., a woman who "rebels" against her husband by refusing to fulfill any of the stipulated legal duties of a wife to her husband, including that of having sex with him). In the previous mishnah (M. *Ketubbot* 5:6), the Mishnah defines the conjugal duties of a husband to-

ward his wife, and the metaphoric meaning of M. *Ketubbot* 7:5 would require the husband to divorce his wife if he imposes on her an oath "that you draw water and empty it on a dunghill" —i.e., accept his resolve to interrupt coitus and masturbate. In any case, later Jewish law required a man who refused to engage in conjugal relations with his wife to divorce her—assuming, of course, that she brought him to court to object; see S. A. *Even ha-Ezer* 154:6–8. All of these sources are translated and discussed in Dorff and Rosett (1988), pp. 472–480.

7. Note that Naḥmanides (1194–1270) titles his letter to men about how to make love to their wives *Iggeret ha-Kodesh*, "The Letter of Holiness," translated and edited by Seymour J. Cohen under the title *The Holy Letter: A Study in Medieval Sexual Morality*, (New York: Ktav, 1976). Similarly, in the book by Rabbi Abraham ben David of Posquieres (1125–1198) on family law, *Ba'alei ha-Nefesh*, the seventh section, dealing with the moral and theological prisms through which one should approach sexual activity, is called *Sha'ar ha-Kedushah*, "The Gate of Holiness." On Judaism's approach to sexuality generally, see Dorff (1996).

8. The biblical command to "be fruitful and multiply": Genesis 1:28. The Mishnah's determination that it is only the man who is subject to the commandment: M. *Yevamot* 6:6 (61b), where the ruling is recorded as the majority opinion (i.e., without ascription) but without textual support and where Rabbi Yoḥanan ben Beroka immediately objects: "With regard to both of them [i.e., the male and female God first created] the Torah says, 'And God blessed them and said to them . . ."Be fruitful and multiply.""" The Talmud (B. *Yevamot* 65b–66a) brings conflicting evidence as to whether or not a woman is legally responsible for procreation and ultimately does not decide the matter. That is left for the later codes; cf. M.T. *Laws of Marriage* 15:2; S.A. *Even ha-Ezer* 1:1, 13. The Talmud there also brings conflicting exegetical grounds for the Mishnah's ruling restricting the command to men, basing it alternatively on, "Replenish the earth and subdue it" (Genesis 1:28) or on Genesis 35:11, "I am God Almighty, be fruitful and multiply." There are problems in using both texts, however. The traditional pronunciation of the Hebrew verb in the first verse (Genesis 1:28) is in the plural, making propagation a commandment for both the man and the woman; it is only the written form of the text that is in the masculine singular (and even that can apply, according to the rules of Hebrew grammar, to either men alone or to both men and women). The second verse (Genesis 35:11) is indeed in the masculine singular, but that may be only because there God is talking to Jacob; the fact that Jacob is subject to the commandment proves nothing in regard to whether his wives were or were not.

These problems make it likely that the real reason for limiting the commandment of procreation to men is not exegetical at all, and we have to look elsewhere for what motivated the rabbis to limit it in that way. I would suggest that that reason is to be found in the economic sphere—specifically, that since men were going to be responsible for supporting their children (although there is some question as to whether they were legally obligated to support their daughters), it was against the man's best economic interests to have children, and so it was precisely the men who had to be commanded. Alternatively, since the man has to offer to have conjugal relations with his wife for procreation to take place, that physical factor may be what prompted the rabbis to impose the commandment on men.

9. M. *Yevamot* 6:6 (61b). In that mishnah, the School of Shammai says that one has to have two boys, and the School of Hillel says that one must have a boy and a girl. The Talmud understands the School of Shammai's position to be based on the fact that Moses had two sons, Gershom and Eliezer (I Chronicles 23:15); while the Mishnah already states that the School of Hillel's ruling is based on Genesis 1:27, according to which God created the human being, "male and female God created them." A Tosefta (T. *Yevamot* 8:3), included in the Talmud (B. *Yevamot* 62a), asserts that the School of Shammai actually requires two males and two females, while the School of Hillel requires one male and one female. Yet another talmudic tradition (ibid.), in the name of Rabbi Nathan, states that the School of Shammai requires a male and a female, while the School of Hillel requires either a male or a female. The Jerusalem Talmud (J. *Yevamot* 6:6 [7c]) records the position of Rabbi Bun (Abun), which takes note of the context of the School of Hillel's ruling right after that of the School of Shammai's ruling requiring two boys. Rabbi Bun therefore reads the School of Hillel as agreeing that two boys would suffice to fulfill the obligation, but "*even* a boy and a girl" would, and thus the School of Hillel is offering a leniency over the School of Shammai's requirement of two boys, in line with the School of Hillel's general reputation. Rabbi Bun also notes that if that were not the case, such that the School of Hillel were saying that *only* a boy and a girl would fulfill the obligation, then this ruling should appear in the various lists of the stringencies of the School of Hillel in chapters 4 and 5 of M. *Eduyot*, but it does not. Despite Rabbi Bun's arguments, the codes rule that the obligation is fulfilled only when one has a boy *and* a girl: M.T. *Laws of Marriage* 15:4; S.A. *Even ha-Ezer* 1:5.

Ironically, in our own day, when modern technology has suddenly provided us with some control over the gender of our children but when the Jewish community simultaneously suffers from a major population deficit, we would affirm that technologically assisted gender selection should *not* take place, that we welcome children into our midst regardless of their gender, and that we see any two of them as fulfillment of the commandment to procreate.

10. The Talmud (B. *Yevamot* 62b) encourages couples to have as many children as possible on the basis of Isaiah 45:18 ("Not for void did He create the world, but for habitation *[lashevet]* did He form it") and Ecclesiastes 11:6 ("In the morning, sow your seed, and in the evening *[la'erev]* do not withhold your hand"). When codifying this law, Maimonides adds the explanation quoted; see M.T. *Laws of Marriage [Ishut]* 15:16. Maimonides' theme of a whole world being created with the birth of a child is echoed in M. *Sanhedrin* 4:5, "If anyone keeps a person [according to some manuscripts, "within the People Israel"] alive, it is as if he has sustained an entire world," and the converse appears in B. *Yevamot* 63b: "If someone refrains from propagation, it is as if he commits murder [literally, 'spills blood'] and diminishes the image of God."

11. The Jewish community, which numbered approximately eighteen million before the Holocaust, lost a third of its numbers during those terrible years. Far from replenishing the numbers we lost, we are now not even replacing ourselves. To do that, we would need a reproductive rate of 2.2 or 2.3 (that is, statistically 2.2 or 2.3 children for every two adults to compensate for those who never marry, those who marry and do not have children, and those who have only one child). The

present reproductive rate for Jews in North America is about 1.6 or 1.7. We Jews are therefore diminishing ourselves as a people to the point that the very existence of Jewry in the coming generations is demographically at risk.

The late age at which Jews marry and first try to have children is a significant factor in Jews' low reproductive rate. Both men and women become increasingly susceptible to the risks of infertility as they age. This is commonly known with regard to women, but it is true for men as well. With aging, there is significant decline in sperm motility and the requisite morphological characteristics for impregnation; see M. Chauhan, "The Influence of Female Fertility on Donor Insemination Success: Possible Reasons for Failure," in Barratt and Cooke (1993), p. 135, citing a study by D. Schwartz, M. J. Mayaux, A. Spira, M-L Moscato, P. Jouannet, and F. Czylik, "Semen Characteristics as a Function of Age in 833 Fertile Men," *Fertility and Sterility* 39 (1983), pp. 530–5. For the effect of age on women's fertility, see, for example, Yovich and Grudzinskas (1990), p. 2, citing M. R. Soules, "Prevention of Infertility," *Fertility and Sterility* 49 (1988), p. 582, according to which 25 percent of women between thirty-five and thirty-nine years of age are infertile, with a sharp rise occurring after that age.

Age affects the reproductive rate in another way as well. Because it often takes older couples longer to conceive, women who begin childbearing in their thirties often have time for only one or two pregnancies before menopause.

Other factors have also contributed to the low reproductive rate among Jews. Contemporary Jews commonly want to provide substantial educational and material benefits to their children, and so they consciously intend to have a small family so that they can afford to do that. Economic necessity and the women's movement have made the dual-career marriage commonplace, and so couples are also reluctant to have many children because of the limited time they will have to care for them.

Some Jews add concern for the world's overpopulation to their personal reasons for having few children. The world suffers from a daunting overpopulation problem. It was not until 1800 that the world had as many as one billion people. By 1930 two billion existed on the planet, by 1960 three billion, by 1974 four billion, and we are now at 5.6 billion and rising. People born before 1950 have seen the number of the people in the world double. (See *World Population by Country and Region, 1990* [Washington, DC: Bureau of the Census, 1990]. I want to thank Dr. Robert Edgar, president of the School of Theology at Claremont, for alerting me to this way of thinking about the overpopulation problem and for providing me with this reference. See also Lester R. Brown [1992], pp. 76–77.) People are already starving in many areas of the world, and although much of that starvation can be attributed to wars and bad distribution of food, there are grounds for real concern about how many people the planet can sustain even under the best conditions of food distribution and world peace.

One does not solve the problem of overpopulation, however, by undermining the existence of one's own people. That is especially true for Jews, who make up approximately one-fifth of 1 percent of the world's population. (For purposes of comparison, Catholics are 25 percent, Catholics and Protestants together make up 33 percent, and Muslims are 17 percent.) This means that if, God forbid, the entire Jewish population of the world were wiped off the map tomorrow, the world's population problem would not be alleviated to any significant degree. If one is really concerned about it, one should go to places like Africa (the continent with the fastest rate of population growth in history), the Middle East, India, China, and Brazil—the regions where the problem is most acute—to persuade people there to use contraceptive devices and to teach them how to do so. One should also foster the responsible use of resources. Sacrificing the existence of the Jewish people is neither an effective nor a warranted solution to the world's major problems of overpopulation and limited resources.

Add to these factors the high rate of intermarriage and assimilation among Jews today, and it becomes clear that Jews as a people are in serious demographic peril. Of course one needs a Jewish education to become an informed, practicing Jew, but people can be educated only if they exist in the first place.

The demographic needs of the Jewish people must also be a factor in communal planning. If we are serious as a community in our attempt to replenish our numbers, we must develop policies and programs to encourage larger families that are also deeply Jewish. Greater discounts could be given, for example, for each added sibling at Jewish day schools, camps, and youth programs; and nationally Jews can and should support profamily legislation such as laws providing for high-quality, affordable day care and family leave for both mothers and fathers. We must, in a phrase, "put our money where our mouths are."

12. God's blessings of the Patriarchs promise numerous children: Genesis 15:5; 17:4–21; 18:18; 22:15–18; 26:4–5; 28:13–15; 32:13. Children figure prominently in the descriptions of life's chief goods in Leviticus 26:9, and often in Deuteronomy (e.g., 7:13–14; 28:4, 11) and in Psalms (e.g., 128:6).

13. The Tosefta (T. *Sanhedrin* 7:3) recognizes this in an unusual setting. It rules that a man who does not have children of his own may not serve as a judge, presumably because his lack of experience in having children makes him insufficiently appreciative of their importance. The accused person, after all, is some couple's child, and if the death penalty is a possibility, the judge must be sensitive to what that means. See B. *Sanhedrin* 36b; M.T. *Laws of Courts (Sanhedrin)* 2:3.

14. Living on in the influence we have on others is often described as one's [good] name surviving—after death as well as in life; see Genesis 48:16; Numbers 27:4. Living on through one's children is most graphically illustrated by the Torah's levirate law, where the living brother was to have children through intercourse with his deceased brother's widow "that his [the dead brother's] name may not be blotted out in Israel"; see Deuteronomy 25:5–10 (the citation is from 25:6) and cf. Genesis 38. God's blessings of the Patriarchs and of the Israelites as a whole if they obey His commandments include the promise of numerous children as the bearers of the Covenant from one generation to another everlastingly, thus carrying on the legacy of the parents even if not their personal existence; see n. 12 above. On the other hand, if the Israelites do not obey God's commandments, one of the repeated curses is infertility and the death of the Israelites' children, to the point that "You shall eat the flesh of your sons and the flesh of your daughters" (Leviticus 26:29; Deuteronomy 28:53–57); see also Deuteronomy 28:18, 32. The Psalmist combines both of these ways in which we live on in praying, with regard to the wicked man, "May his posterity be cut off; may their names be blotted out in the next generation" (Psalms 109:12). If children are the embodiment of one's contin-

ued existence, death is conversely described by the biblical phrase of "being gathered to one's fathers"; see, for example, Genesis 25:8, 17; 35:29; 49:29, 33; Numbers 27:13; Deuteronomy 32:50; Judges 2:10.

For the rabbis, we also live on after death personally, although how we do so is described in varying ways in the sources. See "Afterlife," *Encyclopedia Judaica* 2:336–339; Moshe Greenberg, "Resurrection—In the Bible," *Encyclopedia Judaica* 14:97–98. While early biblical sources affirm the existence of Sheol, a murky place to which people's spirits descend after death, resurrection of the body after death is first affirmed by what is chronologically the last book of the Bible (c. 165 B.C.E.), the Book of Daniel (12:1–3). (Isaiah 26:19, which also affirms it, is, as Greenberg says in the article cited above, understood by almost all commentators to be a much later addition.) Job (e.g., 7:7–10; 9:20–22; 14:7–22), written in about 400 B.C.E., and Ecclesiastes (9:4–5; cf. 3:19–21), written about 250 B.C.E., explicitly deny resurrection and perhaps even any form of life after death. It thus appears that the doctrine of bodily resurrection was first accepted by at least a portion of the Jewish people in the second century B.C.E.

The rabbis (Pharisees), however, made this tenet a cardinal doctrine, asserting that biblical sources clearly and definitively affirm it even though they are, at best, ambiguous about it; see M. *Sanhedrin* 10:1; B. *Sanhedrin* 90a and following. The rabbis, though, were divided in their understanding of life after death, some affirming that the soul lives on after death and is ultimately rejoined with the body on the day of resurrection, others maintaining that when a person dies, the whole human being (i.e., both body and soul) succumbs, and that on the day of resurrection the whole, integrated human being is resurrected. See A. Cohen (1949), chap. 2.

15. Abraham, the patriarch of the Jewish people, is already charged with teaching his children (Genesis 18:19), and the commandment for each Jew to do likewise, which appears several times in the Torah, is enshrined in the sections chosen for the first two paragraphs of the *Shema* (Deuteronomy 6:4–9; 11:13–21), a prayer traditionally recited twice daily. Even when schools developed later on, the primary context for Jewish education remained the home, and the parents continued to be responsible for ensuring that their children would be educated and remain practicing Jews. In our own day, we are rediscovering that no schooling, however good, can be adequate, that family education is crucial for the continuation of the Jewish heritage.

16. See n. 10 above.

17. B. *Yevamot* 61b, where Rabbi Naḥman, quoting Genesis 2:18, asserts that "although a man may have many children, he must not remain without a wife, for the Torah says, 'It is not good that a man should be alone.'" Later Jewish law codes take this as authoritative law: M.T. *Laws of Marriage* 15:16; *Laws of Forbidden Intercourse* 21:26; S.A. *Even ha-Ezer* 1:8. See also n. 1 above.

18. The Mishnah (M. *Yevamot* 6:6), the Talmud (B. *Yevamot* 64a–66a), Maimonides (M.T. *Laws of Marriage* 15:7–15), and Joseph Caro (S.A. *Even ha-Ezer* 154:10–19, 21) all require a man to divorce his wife and marry another if he is not able to have children by her within ten years after marriage. She, in turn, may marry another man, but if she cannot have children with him during a ten-year period, she may not be married to a third man unless he has another wife or has already fulfilled the commandment to propagate. Rabbi Moses Isserles, however,

notes that "in this time we do not force him [a man without children] to divorce his wife at all" (S.A. *Even ha-Ezer* 154:10, gloss), and similarly in our time, infertility no longer requires divorce and should no longer be a source of guilt or shame.

19. Psalms 128:1, 3, 4, 5.

20. Deuteronomy 7:12–14.

21. Julie Stockler (1993), p. 94.

22. Sarah, Rebecca, and Rachel all have trouble having children: Genesis 15:2–4; 18:1–15; 25:21; 30:1–8, 22–24; 35:16–20. Later, Hannah, who ultimately bears the prophet Samuel, also first suffers from infertility; I Samuel 1:1–20.

23. Exodus 32:13; Deuteronomy 7:6–8.

24. The principle is announced in B. *Nedarim* 27a, B. *Bava Kamma* 28b, and B. *Avodah Zarah* 54a. There is some discussion among medieval commentators as to whether in cases of compulsion the obligation continues but the person is not culpable for failing to fulfill it (that is, the exemption applies only to culpability for failure to perform the commanded act), or whether the obligation ceases to apply altogether (that is, the exemption is from the obligation itself). The answer depends on whether the person, although unable to fulfill the obligation now, could fulfill it later, in which case the obligation continues and the principle excludes only culpability at this time, or whether the compulsion will continue indefinitely, in which case the obligation itself ceases. In any case, Tosafot (B. *Gittin* 41a, s.v. *lisa' shifḥah 'aino yakhol*) apply the principle directly to the obligation to be fruitful and multiply, claiming that in such an instance the obligation itself ceases. In general on this topic, see *Encyclopedia Talmudit, "Ones,"* 1:346–360, esp. pp. 347 and 360.

25. See n. 9 above.

26. Yovich and Grudzinskas (1990), pp. 1–2.

27. U.S. Congress (1988 [1]), pp. 1, 3, 4, 6, and 9. According to that report, in 1982, an estimated 8.5 percent of married couples with wives aged fifteen to forty-four were infertile, 38.9 percent were surgically sterile, and 52.6 percent were fertile. As the report notes, however, surgical sterilization masks some couples who were infertile anyway, and so if they are excluded from the population base, the 2.4 million infertile couples account for 13.9 percent of the remaining 17.3 million couples, or roughly one in seven. See also Andrews (1984), p. 160; Lauritzen (1991), pp. 57–58. The optimal age for pregnancy as twenty-two: *The Columbia University College of Physicians and Surgeons Complete Guide to Pregnancy*, as quoted in Weinhouse (1994), which presents a helpful description of the physical factors in pregnancy through the woman's twenties, thirties, and forties. See also chap. 5, n. 22 below.

28. Yovich and Grudzinskas (1990), p. 2.

29. The study conducted by the Office of Technology Assessment of the U.S. Congress (1988 [2]), pp. 3, 15) estimates that in the year 1986–1987, 172,000 women underwent artificial insemination, resulting in 35,000 births from AIH and 30,000 births by DI. See also Andrews (1984), p. 160; Lauritzen (1991), pp. 57–58; and Fader (1994), pp. 12–13. In comparison, in 1990 the number of births in the United States by IVF and GIFT combined was only just over 3,000; see I. D. Cooke, "Introduction," in Barratt and Cooke (1993), p. 1, based on a report of the American Fertility Society and the American Association of Tissue Banks.

30. U.S. Congress (1988 [2]), pp. 48–50. According to the report, on average the woman spends $309 in initial consultations, examinations, and testing and $92 for each of seven inseminations, a total of $953. Within this figure, though, AIH represents an average of $316, whereas DI averages $1,017 to $1,248, clinics handling more than one hundred patients a year being the most costly (averaging $1,718).

31. That approximately half of artificially inseminated women conceived after seven inseminations over a period of 4.4 cycles: U.S. Congress (1988 [2]), p. 45. J. C. Osborn, C. A. Yates, and G. T. Kovacs, "Donor Spermatozoa and Its Use in Assisted Reproduction (IVF, GIFT)," in Barratt and Cooke (1993), pp. 111, 119, and 123, report that "the average cumulative conception rate is approximately 55 percent after 6 cycles and 72 percent after 12 cycles of treatment . . . and the chances of conception after 12 cycles are significantly reduced," and that even after six failed cycles couples have much better results with IVF or, even better, with GIFT than with further attempts at DI.

The U.S. Government report (1988 [2], pp. 3, 8, 45) reported a 37.7 percent success rate for artificial insemination in producing not only conception but live birth—specifically, 65,000 babies born to the 172,000 women inseminated that year. That is more than double the highest success rate (17 percent) claimed by some practitioners of the more complicated methods of IVF, GIFT, and ZIFT — and almost four times as high as the 10 percent success rate reported by many who provide those procedures.

32. The 85–90 percent and 10–15 percent breakdown between conventional treatments and the more technologically sophisticated approaches of IVF, GIFT, and ZIFT is found in the report of the Office of Technology Assessment of the U.S. Congress (1988 [1]), p. 7.

33. Doctor Brenda Fabe, a gynecologist/obstetrician at Kaiser Permanente Hospital in West Los Angeles, supplied these approximate costs for me. See also Royte (1993), pp. 52–55, who reports similar prices.

Royte also notes that success rates "were widely overreported in the early 1980s, with clinics reporting take-home baby rates of 30 to 35 percent. After an Office of Technology Assessment [of the U.S. Congress] investigation in 1987, numbers became more realistic, but because the fertility industry isn't yet regulated by law, there are still no reporting standards." As a result, instead of live births, clinics may count pregnancies, and "they may not disclose the number of babies born with congenital diseases or that die within a month of birth." Moreover, "a woman who has triplets may add three births to the clinic's log, though only one mother takes babies home." (All citations from p. 54.)

The American Fertility Society asserts that IVF has a 15.2 percent success rate, and then only counting couples who produce quality eggs, sperm, and embryos (p. 54). That does not count the couples who drop out because they cannot produce such genetic materials. Still, in the late 1970s and early 1980s, IVF's success rate stood at less than 5 percent; by 1987 it had doubled (p. 55), and by now it has effectively tripled.

34. B. *Hagigah* 14b.

35. Judah Rozanes, *Mishneh le-Melekh* on M.T. *Laws of Women (Hilkhot Ishut)* 15:4; Moses Schick (Maharam Schick), *Taryag Mitzvot*, chap. 1; Solomon Schick, *Responsa Rashbam, Even ha-Ezer*, chap. 8.

36. For example, Rabbi Ḥayyim Joseph David Azulai, quoted in Immanuel Jakobovits, "Artificial Insemination, Birth Control, and Abortion," *Ha-Rofeh ha-Ivri* (1953) 2:169–183 (English) and 114–129 (Hebrew); Rabbi Jonathan Eybeschuetz, *Benei Ahuvah* on M.T. *Laws of Women (Hilkhot Ishut)* 15:6; and Rabbi Jacob Ettlinger, *Arukh la-Ner* on B. *Yevamot* 12b. The sources in this and the previous note are cited in Fred Rosner, "Artificial Insemination," in Rosner and Bleich (1979), p. 116, nn. 4–7. Rabbi Moshe Feinstein also bases his permission to use donor insemination on this source, noting that it specifically classifies the child as legitimate; see *Iggrot Moshe*, 4 *Even ha-Ezer* 1:10, 2:11, 3:11.

37. This is one example of *gematria*, a rabbinic method of interpreting the Bible. Since each Hebrew letter has a numerical equivalent, the rabbis, sometimes fancifully and sometimes seriously, see connections between Hebrew words or names whose Hebrew letters add up to the same number.

38. "Alfa Beta de-Ben Sira" in Eisenstein (1928), p. 43; cf. Preuss (1978), pp. 463–464; Friedenwald (1944), vol. I, p. 386; Jakobovits (1959, 1972), pp. 244–250. The story is denied, however, by Rabbi David Gans, who notes its absence in the Talmud and the classical collections of Midrash, and who quotes Rabbi Solomon ibn Verga as claiming that Ben Sira was the son of the daughter of Joshua ben Jehozadak, a High Priest mentioned in the Book of Ezra. David Gans, *Zemaḥ David* (Offenbach, 1968), 1:1:441, p. 14b. S. Verga, *Shevet Yehudah* (Lemberg, 1846).

39. Quoted by Rabbi Joel Sirkes, *Bayit Ḥadash ("Bah")* on the *Tur, Yoreh De'ah* 195. Also quoted by Rabbi David ben Samuel ha-Lev, *Turei Zahav ("Taz")*, on S.A. *Yoreh De'ah* 195:7.

40. Rabbi Moses ben Naḥman, *Commentary to the Torah*, on Leviticus 18:20. Rabbi Yoel Teitelbaum, *Divrei Yoel* 110, 140. Rabbi Eliezer Waldenberg, 9 *Tzitz Eliezer* 51:4; see also 3 *Tzitz Eliezer* 27:1, where Rabbi Waldenberg vigorously opposes the ruling of Rabbi Peretz, quoting a number of early rabbis who disagree with him on the unqualified legitimacy of a child born without sexual union.

41. Yoel Teitelbaum, 2 *Divrei Yoel* 110, 140. He claims that biblical commentaries may nevertheless be considered a source of law if they engender a stringency rather than a leniency. For Rabbi Moshe Feinstein's reply, see *Dibbrot Moshe, Ketubbot* 238–239.

42. Susan Grossman (1992), p. 14. Rabbi Grossman has suggested calling these the laws of sanctifying the family *(kedushat ha-mishpaḥah)* rather than family purity. She has pointed out to me that sometimes one of the manifestations of a woman's infertility problem, particularly in older women, is that she ovulates early in her cycle or spots during the middle of her cycle, which could mean, according to these laws, that she must refrain from conjugal relations with her husband for three days during her time of ovulation to ensure that her menstrual period is indeed over. To make it possible for such women to have conjugal relations during ovulation despite such spotting, traditional women, sometimes with the collusion of Orthodox rabbis, have invented creative ways to circumvent such possibilities, such as wearing dark underwear during that time so that the spots are not noticeable. For those infertile couples in the Conservative community who observe the laws of family purity, we would heartily endorse such creative solutions to this problem of staining, especially since the time about which we are talking is, at worst, during the

woman's "clean days," which are only rabbinically enacted, while the commandment to have children incumbent upon her husband is biblical.

43. The general imperative to take steps to maintain our health is, according to Maimonides and Isserles, based on Deuteronomy 4:9 and 4:15, "And you shall guard yourselves." The verses in context speak about guarding ourselves against following other gods, but Maimonides and Isserles applied them to guarding our bodies against illness as well. See M.T. *Laws of Ethics (De'ot)*, chaps. 3–5; *Laws of Murder* 11:4–5; S.A. *Yoreh De'ah* 116:5, gloss. Because they are reading the verses out of context, there is a debate in later sources as to whether by quoting these verses they mean to make the requirement biblical or whether the verses are merely a supporting text *(asmakhta)* and the command is therefore rabbinic; see the *Tumim* (27:1), affirming its biblical nature, and the *Leḥem Mishneh* to M.T. *De'ot* 3:5 and the Meiri, who both consider it to be rabbinic. In any case, saving a life *(pikuaḥ nefesh)*, the extreme case of maintaining our health and the issue here, is a well-attested principle in Jewish law, one that the rabbis deduce from Leviticus 18:5, understanding "and you shall live by them [i.e., my commandments]" to mean that you shall not die by them; see B. *Shabbat* 32b, 129a, 132a, 151b; *Yoma* 82a–85b; M.T. *Laws of the Foundations of the Torah* 5:1. The rabbis also asserted the converse, that we may not put ourselves unduly at risk; see chap. 2, n. 2 above.

44. Fader (1994), p. 3. Jakobovits (1959, 1972), p. 244, claims that the first successful human insemination was in 1866.

45. Fader (1994), pp. 8, 11. Average sperm counts over the past fifty years have declined by 50 percent, for reasons researchers are now investigating. "Health Report," *Time*, June 7, 1993, p. 20; Pinchbeck (1996), pp. 79–84, esp. p. 82. Two researchers claimed recently that the decline is due to men's increased exposure to estrogen in milk from hormone-dosed cows and water supplies contaminated by chemical spills.

If the number of sperm in the husband's semen is too small to generate children, or if the sperm are insufficiently motile (that is, not shaped correctly or energized enough to swim up the vaginal cavity), they can sometimes be made effective if several ejaculates are combined. The husband's semen, thus enhanced, is then used for inseminating his wife. According to Meredith F. Small (1991), p. 50, "Doctors look for a sperm count of at least 20 million per milliliter of semen, but they are more interested in sperm motility—the speed and swimming direction of individual sperm—because a few fast swimmers are more likely to succeed than millions of sluggards. Reproductive physiologists believe that at least 40 percent of the sperm viewed under the microscope must be vigorous, well-aimed swimmers for a couple to have a good chance at conception." Of the 300 million sperm in a typical human ejaculation, within ten minutes of landing at the cervix only thousands speed toward the fallopian tubes at the far end of the uterus, where the egg lies in wait after drifting down from the ovaries, and only two hundred sperm typically make it to the egg. Once one sperm has managed to bore into the egg, the shell of the egg releases enzymes that detach the other sperm. Ibid., pp. 51–52. This article also presents the results of recent research to the effect that sperm counts for ejaculations during intercourse decreased the more time couples spent together and, conversely, increased when the male assumed female infidelity. That is *not*, however, a justification for an infertile couple to try promiscuity as a therapy!

46. If, for example, the woman's cervix is damaged, the man's sperm cannot reach the uterus and must be injected artificially into the womb. Semen, though, has proteins that, if injected directly into the woman's uterus, can cause the woman to go into anaphylactic shock, which can be lethal. Before injection into the uterus, the semen must therefore be "washed" or "spun down" with various tissue culture media to separate viable sperm from other components of the semen. Similarly, if the woman's cervix does not make good mucus naturally, or if the drugs she is taking to stimulate her ovaries spoil the effectiveness of her cervical mucus, the sperm must be "washed" first and then artifically implanted into her uterus.

47. See, for example, Jakobovits (1959, 1972), p. 264; Bleich (1981 [1]), pp. 83–84. Dr. Rosner lists, in addition, Rabbis Feinstein, Schwadron, Wolkin, and Zevi Pesaḥ Frank as permitting AIH, while Rabbis Tanenbaum and Waldenberg "frown upon it, stating it is permissible only in extreme situations"—but, of course, that is, by hypothesis, always the case. See Rosner (1970) in Rosner and Bleich (1979), p. 112.

48. B. *Niddah* 13b.

49. Cf. Bleich (1981 [1]), p. 84, n. 3 for a list of sources on this issue.

50. Rabbi Morris Shapiro, "Artificial Insemination in Jewish Law," prepared in August 1978 for the Committee on Jewish Law and Standards, p. 3.

51. Dr. Rosner cites all of the following who claim that the donor is considered the father in Jewish law: Rabbis Moses of Brisk, Samuel ben Uri, Judah Rozanes of Constantinople [a commentator on Maimonides' *Mishneh Torah*], Jacob ben Samuel, Israel Ze'ev Mintzberg, Simeon Zemaḥ Duran, and Jacob Ettlinger. Rabbis Jacob Emden and Moses Schick rule that the child is the son of the donor, but the donor has not fulfilled the commandment of procreation because there has been no sexual act involved. Only Rabbis Hadaya and Moses Aryeh Leib Shapiro on Dr. Rosner's list do not consider the child that of the donor. See Rosner (1970) in Rosner and Bleich (1979), p. 111, with the specific sources in nn. 30–37 on p. 117.

52. B. *Berakhot* 6a; B. *Kiddushin* 40a; J. *Peah* 1. But according to B. *Kiddushin* 39b, there is one exception to the converse of this rule. Specifically, in weighing the culpability of a person, God does not ordinarily connect an evil thought to its act (even if not fulfilled), but God does do so when one thinks of idolatry.

53. Canada (1993). American Fertility Society (1994 [1]), 35S–36S. I would like to thank my friend and colleague, Rabbi Aaron Mackler, for these references and for sharing with me his responsum written for the Conservative movement's Committee on Jewish Law and Standards on IVF, much of which I shall follow in the remainder of this section. See also Yovich and Grudzinskas (1990), pp. 91–92, for this early history of the procedure.

54. American Fertility Society (1994 [2]), pp. 1121–28.

55. American Fertility Society (1994 [1]), pp. 38S–40S.

56. Rabbi Aaron Mackler (1997). Rabbi Ovadiah Yosef, past Sephardic chief rabbi of Israel, has also ruled permissively on IVF; see Drori (1980), pp. 287–88. Similarly, Rabbi David M. Feldman, the Conservative rabbi who has written the most authoritative book on birth control and abortion (Feldman 1968), has permitted the use of IVF for otherwise infertile couples; see Feldman (1986), pp. 71–72.

The major exceptions to this line of permissive rulings for using IVF are Rabbi Eliezer Waldenberg (*Tzitz Eliezer*, vol. 15, no. 45, pp. 115–120; reprinted in *Assia* 33 (1982), pp. 5–13 [both in Hebrew]) and Rabbi J. David Bleich (in Rosner and Bleich [1979], pp. 80–85). I will deal with the substantive objections they raise in the next few paragraphs. Moreover, see the response to Rabbi Waldenberg by Rabbi Avigdor Nebenzal ("In Vitro Fertilization—Comments," *Assia* 35 (1983), p. 5 [Hebrew]), where he points out that prohibiting IVF to those couples who need it would preclude the husband from fulfilling the commandment to procreate and, by increasing the couple's anguish, might even be a prime factor leading to divorce. Again, my thanks to Rabbi Aaron Mackler for these references.

57. Spirtas, Kaufman, and Alexander (1993), pp. 291–292. I want to thank my friend, Dr. Michael Grodin, for sharing this article with me. The 1988 congressional report also reported a number of other possible complications caused by commonly used drugs to stimulate the ovaries, including early pregnancy loss, multiple gestations (fetuses), ectopic pregnancies, headache, hair loss, pleuropulmonary fibrosis, increased blood viscosity and hypotension, stroke, and myocardial infarction; see U.S. Congress (1988 [1]), pp. 128–129. Once again, though, the demonstrated risks are not so great as to make stimulation of the ovaries for egg donation prohibited as a violation of the Jewish command to guard our health, but they are sufficient to demand that caution be taken and that the number of times a woman donates eggs be limited.

58. Canada (1993), pp. 527–30. Rosner (1990), p. 181.

59. I want to thank Rabbi Judah Kogen for calling my attention to the psychological aspects of this situation.

60. Nijs et al. (1993). The Ethics Committee of the American Fertility Society maintained that variations among particular cases argue against establishing a standard numerical limit, but "the number of preembryos transferred should be limited . . . to anticipate that no quadruplet pregnancies will occur and that triplet pregnancies will be minimized to 1 percent to 2 percent." See American Fertility Society (1994 [1]), 37S. This, however, in essence amounts to a limit of two or at most three.

61. Grazi and Wolowelsky (1993–4), p. 20, where they cite the following as all permitting selective abortion in cases in which IVF has produced more than three fetuses: Mordecai Eliyahu, former chief rabbi of Israel; Ḥayyim David Halevi, chief rabbi of Tel Aviv; Yitzḥak Zilberstein, an Israeli rabbi prolific in the area of medical ethics; and, at least reportedly, Rabbi Shlomo Zalman Auerbach, "doyen of leading contemporary rabbinic authorities."

62. Andrews and Douglass (1991), p. 670. Phenylketonuria is a genetic defect that may lead to mental retardation unless identified very early in a child's life. This reference, as well as many in this section on surrogacy, comes from Spitz (1996), and I would like to thank Rabbi Elie Spitz for sharing his manuscript with me and for allowing me to cite from it.

63. The first successful surrogacy (Louise Brown) in 1978: Andrews and Douglass (1991), p. 625. The first paid surrogacy in 1980: Andrews and Douglass (1991), p. 637. The estimate of four thousand children: Andrews and Douglass (1991), p. 670; Edmiston (1991); California Legislature report(1991), p. M8; and Center for Surrogate Parenting Newsletter (1993), where it is reported as the esti-

mate of the New York Health Department. The estimate of one thousand new surrogacy agreements a year: Edmiston (1991), p. 236.

64. Center for Surrogate Parenting (1993), p. 1. Edmiston (1991) puts the number at fifteen; the California Legislature report (1991) cites only ten.

65. Zohar (1991), p. 13.

66. One is Rosner (1991), p. 114.

67. Jakobovits (1959, 1975), pp. 264–265.

68. Sums supplied by the Center for Surrogate Parenting, Beverly Hills, California, in 1994: $12,000 for the surrogate mother; $13,600 for administrative costs; $5,000 for medical costs; $4,000 for psychological costs; $3,000 to retain legal counsel; $4,000 for miscellaneous costs. Cited as endn. 13 in Spitz (1996).

69. Daniel H. Gordis (1988), pp. 14, 16, 18–19. The article he cites for the costs of surrogacy is Anne Taylor Fleming, "Our Fascination with Baby M," *New York Times Magazine*, March 29, 1987, p. 35. Carole Pateman's article is "Charges Against Prostitution: An Attempt at a Philosophical Evaluation," *Ethics* 90:3 (1980), pp. 335–66.

70. Gellman (1987), pp. 105, 107.

71. Pretorius (1994), p. 58, citing *American Medical News* 23 (1987). This ruling was in response to the Baby M case in New Jersey; see n. 76 below.

72. In fairness, I should also mention that the Committee also approved a responsum by Rabbi Aaron Mackler opposing surrogacy. I, however, support Rabbi Spitz's view and so invoke his arguments—and some of my own—here.

73. Spitz (1996), p. 3. California Legislature (1991), p. 16, n. 9, contains a list of the studies, which include the following: "Surrogate Mother Demographics," by H. Daniel and K. Linkins (Harvard Medical School), who conclude that the primary motivation of surrogate mothers is altruism; "Psychiatric Evaluation of Women in the Surrogate Mother Process," *American Journal of Psychiatry*, October 1981, which draws the same conclusion and maintains that surrogate mother candidates are psychologically healthy (on that point see also Andrews and Douglass [1991], pp. 673–674); and "Surrogate Parenting: Reassessing Human Bonding," by Hilary Hanafin, Ph.D., who reports no evidence of regret by surrogates and concludes that open contact between the parties is an important factor in assuring that.

74. William Handel of the Center for Surrogate Parenting, 8383 Wilshire Blvd., Suite 750, Beverly Hills, CA 90211; (213) 655–1974. Reported in Spitz (1996), p. 2.

75. See n. 57 above.

76. *Baby M*: 217 NJ Super 313 323 525 A 2d 1128 1132 Ch. Div. (1987) rev'd in part, 109 NJ 396 537 A 2d 1227 (1988). In that case the court held that the contract was not binding because it violated the rule against payment for adoption, and so the judge treated it as a custody case, awarding custody to William Stern (the father) and later allowing his wife to adopt the child as its mother. The appeal of Judge Sorkow's ruling in that case to the New Jersey Supreme Court (sometimes dubbed "Baby M II") is *In re Baby M* 109 NJ 396 410–11 537 A 2d 1227, 1234 (1988). For a detailed analysis of these cases, see I. Stern, *Journal of Family Law*, 1988–1989, pp. 585–671.

Marriage of Moschetta: 5 Cal. 4th 84, 19 Ca., Rptr. 494 (1993). In that case, the ovum-surrogate claimed that she had agreed to give the baby to a stable couple, but during pregnancy the couple had separated. There again the judge treated the case as one of custody, awarding it to the father and ovum-surrogate jointly.

77. Center for Surrogacy Parenting (1993), p. 1. The latter study, conducted by Carol Wolfe, MFCC, of 250 adoption arrangements found that in 95 of them (38 percent) one or the other party withdrew from the agreement prior to, or following, the birth of the child. If we follow the statistics of the Health Department of the State of New York reported there, in only one case out of four thousand (.025 percent) surrogacy arrangements did the intended parents fail to get the legal right to the child.

78. The four that have outlawed payment altogether: Arizona, Kentucky, Michigan, and Utah. The five that permit paying expenses only: Florida, New Hampshire, New York, Virginia, and Washington. From Spitz (1996), n. 74. Michigan goes the furthest in criminalizing surrogacy. According to its 1988 statute, it is a crime to enter into, or assist in the formation of, a surrogacy contract for compensation. Surrogacy brokers can face fines of up to $50,000 or imprisonment for up to five years; participants in surrogacy contracts with money for more than expenses can be fined up to $10,000 or imprisoned for up to one year. See Pretorius (1994), p. 56. In addition to Spitz's list, Pretorius there says that New Jersey also prohibits "commercial surrogacy," that is, contracts with money for more than expenses. See also Lori B. Andrews (1987); reprinted in Hull (1990). George Annas has argued strongly that surrogacy is tantamount to baby selling; see his article (1986), reprinted in Hull (1990).

79. The father has the duty to maintain his children: M.T. *Laws of Marriage* 13:6; S.A. *Even ha-Ezer* 73:6, 7. Moreover, the father continues to have these responsibilities even if not married to their mother (e.g., in instances of divorce or when the child was born out of wedlock): *Responsa Ribash* 41; *Responsa Rosh* 17:7. See "Parent and Child," *Encyclopedia Judaica* 13:96.

80. Spitz (1996), p. 13.

NOTES TO CHAPTER FOUR

1. Yovich and Grudzinskas (1990), p. 69, citing J. F. Leeton, "The Development and Demand for AID in Australia," in *Artificial Insemination by Donor*, C. Wood, ed. (Melbourne: Brown Prior Anderson, 1980), p. 10.

2. The figure of 50,000 attempts each year: Edmiston (1991), p. 236. The figure of 100,000: Julie Marquis, "Gift of Life, Questions of Liability," *Los Angeles Times*, August 9, 1997, p. A-1. The figure of 45 percent of artificial inseminations using donor sperm: U.S. Congress (1988 [2]), p. 33. The figure of 10,000 to 20,000 births each year through DI: Andrews (1984), p. 160, cited also in Donovan (1986), p. 57, n. 6. The figure of 300,000 births through DI since the 1950s: California Legislature (1991), p. 7, n. 2; Donovan (1986), p. 57—although Donovan there cites Annas (1980), p. 1, for that figure, and if that was true in 1980, then presumably, at the rate of 10,000 to 20,000 births from DI each year, by 1991 the figure should have risen beyond 400,000.

3. Yovich and Grudzinskas (1990), p. 69, citing R. G. Bunge and J. K. Sherman, "Fertilizing Capacity of Frozen Human Spermatozoa," *Nature* 173 (1953), p. 767.

4. That responsum has been published: Dorff (1996[5]).

5. The Torah's ban on marrying *mamzerim*: Deuteronomy 23:3. The opinion of Rabbi Waldenberg based on that ban: *Tzitz Eliezer* IX, 51, chap. 5, sec. 1, p. 251. See also Rabbi Yoel Teitelbaum (1954) and the discussion of this in Grazi and Wolowelsky (1992), pp. 157–158.

6. For the prohibition of adultery, see Leviticus 18:16 and 20:10. For the rationale that observing this will make us holy and pure, see Leviticus 18:24 and 20:8, 26. For separation from the practices of the Egyptians and Canaanites as an explicit component of the meaning of those terms, see Leviticus 18:3, 27, 30; 20:23, 24, 26. For avoiding pollution of the land of Israel as another component of the meaning of these terms: Leviticus 18:25–29; 20:22.

7. Rabbi Paul Plotkin has suggested that, biblically at least, the ban of adultery is based not on the breach of trust involved but on the violation of the husband's acquisition of his wife *(kinyan)*. In DI, though, the husband agrees to the procedure, and so presumably his rights of possession are not violated. Even though most modern Jews do not think of marriage in terms of the man's possession of the woman, even that aspect of the biblical prohibition of adultery is not violated by DI.

8. If both partners agreed to each other's adultery, that, of course, would not make it permissible, for Judaism requires not only honesty and fidelity in marital relationships but exclusivity. (Until the enactment of Rabbenu Gershom's decree in approximately 968 B.C.E., a man could have more than one wife, even though a woman could not have more than one husband.) The vast majority of cases of adultery, however, involve a breach of trust, and it is that which explains much of our abhorrence of adultery, for such lack of trust undermines the honesty and holiness that Judaism wants in marriage.

9. B. *Shevuot* 18a; cf. M. *Yevamot* 6:1 (53b), B. *Yevamot* 54a, and B. *Horayot* 4a. M.T. *Laws of Forbidden Intercourse* 1:10–11. This is also the opinion of Rabbi David Halevi (the "Taz") of the seventeenth century, who bases it on the responsa of Rabbi Peretz, an eleventh-century scholar; see *Turai Zahav* in S.A. *Even ha-Ezer* 1:8. Rabbi Peretz is quoted there as asserting that "in the absence of sexual intercourse, the child resulting from the mixing of sperm and egg is always legitimate." Rabbi Bleich, who vigorously opposes DI, nevertheless notes the following modern authorities *(aḥaronim)* who require sexual contact for a sexual act to be termed adulterous: Rabbi Shalom Mordecai Schwadron, *Teshuvot Maharsham* (Brezany, 1910), III, no. 268; Rabbi Aaron Walkin, *Teshuvot Zekan Aharon* (New York, 1951), II, no. 97; Rabbi Yehoshua Zion Uziel, *Mishpetai Uziel* (Tel Aviv, 1935), *Even ha-Ezer*, I, no. 19; Rabbi Moshe Feinstein, *Iggrot Moshe, Even ha-Ezer*, vol. I (Brooklyn, 1961), no. 10; cf. also no. 71, pp. 169–171; vol. 2 (Brooklyn, 1963), no. 2, pp. 322–324; vol. 3 (Brooklyn, 1973), no. 14, pp. 436f; vol. 4 (Brooklyn, 1985), no. 32(5), pp. 75f; and Rabbi Eliyahu Meir Bloch, *Ha-Pardes*, Sivan 5713. On the other hand, he cites the following who do not require sexual contact for the prohibition of adultery to take effect: Rabbi Yehudah Leib Zierlson, *Teshuvot Ma'arekhei Lev*, no. 73; and Rabbi Ovadiah Hadaya, *No'am*, I (5718), pp. 130–137, with reference also to Rabbi Eliezer Waldenberg, *Tzitz Eliezer*, IX (1985), no. 51, sec. 4. pp. 240–259. These latter authorities stress that Leviticus 18:20 reads literally, "And to the wife of your fellow you shall not give

your intercourse for seed to defile her," which in their view would include providing semen even without sexual intercourse. See Bleich (1981 [1]), p. 84, nn. 1 and
2. See also, on DI generally, Grazi and Wolowelsky (1992); on this aspect of it in
particular, pp. 157–158.

As Rabbi Paul Plotkin has pointed out to me, for those who insist on contact of
the genital organs to establish adultery, this is parallel to the Talmud's insistence
that the Torah's prohibition against eating blood is violated only when the blood
is ingested in the normal way, through the throat. Therefore, contrary to the Jehovah's Witnesses, who interpret the biblical command more broadly, we Jews permit blood transfusions, even when they are precautionary and not clearly essential for the saving of a life. See B. *Sanhedrin* 63a, and Dorff (1991), p. 35, where
I use this precedent along similar lines to permit the withdrawal of artificial nutrition and hydration. See Chapter 8 in this book.

10. See M.T. *Laws of Forbidden Intercourse* 1:1, 9, 12 (and see the commentary
of the *Maggid Mishneh* there).

11. B. *Yevamot* 98a; cf. Tosafot, B. *Yevamot* 22a, s.v. *ervah lakol mesurah*. M.T.
Laws of Forbidden Intercourse 14:13; S.A. *Yoreh De'ah* 269:3.

12. Moshe Feinstein, *Iggrot Moshe, Even ha-Ezer* I (1961), nos. 10, 71, pp. 12–
14, 169–171; II (1963), *Hoshen Mishpat*, no. 11, pp. 322–324. On the pressure
that ultimately caused him to withdraw these responsa, see Zvi Hirsch Friedman,
Sefer Sedeh Ḥemed (Brooklyn, 1965/6), p. 34.

13. In the case of the Orthodox respondents who hold this view, this attitude
toward non-Jews is also, as Daniel J. Lasker has shown, the product of kabbalis-
tic affirmations of original sin, a doctrine roundly rejected by the nonmystic sources
of Jewish thought—and rightly so. See Lasker (1988), esp. pp. 7–11.

14. Currie-Cohen, Lullrel, and Shapiro (1979). Thirty-one per cent of the inseminating doctors surveyed in that study indicated that they use the sperm of several donors within one menstrual cycle, while 51.1 percent reported that they use
a single donor but change donors with each new cycle; one donor had been used
to produce fifty pregnancies (see p. 587). If the subject is a donor for a minority
ethnic group in the area, the chances of intermarriage by the children become even
greater; see p. 589, n. 9. The U.S. Congress report of 1988 ([2], p. 64) included a
summary of a 1986 study by Drs. William Schlaff and Janet Kennedy of hospital-
based sperm banks providing DI. One hundred and thirty facilities responded (out
of four hundred that received the questionnaire), but not all of them answered all
the questions, and hence the disparity of numbers below. Forty-one out of sixty-
one sperm banks that responded to the question asking about limits of pregnancies per donor had a limit of two to twenty pregnancies that could be initiated by
the same donor (with an average of nine). Nineteen of sixty-two facilities that
responded to this question would sometimes tell donors whether pregnancies had
occurred with their semen, with only one facility routinely sharing that information with the donor. This would indicate that using the sperm of one donor for
multiple pregnancies (and keeping the results from him) continued through the
1980s, and the 1992 summary of law regarding artificial insemination published
by the American Bar Association reported no new legislation prohibiting such
multiple uses of one donor's sperm. See Tate (1992). This would mean that the
possibility of incest continues to exist.

The latest information I was able to find, the booklet published by California Cryobank, Inc. (Fader [1994]), states that its practice is that sperm donors must agree to donate sperm twice a week for a minimum of a year, and preferably two. That policy is enforced because the man's sperm is frozen for six months while he continues to be tested for AIDS and venereal diseases to make sure that his sperm is not infected. "Without the year minimum commitment from donors, this safety measure could not be carried out" (p. 21). According to the bank,

> "The number of live births from one donor usually ranges between two and ten" (p. 21), and a donor is retired after his sperm has produced ten live births. Nevertheless, the bank maintains that the chances of offspring from a single donor inadvertently marrying and having children, "although not impossible . . . [are] extremely remote," especially because the frozen sperm is distributed internationally (pp. 21–22).

Only four states (Illinois, Indiana, New York, and Michigan) have specific regulations for sperm banks with regard to the testing for diseases that must be performed with donor sperm and the length of time the frozen sperm must be held before use; another twelve states have laws requiring HIV antibody testing of semen donors. See G. M. Centola, "American Organization of Sperm Banks," in Barratt and Cooke (1993), pp. 146–7. The American Fertility Society published guidelines for the use of donor semen in 1986, however, and in 1988 the American Fertility Society, the Centers for Disease Control, and the Food and Drug Administration recommended that all semen used for DI be frozen and quarantined for a minimum of six months. Currently, the Food and Drug Administration is initiating proceedings to register and certify sperm bank facilities. All of that legal activity, however, is an attempt to ensure the safety of donated semen; it does not include regulations to limit the number of pregnancies for which sperm banks may use the same donor.

15. One case graphically illustrating the need to know the donor's identity in case of diseases that appear in the offspring recently landed in the courts and was reported on the front page of the *Los Angeles Times*. See Julie Marquis, "Gift of Life, Questions of Liability," *Los Angeles Times*, August 9, 1997, pp. A-1, A-18, A-19. Specifically, even though the California Cryobank has been a leader in donor screening, with its doctors pushing for greater accountability in the infertility industry, it was recently sued itself for failing to track the genetic history of a donor thoroughly enough. The sperm of a donor who gave incomplete information about kidney disease in his mother's family was used in 1986 to create a girl who at age eight began to suffer from early onset of adult polycystic kidney disease (APKD). Roughly half of those with the condition experience kidney failure before age fifty, and those who have it (approximately one in 1,000 people) are routinely advised to monitor blood pressure, avoid contact sports, and make other adjustments in diet. The donor supplied 320 vials to the bank over four years, earning $35 per donation. One or two vials are generally used per attempt at conception, but it is impossible to estimate how many children may have resulted.

This particular suit is against the sperm bank exclusively, not against the donor. In addition to suing for monetary damages—including the medical costs of the dialysis and the kidney transplant that will ultimately be needed—the couple are seeking to learn the donor's identity. Two doctors declared in court documents that the donor's complete medical history is needed to predict the course of the girl's disease—whether, for example, she is likely to suffer the potentially lethal complications of brain aneurysms. The couple say they bear Donor 276 no ill will and do not intend to sue him, but they maintain that in addition to receiving an incomplete medical history, they were misled by those who screened him and have a right to talk to him directly.

The case raises a number of sticky moral issues:

1. The natural rate of birth defects is 2 to 5 percent; can a sperm bank be held legally accountable for not doing better? Sperm banks are paid to screen the donor for the recipient, and the relationship of the recipient to the donor is financial rather than romantic, but no battery of tests can guarantee absolute health, and each test would significantly add to the cost of the procedure. Do sperm banks fulfill their duty if they simply disclose what they test for and what they do not, offering the couple the option of further tests at their expense?

2. If precautions fail and a child is born with a serious hereditary defect, does the bank have the duty to warn others who used the same donor? Since the disease is currently incurable, would that just cast a pall over the recipients and their young children's lives, or would telling other recipients spare them the anguish and expense of gradually discovering the nature and origins of their children's disease if and when they contract it?

3. If the donor's identity is revealed in such cases, will that dissuade significant numbers of potential donors? Currently, over 100,000 women each year seek donor sperm to become pregnant. Will they be denied a safe, inexpensive procedure to become pregnant because potential sperm donors have been scared away by the threat of identification and even suit?

16. According to U.S. Congress (1988 [2]), pp. 70–71, "At least 11 of the 15 sperm banks [surveyed] keep detailed records for each donor, which often includes information such as the number of women inseminated, number of pregnancies achieved, number of children born, the donor's physical examination, the donor's family genetic history, and any follow-up examinations of the donor. The majority of facilities will not allow offspring, recipients, recipients' partners, or the donors themselves access to these records." The most some sperm banks will provide, even to the courts and public health officials, is access to donor records without donor names. Moreover, "offspring rights 'to communicate with their genetic fathers' were uniformly and strongly opposed by the surveyed physicians [who perform DI]" (p. 58; see also p. 55). The American Association of Tissue Banks, *Standards of Sperm Banks Practice* (Arlington, VA: 1988), reproduced on p. 71 of U.S. Congress (1988 [2]), specifies that "As of 1988, AATB directed its member sperm banks to maintain complete donor records, but to ensure that the donor's actual identity never be revealed."

17. In 1988, the Conservative movement's Committee on Jewish Law and Standards approved a responsum by Rabbi Avram Reisner according to which a child who is converted to Judaism need not be known as "so-and-so, son or daughter of Abraham, our father, and Sarah, our mother" if Jewish adults are to raise him

or her. Under those circumstances the child may be known by his or her given name(s), son/daughter of the social parents. Moreover, if the child is adopted, even if the natural parents were Jewish and it is known who they are, the child may be known as the child of the social parents when, for example, being called for an honor to the Torah. (See *Summary Index: The Committee on Jewish Law and Standards* [New York: Rabbinical Assembly, 1994], p. 2:6.) In approving my responsum in 1994, on which this chapter is based, the committee extended that ruling to cover children born through DI or egg donation as well.

18. See, for example, Leviticus 21:17, 21; 22:3, 4; etc. While it is clearly true that the word "seed" *(zera)* is often a synonym for children, in both Hebrew and English, the rules of priestly status were not interpreted in that metaphoric way. On the contrary, the genetic line of the priesthood was guarded very carefully; cf. M. *Middot* 5:4; M. *Kiddushin* 4:5. Cf. M.T. *Laws of Entering the Temple* 9:1. The "seed of Aaron" was specifically interpreted not to include girls (B. *Kiddushin* 36a) and not to include even those who were genetic male descendants of Aaron without blemishes but who did not look normal in some way (B. *Bekhorot* 43a–b).

19. Yeh and Yeh (1991), pp. 41–48. That book includes charts on pp. 43–46 that list each state's laws on this as of 1991. The Uniform Parentage Act, 9A U.L.A. 592 (1979), drafted in 1973 by the National Conference of Commissioners on Uniform State Laws and approved by the House Delegates of the American Bar Association in 1974, has since been passed in whole or in part by the following states: Alabama, California, Colorado, Delaware, Hawaii, Illinois, Kansas, Minnesota, Missouri, Montana, Nevada, New Jersey, New Mexico, North Dakota, Ohio, Rhode Island, Washington, and Wyoming. Section 5(A) deals with donor insemination.

This acceptance of donor insemination in American law took some time. In 1964, Georgia became the first state to pass a statute legitimizing children conceived by donor insemination, on condition that both the husband and wife consented in writing, and in 1968 the California Supreme Court became the first American appellate court to hand down a ruling affirming that stance in *People v. Sorenson.* The court there upheld Mr. Sorenson's criminal conviction for not supporting a DI child conceived with his consent during his marriage. The court held that the sperm donor had no more responsibility for the use of his sperm than a blood donor had for the use of his/her blood. This was in sharp contrast to the 1954 ruling of the Supreme Court of Cook County, Illinois, which held that regardless of the husband's consent, DI was "contrary to public policy and good morals, and constituted adultery on the mother's part," so that the child so conceived was the mother's exclusively and "the father has no rights or interest in said child." See Fader (1994), pp. 4–5. Thus the 1973 recommendation of the Commissioners on Uniform State Laws that children born through DI be considered legitimate was, for most jurisdictions, breaking new ground. It has, however, been widely followed: see *S. v. S.*, 440 A.2d 64 (N.J. 1981); *In re* Adoption of Anonymous, 345 N.Y.S.2d 430 (1973); *Noggle v. Arnold*, 338 S.E.2d 763 (Ga. 1985); *R. S. v. R. S.*, 670 P.2d 923 (Kan. 1983); *Mace v. Webb*, 614 P.2d 647 (Utah 1980); *In re* Custody of D. M. M., 404 N.W.2d 530 (Wis. 1987); *L. M. S. v. S. L. S.*, 312 N.W.2d 853 (Wis. 1981); *In re* Baby Doe, 353 S.E.2d 877 (S.C. 1987). Thus the man who consents to the artificial insemination of his wife is now legally obligated to support the resulting children, either on the theory of equitable estoppel (since he, after all, consented to the insemination) or on the theory of adoption, according to which the husband, by his consent, has formally or informally adopted the children.

20. Rabbi Joseph Soloveitchik, however, has said that raising adopted children does fulfill the commandment to procreate (see Melech Schachter [1982], p. 107), and the same reasoning might apply to a child conceived through DI. With regard to semen donors, some rabbis have ruled that while the semen donor has full obligations for the child created through his semen, he does not fulfill the obligation to procreate because there is no sexual act involved. See, for example, Bleich (1981 [1]), p. 80. On this reasoning he incurs the duties of fatherhood without even having the satisfaction of fulfilling the commandment of procreation!

21. Deuteronomy 25:5–10. This law may refer only to inheritance rights, but the language of Deuteronomy seems to indicate a stronger relationship, for the levir is to have a child with his sister-in-law, whom he takes "as his wife," but "the first son that she bears shall be accounted to the dead brother, that his name may not be blotted out in Israel" (Deuteronomy 25:6).

22. *Exodus Rabbah* 46:5. In contrast, another deservedly famous source (B. *Sanhedrin* 19b) proclaims that "whoever brings up an orphan in his home, Scripture ascribes it to him *as if* he had begotten him." This source in *Exodus Rabbah*, however, removes the "as if."

23. M. *Avodah Zarah* 4:4–7; T. *Avodah Zarah* 6:2; B. *Avodah Zarah* 43a, 52a–55a; M.T. *Laws of Idolatry* 8:9–12; S.A. *Yoreh De'ah* 146:1–12.

24. Genesis 48:5–6. Jacob, while not the biological father of Ephraim and Menashe, was their biological grandfather, unlike the social father of a DI child. Furthermore, biblical terminology often does not discriminate between children and grandchildren, and since Joseph was Jacob's firstborn son by Rachel, Ephraim and Menashe may represent Joseph's double portion through primogeniture—although we do not hear of a similar provision for Reuven, Leah's firstborn son. In any case, these factors would argue against using this last example to support the social father's claim to fulfilling the command to procreate, while the specific language of the verses in Genesis, by which Ephraim and Menashe are legally classified as Jacob's sons even though they are not biologically his sons, would seem to support his claim.

25. B. *Sanhedrin* 74a; M.T. *Laws of the Foundations of the Torah* 5:1–3; S.A. *Yoreh De'ah* 157:1.

26. B. *Ketubbot* 50a. See n. 81 below.

27. S.A. *Even ha-Ezer* 15:11.

28. B. *Sotah* 43b. One medieval authority, Rabbi Judah ben Samuel, decreed that such marriages may not be performed; cf. Judah ben Samuel of Regensberg (he-Ḥasid), *Sefer Ḥasidim*, sec. 829. This decree, however, has not been generally accepted; see Rabbi M. Sofer, *Responsa*, 2 *Yoreh De'ah* 125. As Michael Broyde notes, however, although legally permitted, few such marriages are performed; see Michael Broyde (1993), p. 98, n. 15. The rabbinic prohibition I am proposing below takes that reluctance one step further by giving it legal form.

29. The Conservative movement's Committee on Jewish Law and Standards unanimously approved my responsum on this issue, on which this chapter is based, and so Conservative rabbis, at any rate, would uphold these stringencies.

30. I would like to thank Rabbi Gordon Tucker for suggesting this approach in the meeting of the Committee on Jewish Law and Standards on December 8, 1993. The Torah's definition of sex between half siblings as incest: Leviticus 18:9; 20:17. The rabbinic category of incest in the second degree: B. *Yevamot* 21a; M.T. *Laws of Marriage* 1:6; S.A. *Even ha-Ezer* 15:1ff. In line with this treatment of adoptive and DI relationships on a rabbinic rather than a biblical level, we would maintain the rabbinic rulings that award the possessions, earnings, and findings of a minor child to the custodial rather than the natural parents (B. *Bava Metzia* 12b; S.A. *Hoshen Mishpat* 370:2), and despite the laws prohibiting unmarried and unrelated people from living together *(yihud)*, we would permit, for example, an adopted son whose adoptive father has died to continue living alone with his adoptive mother. See Broyde (1993), pp. 98–99.

31. This has been the ruling of the Conservative movement's Committee on Jewish Law and Standards, which validated a responsum in 1988 by Rabbi Avram Reisner to the effect that an adopted child may use the patronymic and matronymic of his/her adoptive parents and, if a convert, need not use *ben/bat Avraham avinu*. The same would apply to children born through DI. That responsum will soon be published in the collection of the committee's responsa from 1985 to 1990.

32. For a brief description of the obligations of children to parents as defined by Jewish tradition, see Dorff (1987), pp. 14–20. For a more extended description, see Blidstein (1975). For a description of the duties of parents toward their children, see Ben-Zion Schereschewsky, "Parent and Child," *Encyclopedia Judaica* 13:95–100. Volume X of *The Jewish Law Annual* (Boston: Boston University Institute of Jewish Law, and Philadelphia: Harwood Academic Publishers, 1992) was devoted in its entirety to legal aspects of the relationships between parents and children. While the Talmud and later Jewish law codes do not speak of DI children specifically, they do require that children honor and respect their stepfather and stepmother (B. *Ketubbot* 103a; S.A. *Yoreh De'ah* 240:21, 21), and the same would clearly apply to the social parents of DI children.

33. I have written about this in several contexts, in addition to Chapter 1 and the Appendix of this book: Dorff (1977); Dorff (1978), esp. pp. 1347–1360; and Dorff and Rosett (1988), pp. 249–257.

34. Bleich (1981 [1]), p. 80.

35. Jakobovits (1959, 1972), pp. 248–249. Cf. pp. 244–250 and 272–273 generally. Cf. also Bleich (1981), pp. 81–84; and Goldman (1978), pp. 74–86. This was also the opinion of Rabbi Jacob Breish, who engaged in a vigorous debate with Rabbi Moshe Feinstein, agreeing with him that donor insemination was technically legal but asserting that it would result in a general decline of moral values, that "from the point of view of our religion these ugly and disgusting things should not be done, for they are similar to the deeds of the land of Canaan and its abominations." 3 *Helkat Ya'akov* 45–51. For the debate with Rabbi Feinstein: *Dibbrot Moshe, Ketubbot*, 232–248.

36. Lauritzen (1991), p. 63. I want to thank Rabbi Aaron Mackler for calling my attention to this article and those listed on this topic in n. 40 below.

37. Ibid., pp. 65, 66.

38. Sissela Bok (1978), p. 224; cited in Lauritzen (1991), p. 69.

39. Lauritzen (1991), p. 69.

40. Ibid. Cf. Rona Achilles (1988); and Patricia P. Mahlstedt and Dorothy A. Greenfeld (1989).

41. Richard Doren has stressed this point in arguing for greater control of sperm donations while yet preserving donor confidentiality; see Richard Doren (1985).

42. Yeh and Yeh (1991), p. 48; S. Cooke, "Counselling in Donor Insemination," in Barratt and Cooke (1993), p. 26.

43. S. Cooke, "Counselling in Donor Insemination," in Barratt and Cooke (1993), pp. 20–21. See also R. Snowden, "Ethical and Legal Aspects of DI," in Barratt and Cooke (1993), esp. pp. 199–202 with regard to the Human Fertilisation and Embryology Act of 1990 in the United Kingdom.

44. *Jhordan C. v. Mary K. and Victoria T.*, 179 Cal. App. 3d 386, 224 Cal. Rptr. 530 (1986).

45. Doren (1985); L. Thomas Styron (1986); Anita M. Hodgson (1993). Styron (1986), at p. 443, n. 190, records the donor agreement recommended by the American Fertility Society to preserve the donor's anonymity while yet making him responsible to notify a designated party "should I contract any contagious or venereal disease."

46. U.S. Congress (1988 [2]), p. 64.

47. Hodgson (1993), p. 359 and n. 10 there. See 1991 Cal. Adv. Legis. Serv. 801 (Deering); FLA. STAT. chap. 381.6105 (1990); IND. CODE, para. 16–8–7.5–6 (1988).

48. Hodgson (1993), p. 360 and n. 12 there.

49. U.S. Congress (1988 [2]), pp. 48–50.

50. *C. M. v. C. C.*, 377 A.2d 82, 152 N.J. Super 160 (Juvenile and Domestic Relations Court, Cumberland County, N.J.), 1977; *Jhordan C. v. Mark K. and Victoria T.*, 224 Cal Rptr 530, 179 Cal. App.3d 386 (1986); *In the Interest of R. C.*, 775 P.2d 27, 34 (Colo. 1989). The condition that the donor show interest in serving as the father through his consistent actions is critical, for the U.S. Supreme Court, in ruling that a biological father who had no relationship with the child was not entitled to notice of the child's adoption proceedings, held in *Lehr V. Robertson* 463 U.S. 248, 103 S.Ct 2985, 77 L.Ed.2d 614 (1983) that ". . . the mere existence of a biological link does not merit equivalent constitutional protection" to one who did maintain a relationship with the child.

51. S. Elias and G. J. Annas (1986), p. 62, cited in Mahlstedt and Greenfeld (1989), p. 911. These laws also prohibit payment for specimens and mixing of donor and husband sperm.

52. Yeh and Yeh (1991), pp. 45–46.

53. S. Cooke, "Counselling in Donor Insemination," in Barratt and Cooke (1993), p. 22. Cooke also discusses the needs of some of the parties for information about the identity of the people involved and, on the other hand, the need for confidentiality of other parties involved; see pp. 21–25.

54. See Fader (1994), pp. 26–27, and n. 16 above.

55. The Health Department is mandated to keep such records in Alabama, Colorado, Minnesota, Montana, Nevada, New Jersey, and Wisconsin; a local court or the Registrar of Vital Statistics keeps such records in Connecticut, Idaho, Kansas, New Mexico, Oklahoma, Oregon, Washington, and Wyoming. See Yeh and Yeh (1991), pp. 45–46.

56. Mahlstedt and Greenfeld (1989), p. 911.

57. Lauritzen (1991), p. 71.

58. S. Cooke, "Counselling in Donor Insemination," in Barratt and Cooke (1993), p. 29, reporting a study by P. Goebel and F. Lubke, "Catamnestic Study of 96 Couples with Heterologous Insemination," *Geburtshilfe und Frauenheilkunde* 47 (1987), pp. 636–40.

59. S. Cooke, "Counselling in Donor Insemination," in Barratt and Cooke (1993), p. 29. The study he cites is that by G. T. Kovacs, D. Mushin, H. Kane, and H. W. G. Baker, "A Controlled Study of the Psychosocial Development of Children Conceived Following Insemination with Donor Semen," Fertility Society of Australia Meeting, Perth, Australia, 1990.

60. Mahlstedt and Greenfeld (1989), p. 913.

61. U.S. Congress (1988 [2]), pp. 64–65. Fourteen percent of practitioners doing artificial insemination say they offer sperm separation for preconception sex selection, but "physicians do not generally perceive the technique as effective" (ibid., p. 41; cf. p. 65). The average charge for this service, offered by about half of the sperm banks surveyed, was $220 (ibid., p. 65).

62. U.S. Congress (1988 [2]), p. 58.

63. U.S. Congress (1988 [2]), pp. 64, 66–70. Diabetes, hemophilia, depression, asthma, cystic fibrosis, mental retardation, obesity, Huntington's chorea, Duchenne muscular dystrophy, sickle cell anemia, thalassemia, hypercholesterolemic heart disease, neurofitromatosis, malignant melanoma, Alzheimer's disease, and severe astigmatism were all tested for in the fifteen sperm banks in the sample, with some sperm banks accepting some of these conditions in their donors (e.g., five would accept asthmatic or obese donors), other sperm banks refusing only donors who had the disease, and still others refusing even those who had a family history of the disease but who were themselves free of it.

64. I spell out some of the advantages of encasing values in law in Dorff (1977) and in Dorff (1992 [1]), pp. 71–75.

65. A brother's sperm was, of course, used in levirate marriages (Deuteronomy 25:5–10), but there the husband had died, and so there was no threat of the complications inherent in the blurring of roles between the brothers. Indeed, in that case it would actually be in the child's best interest if the uncle acted as a substitute father.

66. The talmudic story: B. *Berakhot* 60a. The comment of *Targum Yonatan* is on Genesis 30:21. Maharsha's support of that interpretation: B. *Niddah* 31a. Rabbi J. David Bleich's refusal to use this source to determine the identity of the child's mother on the basis of parturition (along with Rabbi Joshua Feigenbaum) because halakhic principles are not derivable from aggadic sources (quite remarkable, given Rabbi Bleich's usual methodology): Bleich (1981 [2]). See also Fred Rosner (1991), pp. 115–116. I would like to thank Rabbi Aaron Mackler for calling my attention to these materials.

I think that we not only can use aggadic material as the source of general principles but commonly do so in halakhic practice. Moreover, I think we should do so, for only then can our beliefs have impact on our actions. We must just be intelligent enough to understand that stories, unlike laws and judicial precedents, are not generally told in a form intended to be examined in legal detail but rather are to be read as articulating general principles; and we must also remember that stories, perhaps even more than legal precedents, may conflict with each other. Furthermore, in the use of stories for legal purposes, we must examine them, as we analyze potential precedents, for the analogies and dissimilarities between them and the case at hand. In the case here, though, I would agree with Rabbi Bleich that this story is a very thin reed on which to determine the mother's identity, not so much because it is aggadic but because it represents only one reading of what is already a fantastic tale, designed more to indicate the kindness of Leah and the miracles of God than the way rabbis should rule in cases of egg donation. For the general point about the use of stories within the context of legal reasoning, see Dorff (1992 [2]), and more briefly, Dorff (1991), pp. 4–7.

67. Exodus 13:2, 12, 15; 34:19; Numbers 3:12; 18:15.

68. See Mackler (1997), pp. 295–297.

69. See Chap. 3, n. 8 above.

70. M. *Yevamot* 6:6. In mishnaic times, the man legally could have taken a second wife to fulfill the commandment to procreate, but the Mishnah does not mention that possibility, probably because by mishnaic times polygamy, while legal, was already frowned upon. Thus not one of the more than two thousand sages mentioned in the Talmud has a second wife, and a second wife was called a *tzarah*, trouble. See also the story of Rabbi Judah ha-Nasi's son, who could not have children with his wife. His father told him to divorce her, but he said, "People will say, 'This poor one waited all these years in vain.'" His father said, "Take a second wife," but he answered, "People will say, 'This is his wife, and this is his concubine.'" He therefore prayed for her, and she was able to conceive (B. *Ketubbot* 62b). In any case, by the Middle Ages, polygamy was outlawed altogether in Ashkenazic communities through the revision of the law *(takkanah)* accredited to Rabbi Gershom of Mayence (d. 1028).

71. S.A. *Even ha-Ezer* 1:3, gloss.

72. R. Snowden, "Ethical and Legal Aspects of DI," in Barratt and Cooke (1993), p. 201.

73. B. *Hullin* 10a. See B. *Berakhot* 32b; B. *Shabbat* 32a; B. *Bava Kamma* 15b, 80a, 91b; M.T. *Laws of Murder and the Guarding of Life* 11:4–5; S.A. *Orah Ḥayyim* 173:2; *Yoreh De'ah* 116:5, gloss.

74. B. *Sanhedrin* 73a; M.T. *Laws of Murder* 1:14; S.A. *Hoshen Mishpat* 426:1.

75. Spirtas, Kaufman, and Alexander (1993), pp. 291–292.

76. For example, Genesis 15:2–3 and 48:5–6 are probably the most plausible cases, but some suggest that all or some of the following passages refer to adoption as well: Genesis 16:2, 30:3, 38:8–9, 50:23; Exodus 2:10; Leviticus 18:9; Deuteronomy 25:6; Psalms 77:16; Ruth 4:16–17, Esther 2:7, 15, Ezra 2:61, 10:44, and I Chronicles 2:35–41; 4:18. The evidence is murky, especially when one tries to differentiate adoption from fosterage and from inheritance rights alone. See Jeffrey Tigay, "Adoption," *Encyclopedia Judaica* 2:298– 301; and Michael Broyde (1993), p. 97, n. 11.

77. B. *Bava Kamma* 37a; B. *Gittin* 37a.

78. *Wener v. Wener* 59 Misc. 2d 959, 301 N.Y. Supp. 2d 237 (Sup. Ct. 1969); and cf. appeal, 35 App. Div. 2d 50, 312 N.Y. Supp. 2d 815 (2d Dept. 1970), where the judgment was affirmed but not its religious grounds.

79. Michael Broyde (1993), p. 97, n. 11, claims that there are four instances in the Bible in which adoptive parents are called natural parents, but as noted in n. 76 above,

all of the biblical instances of possible adoption are unclear. In any case, the Talmud assumes those ascriptions of parentage to be not legal pronouncements but rather descriptions of the close relationships between the children and adoptive parents: see I Chronicles 4:18; Ruth 4:17; Psalms 77:16; 2 Samuel 21:8; and B. *Sanhedrin* 9b.

Broyde (ibid., n. 10) calls attention to the disparate approaches taken by Roman and American law, which severed all previous relationships between the biological parents and the adopted children (to the point that, until recent amendments, the parties to the adoption were to remain anonymous to each other), as against English common law, which rejected the institution of adoption altogether, as against the intermediate position taken by Jewish law, which saw the adopted parents as agents of the biological parents. He cites, among other articles, C. M. A. McLauliff, "The First English Adoption Law and Its American Precursors," 16 *Seton Hall Law Review* 656, 659–660 (1986); and Sanford N. Katz, "Re-writing the Adoption Story," 5 *Family Advocate* 9–13 (1982). Because of the theory underlying American law, most states still ascribe to adoption law the ability to re-create maternal and paternal relationships even if the child, under the new legislation passed in many states, knows the biological parents.

80. Cf. *Encyclopedia Judaica*, "Adoption," 2:298–303; "Apotropos," 3:218–222; and "Orphan," 12:1478–1480 for a summary of all of the laws in this and the last paragraph. See especially B. *Sanhedrin* 19b; S.A. *Even ha-Ezer* 15:11. Cf. also Michael Broyde (1993), pp. 96–100, who points out that in this way Jewish law is in marked contrast to Roman law as well as American law, but in agreement with English common law.

81. As if giving birth: B. *Megillah* 13a. Doing right at all times: B. *Ketubbot* 50a. See also *Exodus Rabbah*, chap. 4; S.A. *Oraḥ Ḥayyim*, 139:3; Abraham Gumbiner, *Magen Avraham* on S.A. *Oraḥ Ḥayyim* 156; Moshe Feinstein, *Iggrot Moshe*, on *Yoreh De'ah* 161.

82. B. *Sanhedrin* 12b awards such possessions to the child's father; S.A. *Hoshen Mishpat* 370:2 specifies that this means the child's custodial father; and Rabbi J. Falk, *Me'irat Einaim*, on S.A. *Hoshen Mishpat* 370:2, suggests that this is a matter of equity. Thus a financially independent minor does not transfer his income to his parents because he is supporting himself; cf. S.A. *Hoshen Mishpat* 370:2.

83. M. Sofer, *Responsa*, 1 *Oraḥ Ḥayyim* 164. Sofer assumes that mourning is a rabbinic institution, which itself is a matter of dispute: compare S.A. *Yoreh De'ah* 398:1 with Moses Isserles, *Yoreh De'ah* 399:13, gloss. For other examples of rabbinic institutions not strictly applied in the context of custodial parentage, see, generally, S.A. *Oraḥ Ḥayyim* 139:3; Abraham Gumbiner, *Magen Avraham*, on S.A. *Oraḥ Ḥayyim* 156; Moshe Feinstein, *Iggrot Moshe*, *Yoreh De'ah* 161.

84. This was part of the responsum I wrote for the Committee on Jewish Law and Standards, approved unanimously in March 1994, entitled "Artificial Insemination, Egg Donation, and Adoption," on which much of this chapter is based. It was published in the fall 1996 issue of the journal *Conservative Judaism*. See Dorff (1996[5]). On naming an adopted child, see n. 31 above.

85. Despite the thousands of black children waiting to be adopted, it may not be easy for white people to adopt them, for state and private adoption agencies, often backed by state laws, prohibit such adoption for fear that white parents will undermine the ethnic identity of the child. See Lynn Smith (1993), pp. E-1, 3.

86. Ingrassia (1993 [1]).

87. For a poignant article about this, see Susan Chira (1993). I would like to thank Professor Vicki Michel and Rabbi Elie Spitz for calling my attention to this. In addition, the 1996 film *Flirting with Disaster* provides a humorous, but graphic, illustration of some of the problems involved for all concerned when adopted children search for their genetic parents. The film *Secrets and Lies*, in contrast, portrays the same situation in poignant, heart-wrenching terms.

88. U.S. Congress (1988 [2]), p. 23. Of the 4 percent, 3 percent came from women identifying themselves without partners and 1 percent from women who were part of a lesbian couple. That same study (p. 29) reports that 49 percent of physicians would reject for DI an unmarried person with a partner, 61 percent would reject an unmarried person without a partner, and 63 percent of the surveyed fertility society physicians regularly doing artificial insemination would reject lesbians as patients.

89. According to the 1987 national survey commissioned by the U.S. Office of Technology Assessment (U.S. Congress, 1988 [2]), 11,000 physicians around the country provided artificial insemination services to approximately 172,000 women. Eighty percent of the requests for artificial insemination were prompted by male infertility in the husband of a couple; only 4 percent (approximately 5,000 women) were cases of single women seeking to become pregnant. On the other hand, the California Cryobank, based on its own records, estimates that approximately 25 percent of the women requesting artificial insemination today (1994) are without male partners. That is quite some discrepancy! Still, even with the 25 percent figure, the vast majority (75 percent) of artificial inseminations are still done for infertile couples. See Fader (1994), pp. 6, 11.

90. Thus in the case of divorce, children below the age of six must be put in the custody of their mother, for they are mainly in need of the physical care and attention that mothers typically give children at that age. Above six years of age, boys must be with their father so that he can carry out his obligation to teach his male children Torah, while girls must be with their mother so that she can instruct them in the ways of modesty; see B. *Ketubbot* 102b, 103a; M.T. *Laws of Marriage (Ishut)* 21:17; S.A. *Even ha-Ezer* 82:7. One talmudic passage even describes the differing contributions of each parent in the physical makeup of the child, the mother contributing red matter (probably because menstrual blood is red) and the father contributing white matter (probably because semen is white), while God, each person's third parent according to the rabbis, breathes life into the child; see B. *Niddah* 31a. These differing roles lead to differing reactions of the child to each parent, which, according to the rabbis, explains why the Torah commands us to honor the father before the mother (Exodus 20:12) but to revere the mother before the father (Leviticus 19:3); see *Mekhilta*, "Massekhta de-Bahodesh" (ed. Horowitz-Rabin), 8, p. 232 and its parallel in B. *Kiddushin* 30b–31a (although that version lacks the significant phrase, "Where a deficiency exists, He filled it"); and see *Sifra*, "Kedoshim" 1:9 (p. 87a) and M. *Keritot*, (trans. H. Danby, p. 572), according to which even the mother must honor the father.

In modern times, we would certainly have a different understanding of what and how each parent contributes to the biological makeup of the child, and we would probably dispute the rigid roles for mothers and fathers delineated in the sources too; but the underlying point that parents of both genders have distinctive roles to play is, I think, still right. This is one instance of my general approach to matters of gender, for I have long affirmed that men and women are equal but, at least in some significant ways beyond their anatomies, different; see Dorff (1984). More current research—e.g., Deborah Tannen (1990)—confirms that thesis all the more. This makes it all the more important for children to have caring adults of both genders in their lives.

91. Lee Smith (1994); the citation is on p. 82.

92. Ibid., p. 82.

93. Ibid., p. 94.

94. Children born to single women through donor insemination manifest the need to find their fathers, possibly even more than children born to couples through that method. A recent movie, *Made in America* (1993), with Whoopi Goldberg and Ted Danson, depicted exactly that situation. The daughter, born from the sperm Danson's character donated to a sperm bank in his teens, seeks him out when she is a senior in high school. The movie bespeaks two worries about DI— that the children will have a deep-seated need to know their biological fathers, and that sperm banks will not keep accurate records.

95. Michele Ingrassia et. al. (1993 [2]).

96. Thus the only Conservative rabbi who has so far written a formal respon- sum on donor insemination of single women has ruled that it is inconsistent with Jewish law, for some of the same reasons I have delineated above. See Rabbi Dav- id Golinkin (1989). The reverse phenomenon, where single men become parents through surrogacy or adoption, is too new and too rare for there to be good data on the long-term effects on children growing up in that family configuration. One would guess that since children need mothers as well as fathers, some adult female role models must be made an integral part of the children's lives, just as the re- verse is true for children living with single mothers.

97. That was the ruling of the Juvenile and Domestic Relations Court in *C. M. v. C. C.* (1977), the California Court of Appeals in *Jhordan C. v. Mary K. and Victoria T.*, and the Colorado Supreme Court in *In the Interest of R. C.* (1989) (all at n. 50 above), and also the Oregon Court of Appeals in *McIntyre v. Crouch*, 780 P.2d 239, 98 Or. App. 462 (1989).

98. This was the basis of the recent Virginia ruling that Sharon Bottoms could not retain custody of her daughter, born by artificial insemination. Virginia is one of just four states where legal precedent deems gay parents unfit (Arkansas, Mis- souri, and North Dakota are the others), and New Hampshire and Florida cate- gorically bar gays as adoptive parents. On the other hand, in the nation's capital, local officials held a seminar in the summer of 1993 to instruct gays on how to adopt; and New Jersey, Massachusetts, and six other states explicitly permit a les- bian to adopt her lover's child and become a second parent. See "Gay Parents: Under Fire and on the Rise," *Time*, September 20, 1993, pp. 66–71. American law in all its diversity, then, is another factor that must be considered in artificial insemination of single women, and the matter is clearly complicated further if the women involved are lesbians.

99. Gina Kolata (1993). I would like to thank Rabbi Avram Reisner for draw- ing my attention to this. Fader, though, maintains that Alan Trounson reported

success with microinjection of an individual human sperm into a human egg at the Sixth World Congress on Human Reproduction in Tokyo in 1987; see Fader (1994), p. 10.

100. In any case, the health care reforms planned by the Clinton administration did not include payment for IVF, and all the more so have the Republicans excluded coverage for that in their various proposals. Since egg donation requires considerable funds, it may become the privilege of only the rich and therefore quite rare. See Edwin Chen and Robert A. Rosenblatt (1993), especially the exclusions listed on p. A17.

NOTES TO CHAPTER FIVE

1. See, for example, Leitenberg, Detzer, and Srebnik (1993); Laan, Everaerd, Van Aanhold, and Rebel (1993).

2. See J. P. Elia (1987) for the attitudes toward masturbation in ancient Egypt, Greece, and Rome.

3. Maimonides, *Commentary to the Mishnah*, Sanhedrin 7:4.

4. M.T. *Laws of Ethics*, 4:19.

5. Cf. David Feldman (1968), p. 120, and Part 3 of that book generally on this topic.

6. For both men and women: Leviticus 15:16–33. See also Leviticus 18:19 and 20:18 with regard to menstruation, and Leviticus 22:4 and Deuteronomy 23:10–12 with regard to seminal emission. Deuteronomy 23:13–15 treats defecation in a similar way.

7. The Mishnah prohibits a man who had had a seminal emission from reciting the *Shema* or the *Amidah* (M. Berakhot 3:4–5). According to the Talmud (B. Bava Kamma 82a; J. Yoma 1:1; etc.), it was Ezra who instituted the decree that men who have had a seminal emission must immerse themselves in a mikveh before reading the Torah (which, for some interpreters, meant studying any classical Jewish text [cf. B. *Berakhot* 22a]), and, according to some *rishonim* (rabbis of the eleventh through the sixteenth centuries), a later court also required such men to immerse themselves in a mikveh before they prayed (M.T. *Laws of Prayer* 4:4 [but see the comment of the *Kesef Mishneh* there]; Meiri on *Berakhot* 20a; Rosh on *Bava Kamma*, chap. 7, no. 19). This is not required by the Torah, for people in a state of impurity of any sort are permitted by the Torah, as the rabbis understand it, to engage in study and prayer; see Rif, *Berakhot*, chap. 3; M.T. *Laws of Reading the Shema* 4:8; M.T. *Laws of Prayer* 4:5. Indeed, the purpose of this decree, according to these interpreters, was not motivated by concerns of purity at all but was rather to ensure that rabbinic scholars would not have conjugal relations with their wives as often as roosters do with chickens or, alternatively, to make Torah study like the revelation at Sinai, when men were not allowed to have relations with their wives in preparation for the event (Exodus 19:15) and in honor of the Torah that they were to receive and learn.

The decree of Ezra was annulled (B. Berakhot 22a; Bertinoro on M. Berakhot 3:4; M.T. *Laws of Reading the Shema*, 4:8; M.T. *Laws of Prayer* 4:4–6; S.A. Orah Hayyim 88:1; and the commentaries on M.T. and S.A. there). As the *Kesef Mish-*

neh to M.T. *Laws of Reading the Shema* 4:8 asserts and demonstrates, the annulment occurred not because the rabbis voted to do so, for no later court had the authority to overturn a decree of Ezra's court, but rather "because there was not enough strength in the majority of the community to uphold it, the Sages did not force the men to immerse, and it was annulled by itself." Maimonides, however, records the laws concerning a man's impurity through seminal emission fully (M.T. *Laws of the Other Forms of Impurity*, chap. 5, based primarily on M. *Mikvaot* 8:1–4), and to my knowledge those laws have never been formally abrogated but are simply not observed. On this entire subject, see *"Ba'al Keri," Encyclopedia Talmudit* 4:130–148 (Hebrew).

The inequality imposed by these laws is most apparent in a comment by Rabbi Moses Isserles (S.A. *Orah Hayyim* 88:1, gloss), according to which even though men who had had a seminal emission could read the Torah and recite the *Shema* and *Amidah* because Ezra's decree had been annulled, the custom in Askenazic communities was that women who were in their menstrual flow could not do any of those things (even though they were never covered by Ezra's decree!). Moreover, except for the High Holy Days and similar events, when everyone else was attending services and when remaining at home would thus cause great pain, women were even asked to stay away from synagogue services altogether during their menstrual period. This presents quite a gap between what women and men were allowed to do after emissions from their sexual organs.

8. Baruch A. Levine (1989), pp. 243–248; Jacob Milgrom (1990), pp. 344–346; and especially Jacob Milgrom (1991), pp. 766–768, 1000– 1004, where he presents alternative theses about the underlying rationale for the purity laws and argues for his own explanation, namely, that the real issue behind them is preserving life (of which God is the Author) and avoiding its opposite, death.

9. The same theory existed as early as 600 B.C.E. in India, and it was the basis of the degeneracy theory of all disease and the hysteria concerning masturbation in the nineteenth and twentieth centuries. See Money, Prakasam, and Joshi (1991). Another study, comparing attitudes and cases in Sri Lanka and Japan, demonstrated that men presume that semen loss will cause illness, anxiety, and loss of energy and power if the predominant attitude in society supports that belief, as in Sri Lanka, but men will not presume that semen loss produces those negative effects if that is not the prevailing social attitude, as in Japan. See Dewaraja and Sasaki (1991).

10. *Zohar*, Vayehi 219b.

11. *Zohar*, Emor, 90a.

12. *Zohar*, Genesis 19b, 54b.

13. Isaac Bashevis Singer (1957), p. 135.

14. See, for example, H. Leitenberg, M. J. Detzer, and D. Srebnik (1993).

15. The language of the Mishnah (M. *Yevamot* 6:6) suggests that the man may use contraceptives after having fulfilled the commandment by having two children. It reads: "A man may not cease from being fruitful and multiplying *unless* he has children. The School of Shammai says: two males; the School of Hillel says: a male and a female . . . ." That, however, was not the position of later Jewish law (B. *Yevamot* 62b), which encouraged as many children as possible on the basis of Isaiah 45:18 ("Not for void did He create the world, but for habitation *[lashevet]*

did He form it") and Ecclesiastes 11:6 ("In the morning, sow your seed, and in the evening *[la'erev]* do not withhold your hand"). Subsequently these precepts were codified by Maimonides (M.T. *Laws of Marriage [Ishut]* 15:16): "Although a man has fulfilled the commandment of being fruitful and multiplying, he is commanded by the Rabbis not to desist from procreation while he yet has strength, for whoever adds even one Jewish soul is considered as having created an entire world."

16. British researchers, citing World Health Organization statistics and their own study of three hundred men at a south London clinic, have suggested that the failure of condoms may largely be due to the use of the same size for all men, a size too small for one-third of the men of the world. See "One Size of Condom Doesn't Fit All," *Men's Health*, March 1994, p. 27 (no author mentioned).

17. For more on the Jewish imperative of safe sex, see Michael Gold (1992), pp. 112ff; and Dorff (1996 [1]), pp. 12–13, 32–33.

18. B. *Yevamot* 12b.

19. Rashi (eleventh century), the most famous commentator on the Talmud, takes this position. Those who follow him, however (e.g., Rabbi Meir Posner of eighteenth-century Danzig, Rabbi Akiva Eger of nineteenth-century Posen in Prussia, Rabbi Moses Sofer of nineteenth-century Pressburg), were generally convinced that the Sages would permit the use of contraception when someone's life or health depended upon it, and they consequently interpreted the prohibition in the rabbinic source quoted above as applying exclusively to cases where the woman incurs only minor risk. They thereby allowed contraception when medical reasons required it, but not otherwise. See David M. Feldman (1968), pp. 194–226.

20. Rabbenu Tam, one of Rashi's grandsons, adopted this approach, and there are many (probably a majority) who follow him (e.g., Rabbi Asher ben Yeḥiel [the "Rosh"] in late thirteenth- and early fourteenth-century Germany and Spain; Rabbi Solomon Luria in sixteenth-century Poland; and Rabbi Isaac Halevi Herzog, first Ashkenazic chief rabbi of the State of Israel). While Rabbi Luria would permit all women to use contraceptive devices even for nontherapeutic purposes, others of this school would restrict their use in one way or another. Again, see David M. Feldman (1968), pp. 194–226.

21. See David M. Feldman (1968), pp. 224–225.

22. Infertility increases with age: 13.9 percent of couples where the wife is between thirty and thirty-four are infertile, 24.6 percent where the wife is between thiry-five and thirty-nine, and 27.2 percent where the wife is between forty and forty-four. U.S. Congress, Office of Technology Assessment, *Infertility: Medical and Social Choices*, OTA-BA-358 (Washington, DC: U.S. Government Printing Office, May 1988), pp. 1, 3, 4, and 6. See also Lori B. Andrews, *New Conceptions* (New York: St. Martin's Press, 1984), p. 160; Paul Lauritzen, "Pursuing Parenthood: Reflections on Donor Insemination," *Second Opinion* (July 1991), pp. 57–58.

23. Cf. M.T. *Laws of Forbidden Intercourse* 16:2, 6; S.A. *Even ha-Ezer* 5:2.

24. B. *Shabbat* 110b.

25. Cf. J. David Bleich (1981 [1]), p. 65; David Feldman and Fred Rosner (1984), pp. 46–47; Solomon Freehof (1960), pp. 206–208.

26. The National Cancer Insitute, The American Cancer Society, and doctors generally remind men that they must periodically examine their testicles for early

signs of cancer as much as women need to examine their breasts. If detected early enough, orchiectomy (that is, removal of one or, rarely, both testicles) is a proven measure of preventing the spread of the disease to other parts of the body, where it is often fatal. See the publications of the National Cancer Institute, *Testicular Self-Examination* and *What You Need to Know About Testicular Cancer*. I would like to thank Dr. Samuel Kunin, a urologist and good friend, for this information.

27. His mental health may be seriously threatened, though, for if his wife falls ill and perhaps dies from a future pregnancy, he will surely feel the effects. Nevertheless, that is a future and possible risk, while the one to his wife is, by hypothesis, a present and definite one. It is therefore better to rely on the woman's current physical state for this legal permission to undergo a vasectomy, even though that involves extending the duty to preserve life and health to someone other than himself so as to override the prohibitions against castration and self-mutilation.

28. For the general duty we all have to preserve life and health in others, see Chapter 2. The special obligation of husbands to provide for the medical care of their wives refers, in Jewish law, to the provision of monetary resources to provide for her physical care (see M. *Ketubbot* 4:9 (51a); B. *Ketubbot* 52b; M.T. *Laws of Marriage* 14:17; cf. 18:5; S.A. *Even ha-Ezer* 79:1; cf. 94:7; and see the discussion of the cost of health care in Chapter 12 in this book. Saying that the man must, or at least may, undergo a vasectomy for his wife's sake is, admittedly, an extension of this obligation, as it is an extension of his duty to preserve his own life and health and that of others; but for the reasons suggested here, it is an extension that I think is warranted.

29. Exodus 21:22–25.

30. B. *Yevamot* 69b. Rabbi Immanuel Jakobovits (1959, 1975), p. 275, notes that "forty days" in talmudic terms may mean just under two months in our modern way of calculating gestation due to improved methods of determining the date of conception.

31. B. *Niddah* 17a.

32. B. *Hullin* 58a and elsewhere. According to B. *Yevamot* 69b, during the first forty days of gestation, the zygote is "simply water," but even then the rabbis required justification for an abortion based on the mother's life or health. On this topic generally, see David M. Feldman (1968), chaps. 14–15.

33. Cf. David M. Feldman (1968), pp. 265–266, and chap.15.

34. M. *Niddah* 3:5.

35. M. *Oholot* 7:6. There are various versions of this. Like our Mishnah, J. *Shabbat* 14:4 reads "its greater part"; T. *Yevamot* 9:9 and B. *Sanhedrin* 72b have "its head"; and J. *Sanhedrin* 8, end, has "its head or its greater part."

36. Cf. Immanuel Jakobovits (1959, 1975), pp. 186–187 and n. 173 on pp. 378–379.

37. *Responsa Pri ha-Aretz*, vol. 3 (Jerusalem, 1899); *Yoreh De'ah*, no. 2.

38. Cf. David M. Feldman (1968), pp. 284–294; Moshe Halevi Spero, (1980), chap. 12.

39. Ibid., and Immanuel Jakobovits (1959, 1975), pp. 189–190.

40. J. David Bleich (1977 [2]), pp. 112–115; J. David Bleich (1968), esp. pp. 161 and 175, n. 97 (in the 1979 reprint).

41. Cf. David M. Feldman (1968), pp. 284–294.

42. Eliezer Waldenberg, *Responsa Tzitz Eliezer*, 9:51 (1967) and 13:102 (1978); S. Israeli, *Amud ha-Yemini*, no. 35 cited in *No'am*, 16 (K.H.) 27 (note); Lev Grossnass, *Responsa Lev Aryeh* 2:205; Alex J. Goldman (1978), chap. 3, esp. pp. 52–62.

43. Jakobovits (1959, 1975), pp. 278–279.

44. Dorff (1996 [1]), the official policy statement of the Conservative rabbinate on sexual matters, Section B-9, pp. 25–28.

NOTES TO CHAPTER SIX

1. For more on this, see Elliot N. Dorff (1996 [1]), sec. C, pp. 30–36.

2. "54 percent of High School Youth Have Had Sex, Report Says," *Los Angeles Times*, January 4, 1992, p. A-2. As the article points out, the survey conducted by the federal government's Centers for Disease Control of 11,631 high school students revealed that 54 percent of the whole group had had sex—40 percent of ninth graders, 48 percent of tenth graders, 57 percent of eleventh graders, and 72 percent of twelfth graders. Ninety percent of twenty-two year olds: See Robert T. Michael et al. (1994), p. 91.

3. This is Jacob Milgrom's thesis. See Milgrom (1993).

4. The rabbis see female homosexual relations as prohibited under the Torah's command, "You shall not follow the acts of the land of Egypt . . . or the acts of the land of Canaan" (Leviticus 18:3): *Sifra*, "Aharei Mot," 9:5. Since, however, there is no specific verse that prohibits lesbian relations, and since there is no intercourse involved, the penalty prescribed in the law is not that for violating a Torah commandment (i.e., thirty-nine lashes), but rather that of violating a rabbinic enactment: M.T. *Laws of Forbidden Intercourse* 21:8.

Rava in B. *Yevamot* 76a refers to lesbian relations as "simple lewdness," but that does not mean that he thinks of it as being a minor offense; he is there maintaining, in contrast to Rav Huna, that a woman who engages in such relations is not a prostitute but is simply engaging in lewdness and therefore still eligible to marry a *kohen*. Apparently, for Rava, what precludes a lesbian from being a prostitute is that there is no intercourse involved; Rav Huna, though, categorizes lesbian relations as forbidden intercourse.

5. M. *Sanhedrin* 7:4; B. *Sanhedrin* 54a; M.T. *Laws of Forbidden Intercourse* 1:14.

6. Rabbi Judah forbade the practice, but the Sages permitted it (M. *Kiddushin* 4:14; B. *Kiddushin* 82a). Maimonides also permits the practice and provides the rationale quoted (M.T. *Laws of Forbidden Intercourse* 22:2). Caro, however, says, "Nevertheless, in our times, when lewdness is rampant, one should abstain from being alone with another male" (S.A. *Even ha-Ezer* 24); but a century later Rabbi Joel Sirkes again suspended the restriction on the ground that "in our lands [Poland] such lewdness is unheard of" (*Bayit Hadash* to *Tur, Even ha-Ezer* 24).

7. Aristotle, *Nicomachean Ethics*, chap. 3; cf. chap.7.

8. Orthodox defenders of the ban against homosexuality have generally taken a textualist approach. Many rely on the prohibition in Leviticus and its rabbinic commentaries alone as sufficient ground to oppose homosexual sex; others also cite family values. See, for example, Norman Lamm (1974) and Barry Freundel

(1993). But see Rabbi Yaakov Levado [a pseudonym] (1993). Textualists within the Conservative movement include Joel Roth, whose unpublished rabbinic ruling of October 1991 for the Committee on Jewish Law and Standards is based largely on the meaning of *to'evah* (abomination) in the sources and the inability, in his opinion, of any other factor to overcome that; Rabbi Meir Rabinowitz, whose unpublished ruling for the same committee is based on the legal incapacity, in his opinion, of contemporary rabbis to uproot a law in the Torah; and Rabbi Reuven Kimmelman, whose opinion for the same committee, published in large part in Kimmelman (1992–1993) and in Kimmelman (1994), is based on what he perceives to be the undermining of family values inherent in homosexual sex.

9. See Dorff (1977 [2]), pp. 110–157; Dorff (1996 [4]), pp. 101–150.

10. See, for example, Dorff and Rosett (1988), pp. 187–245; Dorff (1996 [4]), pp. 69–95.

11. B. *Bava Batra* 131a.

12. Artson (1988) and, more thoroughly, Artson (1990–1991).

13. *Sifra, "Aharei Mot"* 9:8 (on Leviticus 18:3); B. *Hullin* 92a–92b; *Genesis Rabbah* 26:5 (on Genesis 6:2).

14. See, for example, Simon LeVay and Ean H. Hamer (1994) and William Byne (1994). See also John P. De Cecco and David Allen Parker, eds. (1995), esp. the introduction by the editors, pp. 1–27. I would like to thank Dr. Holly Devor of the University of Victoria for alerting me to this last source.

15. B. *Yoma* 83a; M.T. *Laws of the Sabbath of the Tenth Day (Hilkhot Shevitat Asor)* 2:8; S.A. *Orah Hayyim* 618:1.

16. Thus the American Psychiatric Association, in its April 1993 *Fact Sheet* (p. 1), stated the following:

> There is no evidence that any treatment can change a homosexual person's deep-seated sexual feelings for others of the same sex. Clinical experience suggests that any person who seeks conversion therapy may be doing so because of social bias that has resulted in internalized homophobia, and that gay men and lesbians who have accepted their sexual orientation positively are better adjusted than those who have not done so.

In 1973 the American Psychiatric Association passed a resolution declassifying homosexuality as a mental illness, but those opposed to this move have noted that much political pressure was applied to the association at that time and that the vote was close. In December 1992, however, the association reaffirmed its 1973 analysis of homosexuality in even stronger language:

> Whereas homosexuality per se implies no impairment in judgment, stability, reliability, or general social or vocational capabilities, the American Psychiatric Association calls on all international health organizations, and individual psychiatrists in other countries, to urge the repeal in their own country of legislation that penalizes homosexual acts by consenting adults in private. And further, the APA calls on these organizations and individuals to do all that is possible to decrease the stigma related to homosexuality wherever and whenever it may occur. (*Fact Sheet* of the American Psychiatric Association, April 1993, p. 2.)

17. I say that even in light of the countervailing evidence of the Holocaust. My own view on the Holocaust and its implications for our faith, expressed some years ago (Dorff 1977 [3]) and restructured in expanded form in my book, *Knowing God: Jewish Journeys to the Unknowable* (Dorff 1992 [1]), pp. 129–148), posits that God was indeed involved in the Holocaust. I, however, still maintain the traditional faith that, even with that unfathomable fact, God is ultimately good. I also understand the elements of our tradition that endorsed immoral commands of God, centered on the binding of Isaac and other manifestations of child sacrifice, so well explored by Jon Douglas Levenson in his book, *The Death and Resurrection of the Beloved Son: The Transformation of Child Sacrifice in Judaism and Christianity* (Levenson 1993). Even if, at worst, we deduce on the basis of this evidence that God is sometimes inscrutable and even immoral, we must interpret Jewish law, it seems to me, in accordance with the underlying faith of Judaism, namely, that God is ultimately good.

18. For more on this theoretical point, see Chapter 1 and the Appendix.

19. B. *Bava Kamma* 28b, et al. See also *Sifra* on Lev. 20:3; *Sifra*, "Tzav," end of chap. 14; M.T. *Laws of the Foundations of the Torah* 5:4; Tosafot on B. *Yevamot* 54a.

20. Rabbenu Nissim's comment is printed on the page of the standard editions of the Babylonian Talmud, B. *Nedarim* 27a. That the vow is canceled automatically follows from M. *Nedarim* 3:1, of which this mishnah is the explanation.

21. M. *Nedarim* 3:3 (27a); B. *Nedarim* 27a; M.T. *Laws of Sanhedrin* 7:10; *Laws of Selling* 11:13, 14; *Tur* and S.A., *Hoshen Mishpat*, chap. 21; 54:5; and 207:15.

22. That we may eat only according to the dietary laws: Leviticus 11; Deuteronomy 14. That we must say blessings before and after eating: Deuteronomy 8:10 and M. *Berakhot* 6:1–8:1. That we must cover our feces: Deuteronomy 23:13–15 (although there it is specifically with regard to a military encampment, this requirement was later applied generally): see B. *Berakhot* 25a, where it is applied to wherever one says the *Shema*.

That we must restrict sex to marriage: Deuteronomy 22:28–29 (the penalties for sexual relations outside marriage); 23:18 (the prohibition of prostitution); B. *Gittin* 81a, etc. ("A man does not [want to] make his sexual intercourse harlotry"); B. *Sanhedrin* 76a (and Rashi, s.v. *b'mosair*); 82a; 94b; B. *Keritot* 3a; M.T. *Laws of Marriage* 1:4 (but see Ra'avad there); *Laws of an Unmarried Maiden* 2:17. In the former passage in M.T., Maimonides imposes lashes on a man who has sex with an unmarried woman, but in the latter he seems to distinguish, as Ra'avad does and as the Talmud itself seems to do in B. *Sanhedrin* 21a, between a prostitute *(kedaishah)* — who has sex with many men and is popularly known to be open for that — and a concubine *(pelegesh)* — who has sex with only one man but without betrothal or a marriage contract. Under that distinction, lashes are imposed only on the man who has sex with a prostitute for violating the Torah's explicit prohibition in Deuteronomy 23:18, not on the one who has sex with a concubine. See also M.T. *Laws of an Unmarried Maiden*, chaps. 1 and 2 generally.

23. Barbara Kantrowitz (1996), p. 52. In that same poll, "36 percent of those surveyed think that gay couples should have the right to adopt, as compared with 29 percent in 1994; 47 percent oppose gay adoption rights, down from 65 percent in 1994" (p. 56).

24. Specifically, the carrier frequency of Tay-Sachs among Ashkenazim is 3–4 percent, Gaucher's disease 4–6 percent, Canavan 1.7–2 percent, and Niemann-Pick 1–2 percent, while the reported carrier frequency among Ashkenazi women of the BRCA1 mutation connected with breast and ovarian cancer is approximately 1 percent. See Struewing et al. (1995), pp. 198, 199. On the last of those, I have written a paper entitled "Jewish Theological and Moral Reflections on Genetic Screening: The Case of BRCA1," Dorff (1997), but the following paragraphs on pp. 157ff reflect my revised position in light of new evidence.

25. J. David Bleich (1981 [1]), p. 105.

26. B. *Yevamot* 64b.

27. Bleich (1981 [1]), pp. 106–108.

28. See, for example, Immanuel Jakobovits (1959, 1971), pp. 274–275.

29. Even Rabbi Reisner, who generally does not apply the legal category of *terefah* to dying patients and who thus forbids the withholding or withdrawal of artificial nutrition and hydration from dying patients, would allow that in the case of infants whose lives are impaired from the moment of birth. See Reisner (1991), pp. 62–64, and, in comparison, Reisner (1995).

30. A very good anthology of papers on these issues is *Genes and Human Self-Knowledge* (Weir, Lawrence, and Fales, 1994). The example of Huntington's disease that I have chosen here is based on the first chapter of that book, "A Few Words from a 'Wise' Woman," by Kimberly A. Quaid, in which she describes the disease and quotes the personal reactions of those who have tested positive, those who have tested negative, and those who have chosen not to take the test in the first place.

31. Struewing et al. (1995), p. 198.

32. D. Ford, D. F. Easton, D. T. Bishop, S. A. Narod, and D. E. Goldgar, and the Breast Cancer Linkage Consortium, "Risks of Cancer in BRCA1-Mutation Carriers," 343 *Lancet* 692–695 (1994), cited in n. 12 of Struewing et al. (1995), pp. 199, 200.

33. Struewing et al. (1995), p. 199.

34. Ibid., p. 198. The researchers report as follows: "Based on studies in very high-risk families, the estimated lifetime penetrance for breast cancer among mutation carriers is about 90 percent . . . . The risk of ovarian cancer is lower, but may be as high as 84 percent in a subset of families." Note that these numbers are for those families at the greatest risk for developing cancer in the first place, based on both a family history of the disease and the presence of BRCA1 mutations, and note also that these numbers are over a lifetime. As they report on the same page, "it can be estimated that the 185delAG mutation might account for 16 percent of breast cancers (range 7.9–23.1 percent) and 39 percent of ovarian cancers (range 22–49 percent) diagnosed in Ashkenazi women before age 50." As bad as that is, 16 and 39 percent are *much* lower than 90 and 84 percent and *much* further away from a 100 percent correlation.

35. "Editorial," *Nature Genetics* (October 1995), pp. 105–106, makes this point poignantly in pointing out the correlation between DDT and other pesticides with the development of cancer.

36. Some biblical verses emphasizing the importance and imperative of truth: Exodus 18:21; Zechariah 8:16, 19; Psalms 15:2; 24:3–4; Proverbs 12:19; 23:23. Conversely, the Torah says, "from falsehood you should stay far away" (Exodus

23:7) and "You shall not deal deceitfully or falsely with one another. . . . You shall not defraud your fellow" (Leviticus 19:11, 13). According to the rabbis, God's very seal is truth (*Genesis Rabbah* 81:2); the world is preserved by truth, justice, and peace (M. *Avot* 1:18); and, in sum, "One's 'yes' should be yes, and one's 'no' should be no" (B. *Bava Mezia* 49a; cf. M. *Bava Mezia* 4:2; J. *Berakhot* 1:8 (3c); *Ruth Rabbah* 7:6 on Ruth 3:18; *Pesikta Rabbati* 108a,b).

37. B. *Ketubbot* 16b–17a with regard to describing a bride on her wedding day as beautiful or ugly; *Ecclesiastes Rabbah* on Ecclesiastes 5:6 and S.A. *Yoreh De'ah* 338:1 on keeping bad news from the dying so as not to undermine hope; B. *Yevamot* 65a on telling an untruth for the sake of peace. A good summary and discussion of the sources on this can be found in Basil F. Herring (1984), pp. 47–66.

38. For an example of a Conservative position, see Golinkin (1994). For Orthodox views, see Bleich (1981 [1]), p. 106; Rosenfeld (1972); and Fred Rosner, "Genetic Engineering and Judaism," in Rosner and Bleich (1979), pp. 409–422. For a Reform position, see Walter Jacob, "Jewish Involvement in Genetic Engineering," in Jacob (1992), p. 252; see generally there pp. 244–252, and also Jacob (1987), pp. 32–34.

39. B. *Berakhot* 20a; B. *Bava Mezia* 84a. As Rabbi Rosenfeld (1972) says in endnote 3 of his article, this was a Jewish version of Roman eugenics, for according to the Talmud, the Roman notables used to hold beautiful figures while engaging in sexual relations; cf. B. *Gittin* 58a, and see also *Numbers Rabbah* 9:34, where the fact that an Ethiopian couple produced a white child is ascribed to their house having white figures in it. On analogous procedures involving animals, see Genesis 30:37ff and B. *Avodah Zarah* 24a.

40. Rosenfeld (1979), p. 403.

41. See Annas and Grodin (1992).

42. Genesis 2:15.

NOTES TO CHAPTER SEVEN

1. Aaron Mackler (1993), based on the responsa of Rabbis Elliot N. Dorff (1991 [1]) and Avram Reisner (1991). See also Chapter 8 in this book, and the Statement on Assisted Suicide of the Committee on Jewish Law and Standards, chap. 8, n. 48.

2. *Ecclesiastes Rabbah* on Ecclesiastes 5:6; S.A. *Yoreh De'ah* 338:1, 2. The Jewish emphasis on life also prompts the rule, which we have cited several times, placing preservation of life above all but three other duties. More pervasively still, a hearty attachment to this life undergirds the strong activist tendencies of Judaism to make this world a better place, and even the traditional toast Jews use—*Leḥayyim*, "to life!"

3. J. David Bleich (1990).

4. A good summary of traditional opinions on this issue can be found in Basil Herring (1984), chap. 2. See also Seymour Siegel (1977).

5. S.A. *Yoreh De'ah* 335:7; 338:1.

6. See Israel Abrahams (1926); Riemer and Stampfer (1983); and Riemer and Stampfer (1991).

7. Richard J. Israel, untitled, in Riemer and Stampfer (1983), pp. 206–207. See that book generally for some poignant examples of ethical wills, including some modern ones. See also Riemer and Stampfer (1991) for some further suggestions on preparing an ethical will.

NOTES TO CHAPTER EIGHT

1. M. *Semahot* 1:1–2; M. *Shabbat* 23:5 and B. *Shabbat* 151b; B. *Sanhedrin* 78a; B. *Avodah Zarah* 18a; M.T. *Laws of Murder* 2:2, 7; S.A. *Yoreh De'ah* 339:2 and the comments of the Shakh and Rama there; S.A. *Yoreh De'ah* 345.

2. As we shall describe in detail below, the economics behind these arguments are real. See (4b) below.

3. *Compassion in Dying v. State of Washington* 79 F.3d 790 (9th Cir. 1996); *Quill v. Vacco* 80 F.3d 716 (2d Cir. 1996). (A subsequent petition for the Ninth Circuit to rehear the case *en banc* was denied: 85 F.3d 1440 [9th Cir. 1996]). The Ninth Circuit also invoked the Supreme Court's past decisions on abortion in interpreting the Fourteenth Amendment's clause on liberty to protect a person's right to make his or her own health care decisions. Thus Judge Stephen Reinhardt, writing for an 8–3 majority, stated that "by permitting the individual to exercise the right to choose, we are following the constitutional mandate to take such decisions out of the hands of government, both state and federal, and to put them where they rightly belong, in the hands of the people." The U.S. Supreme Court, though, refused to ground such rights in the Constitution: *Washington v. Glucksberg* 117 S.Ct. 2258 (1997); *Quill v. Vacco* 117 S.Ct. 2293 (1997). See chap. 2, n. 2 above.

4. As Rabbi Aaron Mackler has pointed out to me, the fact that American states do not criminalize suicide may be a function of the medicalization of suicide in our time rather than recognition of a legal right. That is, instead of putting those who attempt suicide in prison, we sedate them, treat them for depression, and restrain them if necessary. That does not mean, though, that suicide is a legal right, for if it were, we would not try to prevent people from taking their lives. The Ninth Circuit, though, has interpreted suicide, and therefore also assisting in suicide, as a legal privilege embedded in the Fourteenth Amendment's guarantee of liberty. Presumably, then, the only reason for trying to prevent people from committing suicide is that we doubt that they have the mental competence required by law to make that decision.

5. See Chapter 2, n.1.

6. This principle includes even inanimate property that "belongs" to us, for God is the ultimate owner. This is the law of *ba'al tashhit*, the prohibition of destroying the world when human need does not require that. Cf. Deuteronomy 20:19–20; B. *Bava Kamma* 8:6, 7; B. *Bava Kamma* 92a, 93a; M.T. *Laws of Murder* 1:4 (where Maimonides specifically invokes this theological basis for the law against suicide); M.T. *Laws of Injury and Damage* 5:5; *Sefer ha-Hinnukh*, commandment 529; S.A. *Hoshen Mishpat* 420:1, 31. For an extended treatment of the parameters of this law, see Schwartz and Cytron (1993).

7. Tuchinsky (1960), pp. 269–270 (my translation). He adds there that the person who commits suicide "is like one who flees to a place where the hand of the

government will catch him and can bring him back to this place with additional punishment also for his escape"—an understandable metaphor in his theology, but one that unfortunately makes life a prison sentence!

8. I say this even though one Reform writer has maintained the contrary, claiming that contemporary Jews overwhelmingly believe that their bodies are their own and thus refuse to abide by medical directives based on God's ownership of our bodies. See Matthew (Menachem) Maibaum, "A 'Progressive' Jewish Medical Ethics: Notes for an Agenda," *Journal of Reform Judaism* 33:3 (Summer 1986), pp. 27–33.

9. See Chapter 2, n. 2.

10. The prohibition against injuring oneself is stated in M. *Bava Kamma* 8:6 (90b); cf. M.T. *Laws of Injury and Damage* 5:1. Tannaitic sources recorded in the Talmud (B. *Bava Kamma* 91b) state divided opinions as to whether individuals may inflict nonfatal wounds on themselves. The later sources generally agree that people are *not* allowed to injure themselves, although some restrict the prohibition against self-injury to cases where wounds are produced (*Ḥemdat Yisrael*, commandment 310); and some think that the prohibition is not a violation of Genesis 9:5 or Deuteronomy 4:9 (interpreted as a command to maintain one's health) but is rather rabbinic (*Leḥem Mishneh* on M.T. *De'ot* 3:1). In any case, people who injure themselves are not punished specifically for doing that, but they may be punished at the hands of Heaven (T. *Bava Kamma* 9:11), and rabbinic courts may inflict disciplinary flogging *(makkat mardut)* for self-injury (M.T. *Laws of Murder* 11:5; S.A. *Hoshen Mishpat* 420:31; 427:10)—understandable, but more than a bit ironic! See *"Hovel," Encyclopedia Talmudit* 12:681f (Hebrew).

The prohibition against suicide is not recorded in the Talmud itself. The post-talmudic tractate *Semaḥot (Evel Rabbati)* 2:1–5 serves as the basis for most of later Jewish law on suicide, together with *Genesis Rabbah* 34:13, which bases the prohibition on Genesis 9:5. Cf. M.T. *Laws of Murder* 2:3; *Laws of Courts (Sanhedrin)* 18:6; S.A. *Yoreh De'ah* 345:1ff. See "Suicide," *Encyclopedia Judaica* 15:489–491.

11. B. *Sanhedrin* 74a.

12. B. *Avodah Zarah* 18a; S.A. *Yoreh De'ah* 339:1 (with gloss).

13. Ahitophel: II Samuel 17:23. See also the case of Zimri: I Kings 16:18. Burying suicides outside the cemetery: M.T. *Laws of Mourning* 1:11; S.A. *Yoreh De'ah* 345:1—or at its edge: Responsum #763 of Rabbi Solomon ben Abraham Adret (the *"Rashba,"* c. 1235–c. 1310). See Rosenbaum (1976), p. 36 and p. 162, n. 21, for a discussion of the origins of this maxim.

14. King Saul: I Samuel 31:3–4, and see *Genesis Rabbah* 34:21 on this incident. The case of four hundred boys and girls abducted to be sexually violated who intentionally drown themselves instead: B. *Gittin* 57b. For a nice summary of later Jewish comments on the cases of Saul and the four hundred children, see Basil F. Herring (1984), pp. 74–78.

15. B. *Sanhedrin* 74a–74b. Cf. M.T. *Laws of the Foundations of the Torah*, chap. 5; S.A. *Yoreh De'ah* 157:1.

16. For example, Tosafot on B. *Avodah Zarah* 18a, s.v. *ve'al y'ḥabel 'tzmo*; Tosafot on B. *Gittin* 57b, s.v., *ve'kaftzu*.

17. *Kol Bo 'al Aveilut*, p. 319, sec. 50; Tuchinsky (1960), 1:271–273; Klein (1979), p. 282–283 (but note the mistake in citing the passage from *Gesher ha-*

Hayyim: it should be 1:271–273, as noted here, not 1:71–73, as printed there). This may be based on an earlier source—namely, *B'samim Rosh* 345—claiming to be the opinion of the much-respected Rabbenu Asher (the "Rosh," c. 1250–1327), who there permits full Jewish burial of people who commit suicide "because of a multiplicity of troubles, worries, pain, or utter poverty." That source, even if accepted as authentically the opinion of Rabbenu Asher, does *not* permit committing suicide in the first place, and neither do the later Jewish authorities cited above; they only permit normal Jewish burial after the fact.

18. I would like to thank Mr. Frederick Lawrence for pointing out this distinction between justification and excuse during the discussion of the Conservative movement's Committee on Jewish Law and Standards of my rabbinic ruling on assisted suicide, on which the first section of this chapter is based. I would also like to thank the other members of the committee for their insightful comments, many of which led to revisions in the ruling and in this part of the chapter. In some of the notes following, I will acknowledge and thank those whose specific comments produced such clarifications and revisions.

19. Oshry (1983), pp. 34–35. Rosenbaum (1976), pp. 35–40.

20. While it is distinctly uncomfortable to second-guess a rabbi ruling in those dire circumstances, one must also note, as Rabbi Aaron Mackler has pointed out to me, that Rabbi Oshry's decision is, in the end, one rabbi's ruling; and since it extends permission to commit suicide to cases beyond the well-established exceptions of martyrdom, it may simply be an erroneous ruling. I would prefer to deny its relevance as a precedent on the basis of the important distinctions between his case and ours—namely, that the man in his case faced the prospect of endangering the lives of others through no fault of his own, whereas the cases we are discussing include no such factor.

21. The prohibition of putting a stumbling block before the blind: Leviticus 19:14. The rabbinic extension of that prohibition to apply not only to the physically blind, but to the morally blind as well: B. *Pesahim* 22b; B. *Mo'ed Katan* 5a, 17a; B. *Bava Mezia* 75b; etc. (The principle is also applied to prohibit intentionally giving bad advice to people [see *Sifra* on this verse], especially to those who are theologically blind in that they might be tempted to worship idols [B. *Nedarim* 42b].)

22. If the aide additionally persuaded the person to commit suicide, the aide may be considered an "inciter" *(masit)*. One who incites another person to worship idols is subject to death by stoning (Deuteronomy 13:7; M. *Sanhedrin* 7:4, 10). In the case of other sins, though, the defendant can invoke the talmudic principle (B. *Bava Kamma* 56a), *divrei ha-rav ve-divrei ha-talmid mi shom'in?* ("When the words of the Master and the words of the student [conflict], to whom does one listen?)—the Master here being God and the student a human being. According to the Talmud (B. *Sanhedrin* 29a), however, those who incite other Jews to engage in idolatry cannot avail themselves of this defense, because with regard to that offense the Torah (Deuteronomy 13:9) specifically says, "Show him no pity or compassion, and do not shield him." Thus while inducing someone to commit any other sin—like suicide—is certainly not laudable behavior, it is not culpable in law because each of us is responsible for knowing right from wrong and for resisting lures to do the wrong.

23. "Strengthening one to commit a sin": B. *Nedarim* 22a; B. *Gittin* 61a. "Helping one to commit a sin": B. *Avodah Zarah* 55b. I would like to thank Rabbi Ben Zion Bergman for alerting me to this point.

24. See B. *Bava Batra* 22a; and see Tosafot there.

25. B. *Bava Kamma* 56a, which refers, among other such cases, to the one in B. *Bava Kamma* 47b concerning the person who places poison before a neighbor's animal.

26. M. *Bava Kamma* 8:7 (92a); M.T. *Laws of Injury and Damage* 5:11; S.A. *Hoshen Mishpat* 421:12.

27. For Rabbi Avram Reisner, who does not accept my "double-effect argument," it would be outright murder even if the intent were not to bring about death but the physician knew that the given amount of morphine would do that. See nn. 31 and 32 below.

28. For a sampling of varying religious approaches to assisted death, including my own more extensive treatment of Jewish perspectives on this issue (on pp. 141–173), see Hamel and Dubose (1996).

29. M. *Avot* 2:16; B. *Berakhot* 4a; B. *Eruvin* 19a; B. *Ta'anit* 11a; B. *Kiddushin* 39b; *Genesis Rabbah* 33:1; *Yalkut Ecclesiastes* 978. Among later Jewish philosophers, Saadiah is the first to affirm this doctrine (*Book of Opinions and Beliefs*, books 4 and 5), while Maimonides rejects it (*Guide for the Perplexed*, part 3, chaps. 16–23).

30. B. *Berakhot* 5b. I would like to thank Rabbi Baruch Frydman-Kohl for suggesting the use of this source here. See also Jakobovits (1975), chap. 8.

31. See Dorff (1991 [1]), pp. 3–51, esp. pp. 17–19 and 34–39. The Committee on Jewish Law and Standards has validated both that stance and that of Rabbi Avram Reisner, who does not accept the "double-effect" argument that I use but does permit large doses of morphine to relieve pain, stopping short of permitting the withdrawal of artificial nutrition and hydration (although he does permit the withholding and withdrawal of machines and medications from the terminally ill). See Reisner (1991 [1]), pp. 52–89; and, especially, Reisner (1991 [2]).

In Rabbi Reisner's view, I would imagine, if the physician knowingly administers enough morphine to kill a person, then even if she or he does so with the primary intent to reduce pain, the physician would be liable for injuring the patient indirectly *(grama)*. On that analysis, the aide is retroactively free of monetary liability for any harm done. Nevertheless, one may not *ab initio* deliberately cause harm to another, even indirectly. See B. *Bava Batra* 22a; and see Tosafot there.

For me, the primary intent of the physician to reduce pain makes such a case not one of injury at all—even indirect injury—but rather one of permissible benefit. Therefore, the physician would not be liable for violating even the prohibition against indirect injury but would rather be carrying out his or her mandate to heal. This case must be distinguished from acquiescing in a patient's request to die, for since that is an illegitimate request on the patient's part in the first place (in contrast to a legitimate request to reduce pain), to assist in a plan to commit suicide violates Jewish law. That is why the permissibility of administering the amount of morphine in question depends so crucially on the primary intent of the physician: if it is to diminish pain, the physician may use that dose of morphine, even if she or he knows that it will also bring about the patient's death; if, on the other hand, the primary intent is to cause the patient's death, it is forbidden to administer that amount of morphine, even at the request of the patient.

32. Reisner (1991[1]) and, especially, Reisner (1991[2]).

Again, this case must be distinguished from acquiescing in a patient's request to die, even when the death is requested for the express purpose of relieving pain. To kill oneself, or to ask others to help in doing so, is forbidden in Jewish law, and so if that is the intent, the act is illegitimate. In practice, this difference in motive may translate into the amount of medication administered. Specifically, in light of the fact that within a given range of dosages of morphine doctors never know whether a given patient will die or not, these cases never fall into the talmudic category of *p'sik reshai ve'al yamut* ("Can you cut off the chicken's head and it will not die?" [B. *Shabbat* 75a; see Rashi on this principle on B. *Sukkah* 33b]), for within that range the result is never inevitable. Therefore, doctors' attempts to relieve pain are legitimate, in my view, even if they fear that the amount they need to use in the last stages of life may be crossing the line into a fatal dosage for a given patient, for they are still within the range where they do not know that for certain. On the other hand, to administer a dosage that beyond all reasonable doubt will kill the person is to commit murder, even when the stated intent of the physician is to relieve pain and even if the patient requests it. (I want to thank Rabbi Gordon Tucker for calling my attention to the need to make this distinction clearly.)

33. See, for example, Moshe Spero (1980). I would like to thank Rabbi Mayer Rabinowitz for raising the question discussed in this paragraph.

34. B. *Berakhot* 58b; M.T. *Laws of Blessings* 10:12. For an excellent account of these laws and the theology and practice surrounding them, see Astor (1985).

35. M.T. *Laws of Ethics (Hilkhot De'ot)* 3:3; see also 4:1.

36. The argument that assisting a suicide would be to further God's purpose in having made the person sick in the first place is specifically rejected by Rashi and by Tosafot. Commenting on the Talmud's statement (B. *Bava Kamma* 85a) that Exodus 21:19 *(ve-rappoh yerappeh)* serves as permission for physicians to heal, Rashi (s.v., *nitnah reshut larof'im lerappot*) says, "And we do *not* say that the Merciful One struck [the patient] and he [the physician illegitimately] heals." Tosafot there (s.v. *shenitnah reshut larofeh lerappot*) points out that one can derive authorization for the physician to heal from just the first of the words in the phrase in Exodus 21:19, *ve-rappoh yerappeh*, and so why does the Torah state the verb "to heal" in two different forms? Because if it were stated only once, Tosafot suggests, one might think that the physician may heal only those maladies inflicted by human beings but not those inflicted by God; the double presence of the verb in the biblical verse indicates that the physician has permission to heal even illnesses inflicted by God.

37. This is the law of *pikuaḥ nefesh*, saving a life, whether one's own or someone else's; see Chapter 2, nn. 3–4 in this book. While aiding a suicide is against the law in many states, committing suicide itself is not a violation of the law, another manifestation of American individualism. (Most life insurance policies, though, become null and void if the insured commits suicide.)

38. See my short essay, Dorff (1990).

39. See Monmaney (1997).

40. For a fascinating comparative study of how the same diseases are treated differently in the United States, Great Britain, France, and Germany as a reflection of their national cultures, see Payer (1988).

41. On the other hand, in cases where patients are not seeking to die and choose to endure some pain in order to be able to remain conscious, that request must be honored. It is *permissible*, in my view, to use whatever amount of medication is necessary to alleviate pain, but it is *not required* to relieve pain at the cost of consciousness if the patient chooses instead to remain conscious with some degree of pain.

42. This paragraph is based on Monmaney (1997), p. A9.

43. Basil F. Herring quotes and discusses those sources in Herring (1984), chap. 2, entitled "Truth and the Dying Patient," pp. 47–66.

44. See Kubler-Ross (1995) for some striking examples of how meaningful and reconciling the last stages of life and death itself can be. I would like to thank my friend and colleague Rabbi Elie Spitz for calling my attention to this book.

45. The phrase comes from Shakespeare's *Hamlet*, 3.1.67.

46. Leviticus 19:16; B. *Sanhedrin* 73a.

47. Just as bad as recognizing no distinctions is creating sweeping, inviolable categories rather than discerning the fine lines that characterize real moral life. See my response to J. David Bleich in Dorff (1990).

48. The prayer of Rabbi Judah's handmaid: B. *Ketubbot* 104a. Other talmudic instances of praying for God to take a person's life: B. *Bava Mezia* 84a; B. *Ta'anit* 23a. Cf. RaN, B. *Nedarim* 40a. Note that praying for death is not a form of passive euthanasia: in the former, people refrain from acting, but here people ask God to act. See also William Cutter (1995).

The discussion of assisted suicide in this section is based on a *teshuvah* (rabbinic ruling) that I wrote for the Conservative movement's Committee on Jewish Law and Standards. It was passed on March 12, 1997, with 21 in favor, 2 opposed, and 1 abstention. The committee then passed, by the same margin, a summary statement, which will also serve to summarize our discussion on this topic:

Statement on Assisted Suicide: Committee on Jewish Law and Standards—March 12, 1997

- Since God infuses each human life with inherent meaning by creating each of us in the divine image, thereby guaranteeing ultimate value regardless of a person's abilities or quality of life; and
- Since Judaism views life as sacred and understands human beings to have life on trust from God; and
- Since God's creation and ownership of our bodies puts the decision of when life is to end in God's hands; and
- Since we nonetheless have both the right and the duty to seek to cure, to relieve pain, and to provide comfort care, including social, emotional, and psychological support to all who are ill; and
- Since current efforts to rein in costs for medical care threaten to transform any permission to aid a suicide into a perceived duty to commit suicide, shifting the burden of proof to the one who wants to remain alive;

• The Conservative movement's Committee on Jewish Law and Standards has adopted a rabbinic ruling *(teshuvah)* by Rabbi Elliot N. Dorff affirming that:

1. Suicide is a violation of Jewish law and of the sacred trust of our lives given us by God.

2. Assisting a suicide is also a violation of Jewish law and God's sacred trust of life. No human being may take his or her own life, ask others to help them do so, or assist in such an effort.

3. Patients and their caregivers nevertheless have the tradition's permission to withhold or withdraw impediments to the natural process of dying, as described in two responsa by Rabbis Elliot N. Dorff and Avram Israel Reisner, previously adopted by the committee and published in the spring 1991 edition of the journal *Conservative Judaism,* and as applied in the committee's *Medical Directive for Health Care,* written by Rabbi Aaron Mackler on the basis of those responsa.

4. Physicians must assure that patients are given sufficient pain medication as part of their duty to provide medical care, as mandated in Jewish law.

5. In the context of nuclear families, divorce, and far-flung families, the *mitzvah* of *bikkur ḥolim* (visiting the sick) becomes all the more imperative in our day than it was in times past to counteract the loneliness that terminally ill patients often face. Individual Jews and synagogues should see this as an important priority of their Jewish commitment.

6. Requests for assistance in suicide are often an expression of the patient's extreme suffering, despair, psychiatric depression, and loneliness. The Jewish tradition bids us to express our compassion in ways that effectively respond to the patient's suffering while adhering to our mandate to respect the divine trust of life. Among such options is final care at home, with the help of palliative ministrations, including hospice care, to provide the social and emotional support severely sick people need. The approach of death can provide an opportunity for the patient, family, and friends to have meaningful closure and final reconciliation.

---

49. For a discussion of the methodological issues involved in deriving legal guidance from such stories, see the articles by David Ellenson, Louis Newman, Elliot Dorff, and Aaron Mackler in Dorff and Newman (1995), pp. 129–193.

50. B. *Avodah Zarah* 18a.

51. S.A. *Yoreh De'ah* 339:2 gloss.

52. Rabbi Judah the Pious, *Sefer Ḥasidim* nos. 723, 234.

53. *Bet Ya'akov,* no. 59 and *Gilyon Maharsha* on S.A. *Yoreh De'ah* 339:1. Cf. also Moshe Feinstein, *Iggrot Moshe, Yoreh De'ah,* II, no. 174.

54. J. David Bleich (1981 [1]), pp. 141–142. Cf. S.A. *Yoreh De'ah* 339:2, which says that one who has seen a *goses* must begin to mourn for him or her three days later. This gives a retroactive test for the state of *gesisah* in line with Rabbi Bleich's definition, but one based on the medicine of the time, when medical ability to put off death was much more limited. It is on those grounds that others define this period more broadly.

55. For example, Jakobovits (1959, 1975), p. 124 and n. 46; Reisner (1991 [1]), pp. 52–89, esp. pp. 56–58.

56. Dorff (1991 [1]), esp. pp. 19–26; Dorff (1991 [3]). Rabbi Morris Shapiro has also suggested using the *terefah* category in these cases. The sources that Rab-

bi Shapiro adduces in regard to that category are M.T. *Laws of Murder* 2:8; *Minḥat Ḥinnukh*, mitzvot 34 and 296.

Rabbi Shapiro notes that Ezekiel Landau (*Noda Be'yehudah*, Hoshen Mishpat 59), the author of *Tiferet Zvi, Oraḥ Ḥayyim*, 14, and others cited by Rabbi Eliezer Waldenberg in *Tzitz Eliezer*, vol. 5, 28, as well as the Tosafot in B. *Niddah* 44a–b, as Rabbi Reisner points out in n. 19 of Reisner (1991 [1]), all dispute the ruling of the *Minḥat Ḥinnukh* (and that of the Meiri, which Rabbi Shapiro does not mention but which I shall discuss below); but he claims that B. *Nedarim* 22a and the Rosh's comment thereon support the former, permissive opinion, as do the *Oraḥ Ḥayyim* on Exodus 31:16; *Responsa Beit Ya'akov* 59; and, in our own time, Rabbi G. A. Rabinowitz (*Halakhah u'Refuah*, vol. 3, p. 113); and Rabbi N. Goldberg (cf. Rabinowitz, ibid., vol. 2, pp. 146–147).

57. For a more detailed account of these stages, see Dorff (1996 [2]), esp. pp. 172–180.

58. Thus the Talmud specifically says, "We do not worry about mere hours of life" (B. *Avodah Zarah* 27b). The Talmud also says, however, that we may desecrate the Sabbath even if the chances are that it will only save mere hours of life (B. *Yoma* 85a). The latter source has led some Orthodox rabbis to insist in medical situations that every moment of life is holy and that therefore every medical therapy must be used to save even moments of life; see, for example, Bleich (1981 [1]), pp. 118–9, 134–45. The only exception is when a person is a *goses*, which Rabbi Bleich defines as within seventy-two hours of death, at which time passive, but not active, euthanasia may be practiced. He then uses the source in *Avodah Zarah* only to permit hazardous therapies that may hasten death if they do not succeed in lengthening life. Rabbi Bleich's position is *not*, however, necessitated by the sources. On the contrary, they specifically allow us (or, on some readings, command us) not to inhibit the process of dying when we can no longer cure, even long before seventy-two hours before death (however that is predicted).

As we have seen in Chapter 2 in this book, the biblical verse (Deuteronomy 4:15), "Take great care of yourselves," does not, in its context, refer to medical care at all. In rabbinic sources, however, it is used to demand that we take reasonable care of our health. It cannot plausibly be interpreted, though, to require preserving every moment of life regardless of the circumstances, as the rabbis themselves indicate through what they say in the tractate *Avodah Zarah*, cited above. To use that verse to insist on keeping people alive under all conditions would be a new midrash with which I, for one, would not agree.

59. B. *Sotah* 14a. On the general topic of visiting the sick, see Chapter 12 in this book.

60. Ronald Dworkin (1977), p. 22 and, generally, pp. 22–31, where his characterization of the distinctions among rules, principles, and policies appears. As Dworkin points out, however, courts sometimes muddy the waters yet further by interpreting rules with words like "reasonable," "significant," "just," and the like, which invoke the principles or policies that led the legislature to enact the rule in the first place. "But they do not quite turn the rule into a principle, because even the least confining of these terms restricts the *kind* of other principles and policies on which the rule depends." Dworkin (1977), p. 28.

61. The Torah mandates executing people for a long list of offenses; largely through specifying stringent evidentiary rules, the rabbis narrowed the scope of this punishment considerably (cf. M. *Makkot* 1:10), but they retained it, at least in theory. The Talmud (if not the Bible) requires that, even at the cost of killing the attacker, we defend both ourselves (Exodus 22:1; B. *Berakhot* 58a; *Yoma* 85b; *Sanhedrin* 72a) and even others (the law of *rodef*, B. *Sanhedrin* 72b–73a; M.T. *Laws of Murder* 1:6–7; S.A. *Hoshen Mishpat* 425:1). The duty to give up one's own life when the alternative is to commit murder, idolatry, or incest is specified in B. *Sanhedrin* 74a.

62. B. *Avodah Zarah* 27b. In this text, an objection is raised in the name of Rabbi Ishmael to the point made here that we need not be concerned about brief moments of life, but it is deflected.

63. Tosafot, B. *Avodah Zarah* 27b, s.v., *l'hayyei sha'ah lo hyyshenan.*

64. I can imagine someone arguing that I should construe this comment of the Tosafot according to the hermeneutical rule of *kelal u'prat* (a generalization followed by a specification), where one is to interpret the generalization as being limited by the specific example. I would point out, however, that Tosafot follow their discussion of the two examples with another generalization—namely, that we abandon the certain and adopt the uncertain course of action (in order to act for the patient's benefit). Thus this is actually an instance of *kelal u'prat u'kelal* (a generalization followed by a specification followed, in turn, by another generalization), and then the generalizations, rather than the examples, determine the scope of the author's meaning.

For a more extensive explication of how I interpret this source, see Dorff (1991 [1]), pp. 15–17 and p. 43, n. 22. For a contrasting interpretation of this source, see Reisner (1991 [1]), pp. 56–7 and p. 72, n. 21.

65. I first heard Rabbi Immanuel Jakobovits give this exact advice in a conference for physicians and nurses at Cedars-Sinai Medical Center in Los Angeles in 1984. Subsequently, he and others have taken this stance in writing as well. This is one of the many areas in which Rabbi Avram Reisner and I agree in our responsa for the Conservative movement's Committee on Jewish Law and Standards; see Dorff (1991 [1]), pp. 27–33 and Reisner (1991 [1]), p. 64.

66. Cf. Dorff (1986), esp. pp. 33–44.

67. *Cruzan v. Director, Missouri Department of Health* 497 U.S. 261 (1990). For the assisted suicide cases, see note 3 above.

68. B. *Sanhedrin* 63a.

69. Reisner (1991 [1]), pp. 60–62.

70. See Daniel C. Goldfarb (1976); Seymour Siegel (1976); and Discussion, which follows those two articles in that issue of *Conservative Judaism*, pp. 31–39.

71. Cf. Carl Astor (1985).

72. Youngner and Bartlett (1983). I owe this citation and the next, together with the suggestion of this line of reasoning, to Rabbi Avram Reisner. While he articulates it, he does not endorse it. I cannot say that I am thrilled to permit removal of nutrition and hydration tubes from PVS and advanced Alzheimer's patients—such cases are always tragic, no matter what you do—but I do think that, after trying to revive such patients for some time, it is permissible and probably appropriate to do so.

73. M.T. *Laws of the Fundamental Principles of the Torah* 4:8.

74. See, for example, Berman (1982).

75. Once again, we are mandated do what is for the benefit of the patient, in accordance with B. *Avodah Zarah* 27b, but even those who do not attach much weight to this principle have permitted using hazardous therapies when they offer some hope in the name of our duty to preserve life and health. See, for example, Jakobovits (1959, 1975), p. 263, n. 69; Bleich (1981 [1]), chap. 20. The dispute between Rabbi Reisner and me regarding the double-effect argument, described in note 31 above, would not apply to these cases because, by hypothesis, the physician there does not know that the procedure will cause death, as she or he does when administering a high dose of morphine to relieve pain.

76. As noted above, Rabbi Reisner does not accept this double-effect argument, but he would agree that pain should be alleviated as much as possible up to, but not including, the dosage that would inevitably have the effect of hastening the person's death, even if not intended for that purpose. See Reisner (1991 [1]), p. 66 and pp. 83–5, nn. 50–2; and see, in contrast, Dorff (1991 [1]), pp. 17–9 and pp. 43–5, nn. 24–7. See also Rabbi Reisner's summary of the differences between the Dorff and Reisner positions in Reisner (1991 [2]).

NOTES TO CHAPTER NINE

1. *Sifre Deuteronomy*, "Ekev"; B. *Sotah* 14a. In the latter, I have left out the biblical prooftexts that the Talmud uses to demonstrate that God has clothed the naked, visited the sick, etc.

2. I discuss at some length how all of these concepts impinge on the Jewish duty to help others in Dorff (1986), pp. 23–31.

3. See chap. 2, n. 3.

4. Hillel Posek, *Haposek*, vol. 9 (1949; *Av* 5709), no. 3.

5. In Israel, indeed, demonstrations, street riots, and intermittent cabinet crises have periodically occurred over the issue. It was a major factor in the failure of the traditional coalition between the Labor and National Religious Parties to form a government in 1977, the resultant concessions on this issue promised by Menahem Begin to the religious parties, and ultimately (on December 2, 1980) the revision of the Anatomy and Pathology Law, making autopsies subject to family agreement and thus diminishing their number considerably. See, for example, the following articles in the *Jerusalem Post*: "A Matter of Life and Death," June 24, 1977, p. 6 of the magazine; "Medical Progress Must Not Be Prejudiced," August 21, 1977; and several articles and editorials on this topic (all negative!) in the issues of November 13, 1980 and December 1, 2, and 3, 1980, surrounding the passage of the amendment. The new legislation did not prevent further disturbances over this issue, however, as evidenced by the Jewish Telegraphic Agency report of August 27, 1981, that police had to fire tear gas to disperse a crowd of ultra-Orthodox Jews in Jerusalem on the previous day when they tried to prevent police from removing the body of a suspected murder victim (Margalit Cohen) lest an autopsy be performed on her body.

6. Cf. Jakobovits (1959, 1975), pp. 150, 278–283, and, more generally, pp. 132–152. For a thorough discussion of the history of Jewish attitudes toward au-

topsies and dissection against their non-Jewish background, see Jakobovits (1959, 1975), pp. 132–152. The Chief Rabbinate's ruling and the Israeli Anatomy and Pathology Act of 1953 are cited on p. 150. Rabbi Jakobovits's own opinion can be found on pp. 278–283.

7. See Thomas H. Murray (1996).

8. Jakobovits (1959, 1975), p. 291; cf. also pp. 96–98. That this is the generally held opinion regarding living donors is true not only for Orthodox rabbis, to some of whom he refers, but also for Conservative and Reform rabbis. For Orthodox opinions, see Moshe Feinstein, *Iggrot Moshe, Yoreh De'ah* 229 and 230 (Hebrew); Eliezer Waldenberg, *Tzitz Eliezer*, vol. 5, no. 45; vol. 10, no. 25 (Hebrew); Obadiah Yosef, *Dinei Yisrael*, vol. 7 (Hebrew). For a Conservative position (the only one I know of to date on living donors), see Dorff (1985), p. 23. For Reform positions, see Solomon B. Freehof, (1980), pp. 62ff; Freehof (1969), pp. 118–125; and Walter Jacob (1987), pp. 128–133.

9. Cf. Feldman and Rosner (1984), pp. 67–71; Goldman (1978), pp. 211–237.

10. This is the position of Bleich (1981 [1]), pp. 132, 166–167; see generally pp. 129–133 and 162–168.

11. *Proceedings of the Rabbinical Assembly*, vol. 52 (1990), p. 279. Although somewhat dated, a good summary of the positions of all three movements, with relevant quotations from responsa and other official position statements, can be found in Alex J. Goldman (1978), pp. 211–237. That includes quotations from two responsa approved by the Conservative movement's Committee on Jewish Law and Standards. A similar stance can be found in the work of two other Conservative rabbis, namely, Isaac Klein (1975), chap. 5; and David M. Feldman (1986), pp. 103–108.

For a summary of Orthodox positions, see Jakobovits (1959, 1975), pp. 278–291; and Fred Rosner, "Organ Transplantation in Jewish Law," in Fred Rosner and J. David Bleich (1979), pp. 387–400.

For a Reform position on this, see Solomon B. Freehof (1956); Freehof (1968), pp. 118–121 (both of these last two responsa are reprinted in Walter Jacob (1983), pp. 288–296); Freehof (1960), pp. 130–131; Freehof (1974), pp. 216–223. In a March 1986 responsum, the Central Conference of American Rabbis as a body officially affirmed the practice of organ donation, and the synagogue arm of the Reform movement, through its Committee on the Synagogue as a Caring Community and Bio-Medical Ethics, has recently published a manual on preparing for death that specifically includes a provision for donation of one's entire body or of particular organs to a specified person, hospital, or organ bank for transplantation and/or for research, medical education, therapy of another person, or any purpose authorized by law. See Richard F. Address (1992).

12. Prouser (1995).

13. B. *Yoma* 85a; *Pirkei de-Rabbi Eliezer*, chap. 52; *Yalkut Shim'oni*, "Lekh Lekha," no. 72.

14. B. *Yoma* 85a.

15. Cf. Rashi on *Yoma* 85a; Rabbi Tzevi Ashkenazi, *Ḥakham Tzvi*, no. 77; Rabbi Moses Sofer, *Teshuvot Ḥatam Sofer, Yoreh De'ah*, no. 338.

16. Cf. Isserles, S.A. *Yoreh De'ah* 338; Bleich (1981 [1]), pp. 152–154.

17. Daniel C. Goldfarb (1976); Seymour Siegel (1976); and Discussion, *Conservative Judaism*, 30:2 (winter 1976), pp. 31–39.

18. For a summary of some of the varying Orthodox opinions on this subject up to 1978 in America, Great Britain, and Israel, see Goldman (1978), pp. 223–229. Rabbi Immanuel Jakobovits, immediate past chief rabbi of the British Commonwealth, accepted heart transplants from 1966 on. In Israel, Ashkenazi Chief Rabbi Issar Yehudah Unterman permitted heart transplants in 1968 ("Points of Halakhah in the Question of Heart Transplantation," from an address to the Congress of Oral Law, Jerusalem, August 1968; discussed and cited in Rosner and Bleich [1979], pp. 367–371; see also a subsequent, published essay by Rabbi Unterman [1970]); and the Sephardic chief rabbi at that time, Rabbi Yitzḥak Nissim, endorsed that responsum.

On the other hand, Rabbi Moshe Feinstein, president of Agudat ha-Rabanim, the Union of Orthodox Rabbis of America, and the rabbi whose responsa shaped right-wing Orthodox practice in North America throughout his life, issued a strong prohibition against heart transplants, claiming that they involve a double murder (the donor and the recipient) and that physicians who perform them are "evil" (*Hapardes* 43:6 [March–April 1969], p. 4; see also his collection of responsa, *Igrot Moshe, Yoreh De'ah*, part 2 [1973], no. 174, pp. 286–294). However, his son-in-law, Rabbi Moses Tendler, and Dr. Fred Rosner report subsequent conversations with him in which Rabbi Feinstein "clarified" his position to mean that if the donor is absolutely dead by all medical and Jewish legal criteria, then heart transplantation would be permissible, a view he seems to take in his responsum concerning the signs of death (ibid., no. 146, pp. 247–252); see Rosner's article in Rosner and Bleich (1979), p. 370. Rabbi J. David Bleich (1981 [1], pp. 146–157) categorically denies the acceptability of brain-death criteria to determine death, and in his article (1977 [3]), he claims that in oral communications with him, Rabbi Feinstein "in no way is prepared to accept any form of 'brain death' as compatible with the provisions of Halakhah. . . ."

In any case, Israel's Chief Rabbinical Council reaffirmed the acceptability of heart transplants in a responsum issued in 1987. That responsum has been translated by Yoel Jakobovits (1989). For yet other Orthodox opinions, see the article on this by Rosner (in Rosner and Bleich [1979]) and the chapter on this in Goldman (1978).

For Conservative positions, see Jack Segal, "Judaism and Heart Transplantations," in the Rabbinical Assembly archives (August 4, 1969), vol. Y, pp. 90–92; quoted in Goldman (1978), pp. 229–230; Seymour Siegel (1975); Seymour Siegel (1976); and Daniel Goldfarb (1976). No mention of these articles is included in the Index to Law Committee Responsa published in *Conservative Judaism* 34:1 (September/October 1980), pp. 43–54, and so the first official endorsement of the new criteria for the Conservative movement came in the approval of the Conservative movement's Committee on Jewish Law and Standards in December 1990 of the responsa by Rabbis Elliot N. Dorff (1991 [1]) and Avram Reisner (1991), both of which assume and explicitly invoke the new medical definition.

The Reform movement officially adopted the Harvard criteria (presumably, as modified by the medical community) in 1980. See Walter Jacob (1983), pp. 273–274.

19. Adena K. Berkowitz (1995). The 5 percent figure for Orthodox Jews: p. 34. The transplant problems in Israel: pp. 35–36.

20. On the dimension of donation as a gift and the importance of keeping it that way, see Thomas H. Murray (1996).

21. *Genesis Rabbah* 100:7; *Leviticus Rabbah* 18:1; *Ecclesiastes Rabbah* on Ecclesiastes 12:6; J. *Mo'ed Katan* 3:5.

22. S.A. *Even ha-Ezer* 17:26, based on M. *Yevamot* 16:3. See *Genesis Rabbah* 65:20 and *Ecclesiastes Rabbah* on Ecclesiastes 12:6 for a specific linkage of this law to the belief in the soul's association with the body for three days.

23. The quotation is from M. *Semahot* 8:1; the practice is permitted in S.A. *Yoreh De'ah* 144:3. Some moderns, however, maintain that this applied "only in ancient days when they used to place the dead in sepulchral chambers which could be uncovered to reveal the corpse" (Falk, *Perishah*, ad loc.). See also gloss on the Rosh, *Moed Katan* 3:39 in the name of *Or Zarua*.

24. The story of Saul and the witch of En-dor: I Samuel 28. The doctrine of twelve months: B. *Shabbat* 152b–153a; *Tanhuma*, Vayikra 8. The soul after death is quiescent: B. *Shabbat* 152b. The soul is fully conscious: *Exodus Rabbah* 52:3; *Tanhuma*, "Ki Tissa," 33; B. *Berakhot* 18b–19a; B. *Ketubbot* 77b, 104a. The quotation comes from *Pesikta Rabbati* 12:46. The disputes about how much the dead know about the living: B. *Berakhot* 18b.

25. Much of the material for this paragraph and the ones immediately following comes from Joshua Trachtenberg (1939), chap. 5, pp. 61–68. See the original sources he cites there.

26. Adena K. Berkowitz (1995), p. 58.

27. Maccabee Dean (1977).

28. Psalms 115:17. Job 7:6–10; 14:12, 14; 16:22; cf. also 10:20–22; 14:1–2; 17:13–16; 26:5–6. Ecclesiastes 3:19–22; 9:4–6, 10; 11:8; 12:7. Daniel 12:2. Isaiah 26:19 also apparently affirms resurrection of the dead, but scholars construe that verse as imported into the Book of Isaiah in a much later period. On this topic generally, see "Death," *Encyclopedia Judaica* 5:1420–1422.

29. The immortality of the soul was apparently first affirmed in a Jewish source in IV Maccabees 9:8; 17:5, 18. Resurrection, on the other hand, is affirmed in II Maccabees 7:14, 23. Both of these are books of the Jewish Apocrypha coming from the Second Temple period. The rabbis' insistence that Jews believe not only in the world to come but that it is stated in the Torah: M. *Sanhedrin* 10:1; B. *Sanhedrin* 90b–91a. That the Sadducees did not believe this we learn from Josephus, *Wars* 2:162ff. On these topics generally, see *Encyclopedia Judaica* 5:1422–1425 ("Death—In the Talmud and Midrash"); and 2:336–339 ("Afterlife"). Louis Finkelstein has claimed that the second blessing of the *Amidah*, a group of blessings said by traditional Jews three times a day while standing, is deliberately ambiguous in order to accommodate both immortality of the soul and resurrection; it blesses God for being the one who "gives life to the dead." See Louis Finkelstein, (1966), vol. 1, pp. 145–159 (esp. pp. 158–159) and vol. 2, pp. 742–751 (esp. pp. 750–751).

The starkly physical character of the rabbis' understanding of things is illustrated by their beliefs concerning the place where one is buried. Since Israel is, for them, God's promised land and, indeed, the very center of the earth, it is most honorific to be buried there so that one can be resurrected there—and so some Jews to this day arrange to have their bodies flown to Israel for burial. Still, the rabbis recognized that many righteous Jews will be buried outside the land of Israel, and so they affirmed that God creates tunnels through which such dead bodies will roll at the time of resurrection so that they can emerge in Israel! (B. *Ketubbot* 111a; J.

Kilayim 9:4 [end]; *Genesis Rabbah* 96:5; *Tanḥuma*, "Vayeḥi" 3 [6 in some editions]; *Pesikta Rabbati* 43:7.)

As these sources indicate, however, the clear preference is to be buried in Israel or at least to arrange for some earth from Israel to be placed in the coffin as an expression of commitment to the land of Israel, in fulfillment of the biblical verse, "Your servants take delight in its [Zion's] stones and cherish its dust," and also in hopes of assisting the deceased's resurrection. The reasons for burial in Israel are summarized in Yeḥiel Mikhal Tuchinsky (1960), part 1, p. 297. There is some dispute in the sources cited above and in other sources, however, as to whether one who is buried outside Israel may be disinterred and reburied in Israel, but already some of the Amoraim (that is, rabbis of the Talmud living in Persia) were in fact disinterred and moved to Israel (e.g., Rav Huna, according to B. *Mo'ed Katan* 25a), and the law, as codified in the *Tur* and the *Shulḥan Arukh* (*Yoreh De'ah* 363:1), follows this precedent. That is preferably done, though, after the flesh has disintegrated so that it is one's bones that are buried in Israel, as in the case of the biblical Joseph (Genesis 50:25). The verse cited is Psalms 102:15. See Tuchinsky (1960), pp. 299–301, for the sources and explanations of the custom to include some earth from Israel in one's coffin. In any case, this graphically physical depiction of resurrection helps to explain why the traditional rabbinic belief in bodily resurrection is, for some Jews, the source of an important objection to organ donation.

30. Saadiah Gaon, *Book of Doctrines and Beliefs* 2, sec. 1, in Alexander Altmann et al. (1960), sec. 2, pp. 155–156.

31. Moses Maimonides, *Commentary on the Mishnah, Sanhedrin*, chap. 10; in Isadore Twersky (1972), pp. 403–404.

32. Ibid., pp. 410ff. The talmudic citation is from B. *Berakhot* 17a. In his *Commentary to the Mishnah* Maimonides affirms both the immortality of the soul and the resurrection of the body, but by the end of his life, when he wrote the *Guide for the Perplexed*, he makes no mention of resurrection at all, concentrating solely on the eternal nature of the soul. See *Guide* 2:27; 3:54.

33. I. Jakobovits, "The Religious Problem of Autopsies in New York Jewish Hospitals," *Hebrew Medical Journal* (New York, 1961) 34:2:238ff; cited in Jakobovits (1959, 1975), p. 279.

34. See n. 5 above.

35. Cited in Allen S. Maller (1992). His statistics were based on a *Los Angeles Times* poll taken on December 14 and 15, 1991, in the San Fernando Valley section of Los Angeles. The results of that poll were reported, in part, in the metro section of the Valley edition of the *Los Angeles Times* on January 5, 1992, but the *Times* made the full data available to Rabbi Maller, a professional sociologist, for his article in *Heritage*. Another interesting result of that poll: 58 percent of Christians but only 4 percent of Jews did believe in a devil or in a Hell to which sinners are condemned.

36. See "Gilgul," Encyclopedia Judaica 7:573–577.

37. Bleich (1981 [1]), ch. 27.

38. As quoted in Jakobovits (1959, 1975), p. 150; see also n. 231 on p. 362.

39. Isaac Klein (1975), p. 41.

40. Permission of the donor or his family must be procured so that the transplant does not constitute a theft, according to Chief Rabbi Unterman's responsum

in Goldman(1978), p. 226. Feldman and Rosner (1984), p. 68, say that the family's permission is advisable in Jewish law and mandatory in American law. Cf. also Isaac Klein, (1975), pp. 40–41.

NOTES TO CHAPTER TEN

1. *Leviticus Rabbah* 34:3.

2. M.T. *Laws of Ethics (De'ot)*, chaps. 3–5.

3. M.T. *Laws of Ethics (De'ot)* 3:3.

4. Maimonides' specific treatment of the dietary laws: Maimonides, *Guide for the Perplexed*, part 3, chaps. 33, 35, 48. His overarching theory that God did not command anything arbitrarily (except perhaps the details of the laws) but rather intended all the commandments for the sake of promoting our welfare: *Guide*, part 3, chaps. 26, 27.

5. B. *Berakhot* 53b. This was an application of the priestly practice to the masses, for the meal was considered to be like a sacrifice on the altar; consequently, priestly rituals appropriate to handling sacrifices were also appropriate to eating an ordinary meal. See B. *Berakhot* 55a; B. *Sotah* 4b.

6. B. *Sanhedrin* 17b; B. *Avodah Zarah* 20b; J. *Shabbat* 1:3. Cf. *Kitzur Shulḥan Arukh,* part 1, chap. 2:1. The required morning ablution was seen as a reenactment of the priestly practice of washing hands before performing the Temple service.

7. B. *Berakhot* 28b. Several interpretations are possible for the Hebrew here, *yoshvei keranot:* those who sit (a) at street corners; (b) in wagons; (c) in markets; (d) a company [of musicians], connecting the word with the Latin *corona*—all of which are just not privileged to spend time in study—or, (e) most probably, *keranot* is a corrupted abbreviation for *kirkisayot ve'te'atrot*, those who sit in the circuses and theaters, in which case they not only lack time for study due to work but, worse, spend their free time in the pagan temples of Roman culture. See Soncino, *Sanhedrin*, p. 6, n. 4 (on *Sanhedrin* 3a, where the expression also appears).

8. B. *Shabbat* 32a; B. *Bava Kamma* 15b, 80a, 91b; M.T. *Laws of Murder* 11:4–5; S.A. *Yoreh De'ah* 116:5 gloss; S.A. *Hoshen Mishpat* 427:8–10.

9. B. *Hullin* 10a; S.A. *Oraḥ Ḥayyim* 173:2; S.A. *Yoreh De'ah* 116:5 gloss.

10. S.A. *Yoreh De'ah* 255:2.

11. J. David Bleich (1977); Solomon Freehof (1977), chap. 2; *Proceedings of the Rabbinical Assembly*, 44 (1983), p. 182. All of the above are reprinted in Elliot N. Dorff and Arthur Rosett (1988), pp. 337–362.

12. Psalms 104:15; cf. Judges 9:13, Proverbs 31:6–7; Ecclesiastes 10:19. Wine was also used for libations in the cult (Exodus 30:40–41) and in the festive sacred meal (Deuteronomy 14:26).

13. Intoxication was forbidden in the cult to avoid the Dionysian element of pagan religions (Leviticus 10:8–11; I Samuel 1:13–16; Ezekiel 44:21) and in everyday life. Biblical wisdom literature warns that drunkenness brings poverty, quarrels, strange visions, and woes of other sorts (Proverbs 20:1; 21:17; 23:19–21, 29–35; 31:4–5), causing leaders to err in judgment (Proverbs 31:4–5; cf. Leviticus 10:8–11; Isaiah 28:7). Biblical narratives depict the disgrace and sometimes the

death of drunkards (Noah, Genesis 9:20–27; Lot, Genesis 19:31–38; Nabal, I
Samuel 25:36; Elah, I Kings 16:9; Ben-Hadad, I Kings 20:16; Ahasuerus, Esther
1:10). According to the Talmud, a person under the influence of alcohol is legally
responsible for his actions unless he has reached the state of oblivion attributed to
Lot in the Bible (Genesis 19:31–36; B. *Eruvin* 65a–65b). In general on this topic,
see "Drunkenness," *Encyclopedia Judaica* 6:237–241.

14. B. *Nedarim* 28a; B. *Gittin* 10b; B. *Bava Kamma* 113a; B. *Bava Batra* 54b–
55a. See Dorff and Rosett (1988), pp. 515–545 for a description of the developing definition and application of this principle, especially as it relates to Jewish
marriage and divorce.

15. See Dorff [1], pp. 30–36.

NOTES TO CHAPTER ELEVEN

1. *Zohar*, I, 229b.
2. Rabbi Nissim Gerondi (c. 1360) is the first to mention such societies, perhaps because in earlier times Jews lived in communities sufficiently small to ensure that everyone would be visited even without such a formal structure to make
sure that that happened. See *Encyclopedia Judaica* 14:1498.
3. B. *Nedarim* 39b–40a.
4. B. *Berakhot* 6a; 7b–8a; J. *Berakhot* 5:1; cf. M.T. *Laws of Prayer* 8:1.
5. B. *Nedarim* 41a.
6. B. *Ta'anit* 8a; cf. M.T. *Laws of Prayer* 8:1.
7. B. *Nedarim* 39b–40a.
8. As the endnotes in the various paragraphs of this list will indicate, the primary places where the classical codes deal with this topic are in M.T. *Laws of
Mourning*, chap. 14, and in S.A. *Yoreh De'ah* 335. Other sources in English on
Jewish practices regarding visiting the sick include Klein (1979), pp. 271–272;
Krauss (1988), esp. chaps. 16 and 17, pp. 123–139; Schur (1987), esp. chap. 6,
pp. 66–69; Abraham (1980), chap. 35, pp. 135–138; and a new pamphlet, *Bikkur
Holim* (1992), for all the Conservative congregations.
9. B. *Shabbat* 127a; B. *Sotah* 14a; B. *Nedarim* 39–40b; B. *Bava Kamma* 100a;
M.T. *Laws of Mourning* 14:4.
10. B. *Gittin* 61a; M.T. *Laws of Mourning* 14:12; M.T. *Laws of Kings* 10:12;
S.A. *Yoreh De'ah* 335:9.
11. M.T. *Laws of Mourning* 14:4.
12. Thus Maimonides (M.T. *Laws of Mourning* 14:5) says this: "We visit neither those with bowel disease nor those with eye disease nor those with headaches,
for visits are hard on them," either because the patient will be embarrassed by the
disease, as in bowel trouble, or because a visit will add to the patient's pain and
impede recovery, as in the cases of patients with eye trouble or frequent headaches,
for whom speaking with visitors is, according to talmudic medicine (B. *Nedarim*
41a), physically and psychologically burdensome.
13. J. *Pe'ah* 3:9. Other sources (e.g., *Bayit Hadash* on *Tur* 335; M.T. *Laws of
Mourning* 14:5; S.A. *Yoreh De'ah* 335:1 and *Turei Zahav* there) tie this to the
talmudic story (B. *Nedarim* 40a) of Rava, who, when he fell sick, asked that on

the first day of the illness his servants not make it known, "lest his fortune be impaired"—that is, lest people talk about it generally and thus attract evil spirits. Relatives and close friends who commonly came into the house to visit would not arouse such spirits.

14. Thus Maimonides (M.T. *Laws of Mourning* 14:5) says: "We do not visit the sick in the first or last three hours of the day because at those times the caregivers are busy with the needs of the sick person." The Talmud (B. *Nedarim* 40a) and, following that, the *Shulḥan Arukh* (*Yoreh De'ah* 335:4) give a less medical and more theological reason: During the first three hours of the day, the illness is generally less acute than it is later, and so visitors will not remember to offer prayers on behalf of the sick because they will not think it necessary. During the last three hours of the day, the illness may appear so serious that visitors will despair from offering prayers for the sick, thinking that prayer in such serious cases would inevitably be ineffective. This would be theologically spurious reasoning, for God, according to the tradition, is always open to hear prayer and may respond in even the direst of circumstances, but the *Shulḥan Arukh* is here reflecting what people may think anyway.

15. M.T. *Laws of Mourning* 14:4: "People should visit many times during the day, and all who add to their visits are to be praised—as long as they do not burden the patient."

16. M.T. *Laws of Mourning* 4:6; Tosafot on B. *Shabbat* 127a; S.A. *Yoreh De'ah* 35:3, gloss.

17. Ramban (Naḥmanides), *Torat ha-Adam*, "Sha'ar ha-Mehush"; S.A. *Yoreh De'ah* 335:4, gloss.

18. B. *Shabbat* 12b; S.A. *Yoreh De'ah* 335:6.

19. S.A. *Yoreh De'ah* 335:5. Hebrew and/or the vernacular may be used in the presence of the patient; presumably the visitor should base the decision his or her own abilities and the knowledge and sensitivities of the patient. In the synagogue, though, Jewish law states that the prayer for healing should be done in Hebrew.

20. Nel Noddings (1984). I raise these questions even though years before Noddings wrote her book claiming that women resolve moral questions on the basis of caring rather than the moral rules that men tend to use; a man, Milton Mayeroff, wrote a book with almost the exact same title claiming, "In the sense in which a man can ever be said to be at home in the world, he is at home not through dominating, or explaining, or appreciating, but through caring and being cared for." See Milton Mayeroff (1971).

21. Carol Gilligan (1982). Deborah Tannen (1990).

22. The custom of using the mother's name in a prayer for the sick (instead of the more usual custom of identifying the person as so-and-so, son or daughter of *the father*): Scherman (1986), pp. 144–145, 442–443. No explanation is given there, and the explanation I found in two published sources links it to the question the Zohar raises in interpreting Psalm 86:16, namely, why did David, the presumed author of the Psalm, identify himself as "the son of your maidservant" rather than "son of Yeshai," his father? From this the Zohar concludes that when asking for God's deliverance, individuals should identify themselves by the name of their mother, whose identity is beyond question. See also Psalms 116:16; J. D. Eisenstein (1938), p. 220; and Abraham Isaac Sperling (1957), p. 164, para. 353.

The rationale in the folklore, though, as told to me by my father, is that one uses one's mother's name when praying for healing since mothers generally take care of their sick children more than fathers do—or did! Moreover, the Hebrew term for mercy, *raḥamim*, is etymologically related to the word for womb, *reḥem*, and so mothers are associated linguistically in Hebrew with mercy, and that has an effect on the popular imagination. (Along these lines, though, it is interesting that Sperling [1957], in a note on p. 164, cites one source saying that to acquire God's mercy it would be better to identify the patient by his or her *father's* name. Although Sperling himself rejects that custom and quotes another source to reaffirm the custom of using the mother's name, the very existence of a source that suggests using the father's name specifically to induce God to be more merciful is a clear blow against sexual stereotypes!)

23. B. *Sotah* 14a.

24. B. *Shabbat* 127a. See also M. *Pe'ah* 1:1, where acts of lovingkindness, such as visiting the sick, are described as deeds for which there is no prescribed measure since they are limitless in their benefit—although only, as the rabbis said, when visitors are sensitive to the needs of the patient so that their visits do not become a burden and a source of suffering (cf. B. *Nedarim* 40a). The first two passages cited in this note are included at the very beginning of the daily morning service; see, for example, Harlow (1985), pp. 8–9.

25. Preuss (1978), chap. 11. Rosner (1977), p. 32, classifies Saul as suffering from "paranoid psychopathia." See also Gorlin (1970).

26. B. *Hagigah* 3b–4a; see also T. *Terumot* 1:3; B. *Shabbat* 105b; B. *Sanhedrin* 65b; B. *Niddah* 17a.

27. M.T. *Laws of Testimony* 9:9–11, and see the commentary of the *Kesef Mishneh* there.

28. Moshe Halevi Spero (1980), p. 175.

29. M. *Hagigah* 1:1; M. *Bava Kamma* 8:4; B. *Gittin* 23a; S.A. *Hoshen Mishpat* 188:2.

30. See Spero (1980), chap. 9, pp. 120–141.

31. See I Samuel 10:5–12; 19:8–24.

32. T. *Terumot* 1:3; see also B. *Rosh Hashanah* 28a; B. *Yevamot* 31a, 113b; B. *Ketubbot* 20a. On all of these legal ramifications, cf. Spero (1980), chaps. 3, 9, 11, and 12.

33. B. *Shabbat* 128b.

34. Chavel, (1968), 2:43.

35. M.T. *Laws of Ethics*, chaps. 1–3.

36. English translations of these works are available. Bahya's *Ḥovot ha-Levavot* has been translated as *Duties of the Heart* by Hyamson (1970); *Sefer ha-Ḥinnukh* has been translated by Chavel; and *Kad ha-Qemaḥ* has been translated into English by Chavel (1980) under the title *Encyclopedia of Torah Thoughts*. Luzzato's *Mesillat Yesharim* has been translated as *The Path of the Upright* by Kaplan (1936, 1964).

37. See Exodus 32:3, 35:22; Numbers 31:50; Judges 8:24; Isaiah 3:21; Ezekiel 16:11.

38. B. *Shabbat* 113a. Note that the converse of this is also true. In contexts of prison or captivity, one way in which people are disgraced is by stripping them naked.

39. Leviticus 19:28; cf. Leviticus 21:5; Deuteronomy 14:1. For some of the research on tattooing and body piercing included in this section, I am indebted to Rabbi Alan Lucas's responsum on these subjects, approved by the Committee on Jewish Law and Standards in 1996.

40. M. *Makkot* 3:6; B. *Makkot* 20b.

41. Isaiah 44:5; cf. also Isaiah 49:16 and Job 37:7.

42. M.T. *Laws of Idolatry* 12:11; Tur, *Yoreh De'ah* 180, and see the comments of the Beit Yosef and Bayit Ḥadash there; S.A. *Yoreh De'ah* 180:1. Tattoos may be used for medical purposes: S.A. *Yoreh De'ah* 180:3. Those tattooed against their will are free of liability: S.A. *Yoreh De'ah* 180: 2. The Torah's laws against following pagan practices, interpreted to apply generally and not just to cultic matters: Leviticus 20:23.

43. Exodus 21:6. The rabbis clearly saw the ear piercing in this instance as a mark of shame: "Rabbi Yoḥanan, son of Zakkai, would interpret [the verse this way]: How is the ear different from all other parts of the body? The Holy One, blessed be He, said: The ear heard on Mount Sinai at the time that I said 'for the Children of Israel are servants to Me'[Leviticus 25:55] and not servants to servants, and this person went and acquired for himself another master. His ear should therefore be pierced." B. *Kiddushin* 22b. In Genesis 24:47, Eliezer puts a ring on Rebecca's nose and bands on her arms as gifts, but these acts may also foreshadow his expectation that she will enter the bonds of marriage with his master's son, Isaac.

44. B. *Shabbat* 11b (forbidding the practice on the Sabbath, when business and carrying are prohibited); Rashi, ibid., s.v. *b'kisam she-b'ozno.*

45. M. *Bava Kamma* 8:6–7. Many of those who tattoo their bodies would also claim that it should be permitted as an adornment, but the Torah, as interpreted by the rabbis, explicitly prohibits tattoos, even for that purpose. No such prohibition exists with regard to body piercing, and hence it becomes a matter of aesthetics, modesty, and health.

46. Proverbs 31:30.

47. Milton R. Konvitz (1980) has emphasized that Judaism and American ideology share this underlying perspective and thus both seek to protect minorities and the disabled; see chap. 1, esp. pp. 33–41.

48. Numbers 15:15–16; cf. Exodus 12:49; 22:20; Leviticus 24:22; Numbers 9:14; 15:29; Deuteronomy 24:14–15; etc. Note that these include equality in civil law as well as in ritual law. So, for example, a stranger had recourse to Israelite courts: Exodus 22:21; 23:9; Deuteronomy 24:17; 27:19. One must even "love" strangers and treat them as citizens: Leviticus 19:33–34; cf. Deuteronomy 10:18. The rabbis' count that the law of treating the alien as a citizen appears thirty-six times: B. *Bava Mezia* 59b.

Along these lines, rabbinic Judaism respects the rights of non-Jews to live as such, as long as they obey the seven laws given, according to tradition, to the descendants of Noah. See T. *Avodah Zarah* 8:4; B. *Sanhedrin* 56a; *Seder Olam*, chap. 5; *Genesis Rabbah* 16:6, 34:8; *Canticles Rabbah* 1:16; M.T. *Laws of Kings* 9:1. For a thorough description and discussion of this doctrine, cf. David Novak (1983).

Although the attitude of Jews toward non-Jews varied according to the specific conditions of their interaction, and although there were exceptions to the general principle of equal treatment, the rabbis applied the principle not only to the ritual context in which it appears most often in the Bible but also to broad areas of civil legislation as well. See B.*Gittin* 5:8–9; *Mekhilta*, "Pisha," 15; B. *Gittin* 61a; B. *Bava Metzia* 70b; B. *Bava Batra* 113a; Maimonides, *Commentary to the Mishnah, Kelim* 12:7; M.T. *Laws of Sale* 18:1. Cf. "Gentile,"*Jewish Encyclopedia,* 5:615–626; "Gentile," *Encyclopaedia Judaica* 7:410–414. Furthermore, Judaism does not missionize, except by example: B. *Yevamot* 47a–47b; J. *Kiddushin* 4:1 (65b); M.T. *Laws of Forbidden Intercourse* 13:14–14:5; S.A. *Yoreh De'ah* 268:2. Cf. "Proselytes," *Encyclopedia Judaica* 13:1182–1194. Jews were, though, to serve as an example to other nations: Isaiah 2:2–4; 11:10; 42:1–4; 49:6; *Genesis Rabbah* 43:7; *Leviticus Rabbah* 6:5; etc.

49. T. *Sanhedrin* 13:2; B. *Bava Batra* 10b; M.T. *Laws of Repentance* 3:5. According to Samuel, on the Day of Judgment there is no distinction between Jew and Gentile; J. *Rosh Hashanah* 1:3 (57a).

50. Cf., for example, Aaron Kirschenbaum (1970); Norman Lamm, (1971), chs. 10, 11; Milton R. Konvitz (1972).

51. B. *Eruvin* 13b. But cf. its correlative in B. *Sotah* 47b. See Dorff (1992[4]) for a discussion of how these and other traditional Jewish sources constitute a basis for pluralism.

52. For example, Deuteronomy 24:10–22; cf. also Exodus 22:21–26; 23:6; Leviticus 25:25–55; Deuteronomy 15:7–11. Biblical law condoned slavery to pay debts, but it restricted the length and conditions of servitude; cf. Exodus 21:2–11, 20–21, 26–27; Deuteronomy 15:12–18; 23:16–17. For one poignant example of Jewish provision for the poor in the Middle Ages, cf. S. D. Goitein (1971), vol. 2, pp. 139–142; cf. also p. 128. Cf. also my paper, Dorff (1986), for a general treatment of the topic.

53. Rabbi Avram Reisner reasons this way in an as yet unpublished responsum entitled "Peri- and Neo-Natology," approved by the Conservative movement's Committee on Jewish Law and Standards in fall 1995. That a child's life is not confirmed until thirty days of age: B. *Shabbat* 135b. M. *Niddah* 5:3, however, states that from the moment of birth a child is, to his or her parents and relatives, "like a bridegroom [or bride]"—that is, that the parents and relatives, if not the rest of society, assume that the child is alive and well and will ultimately marry. Based upon that and upon our advanced scientific knowledge, which enables us to determine the gestational age of a child with accuracy, the Conservative movement's Committee on Jewish Law and Standards endorsed a responsum by Rabbi Stephanie Dickstein requiring that full mourning rites be used for a child who dies within the first thirty days of life (contrary to the traditional practice of simply burying the child privately without communal participation and without the traditional rites of the seven days of mourning following burial). See Stephanie Dickstein's as yet unpublished responsum, "Mourning Practices for Infants Who Die Prior to the Thirty-first Day of Life," approved by the Committee on June 3, 1992.

54. Leviticus 19:14. For an excellent summary of Jewish law on the disabled, including some of the provisions mentioned in the next few paragraphs, see Carl Astor (1985).

55. Ecclesiastes 12:3–8. I am following the Jewish Publication Society translation (*Tanakh*, 1985) and notes here on pp. 1454–1455.

56. Thus the rabbis (*Genesis Rabbah* 9:5–9) explained the insertion of the adverb "very" in the Torah's judgment, "God saw all that He had made and found it very good" (Genesis 1:31) as including death and the evil impulse in people, for they both contributed in the end to the welfare of the human species.

NOTES TO CHAPTER TWELVE

1. M. *Kiddushin* 4:14 (82b). Exactly why "the best of physicians are destined for hell" is disputed. Rashi suggests several reasons: (a) being unafraid of illness, they do not appropriately adjust the diet of the sick and feed them instead food for healthy people; (b) again, because they do not fear illness and sometimes cure it, they are haughty before the Almighty; (c) their treatment is sometimes fatal; and finally (d) on the other hand, by refusing treatment to the poor, they may indirectly cause their death. Ḥanokh Albeck (1958), in his commentary to the Mishnah, vol. 3, p. 330, suggests that it is because they are not careful in their craft and thus cause sick people to die (similar to Rashi's first and third explanations combined). Philip Blackman (1963) suggests in his commentary to the Mishnah, vol. 3, p. 484, n. 27, that the subject of this curse is not doctors per se but "one who pretends to be a specialist and in consequence brings disaster to his patients." The Soncino translation and commentary to the Talmud (1936), Nashim, vol. 4, p. 423, n. 9, citing the *Jewish Chronicle* of 1.3.35, says that "it is probable that it is not directed against healing as such, but against the 'advanced' views held by physicians in those days."

2. B. *Sanhedrin* 17b.

3. Cf. Joshua 9:3ff; Ezra 2:43, 8:20; Neḥemiah 3:26; I Chronicles 9:2.

4. B. *Horayot* 3:7–8.

5. B. *Horayot* 13a; *Tur* and S.A. *Yoreh De'ah* 242 and 252. Saving oneself first is demanded by Rabbi Akiba's position on B. *Bava Mezia* 62a, which becomes the accepted law.

6. S.A. *Yoreh De'ah* 251:9.

7. B. *Bava Mezia* 62a. I would like to thank my friend and colleague Rabbi Elijah Schochet for pointing out this glaring absence to me and for discussing with me the conclusions we should draw about how the rabbis themselves thought of deciding such matters on the basis of a social hierarchy.

8. This is especially interesting against the background of the Greek Stoic Hecaton, who makes such decisions precisely on the bases of social status and worth; see Saul Lieberman (1963), pp. 124–126.

9. S.A. *Yoreh De'ah* 251:3.

10. T. *Pe'ah* 4:9.

11. S.A. *Yoreh De'ah* 249:16.

12. S.A. *Yoreh De'ah* 251:7–8.

13. S.A. *Yoreh De'ah* 252:1, 3.

14. S.A. *Yoreh De'ah* 252:8.

15. S.A. *Yoreh De'ah* 252:9.

16. This principle is enunciated in B. *Bava Mezia* 62a, where it is based on Leviticus 25:36, "so that your brother may live with you": since your brother cannot

live with you unless you yourself are alive, Rabbi Akiba deduces that saving your own life comes first.

17. M. *Sanhedrin* 4:5.

18. J. *Nedarim* 9:4 (41c).

19. B. *Berakhot* 17a. The text quoted in this is from B. *Menaḥot* 110a.

20. J. *Terumot* 7:20; *Genesis Rabbah* 94:9.

21. The reference of Rabbi Judah's question is unclear. If we follow the usual stylistic conventions, where the phrase, "where does that apply" comes to narrow a previous ruling to make it more lenient, Rabbi Judah comes to limit the first opinion mentioned (the *tanna kama*). Specifically, while the first opinion says that if the enemy does not designate a particular person, nobody may be handed over, Rabbi Judah would say that that ruling applies only if the enemy is still outside the city walls so that there is still a chance that they would all survive; but if the enemy has already managed to break into the city, someone may be handed over to save the rest, since that is the only chance that any of them will be saved.

The problem with interpreting Rabbi Judah that way, though, is that if the enemy had not designated someone, how would the city dwellers choose whom to hand over? Moreover, Rabbi Judah says that "he" may be handed over if the enemy is inside the city walls, which would seem to indicate that the enemy has designated someone. This, then, leads us to interpret the first opinion and Rabbi Judah as we do here, namely, that the first opinion permits handing over only someone who is both designated by the enemy and also liable for the death penalty, whereas Rabbi Judah says that if the enemy designated someone and the lives of the rest of the city dwellers are at stake, the citizens may hand over the designated party in order to save themselves, even if he is not liable for the death penalty. In the next generation, under this interpretation Rabbi Shimon ben Levi (Resh Lakish) in the next clause agrees with the first opinion, and Rabbi Yoḥanan agrees with Rabbi Judah. See Saul Lieberman (1955), *Zeraim*, pp. 420–422 [Hebrew]; Elijah J. Schochet (1973), pp. 6–7; and David Daube (1965), pp. 31–36.

22. Thus God inflicts illness for sin according to Leviticus 26:16 and Deuteronomy 28:59–60, and the Talmud follows suit, claiming, "There is no sickness without iniquity" (B. *Shabbat* 55a; cf. B. *Sanhedrin* 101a). A tenth–century commentary (*Midrash Tadshe* 16) put it graphically: "If a subject sins against his ruler, a blacksmith is commanded to fashion chains in which the ruler imprisons the sinner. When a man sins against the Lord, his limbs become his fetters."

23. The Book of Job is probably the most famous challenge to the linkage between sickness and sin, and B. *Menaḥot* 29b provides a powerful talmudic example of such a challenge. In contemporary times, doubts about this linkage are articulated eloquently in Harold Kushner (1981).

24. M.T. *Hilkhot Rozeaḥ* 2:8. Since the death of a *terefah* is inevitable, evidence of *tarfut* is equivalent to evidence of death, and therefore, according to the Talmud and later Jewish law, the deserted wife of a *terefah* may remarry (B. *Yevamot* 120b–121a; M.T. *Hilkhot Gerushin* 13:16–18; *Tur, Even ha-Ezer* 17; S.A. *Even ha-Ezer* 17:3–32). According to most authorities, twelve months must elapse before permission to remarry may be granted, analogous to the presumption regarding animal *terefot*. Cf. M. *Yevamot* 16:4; Ramban, *Yevamot* 120b, s.v. *umi matsit*; Rashba, *Yevamot* 120, s.v. *umi matsit; Maggid Mishneh, Hilkhot Gerushin* 13:16,

s.v. *vekakh nireh; Kesef Mishneh, Hilkhot Gerushin* 13:16, s.v. *vekhen im; Tur, Even ha-Ezer* 17; S.A. *Even ha-Ezer* 17:32. Also see *Responsa Mishpetei Uziel, Even ha-Ezer* 79; *Responsa Ziz Eliezer* I, 23. *Tosafot,* however, argues that fundamental physiological differences between humans and other animals (and, I would add, the expenditure of considerably more human energy and resources in caring for sick humans) often enable people to survive for a longer period. These factors underscore the fact that for all of these authorities, the twelve-month period with regard to humans is only an estimate, and the crucial factor in the definition of *terefah* is the medical diagnosis of incurability.

25. Meiri, *Sanhedrin* 74a, s.v. *yera'eh li* (p. 271). Also see *Tiferet Yisrael, Yoma* 8:7, s.v. *venireh li,* and Ḥayyim Benviniste, *Seyarei Knesset ha-Gedolah* on S.A. *Yoreh De'ah* 156, no. 36. In general on this, see Dorff (1991 [1]), pp. 22–23.

26. J. *Terumot* 47a.

27. B. *Shabbat* 46a.

28. B. *Yevamot* 36a, according to which the law is always according to Rabbi Yoḥanan when he argues with Resh Lakish except in three instances, and this is not one of those three. Rabbi Yoḥanan generally wins the day even though on two occasions (B. *Ketubbot* 54b, 84b), when confronted with the differing ruling by Resh Lakish, Rabbi Yoḥanan himself remarked, "What can I do when a rabbi of equal status disagrees with me?" I would like to thank my teacher and colleague at the University of Judaism, Dr. Elieser Slomovic, for discussing these sources with me.

29. M.T. *Hilkhot Yesodei ha-Torah* 5:5 The basis for this ruling is discussed in *Kesef Mishneh* there; *Responsa Habah ha-Yeshanot,* 43; *Responsa Seridei Esh* 2, no. 78. Those who rule with Maimonides include *Bah, Tur, Yoreh De'ah* 153; *Taz, Shulḥan Arukh, Yoreh De'ah* 157:7; and *Responsa Noda Beyehudah* 2, *Yoreh De'ah* 74. The Tosefta and its variations were used also in responsa to determine how a Jewish community should supply men for the army; cf. Schochet (1973), pp.47–48.

30. B. *Bava Kamma* 85a.

31. B. *Ta'anit* 21b.

32. Rabbi Eliezer Fleckeles, *Teshuvah Meahavah,* III, on S.A. *Yoreh De'ah* 336.

33. M.T. *Laws of Gifts to the Poor* 7:5. See also S.A. *Yoreh De'ah* 248:1–2.

34. S.A. *Yoreh De'ah* 252:11.

35. B. *Bava Metzia* 62a. The verse that Rabbi Akiba interprets for his ruling is Leviticus 25:36.

36. M. *Ketubbot* 4:9.

37. S.A. *Yoreh De'ah* 252:10. This is ultimately based on the Mishnah's insistence that a man redeem his wife from captivity before being able to divorce her; cf. M. *Ketubbot* 4:9.

38. S.A. *Yoreh De'ah* 252:12. Rabbi Joseph Caro wrote the *Shulḥan Arukh,* completing it in 1565. He was a Sephardic Jew. Rabbi Moses Isserles, an Ashkenazic Jew from Cracow, Poland, added glosses to that work to note where Ashkenazic Jewish practices differed from, or added to, the Sephardic practices. He cleverly called his work the *Mappah,* "the tablecloth," to Caro's *Shulḥan Arukh,* "set table."

In standard editions of the *Shulḥan Arukh,* Isserles's glosses appear embedded in the text of the *Shulḥan Arukh* itself but are printed in "Rashi script" to differentiate it from Caro's text, printed in block letters.

39. M.T. *Laws of Gifts to the Poor* 7:10. See also S.A. *Yoreh De'ah* 248:2.

40. S.A. *Yoreh De'ah* 249:16; 255:2.

41. Baron (1942, 1972), vol. 2, pp. 115, 329.

42. S.A. *Yoreh De'ah* 252:6.

43. S.A. *Yoreh De'ah* 255:2.

44. S.A. *Yoreh De'ah* 252:4.

45. I am following Robert Cover's theory of law in this last phrase. See Cover (1983).

46. Recent California cases have imposed considerable penalties on HMOs failing to provide sufficient benefits: *Fox v. Health Net* (an $89 million jury award for bad faith); *De Meruers v. Health Net* (a $1.3 million arbitration verdict for denial of HMO benefits); and *Ching v. Gaines* (a $3 million jury verdict in a case that challenged the entire HMO distribution system). Federal regulations now forbid HMOs to impose gag rules on their doctors, and California, among other states, has passed legislation to that effect (AB 3013).

47. See Friedenwald (1944) and Nevins (1996).

48. Rava's golem: B. *Sanhedrin* 65b. On the golem legend generally, including the most popular (and menacing) legend ascribed first to R. Elijah of Chelm and then to R. Judah Loeb of Prague, see "Golem," *Encyclopedia Judaica* 7:753–756; Sherwin (1985); Idel (1990).

49. For extended treatments of Judaism and ecology, see, for example, "Ecology and the Judaic Tradition," in Robert Gordis (1986), pp. 13–22, reprinted in Dorff and Newman (1995), pp. 327–335; Waskow (1995), esp. pp. 94–96, 117–143, 214–217, 224–239; Bernstein and Fink (1993); Waskow and Elon (1996).

50. See Annas and Grodin (1992).

51. A recent film, *The Twilight of the Golds*, produced by Showtime and first aired on March 23, 1997, depicts a Jewish family in which the adult son is gay and the daughter, who is married and pregnant, finds out that the child that she is carrying has the gene for being gay. The woman's husband and parents want her to abort the child, whereas the brother sees their response as a rejection not only of homosexuality but of him personally. The woman chooses not to abort the child, but it costs her her marriage. These dilemmas are bad enough when the only option is to abort; they will become even worse if we can one day not only identify a gene for homosexuality but also change it. Under those circumstances, would we alter it? On what grounds? Would we leave it as is? On what grounds? Either way, the issue is no longer the health of the mother or child; it is our evaluation of what constitutes a good state of being—a very dangerous standard for making such decisions.

52. M. *Sanhedrin* 4:5.

53. See "Afterlife," *Encyclopedia Judaica* 2:336–339; Moshe Greenberg, "Resurrection—In the Bible," *Encyclopedia Judaica* 14:97–98. While early biblical sources affirm the existence of Sheol, a murky place to which people's spirits descend after death, resurrection of the body after death is first affirmed by what is chronologically the last book of the Bible (c. 150 B.C.E.), the Book of Daniel (12:1–3). (Isaiah 26:19, which also affirms it, is, as Greenberg says in the article cited above, understood by almost all commentators to be a much later addition.) Job (e.g., 7:7–10; 9:20–22; 14:7–22), written in about 400 B.C.E., and Ecclesiastes (9:4–

5; cf. 3:19–21), written about 250 B.C.E., explicitly deny resurrection and perhaps even any form of life after death. It thus appears that bodily resurrection made its first appearance in Judaism in the second century B.C.E. The rabbis (Pharisees), though, made it a cardinal doctrine, even asserting that biblical sources, which are at best ambiguous about this, clearly and definitively affirm it; see M. *Sanhe-drin* 10:1; B. *Sanhedrin* 90a and following.

Appendix:
The Philosophical Foundations of My Approach to Bioethics

Religion and Morality

The Role of Religion in Making Moral Decisions

THE MORE WE DEAL WITH CONTEMPORARY MICRO AND macro issues in bioethics, the more we realize that deciding how to resolve them is not just a matter of determining what works or what is affordable; it is also critically a matter of our ultimate hopes and fears, of what we value in life, and of how we conceive of life in the first place. These concerns are the province of religion. The word *religion* etymologically means "linkages," coming from the same Latin root meaning "to tie or bind," from which we also get the word *ligament*. And so it is that religions address the nature of our links to one another, to the environment, and to the transcendent. From such large pictures of how the world is, we base our hopes for how it should be, and thus our values are rooted in the broader world views that religions provide. It is only when we have these ultimate perceptions and convictions in mind that we can sensibly make the specific decisions contemporary medicine calls upon us to make.

Secular philosophies like those of Plato, Aristotle, Hobbes, and Marx also portray such pictures of reality, but they lack religion's popularity and emotional power. That is because religions do not merely present a given view of reality and a set of values deriving from it; they also link us to a community that shares these perceptions of reality, cherishes those values, and works for the realization of those hopes. Religions create communities committed to their ideologies by putting their specific understanding of reality into stories that can be easily shared, rituals that can help people live out their understanding of life and feel part of a group that shares it, and institutions that make it possible to teach and share the group's common convictions. These features make religion a powerful and popular way to speak about reality and to guide important decisions in life.

The Relationship Between Religion and Morality:
Four Theories

Religion, though, has not guaranteed moral behavior; in fact, sometimes religion itself is utterly hostile to it. Take, for example, the Crusades and the Inquisition, during which moral atrocities were committed in the very name of religion. Indeed, even some passages in the Bible are morally ambiguous at best and downright immoral at worst—texts such as God's commands to bind and presumably murder Isaac, to kill all of the Canaanites as part of the conquest of the Holy Land, and to enslave non-Jews.[1] In the twentieth century, the worst atrocities were inflicted by the avowedly secular regimes of Stalinist Russia, Maoist China, and Nazi Germany. But moral abominations explicitly in the name of religion have continued, as fundamentalist Muslims terrorized or murdered all who opposed them, including other Muslims, and as Baruch Goldstein and Yigal Amir killed in the name of their understandings of Judaism.

Why does religion sometimes lead to immoral action? For one thing, religious faith is built upon trust in God, but all too often that trust turns into credulity and superstition. More pervasively, the blind loyalty religion summons in its adherents, at least in some forms, works against their retaining a critical, moral sense that could criticize religion itself. Indeed, religious authorities have often discouraged or totally suppressed dissent, sometimes even to the point of executing dissenters and heretics.[2] In addition, religions have of necessity been organized into institutions, and so they suffer from all the moral weaknesses inherent in any institution. Conversely, many people we would clearly consider moral are avowedly secular, denying belief in any religion.

Since religion is neither sufficient nor necessary for moral behavior, then, and since sometimes religion actually produces immorality, some people conclude that religion and morality logically have nothing to do with each other. The two may affect each other, but like other independent agents, their interaction may either benefit or harm.[3]

Others take the opposite view. Despite the evidence that religion can undermine morality, they hold, logic requires a religious basis for morality (a logical claim), or that social order and moral education both require a religious framework (an empirical claim). George Washington, Thomas Jefferson, and James Madison all endorsed some variation of this theory. Most Americans today likewise believe that even if nothing can absolutely guarantee morality, religion substantially increases its chances.[4]

Still others argue for a third way of viewing the relationship between religion and morality. Robert Gordis and David Hartman, among others, maintain that to be accurately described as religious, a person must behave morally. In other words, they view morality as a logical prerequisite for religion.[5]

The problem with this theory, however, is that it runs counter to how people understand themselves and others. That is, some people who consider themselves and are generally considered religious nonetheless engage in gross moral turpitude, sometimes even being jailed for their behavior. Indeed, Jews' deep embarrassment at seeing newspaper photographs of Ḥasidim convicted of crimes would be unintelligible if such people automatically lost their religious status (and therefore ceased representing Judaism in the public mind) upon committing an immoral act. Thus, as much as Judaism demands and supports morality, morality is not by definition inextricably linked to Judaism.

In light of all the above, I hold yet a fourth thesis—namely, that *in Judaism, ethics and religion interact, and that they do so in both directions.* That is, some features of ethics can and should be used to direct and criticize religion, and conversely, some features of Judaism can both deepen and foster moral life. Thus each can guide and enrich the other, but it is also true that each can impede the other. Religion has been used to justify immoral behavior ranging from slaveholding to the assassination of Israeli Prime Minister Yitshak Rabin. Moreover, moral claims can produce conflicts with religion—as, for example, when a rally to help the poor takes place on Shabbat, or when moral considerations challenge norms embedded in religious texts (for example, the ban against homosexual sex). Yet because neither perspective controls the other or acts as a logical or empirical prerequisite for the other, religious people and institutions commit many amoral and even completely immoral acts, whereas secular people often behave quite morally. Often and ideally, though, morality and religion correct and support each other.

The Contributions of Ethics to Religion

How do morality and religion interact to their mutual benefit? Let us first look at how ethics can and should be used to guide and criticize religion—or rather, more specifically, the theology and practice of Judaism.

Theologically, the relationship between God and goodness as depicted in Jewish sources from the Bible to our own day has been ambiguous. Although God is generally held to be good, sometimes God commands or does things that are hard, if not impossible, to justify morally.[6] Moreover, in the experience of individuals and of the people Israel as a whole, both natural and human evils occur that make us question God's goodness or power—or even God's very existence.

Nevertheless, most of Jewish tradition teaches—and I concur with this view—that God must be construed as morally good, indeed, as the paradigm of what it means for us to be morally good.[7] Phenomena like childhood leukemia, where there is no human complicity on the part of the person afflicted and where the innocent suffer, though inscrutable, do not constitute sufficient proof that God does not exist or that God is amoral, immoral, or powerless; such phenomena are offset by the many instances of God's beneficence.[8] Thus, when faced with morally troubling phenomena devoid of human complicity, we must accept that we will never understand them and instead learn to cope with them. Such are the limits of human knowledge and understanding.[9]

On the other hand, when confronted with evils caused by human beings, our Jewish belief in a moral God who demands goodness requires that we do what we can to alleviate the effects of such evils and to prevent their recurrence in the future. This is the holy mission that Judaism establishes for us. Therefore, we dare not leave an immoral situation unchallenged, merely attributing it to the unchangeable will of an inscrutable or downright evil God.

Legally, this theology has even more far-reaching implications. For if God is "good to everything, and God's mercies are over all God's works," and furthermore, if God's laws are a manifestation of God's deep and abiding love, as the Psalmist and traditional prayer book proclaim,[10] then Jewish legal decisions must reflect these beliefs. Therefore, if a legal decision that seems justified by traditional sources, or even mandated by the majority of them, is not moral, it must be changed.

The classical rabbis made it very clear that the Jewish tradition they were shaping, which we identify today as normative Judaism, is *not* fundamentalist, even with regard to the Torah; it rests rather in the hands of the rabbis of each generation who interpret and apply it according to their own understanding of God's will.[11] It is, then, the way in which the rabbis of each generation understand morality that must govern how Jewish law is shaped to be morally good and, therefore, Godlike.

Because intelligent, morally sensitive, and committed Jews may disagree about the ethics and wisdom of any proposed decision, this methodological principle does not automatically require, or justify, any given decision in Jewish law. Yet the underlying morality of Jewish law, reflecting a moral God who commands it, should motivate its interpreters to aspire to make

their legal decisions as morally exemplary as possible. Conversely, laws that are patently immoral must either be annulled altogether or at least so restricted in their scope as to make them
effectively inoperable. Indeed, such reinterpretations of Jewish
law on moral grounds have occurred in our own day, especially
in respect to many laws defining the status of women. And by
the same token, conflicting moral perspectives today fuel the
arguments surrounding the status of homosexual relations.

Similarly, this fundamental commitment of Jewish law to
morality, based on an underlying theology of a moral God who
commands it, should also guide us as we face the many new
issues in contemporary bioethics. In many such issues, the radical innovations of modern medical care make a mechanical or
literal reading of traditional texts inappropriate. Instead, those
who would apply Jewish law to these new circumstances must
supplement their traditional learning with a keen moral sense
of when and how to apply classical Jewish sources as a good
God would direct us to do.

The Contributions of Judaism to Moral Theory and Practice

The second half of my argument—namely, that Judaism can
contribute significantly to morality—applies to both moral theory (or "ethics") and moral practice ("morality").

On a theoretical level, Judaism affirms a particular picture of
the world as it is and as it ought to be. It defines who we are as
individuals, as a community, as parts of the environment, and
as partners of God; and it provides ideals toward which we can
and should strive. In so doing, Judaism places our moral decisions into the *context* of a larger vision of the world and our
goals within it. Judaism thereby gives *meaning* to each of our
moral efforts and provides *motivation* to meet our moral challenges. The beliefs of Judaism thus establish moral moorings for
our specific judgments and acts.

Judaism also contributes to our moral behavior on a pragmatic level by strengthening the family and self-worth of both ourselves and others, as well as our moral restraints and aspira-
tions. Through values, stories, rituals, and laws, Judaism

reinforces the cohesiveness and moral effectiveness of our families and communities.

Another pervasive feature of Judaism that contributes mightily to our moral framework but is less often acknowledged in that capacity is *Jewish law*. Like Judaism as a whole, Jewish law does not guarantee moral sensitivity or behavior, but it makes their presence more likely in a number of ways. Since Judaism focuses so much on the legal expression of its views and values, much of our treatment of Jewish bioethics must be framed in legal terms. It is therefore worth spelling out here some of the ways in which Jewish law as a whole, and Jewish bioethical law in particular, helps to make people behave morally.

1. *Establishing a moral bottom line.* Law establishes a minimum standard of practice. Because many moral values depend on the mutual action of a number of people, the enforcement as law of a minimum moral standard enables a society to secure the cooperation necessary for such moral attainment. Furthermore, a beneficent act, whether done for the right reason or not, has its own objective value.

2. *Translating moral goals into concrete rules.* It is not just on a minimal level that law is important for morality; at every level of moral aspiration law translates moral insight and fervor into modes of daily action. Without that translation, our moral vision and courage lose their meaning and influence.

3. *Setting priorities among conflicting moral goals.* When moral values conflict, law provides a method for determining which value will take precedence over which, and under what circumstances. Nonlegal systems commonly rely on the sensitivity and analytical ability of the individual or an authority figure to do that; law enlists the minds and hearts of legislators, judges, and the public at large. Although such a process does not guarantee wisdom, it does at least provide a greater measure of objectivity and hence a more thorough consideration of relevant elements.

4. *Appreciating the reality, nuances, and immediacy of moral issues.* In contrast to moral treatises, which are usually general and nondirective, judicial rulings respond to concrete cases in

which judges make practical decisions. Thus in contrast to many "ivory tower" moral essays, legal precedents address reality in all its complexity and provide specific instructions for action. Much of the rabbis' sheer wisdom, in truth, can be attributed to the fact that they served as judges as well as scholars and teachers. Thus the legal context adds a sense of immediacy, nuance, and reality to moral deliberation.

5. *Preserving the integrity of moral intentions.* Law brings our motives into the arena of action, where we can see them clearly and work to change them if necessary. Law thus helps to preserve the integrity of moral intentions themselves, clarifying and verifying them in action.

6. *Balancing continuity with flexibility.* Because law operates on the basis of precedent, it preserves a strong sense of continuity in a moral tradition. On the other hand, through various legal techniques—differentiating the present case from previous ones; limiting the scope of previous cases; finding other analogous cases in the tradition that lead to a different conclusion; redefining some of the critical terms involved; or, ultimately, issuing a *takkanah*, that is, a "fixing" or changing of the law—law preserves a reasonable amount of flexibility and adaptability. Since this process is in the hands of rabbis, whose ordination signifies that they are both committed to the tradition and schooled in it, such changes will not happen cavalierly—especially if any one rabbi's decision enters into a larger discussion among many rabbis—but will instead enable appropriate change to take place over time.

7. *Preserving the coherence of a moral system.* If authorized judges in each generation—namely, rabbis—are entrusted with the task of legal interpretation for their communities, then even if there is disagreement among them, we can learn from their deliberations what counts as a Jewish approach— a norm formulated in the judicial line of precedents within Judaism—to a given issue. This is all the more true if the rabbis have a communal method of setting parameters for legitimate dissent among them; the Sanhedrin did that in times past, and the Conservative movement's Committee on Jew-

ish Law and Standards functions in that way for the Conservative movement now.[12] To achieve a measure of coherence, even the Reform movement, which puts so much emphasis on individual autonomy, has shown renewed interest and creativity in developing its own legal response to moral issues by creating a Committee on Halakhic Inquiry and by publishing books of responsa.[13]

8. *Establishing and preserving the authority of moral norms.* Jews have historically adopted legal methods primarily because they believed that this was the only way to preserve the divine authority of the tradition. Rabbinic authority ultimately rests on Deuteronomy 17:8–13, which provides that in each generation questions about the law (and hence about what God wants) should be addressed to the judge of that generation. One may not, as the rabbis warn us, complain that this generation's judges pale by comparison with those of previous generations; instead, one must accept that "Jephthah in his generation is like Moses in his." Thus divine authority—and indeed continuing divine revelation—takes place in the form of judicial decisions throughout the generations.[14]

9. *Teaching morality.* The law serves as a tool for moral education as well. Although theories of moral education are many and diverse, the Jewish tradition has a clear methodology for teaching morality:

> Rav Judah said in Rav's name: A man should always occupy himself with Torah and good deeds, even if it is not for their own sake, for out of [doing good] with an ulterior motive he will come to [do good] for its own sake.[15]

Study of the tradition complements this largely behavioristic approach to moral education. On balance, though, the emphasis is on action:

> An excellent thing is the study of Torah combined with some worldly occupation, for the labor demanded by both of them causes sinful inclinations to be forgotten. All study of the Torah without work must in the end be futile and become the cause of sin.[16]

The same educational theory is applied to moral degeneracy and repentance:

> Once a man has committed a sin and repeated it, it appears to him as if it were permitted.

> Run to fulfill even a minor precept and flee from the slightest transgression; for precept draws precept in its train, and transgression draws transgression. If a transgression comes to a man a first and second time without his sinning, he is immune from the sin.[17]

Formulating moral norms in terms of law is thus very important educationally; for by so doing people are *required* to act in accordance with moral rules as a step in teaching them how to do the right thing for the right reason.

In all of these ways, and undoubtedly in others, law contributes to our moral sensitivity and behavior as much as morality informs our law. The *interaction* between them improves both, especially when they are both put into the larger contexts of theology and religion.

Judaism has gone further than most other religious or secular systems of ethics in trying to deal with morality in legal terms. It is therefore not surprising that contemporary decisions in Jewish medical ethics flow out of the continuing interactions among Jewish religious thought, law, and morality. To isolate any one of these perspectives is to distort Jewish tradition. But to see and apply their interactions to contemporary concerns requires knowledge of and commitment to all three; a developed moral and legal sense; and the capacity for sound judgment, compassion, and wisdom.

Legal Versus Nonlegal Methods of Accessing the Tradition

If religion can contribute to both moral theory and practice, as I have argued, how can someone looking for moral guidance access the tradition for its direction and moral insight? In other words, how can the tradition help us to confront the moral challenges of our age—especially those as markedly new as many of those in contemporary bioethics?

Judaism has historically depended upon a judicial mode for resolving moral quandaries, blending exegeses of the Torah and later rabbinic literature, precedents, and customs to arrive at a decision. Accordingly, almost all Jews who have written about biomedical issues in our day have used Jewish legal sources and methods primarily, if not exclusively. Yet within this commonality there are considerable differences. Conservative and Reform authors, for instance, differ from Orthodox writers in their ways of interpreting classical texts, the former two groups adding historical and cross-cultural considerations to the traditional commentaries used by the latter. Authors from these three denominations of American Judaism, and their counterparts elsewhere, differ even more in the ways in which they apply those sources to contemporary circumstances and the degree to which they and their intended audiences feel obligated to follow the tradition, however it is interpreted. But most rabbinic writers in all three movements are united in their assumption that identifiably *Jewish* moral positions can emerge only through interpreting and applying the *legal* precedents and statutes of the Jewish tradition.

While this methodology is central to Judaism, it is by no means the only way to approach these matters. One could claim, for example, any of the following:

1. That the ultimate authority for differentiating right from wrong and good from bad is God (a "divine command theory"). Some who hold this theory maintain that God's will can be determined only by a literalist reading of a revealed text (for example, the Hebrew Bible, the Christian Bible).

2. That the authority to define God's will, including its moral aspects, should be invested not in a text but in a religious leader. Catholics, for example, understand the Pope as the ultimate authority in faith and morals, even when they disagree with him or disobey him.

3. That it is an individual's conscience that discerns God's will and thus determines what is moral and immoral. Both Cath-

olics and Protestants assign such a role to the individual conscience, which is emphasized more or less according to the specific interpreter or adherent. The Reform movement in Judaism has similarly made individual autonomy the centerpiece of its ideology and methodology.[18]

4. That the person who makes moral decisions should not be a religious leader, whose authority is based on God, but rather a political one, whose authority is based on the power to enforce it ("Might makes right"). This is a secular version of the last two theories. In varying forms, this is the theory of Thrasymachus and Callicles in Plato's dialogues, and of Machiavelli and Nietzsche much later on,[19] and in practice it is the theory asserted by monarchs and dictators throughout history.

5. That moral decisions made for an entire democratic community should be determined by the will of the majority of citizens or their representatives or by some other expression of the communal will. This theory is either grounded on the pragmatic rationale that democratic decisions are the only way in which people with conflicting moral convictions can live together peacefully; or it is based on theories, such as those of Aristotle and Rousseau, holding that moral vision and consensus emerge from public debate. Since communities and nations do, and on this theory may, decide about the morality of a given act in different ways, such theories are inherently relativist—that is, they make moral judgments dependent upon, and only valid in, a given society. Even regions of a given country may, according to this theory, take different moral positions. Consider, for example, the disparity between the laws governing sodomy in California, where sex between consenting adults in private is legal regardless of the gender of the partners, and those in Georgia, where there is a law against even private, consensual homosexual sex between adults, a law that the United States Supreme Court has affirmed Georgia's right to enact and enforce.[20]

6. That good actions and policies are those that afford the greatest good for the greatest number, a view held by utilitarians and many American pragmatists. Theoretically at least, an

objective calculus of benefits and burdens should be able to determine the correct moral decision in any given case.

7. That right and wrong can be determined on objective grounds, independent of the wishes or views of individual people or communities. Divine command and utilitarian theories are two forms of moral objectivism. Likewise one could claim, along with Immanuel Kant, that moral principles are built into the structure of the human mind or, along with Saint Thomas Aquinas, that they are built into the very structure of nature. These principles define right and wrong and good and bad.[21] Although the methods by which one discerns these principles differ according to the particular theory, they usually involve an appeal to reason in some form.

8. That "good" simply means that the person using the term has a positive emotion toward the person or action being mentioned, and "bad" means the reverse. This view, advocated by the philosophers A. J. Ayer and Leslie Stevenson in the middle of the twentieth century,[22] stands at the other end of the objectivist-relativist-subjectivist spectrum. Such an emotivist theory of morality asks that we each simply consult our feelings toward the person or act being evaluated, without claiming that other people must or should share our own emotional reactions.

9. That there is no moral realm, that no decision is better or worse than any other, and that people should just do what pleases them.[23]

This is only a partial list of the methods people use to determine what is moral. Clearly, then, the Jewish preference for defining morality through a legal approach, while certainly long-standing and deeply entrenched within Judaism, is by no means the only way to do this.

Each of these methods has its benefits and drawbacks; none is perfect or totally without merit. I believe, though, that the Jewish tradition was wise in choosing to confront contemporary moral issues by using law because of the strengths of that method delineated above and the corresponding weaknesses of the alternatives.

APPENDIX

Rules Versus Principles and Policies

To apply a legal method to contemporary medical issues, however, is not easy, for there are not many legal sources to ground
such decisions. Although Jews have had a veritable love affair
with medicine throughout the last millennium and even before,
they have been no more able than non-Jews to extend or
significantly improve a person's medical history. It is therefore
surprising that there are *any* precedents whatsoever on many
of the subjects that currently concern us.

As soon as we look at the precedents that do exist, however,
we see the difficulties in applying them to contemporary circumstances. For example, when we examine the precedents that
have been widely cited to shed light on issues at the end of life,
we find that some of them are not actually medical. They speak
rather of Rabbi Hananyah ben Teradiyon's responses to his students as they tried to relieve his suffering while he was being
burned at the stake, and of Rabbi Judah ha-Nasi's handmaid-
en's interruption of his students' prayers on her master's behalf
so that he could die. Other sources, though medical, bear little
resemblance to modern medical contexts. They speak, for example, of the efficacy of putting salt on the tongue or hearing a
knocking noise coming through an open window as ways to
extend life. That is hardly the world of respirators and gastrointestinal tubes.

To address today's medical issues, then, Jewish law needs to
be extended considerably. Contemporary rabbis must take on
this challenge if Jewish law is going to be at all relevant to some
of the most critical issues of our time. To do so, however, rabbis
must face some deeply rooted philosophical questions about
how to reconcile constancy with change—and, indeed, how to
interpret and apply texts in the first place. What *should* be the
methodology of Jewish law in addressing these radically new
realities?

Contemporary legal philosopher Ronald Dworkin has eluci-
dated an important distinction—between rules on the one hand
and principles and policies on the other—that must inform such
discussions.[24] Rules are norms to which there are no exceptions;

they must either be followed at all times, or they must be changed. If rules conflict with each other, the conflict must be resolved by a higher-order rule specifically created to govern the authority and application of rules. A principle or policy, on the other hand, is a general guideline, set for either moral reasons (our "principles") or pragmatic ones (our "policies"), which can admit of exceptions when weighed against other moral or practical concerns.

Rules are most common in logic, mathematics, and games; but they exist in law as well. Such rules determine the hierarchy of laws—for example, a federal law takes precedence over a state law if the federal government has jurisdiction over the matter, and in Jewish law, a mishnah has more authority than a *baraita*. Rules can also affect matters of content, but here it is often hard to determine whether a given norm is indeed a rule rather than a principle or policy. For example, does the First Amendment to the United States Constitution ban Congress from *any* impediment to freedom of speech—that is, is it a rule?—or does it establish a general norm restraining Congress from banning freedom of speech *unless* there is some important social reason to do so—that is, is it a principle or a policy? The language of the amendment itself can be interpreted either way, but later courts determined that the law was to be construed and used as a principle, not a rule. That is why yelling "Fire!" in a crowded theater is not constitutionally protected speech. Similarly, in Jewish law, the sixth of the Ten Commandments, "You shall not murder," sounds like an inviolable rule banning all forms of homicide, but the Torah itself permits killing others in war and self-defense.

This distinction has important implications for medical ethics. For example, one overarching axiom informing most Orthodox responsa on medical issues generally, and on euthanasia in particular, is that human life is sacred and therefore even small moments of it *(ḥayyei sha'ah)* must be preserved, whatever its quality. However, although Judaism certainly cherishes human life, it does *not* mandate the duty to preserve all human life under all circumstances and at all costs. On the contrary, in some situations we are actually commanded to *take* a human life (for example, when execution is mandated by law, or when killing another is required to defend oneself), and in other cases we are obligated to give up our own life (specifically, when the alternative is that we ourselves must commit murder, idolatry, or incest).[25] In other words, Jewish law establishes a clear general *principle* to preserve life; but like all other principles and policies, this one is open to being supplanted in given circumstances by specific considerations.[26]

Some rabbis have historically tried to establish general rules and to deduce rulings in specific cases from them, whereas others—the vast majority—have understood generalizations in the law as summaries of some decisions but not prescriptions for others. The former deductive approach was undoubtedly influenced by the medieval penchant for systematic structuring of both thought and law, and it produced the genre of codes; the latter casuistic method has its roots in the Bible and the Babylonian Talmud, and it has led to the genre of responsa.[27] Many rabbis in the last millennium have used both methods at various times; some (for example, Maimonides) have tried as much as possible to fit their decisions under the rubric of a well-defined rule, while most have preferred to reason analogically from a variety of precedents.

In any case, this distinction in method is crucial in contemporary biomedical cases for both methodological and historical reasons. Methodologically, a generalization that seems unexceptionable in one era may be subject to serious criticism in another when circumstances have changed. If it is seen as a rule, to change it would require the wrenching task of either discarding the long-standing rule or weakening the absolute authority of all rules in the system by making an exception to this one. Normal legal reasoning, on the other hand, simply searches for other precedents within the law that seem more appropriate to the case at hand. One may not always find such precedents—in which case some serious revision of the law may be necessary— but this approach offers a considerably greater chance of extending the law aptly than merely invoking hard-and-fast rules.

Moreover, arguing analogically from precedents is historically the *standard* method in Jewish law, and so following this method is actually adhering to the more traditional approach.[28]

Balancing General Guidelines and Individual Cases

The point needs to be taken yet further. Contemporary physicians and ethicists underscore the *complexity* of each case. Even when the medical diagnosis and prognosis of two people are identical, there may well be differences in temperament, values, family support, financial resources, and the like. Although these factors may not be relevant in analyzing the patient's *physical* status, they may well be very important in designing appropriate medical and nonmedical responses. Some scholars have therefore urged all concerned to pay attention not only to what Carol Gilligan has called the "masculine voice" in ethics—concerned primarily with rules and abstract principles—but also to what she calls the "feminine voice," which pays more attention to the specific human situation in which the decision is made, the relationships of the people involved, and the question of how a course of action will help or hurt the people *in this case.*[29] This approach has been compared to the more internally Jewish model of the Ḥasidim, who, at least by reputation, followed their emotions when dealing with specific cases that cried for compassion, in contrast to the *misnagdim*, who were said to rely excessively on general norms framed by the intellect.

In large measure I agree with this call for increased attention to the details and nuances of specific cases. But this approach is neither distinctly feminine nor specifically hasidic.[30] Rather it bespeaks the Jewish tradition's long-standing insistence that individual cases must be decided on their own merits; that general rules may not substitute for careful consideration of the particular circumstances of the people involved; and that, more generally, law and morality are, and must remain, intertwined. Making decisions in specific cases does not eliminate the importance of articulating general standards—that is, commonly used principles and policies; one must just know when and how to use them. In the technical terms of contemporary ethicists, I am arguing neither for an exclusively situational ethic nor for a solely rule-based one (regardless of whether the rules are seen as deontological or consequentialist); I am arguing instead for a character-based ethic, in which both rules and contexts combine with moral moorings in philosophical/religious sources and moral education to produce moral sensitivity.[31] This approach represents a much richer—and, I think, much more realistic—view of how moral norms evolve and operate than the exclusive attention to principles that has characterized much of moral theory until this century.

Weighing the Applicability of Precedents

This analysis, then, brings us back to our original question, namely, how can Judaism address contemporary medical realities radically different from those of the past? The methodological points I have made so far—that we must interpret Judaism's general rules as policies, not inviolable principles; that even general policies must be applied with sensitivity to the contexts of specific cases; and that we must nevertheless retain a legal method in making our decisions—all inform how we should apply Judaism to modern medicine. How, though, can we use ancient precedents that have at best a questionable relationship to contemporary medical contexts?

Despite radical differences between medicine in the past and in the present, Orthodox rabbis, by and large, have taken their customary, literalist approach. Some have indeed been ingenious in making it appear that the few ancient precedents available can reasonably determine the outcome of modern questions.[32] This process, however, ignores the historical context of past medical decisions and the crucial differences between medical conditions then and now. In Arthur Danto's felicitous phrase, such responses to the issues are paradigmatic examples of "misplaced slyness." Rabbinic sources, after all, did not contemplate the realities of modern medicine; nor, for that matter, did American legal sources as late as the 1940s. Therefore, depending closely on laws and precedents from times past to arrive at decisions about contemporary medical therapies all too often amounts to sheer sophistry. In such attempts the texts themselves are not providing clear guidance but are rather being twisted to mean whatever a particular rabbi or judge wants them to mean.

In a different form, though, this is simply legal method. To bring new situations under the umbrella of the law, judges in any legal system must often stretch precedents to make them relevant to new circumstances. Indeed, for a legal system to retain continuity and authority in current decisions, this *must* be done. Thus in our case, if a decision is going to be *Jewish* in some recognizable way, it *must* invoke the tradition in a serious, not perfunctory, way. One *can* do this without being devious or anachronistic *if one does not pretend that one's own interpretation is its originally intended meaning (its* peshat*) or its only possible reading.* The Conservative objection to many Orthodox readings of texts is thus based on both tone and method: not only do many Orthodox responsa make such pretensions, often with an air of dogmatic certainty, they do so with blatant disregard for the effects of historical and literary context on the meaning of texts and indifference to the multitude of meanings that writings can often legitimately have.

In addition to such matters of intellectual honesty, literalist efforts to arrive at medical decisions today seem to be misguided on a purely practical basis. Even if we presume that our ancestors were consummately wise and perhaps even divinely inspired in making the decisions they did, there is no reason to suppose that their decisions would retain those qualities in our own setting. On the contrary, I am sure that they themselves would have insisted, as the Talmud does, that each rabbi now take a good look at "what his own eyes see" to be sure that his or her application of the tradition is deserving of the godly qualities of wisdom and kindness that we ascribe to Jewish law.

In our topic, this means that we, like medieval Jewish physicians and rabbis, should be prepared to deviate from the specific medical directions given in a particular precedent if contemporary medical conditions require a new application of Jewish concepts and values.[33] We want to root our decisions as strongly as possible in the tradition, but not at the cost of ignoring the significant differences between the medical setting of our own time and that of the past. We must therefore first judge whether or not medicine has changed significantly in the area we are considering, and, if it has, be prepared to stretch some halakhic and aggadic sources beyond their original meanings. We *should* do this in order to retain clear connections to the tradition, not only in spirit and concept but even in expression. At the same time, we should openly state what we are doing—namely, that we are choosing both the texts to apply and specific interpretations of those texts in order to develop a Jewish medical ethic that carries traditional Jewish concerns effectively into the contemporary setting.

In insisting that we retain the legal form and substance of past Jewish law, I am disagreeing with Reform positions such as that articulated by Matthew Maibaum. He claims that the radical individualism and secularism of contemporary American Jews means that "to an increasing degree, trying to talk about Jewish medical ethics from a traditionalist point of view will impress no one." He objects to using not only the precedents of the past but even many of the concepts that underlie those precedents—concepts such as God's ownership of our bodies. Individual Jews, then, according to him, should not feel themselves bound by the tradition's laws or concepts but should rather use the tradition however they wish in arriving at their own decisions.[34]

It seems to me that his analysis makes one's claim to articulate a *Jewish* position much too tenuous. With such an approach, for example, how does one rule out anything as being contrary to Judaism? Why, indeed, would one be interested in developing a specifically Jewish approach to medical matters in the first place?

From one perspective, then, there is a methodological spectrum, in which positions are differentiated according to the *degree* to which individual Jewish sources are allowed to determine specific, contemporary medical practices. For most Orthodox rabbis, who read the classical texts of the Jewish tradition in a literalist way, such texts are totally determinative, and so the only substantive question is how a decision can be read out of, or into, those sources. For at least a segment of the Reform movement, the goal, as Maibaum says, is to show secular Jews that a given Jewish position "also happens to be immediately and centrally good for them." If this cannot be shown, then the whole tradition is "like a fine fossil or an elegant piece of cracked statuary; it is venerable, but is not relevant today."[35] I am taking a methodological position somewhere in between those two poles, affirming the necessity to root a contemporary Jewish medical ethic in the Jewish conceptual and legal structure of the past but recognizing that to do so honestly and wisely, we will have to make difficult judgments as to when and how to apply that material to substantially new settings.

The position I am affirming, however—largely identified with the Conservative movement in American Judaism—is not defined solely either by what it denies or by its comparison with others. On the contrary, central to its identity are its positive convictions about the proper way to understand and apply Jewish sources. In brief, Conservative Judaism affirms that to understand Jewish conceptual and legal sources properly—both early texts and their later interpolations through the generations—they must be studied in their historical contexts. The relevant similarities and differences between previous settings and our own can then be identified. With those in mind, to arrive at an authentically Jewish and wise decision, we should use legal reasoning, with appropriate attention to moral, economic, and sociological concerns and with continued awareness of the Jewish theological foundation concerning our nature as human beings created by and in the image of God. Sometimes traditional sources must be extended considerably to arrive at an apt decision, but the more a decision can be connected to classical Jewish legal and theological texts the better, for then continuity and the other advantages of a legal approach are more confidently assured. At the same time, we should always be careful to declare that ours is *a* possible reading of the tradition, among other possible readings, and we must argue for the one we choose by explaining the reasons that motivate us to adopt it.

The Impact of the Reader

This Appendix on methodology must also include a reference to the discussion in Chapter 1 of the impact of the reader on how one reads any text and applies it to current circumstances. I will not repeat that discussion here, but I do want to remind the reader of it and thereby to incorporate it into this short treatise on methodology.

A Traditional, Dynamic Ethic for Our Time

I have described above a number of methodological principles:

- We should make our individual moral decisions within the context of our broader, religious convictions to give them intelligibility, coherence, and meaning.
- We should seek to maximize the contributions of religion and morality to each other and to minimize the dysfunctions in the relationship between them.
- We should retain a legal method with its inherent discipline, authority, continuity, coherence, and educational utility in making our moral decisions and in teaching moral sensitivity, recognizing all the while that the law must be continually tempered by its traditional and necessary interaction with morality.
- We should understand that Jewish law most often prescribes policies, not inviolable rules, and interpret and apply Jewish law accordingly.
- We should implement general policies with an appreciation for the nuances of a specific case.
- We should read texts in their historical contexts to understand them properly and to apply them intelligently to our times.
- We should be ever cognizant of the inevitable and proper impact of the reader and his or her context, goals, and values in interpreting and employing a text.

- We should understand that our awareness of the contemporary context does not vitiate the authority of the text but nevertheless opens the door, with appropriate argumentation, to contemporary moral perceptions and judgments.

In my view these principles must collectively shape the way in which we approach issues of bioethics in our time. Only then can our methodology be sufficiently dynamic to accommodate the revolutionary changes occurring in the world of medicine on an almost daily basis and yet remain unmistakably Jewish. Only then can we responsibly and wisely carry on the vital and religiously rooted tradition of medical care that we have inherited.

Notes to the Appendix

1. The binding of Isaac: Genesis 22. The fate of the seven Canaanite nations: Deuteronomy 20:10–18; see also Exodus 34:11–16; Deuteronomy 7:1–6. The permission to enslave gentiles: Leviticus 25:35–46. For more discussion of biblical understandings of the relationship between God's word and the moral norm, see Elliot Dorff and Arthur Rosett (1988), pp. 110–123. For rabbinic understandings of the relationship, see ibid., pp. 249–257.

2. Morris Raphael Cohen (1945, 1977) has written polemically, but convincingly, on this—although with more examples from ancient religions and from Christianity than from Judaism. See chap. 41, "The Dark Side of Religion," pp. 337–361.

3. Two people who hold that position, but for different reasons, are Kai Nielson (1973; reprinted in part in Nielson, 1976) and David Sidorsky (1975).

4. The evidence on that is, however, ambiguous. To take just one example, religious people (including some leaders of the Church) were counted among both those who actively cooperated with the Nazis as well as "the righteous gentiles"— that is, those who, at the risk of their own lives and those of their families, hid Jews from the Nazis. To make matters yet more complicated, while most righteous gentiles affirmed a belief in Christianity, they did not generally attribute their heroic acts to their religious beliefs but rather to their often unsophisticated, albeit deeply held, moral conviction that it simply was not right to surrender Jews to the Nazis. See Pearl and Sam Oliner (1988); Nechama Tec (1986); and Mordecai Paldiel (1993). I would like to thank my friend, colleague, and mentor, Rabbi Harold Schulweis, for these references.

A recent experiment by *Reader's Digest* provides another intriguing example of this ambiguity. The magazine's agents planted ten wallets filled with fifty dollars and identification information in twelve places in a variety of cities across the United States to determine whether the rate of return of the "lost" wallets would vary by the gender or age of the finders, the size of the city in which the wallets were found, or the depth of religious belief of the finders. A large number of those who returned the wallets said that they were motivated to do so by their belief in God: "Even those who don't regularly attend services credited religious lessons as a moral prod." The moral training received within the family, a personal sense of moral responsibility, and/or the desire to be treated similarly if they had lost their own wallet were, however, even more commonly mentioned as factors that prompted their honesty. See Bennett (1995); the quotation is on p. 55.

5. Robert Gordis (1990), pp. 50–68. Gordis maintains that, both according to the theory (aggadah) and practice (halakhah) of Judaism, ethics takes precedence over ritual, and moreover, the possibility "that God could command an immoral act is a notion completely unacceptable to Judaism" (p. 67). He thus titles the chapter where he makes and supports these claims "The Primacy of Ethics," by which he means both the legal and logical primacy of ethics over ritual and theology. Similarly, David Hartman maintains that "the divine power and mystery must never be used as a justification to undermine the category of the ethical" (David Hartman [1985], p. 97).

6. See Elliot Dorff and Arthur Rosett (1988), pp. 110–123, for a discussion of such passages.

7. See, for example, Deuteronomy 32:4; Psalms 145:9, 17; B. *Sotah* 14a; *Sifre Deuteronomy*, Ekev.

8. I first argued this in response to Richard Rubenstein, who has articulately held in his various writings that the Holocaust, the nuclear threat, and overpopulation make it impossible any longer to believe in a beneficent God or, indeed, in a personal God altogether. See Richard Rubenstein (1974) and my response (Elliot N. Dorff [1974]).

9. To strip God of power or personality on this basis, as Harold Kushner (1981) and Harold Schulweis (1994) have done in their theologies, is, I think, radically to diminish what we mean by God, as well as to pretend that the complexities of our existence are simpler than they are. I would rather have honest perplexity in the face of some phenomena I cannot understand than believe in a neat, consistent system that ignores or sets aside by definition the parts of reality that do not fit it. That will mean, of course, that I must have some intellectual humility, but part of what it means not to be God, after all, is not to be omniscient. For more on this, see Dorff (1992), pp. 129–148.

10. The verse from Psalms: Psalms 145:9. The liturgist's understanding of God's law as the gift of God's love is expressed in the *ahavah rabbah* prayer in the morning service and in the *ahavat olam* prayer in the evening service, both immediately before the *Shema*; see Harlow (1985), pp. 98–99 and 200–201.

11. For a thorough discussion of the rabbinic justification of the interpretive process, including the limits of its flexibility, see Elliot N. Dorff and Arthur Rosett (1988), pp. 185–245. That rabbis must judge according to how their own eyes see things: B. *Bava Batra* 131a, cited on p. 389 in Dorff and Rosett. For the impact of morality on the making and practice of Jewish law, see Dorff, "The Interaction of Jewish Law with Morality" (1977).

12. There is no equivalent body among North American Orthodox Jews, who are badly splintered and who tend to follow a particular rabbi revered by their particular segment of the Orthodox community. Thus, until their deaths during

the last decade, Rabbis Dov Baer Soloveitchik, Moshe Feinstein, and Menachem Mendel Schneerson served in the capacity of ultimate authority for the modern Orthodox, Agudat Yisrael, and Lubavitch portions of the Orthodox community, respectively. The Israeli Orthodox community has a Sephardic and an Ashkenazic chief rabbinate, but that office does not deter sharp criticism from other Orthodox rabbis, even of the same stripe—as, for example, the roundly maligned decision of the Ashkenazic chief rabbi to allow heart transplants. See *Assia* 14:1–2 (August 1994) (Hebrew), where ten rabbis take issue with Rabbi Abraham Kahana-Shapira's decision to permit heart transplants. The three American rabbis mentioned above were rarely, if ever, subjected to such open rebellion.

The Central Conference of American Rabbis (Reform) has constituted a Committee on Halakhic Inquiry, and its chair, Rabbi Walter Jacob, has edited three books of Reform responsa: Jacob (1983), Jacob (1987), and Jacob (1992). Since Reform ideology champions the individual autonomy of each Jew to make religious decisions, however, these responsa function exclusively in an advisory capacity for Reform Jews. For two Reform theories on how that process should work, see the articles by Eugene B. Borowitz and David Ellenson in Dorff and Newman (1995), pp. 106–117 and 129–139. In the end, even a policy against intermarriage, overwhelmingly approved by the delegates to the 1985 convention of the Central Conference of American Rabbis, could not become binding on individual Reform rabbis, and in the intervening years it has actually become hard for Reform rabbis to refuse to perform intermarriages.

The Conservative movement tries to balance the authority of the individual rabbi for his or her community with communal norms. The Committee on Jewish Law and Standards validates acceptable options on issues that individual rabbis raise; if a responsum attains six votes or more (out of twenty-five), it becomes a validated option within the movement. If two or more are validated, individual rabbis may use their own discretion as to which to follow. Even if only one option is validated, individual rabbis may choose to do otherwise. Three "standards" of the movement, however, have been adopted—forbidding intermarriage, requiring a Jewish writ of divorce *(get)* for remarriage, and defining Jewish identity through birth to a Jewish mother or halakhic conversion—and no Conservative rabbi or synagogue may violate those standards on pain of expulsion. For more on this, see Dorff (1989), pp. 278–283. This structure makes for plural practices in the movement within a given framework.

13. Three sets of books come especially to mind: the many books of responsa by Solomon Freehof, published by the Central Conference of American [Reform] Rabbis; the three books of new responsa that have already been published by that same body under the editorship of Walter Jacob; and the books published by the Freehof Institute of Progressive Halakhah, edited by Walter Jacob and Moshe Zemer.

14. For a thorough discussion of how this line of divine authority is understood in the biblical and rabbinic sources, see Elliot N. Dorff and Arthur Rosett (1988), pp. 123–133, 187–198, and 213–245. The specific sources mentioned in this paragraph are the following: the Torah's attempts to differentiate true from false revelation: Deuteronomy 13:2–6; 18:9–22; examples of problems with false prophets: Jeremiah 23:16–40; that prophecy ceased after the Haggai, Zechariah, and Malachi died: B. *Sanhedrin* 11a; that interpretation (Midrash) took the place of

prophecy: B. *Bava Batra* 12a; the comparative lenses through which Moses and other prophets see: *Leviticus Rabbah* 1:14; Jephthah in his generation is like Moses in his: T. *Rosh Hashanah* 1:18; B. *Rosh Hashanah* 25a–25b.

15. B. *Pesaḥim* 50b and elsewhere.

16. M. *Avot* 2:1.

17. B. *Yoma* 86b; M. *Avot* 4:2; B. *Yoma* 38b.

18. See, for example, Eugene Borowitz (1984 [1]). Rabbi David Ellenson, another important ideologue of the Reform movement, has pointed out that primarily because of the wide disparity between contemporary medical conditions and those of times past, some rabbis in all three movements have suggested using a "covenantal" model for making medical decisions centering on the individual's conscience. See David Ellenson (1990), esp. pp. 228–29; reprinted in Elliot N. Dorff and Louis E. Newman, eds. (1995), pp. 129–139, esp. pp. 136–137. The articles he cites are these: Daniel H. Gordis [a Conservative rabbi] (1989); Irving Greenberg [an Orthodox rabbi] (1986); David Hartman [an Orthodox rabbi] (1979), pp. 100ff; and Eugene B. Borowitz [a Reform rabbi] (1983), esp. pp. 367–368, and (1984 [2]), pp. 48–49. I would object to this approach on three grounds: (a) my appreciation of the *strengths* of a legal approach to the moral issues in life, as delineated above, and the corresponding weaknesses of the suggested alternative; (b) my conviction that personal responsibility *can* be retained in a properly understood halakhic system; and (c) my confidence that, when properly understood and applied, legal methods can enable Jewish law to treat realities as new as contemporary medical phenomena sensitively and wisely. For more on this, see Dorff (1991 [2]).

19. Thrasymachus: Plato, *Republic* 336B–354C. Callicles: Plato, *Gorgias* 482ff; 491ff. Niccolo Machiavelli (1950). Friedrich Nietzsche (1914), secs. 259–260; Nietzsche (1956), pp. 166–168.

20. *Bowers v. Hardwick* 478 U.S. 186 (1986).

21. Immanuel Kant (1898), pp. 9–44. Thomas Aquinas (1945), vol. 2, pp. 3–5, 59–60, 85, 234–238, 335–342, 356–357, 748–750, 774–775; these are selections from Aquinas's *Summa Contra Gentiles*, book 3, chaps. 1, 2, 37, and 48, and from his *Summa Theologica*, questions 19, 20, and 91. All of these selections are reprinted in Albert et al., eds (1988), pp. 106–125 and 178–197.

22. A. J. Ayer (1936, 1950), pp. 103–112. C. L. Stevenson (1947–48); reprinted in C. L. Stevenson (1963). Both of these selections are reprinted in Albert, Denise, and Peterfreund (1988), pp. 309–329.

23. For a good overview of how biomedical decisions have been made historically in other religions, both in theory and in practice, cf. Ronald L. Numbers and Darrel W. Amundsen, eds (1986). For greater detail, see the series of books published by Crossroad (New York), in conjunction with the Park Ridge Center in Illinois, entitled *Health and Medicine in the Tradition*, with volumes on the bioethics principles and practices of the Anglican, Catholic, Islamic, Jewish, Lutheran, Methodist, and Reformed traditions. There is a plethora of books on secular approaches to medical ethics; two good ones, of many, are Tom L. Beauchamp and James F. Childress (1979) and William J. Winslade and Judith Wilson Ross (1986). On the topic of our example, euthanasia, see, for example, Marvin Kohl, ed. (1975) and John Ladd, ed. (1979).

24. Dworkin (1977), pp. 22–31. That distinction is parallel to one commonly cited in Anglo-American law between absolute and rebuttable assumptions of the law.

25. The Torah mandates executing people for a long list of offenses; largely through specifying stringent evidentiary rules, the rabbis narrowed the scope of this punishment considerably (cf. M. *Makkot* 1:10), but they retained it, at least in theory. The Talmud (if not the Bible) requires that, even at the cost of killing the attacker, we defend both ourselves (Exodus 22:1; B. *Berakhot* 58a; *Yoma* 85b; *Sanhedrin* 72a) and even others (the law of *rodef,* B. *Sanhedrin* 72b–73a; M.T. *Laws of Murder* 1:6–7; S.A. *Hoshen Mishpat* 425:1). The duty to give up one's own life when the alternative is to commit murder, idolatry, or incest is specified in B. *Sanhedrin* 74a. Note that the biblical phrase, "and you shall live by them" (Leviticus 18:5) is a divine *promise* in the Torah, not a command; and in Jewish law it functions as the ground to justify the overriding of other commandments in order to save a life; it is *not* meant, either in the Bible or in later rabbinic literature, as a general command to save all human life in all cases.

26. Daniel B. Sinclair (1989), pp. 80–81, 88–89.

27. Umberto Cassuto has made this point with reference to biblical law codes, which, he says, "should not be regarded as a code of laws, or even as a number of codes, but only as separate instructions on given matters." See Cassuto (1967), pp. 260–264. The Babylonian Talmud in B. *Eruvin* 27a and B. *Kiddushin* 34a expressly objects to treating the Mishnah's general rules as inviolable principles; moreover, in practice it recurrently interprets general principles announced in the Mishnah (with phrases like *zeh ha-klal*) not as generalizations at all but rather as additions of further specific cases. See Jacob Eliyahu Efrati (1973), part 2, pp. 157–278, who points out that the Talmud interprets the phrase this way explicitly sixteen (or possibly eighteen) times among the eighty-five unrepeated instances in the Mishnah where this expression occurs. He claims that these discussions, limited to the Babylonian Talmud, are Saboraic in origin (i.e., from 500–689 C.E.). (I want to thank my colleague at the University of Judaism, Dr. Elieser Slomovic, for this reference.) With regard to the genre of Jewish codes, its methodological pros and cons, and its origins in medieval systematics, see Elliot N. Dorff and Arthur Rosett (1988), pp. 366–401.

28. The more radical option of instituting revisions in the law *(takkanot)* is also an available alternative within the methods of classical Jewish law, and given the radically new realities of contemporary medical practice, one might reasonably argue that such revisions can be more easily justified in this area than in most others. I would agree, but I share the tradition's reticence to employ this method unless absolutely necessary (cf. Elliot N. Dorff and Arthur Rosett [1988], pp. 402–420). We do not have much experience in dealing with many of the morally excruciating questions posed by modern medicine, and so at this point we have not yet had time to see if revisions are required. I, for one, think that the classical methods of legal exegesis and analogizing, if used creatively and sensitively, are fully capable of producing appropriate guidelines to modern Jewish medical decisions; and I certainly think that we owe it to the tradition to try to use these more conservative methods for a period of time before resorting to *takkanot.*

29. Carol Gilligan (1982).

30. The first story I heard about Jewish law, in fact, came from my father. My grandparents and their children lived across the street from a large, Orthodox synagogue, of which they were members. Because of their proximity, my grandparents often hosted guests of the congregation for the Sabbath. One Friday afternoon my grandmother sent my father, then a lad of fifteen or so, to ask Rabbi Solomon Scheinfeld when the guests for that week were expected. Rabbi Scheinfeld served that congregation from 1902 to 1943, and according to the *Encyclopedia Judaica*, he "was the recognized head of the city's Orthodox congregations during his tenure." The encyclopedia clearly refers to the camp of the *misnagdim*, for the Twersky family was firmly in charge of Milwaukee's Ḥasidim. When my father entered the rabbi's office, Rabbi Scheinfeld was literally in the process of deciding whether a chicken was kosher. As he turned the chicken over in his hands, he asked the woman who had brought it many questions about the physical and economic health of her husband and family. After he pronounced the chicken kosher and the woman left the room, my father asked him why he had asked so many questions about her family. The rabbi turned to my father and said, "If you think that the kosher status of chickens depends only on their physical state, you understand nothing about Jewish law!" This, of course, attests only to the attitude of one rabbi in one instance, but if this is true for chickens, how much more so for human beings.

31. Stanley Hauerwas has probably been the preeminent exponent of this theory in the Christian world, as the very titles of his books indicate; cf. his *Vision and Virtue* (1974); *Character and the Christian Life: A Study in Theological Ethics* (1975); *Truthfulness and Tragedy* (1977); and *A Community of Character: Towards a Constructive Christian Social Ethic* (1981). Cf. also James William McClendon, Jr. (1987); and Alasdair MacIntyre (1981) and (1988).

32. Basil Herring (1984) gives an especially thorough and fair presentation of the various attempts to do this on many issues, including a number in bioethics.

33. Tosafot, *Mo'ed Katan* 11a; Jacob ben Moses Mollin, *Yalkutai Maharil* (Segal), cited in Fred Rosner (1977), p. 21; Solomon Luria, *Yam Shel Shelomo*, "Kol Basar," sec. 12; Joseph Caro, *Kesef Mishneh* commentary to M.T. *Hilkhot De'ot (Laws of Ethics)* 4:18; Abraham Gombiner, Magen Avraham commentary to S.A. *Oraḥ Ḥayyim* 173.

34. Matthew (Menachem) Maibaum (1986), p. 29.

35. Ibid. Despite my problems with Maibaum's position, he is definitely right in his call for Conservative, Reconstructionist, and Reform rabbis to articulate their respective views on medical matters in written form and to cull them into easily accessible collections so that lay Jews do not mistakenly think that the only Jewish views on these matters are those of the Orthodox, simply because they are the only ones in print. (And the Orthodox, who publish books with titles like "Jewish Bioethics," certainly do not let on that there are other possible Jewish approaches!) This book, in fact, is just such an effort.

Bibliography

Abraham, Abraham S. 1980. *Medical Halachah for Everyone*. New York: Feldheim.

Abrahams, Israel. 1926. *Hebrew Ethical Wills*. 2 vols. Philadelphia: Jewish Publication Society.

Achilles, Rona. 1988. "Anonymity and Secrecy in Donor Insemination: In Whose Best Interests?" In *Sortir la maternité du laboratoire*. Montreal: Government of Quebec, Conseil du Statut de la Femme, pp. 156–163 (notes on pp. 407–408).

Address, Richard F. 1992. *A Time to Prepare: A Practical Guide for Individuals and Families in Determining One's Wishes for Extraordinary Medical Treatment and Financial Arrangements*. Philadelphia: Union of American Hebrew Congregations Committee on Bio-Medical Ethics.

Adler, Morris. 1963. *The World of the Talmud*. New York: Schocken.

Albeck, Ḥanokh. 1958. *The Six Orders of the Mishnah*. 6 vols. Tel Aviv: Dvir.

Albert, Ethel M., Theodore C. Denise, and Sheldon P. Peterfreund, eds. 1988. *Great Traditions in Ethics*, 6th ed. Belmont, CA: Wadsworth.

American Fertility Society, Ethics Committee of. 1994 [1] *Ethical Considerations of Assisted Reproductive Technologies, Fertility and Sterility 62*.

———. 1994 [2]. "Assisted Reproductive Technology in the United States and Canada: 1992 Results Generated from the American

Fertility Society/Society for Assisted Reproductive Technology Registry." In *Fertility and Sterility* 62, pp. 1121–28.

Andrews, Lori B. 1984. *New Conceptions*. New York: St. Martin's Press.

—————. 1987. "The Aftermath of Baby M: Proposed State Laws on Surrogate Motherhood." *Hastings Center Report* 17:5 (October/ November), pp. 31–40.

————— and Lisa Douglass. 1991. "Alternative Reproduction." *Southern California Law Review* 65:623ff.

Annas, George. 1980. "Fathers Anonymous: Beyond the Best Interests of the Sperm Donor." 14 *Family Law Quarterly* 1ff.

—————. 1986. "The Baby Broker Boom." *Hastings Center Report* 16:3, pp. 30–32. Reprinted in Hull (1990).

————— and Michael A. Grodin. 1992. *The Nazi Doctors and the Nuremberg Code: Human Rights in Human Experimentation*. New York: Oxford University Press.

Aquinas, Thomas. 1945. *Basic Writings of St. Thomas Aquinas*, A. C. Pegis, ed. 2 vols. New York: Random House.

Artson, Bradley S. 1988. "Judaism and Homosexuality." *Tikkun* 3:2 (March/April), pp. 52–54.

—————. 1990–1991. "Gay and Lesbian Jews: An Innovative Jewish Legal Position." *Jewish Spectator* 55:3 (Winter), pp. 6–14.

Astor, Carl. 1985. *". . . Who Makes People Different:" Jewish Perspectives on the Disabled*. New York: United Synagogue of America.

Ayer, A. J. 1936, 1950. *Language, Truth, and Logic*. New York: Dover.

Baron, Salo. 1942, 1972. *The Jewish Community*. Philadelphia: Jewish Publication Society (1942); Westport, CT: Greenwood Press (1972).

Barratt, C. L. and I. D. Cooke, eds. 1993. *Donor Insemination*. Cambridge, England, and New York: Cambridge University Press.

Beauchamp, Tom L. and James F. Childress. 1979. *Principles of Biomedical Ethics*. New York and Oxford: Oxford University Press.

Bennett, Ralph Kinney. 1995. "How Honest Are We?" *Reader's Digest* (December), pp. 49–55.

Berkovits, Eliezer. 1983. *Not in Heaven: The Nature and Function of Halakha*. New York: Ktav.

Berkowitz, Adena K. 1995. "All Take and No Give?" *Moment* (August), pp. 32–35, 58–59.

Bernstein, Ellen and Dan Fink. 1993. *Judaism and Ecology*. New York: Hadassah.

Berman, Louis A. 1982. *Vegetarianism and the Jewish Tradition*. New York: Ktav.

Besser, Anne Cucchiara and Kalman J. Kaplan. 1994. "The Good Samaritan: Jewish and American Legal Perspectives." *The Journal of Law and Religion* 10:1 (Winter), pp. 193–219.

Blackman, Philip, trans. and ed. 1963. *The Mishnah*. New York: Judaica Press.

1992. *Bikkur Holim*. New York: Women's League for Conservative Judaism.

Bleich, J. David. 1968. "Abortion in Halakhic Literature." *Tradition* 10:2 (Winter), pp. 72–120. Reprinted in Rosner and Bleich (1979), pp. 134–177.

————. 1977 [1]. "Smoking." *Tradition* 16:4 (Summer), pp. 130–133.

————. 1977 [2]. *Contemporary Halakhic Problems*, vol. 1. New York: Ktav.

————. 1977 [3]. "Time of Death Legislation." *Tradition* 16:4 (Summer), pp. 133–139.

————. 1981 [1]. *Judaism and Healing*. New York: Ktav.

————. 1981 [2]. "Maternal Identity." *Tradition* 19:4 (Winter), pp. 359–360.

————. 1983. *Contemporary Halakhic Problems*, vol. 2. New York: Ktav.

————. 1989. *Contemporary Halakhic Problems*, vol. 3. New York: Ktav.

————. 1990. "The Jewish Entailments of Valuing Life." *Sh'ma*, November 16, pp. 1–3.

Blidstein, Gerald. 1975. *Honor Thy Father and Mother*. New York: Ktav.

Bok, Sissela. 1978. *Lying: Moral Choice in Public and Private Life*. New York: Vantage Books.

Borowitz, Eugene B. 1983. *Choices in Modern Jewish Thought*. New York: Behrman House.

————. 1984 [1]. "The Autonomous Jewish Self." *Modern Judaism* 4:1 (February), pp. 39–56. Reprinted in revised form in Borowitz (1991), pp. 284–299, and in Dorff and Newman (1995), pp. 106–117.

————. 1984 [2]. "The Autonomous Self and the Commanding

Community." *Theological Studies* 45:1 (March), pp. 34–56.

————. 1991. *Renewing the Covenant: A Theology for the Postmodern Jew.* Philadelphia: Jewish Publication Society.

Brown, Lester R. 1992. "Population Growth Sets Record." *Worldwatch.* Washington, DC: Worldwatch Institute.

Broyde, Michael J. 1993. "Marital Fraud." *Loyola of Los Angeles International and Comparative Law Journal* 16:1 (November), pp. 95–106.

Buber, Martin. 1948, 1961. *Tales of the Ḥasidim: Later Masters.* 2 vols. New York: Schocken.

Byne, William. 1994."The Biological Evidence Challenged." *Scientific American* 270:5 (May), pp. 50–55.

California Legislature (1991). *Minority Report of the Advisory Panel to the Joint Legislative Committee on Surrogate Parenting.*

Canada, Government of. 1993. *Proceed with Care: Report of the Royal Commission on New Reproductive Technologies.* Ottawa: Government of Canada.

Cassuto, Umberto. 1967. *A Commentary on the Book of Exodus.* Jerusalem: Magnes Press [Hebrew University].

Center for Surrogate Parenting. 1993. *Newsletter,* vol. 1 (Spring).

Chavel, Charles B., ed. 1963. *Kitvei Haramban.* 2 vols (Hebrew). Jerusalem: Mosad ha-Rav Kook.

————, ed. 1966. *Sefer ha-Ḥinnukh.* (Hebrew). Jerusalem: Mosad ha-Rav Kook.

————, trans. 1978. *Naḥmanides: Writings and Discourses.* 2 vols. New York: Shilo Publishing House.

————. 1980. *Encyclopedia of Torah Thoughts.* New York: Shilo.

Chen, Edwin and Robert A. Rosenblatt, "Clinton Promises Sweeping Coverage in Health Care Plan." 1993. *Los Angeles Times,* September 11, pp. A1, A16–17.

Chira, Susan. 1993. "Years After Adoption, Adults Find Past, and New Hurdles." *New York Times,* August 30, pp. A1, C11.

Cohen, A. 1949. *Everyman's Talmud.* New York: Dutton.

Cohen, Morris Raphael. 1945, 1977. *The Faith of a Liberal.* Salem, NH: Ayer.

Cover, Robert. 1983. "Nomos and Narrative." *Harvard Law Review* 97/1 (November), 4–68.

Currie-Cohen, Lullrel, and Shapiro. 1979. "Current Practice of Artificial Insemination by Donor in the United States." 300 *New England Journal of Medicine,* pp. 585–9.

Cutter, William. 1995. "Rabbi Judah's Handmaid." In Jacob and Zemer (1995), *Death and Euthanasia in Jewish Law*, pp. 61–88.

Daube, David. 1965. *Collaboration with Tyranny in Jewish Law*. New York: Oxford University Press.

De Cecco, John P. and David Allen Parker, eds. 1995. *Sex, Cells, and Same-Sex Desire: The Biology of Sexual Preference*. New York: Haworth Press.

Dean, Macabee. 1977. "A Matter of Life and Death." *Jerusalem Post*, June 24, magazine section, p. 6.

Dewaraja, R. and Y. Sasaki. 1991. "Semen-Loss Syndrome: A Comparison Between Sri Lanka and Japan." *American Journal of Psychotherapy* 45:1 (January), pp. 14–20.

Dickstein, Stephanie. 1992. "Mourning Practices for Infants Who Die Prior to the Thirty-First Day of Life." Unpublished manuscript approved by the Committee on Jewish Law and Standards on June 3, 1992.

Donovan, Patricia. 1986. "New Reproductive Technologies: Some Legal Dilemmas." *Family Planning Perspectives* 18:2 (March/April), pp. 57–60.

Doren, Richard. 1985. "The Need for Regulation of Artificial Insemination by Donor." *San Diego Law Review* 22:1193–1218.

Dorff, Elliot N. 1974. "A Response to Richard Rubenstein." *Conservative Judaism* 28:4 (Summer), pp. 33–36.

————. 1977 [1]. "The Interaction of Jewish Law with Morality." *Judaism* 26:4 (Fall), pp. 455–466.

————. 1977 [2]. *Conservative Judaism: Our Ancestors to Our Descendants*. New York: United Synagogue of Conservative Judaism. 2nd ed.: 1996.

————. 1977 [3]. "God and the Holocaust." *Judaism* 26:1 (Winter), pp. 27–34.

————. 1978. "Judaism as a Religious Legal System." *Hastings Law Journal* 29:6 (July), pp. 1331–1360.

————. 1984. "Equality with Distinction." In Judith Glass and Elliot N. Dorff, *Male and Female God Created Them*. Los Angeles: University of Judaism (the *University Papers* series) (March), pp. 13–23.

————. 1985. *"Choose Life:" A Jewish Perspective on Medical Ethics*. Los Angeles: University of Judaism.

————. 1986. "Jewish Perspectives on the Poor." In Gary Rubin, ed., *The Poor Among Us*. New York: American Jewish Committee, pp. 21–55.

————. 1987. "Honoring Aged Mothers and Fathers." *Reconstructionist* 53:2 (October–November), pp. 14–20.

————. 1989. *Mitzvah Means Commandment.* New York: United Synagogue of America.

————. 1990. "Moral Distinctions." *Sh'ma: A Journal of Jewish Responsibility* 21/401 (November 16), pp. 6–8.

————. 1991 [1]. "A Jewish Approach to End-Stage Medical Care." *Conservative Judaism* 43:3 (Spring), pp. 3–51.

————. 1991 [2]. "A Methodology for Jewish Medical Ethics." *Jewish Law Association Studies* 7:35–57. Reprinted in Dorff and Newman (1995), pp. 161–176.

————. 1991 [3]. "A Time to Live and a Time to Die." *United Synagogue Review* 44:1 (Fall), pp. 21–22.

————. 1992 [1]. *Knowing God: Jewish Journeys to the Unknowable.* Northvale, NJ: Jason Aronson Press.

————. 1992 [2]. "Methodology in Jewish Medical Ethics." In B. S. Jackson and S. M. Passamaneck, eds. *Jewish Law Association Studies 6: The Jerusalem 1990 Conference Volume.* Atlanta, GA: Scholars Press, pp. 35–57. Reprinted in Dorff and Newman (1995), pp. 161–176.

————. 1992 [3]. "Individual and Communal Forgiveness." In Daniel Frank, ed., [1992], *Autonomy and Judaism: The Individual and the Community in Jewish Philosophical Thought,* pp. 193–218.

————. 1992 [4]. "Pluralism." In *Frontiers of Jewish Thought,* Steven Katz, ed. Washington, DC: B'nai Brith Books, pp. 213–234.

————. 1996 [1]. *"This Is My Beloved, This Is My Friend": A Rabbinic Letter on Intimate Relations.* New York: Rabbinical Assembly. Written for and with the Commission on Human Sexuality of the Rabbinical Assembly.

————. 1996 [2]. "Choosing Life: Aspects of Judaism Affecting Organ Transplantation." In Youngner, Fox, and O'Connell (1996), pp. 168–193.

————. 1996 [3]. "Assisted Death: A Jewish Perspective." In Hamel and Dubose (1996) *Must We Suffer Our Way to Death?* pp. 141–173.

————. 1996 [4]. *Conservative Judaism: Our Ancestors to Our Descendants.* 2nd ed. New York: United Synagogue of Conservative Judaism.

————. 1996 [5]. "Artificial Insemination, Egg Donation, and

Adoption." *Conservative Judaism* 49:1 (Fall 1996), pp. 3–60.

————. 1997. "Jewish Theological and Moral Reflections on Genetic Screening: The Case of BRCA1." *Health Matrix: Journal of Law-Medicine* 7:1 (Winter), pp. 65–96.

Dorff, Elliot N. and Louis E. Newman, eds. 1995. *Contemporary Jewish Ethics and Morality.* New York: Oxford University Press.

Dorff, Elliot N. and Arthur I. Rosett. 1988. *A Living Tree: The Roots and Growth of Jewish Law.* Albany, NY: State University of New York Press, and New York: The Jewish Theological Seminary of America.

Dror, Gilah. 1994. "The Donation of Bodies to Medical Schools." *Responsa of the Va'ad Halakhah of the Rabbinical Assembly of Israel.* Jerusalem: The Rabbinical Assembly and the Masorti Movement, vol. 5, pp. 143–160.

Drori, Moshe. 1980. "Genetic Engineering—Preliminary Discussion of Its Legal and Halakhic Aspects." *Teḥumin* 1, pp. 280–96 (Hebrew).

Dworkin, Ronald. 1977. *Taking Rights Seriously.* Cambridge, MA: Harvard University Press.

————. 1985. *A Matter of Principle.* Cambridge, MA: Harvard University Press.

Edmiston, Susan. 1991. "Whose Child Is This?" *Glamour* 89 (November), pp. 234, 276.

Efrati, Jacob Eliyahu. 1973. *Tekufat ha-Saboraim v'Sifrutah.* Petah Tikvah: Agudat Benai Asher [New York and Jerusalem: Philip Feldheim, Inc., distr.] (Hebrew).

Eisenstein, J. D. 1928. *Otzar Midrashim.* New York: Hebrew Publishing Co. (Hebrew).

————. 1938. *Ozar Dinim u'Minhagim (A Digest of Jewish Laws and Customs).* New York: Hebrew Publishing Co. (Hebrew).

Elia, J. P. 1987. "History, Etymology, and Fallacy: Attitudes Toward Male Masturbation in the Ancient Western World." *Journal of Homosexuality* 14:3–4, pp. 1–19.

Elias, S. and G. J. Annas. 1986. "Social Policy Considerations in Noncoital Reproduction." *Journal of the American Medical Association* 255, pp. 62ff.

Eliash, Ben Zion. 1994. "To Leave or Not to Leave: The Good Samaritan in Jewish Law." *Saint Louis University Law Journal* 38:3 (Spring), pp. 619–628.

Ellenson, David. 1990. "Religious Approaches to Mortal Choices:

How to Draw Guidance from a Heritage." In Barry S. Kogan, ed., *A Time to Be Born, A Time to Die: The Ethics of Choice,* New York: Aldine de Gruyter, pp. 219–232.

Encyclopaedia Judaica. 1971, with subsequent supplements. Jerusalem: Keter Publishing House.

Encyclopedia Talmudit. 1978–present. Jerusalem: Talmudic Encyclopedia Publishers, Ltd. (Hebrew).

Fader, Sonia. 1994. *Sperm Banking: A Reproductive Resource.* Los Angeles: California Cryobank, Inc.

Feinstein, Moshe. 1979. *Dibbrot Moshe.* Bnei Brak, Israel: Yeshivat Ohel Yosef (Hebrew).

_____. 1961 (vol. 1); 1963 (vol. 2); 1973 (vol. 3); 1985 (vol. 4). *Iggrot Moshe.* Brooklyn, NY: Moriah (Hebrew).

Feldman, David M. 1968. *Birth Control in Jewish Law.* New York: New York University Press. Reprinted as *Marital Relations, Abortion, and Birth Control in Jewish Law.* New York: Schocken.

_____. 1986. *Health and Medicine in the Jewish Tradition.* New York: Crossroad.

_____ and Fred Rosner, eds. 1984. *Compendium on Medical Ethics: Jewish Moral, Ethical and Religious Principles in Medical Practice.* New York: Federation of Jewish Philanthropies of New York.

Finkelstein, Louis. 1966. *The Pharisees.* 2 vols. Philadelphia: Jewish Publication Society of America.

Fish, Stanley. 1980. *Is There a Text in This Class?* Cambridge, MA: Harvard University Press.

Frank, Daniel, ed. 1992. *Autonomy and Judaism.* Albany, NY: State University of New York Press.

Freehof, Solomon. 1956. "The Use of the Cornea of the Dead." *C.C.A.R. Yearbook,* vol. 66, pp. 104–107.

_____. 1960. *Reform Responsa.* Cincinnati: Hebrew Union College Press.

_____. 1968. "Surgical Transplants." *C.C.A.R. Yearbook,* vol. 78, pp. 118–121.

_____. 1969. *Current Reform Responsa.* Cincinnati: Hebrew Union College Press.

_____. 1974. *Contemporary Reform Responsa.* Cincinnati: Hebrew Union College Press.

_____. 1977. *Reform Responsa for Our Time.* Cincinnati: Hebrew Union College Press.

_____. 1980. *New Reform Responsa.* Cincinnati: Hebrew Union

College Press.

Freeman, Samuel. 1994. "Criminal Liability and the Duty to Aid the Distressed." *University of Pennsylvania Law Review* 142:5 (May), pp. 1455–1492.

Freundel, Barry. 1993. "Homosexuality and Halachic Judaism: An Orthodox View." *Moment* (June), pp. 40, 43–45.

Friedenwald, H. 1944. *The Jews and Medicine*. Baltimore: Johns Hopkins Press.

Gellman, Marc. 1987. "The Ethics of Surrogate Motherhood." *Sh'ma* 17 (334) (May 15), pp. 105–7.

Gilligan, Carol. 1982. *In a Different Voice*. Cambridge, MA: Harvard University Press.

Goitein, S. D. 1971. *A Mediterranean Society: The Jewish Communities of the Arab World as Protrayed in the Documents of the Cairo Geniza*. Berkeley: University of California Press.

Gold, Michael. 1992. *Does God Belong in the Bedroom?* Philadelphia: Jewish Publication Society.

Goldfarb, Daniel C. 1976. "The Definition of Death," *Conservative Judaism*, 30:2 (Winter), pp. 10–22.

Goldman, Alex J. 1978. *Judaism Confronts Contemporary Issues*. New York: Shengold.

Golinkin, David. 1989. "Artificial Insemination for a Single Woman." In *Responsa of the Va'ad Halacha of the Rabbinical Assembly of Israel*. Jerusalem: The Rabbinical Assembly of Israel and the Masorti Movement, vol. 3, pp. 83–92.

————. 1994. "Responsa: Does Jewish Law Permit Genetic Engineering on Humans?" *Moment* (August), pp. 28, 29, 67.

Gordis, Daniel H. 1988. "'Give Me Progeny . . .': Jewish Ethics and the Economics of Surrogate Motherhood." Los Angeles: University of Judaism (*University Papers* series) 8:1 (November), 27 pgs.

————. 1989. "Wanted—The Ethical in Jewish Bio-Ethics." *Judaism* 38:1 (Winter), pp. 28–40.

Gordis, Robert. 1986. *Judaic Ethics for a Lawless World*. New York: Jewish Theological Seminary of America.

————. 1990. *The Dynamics of Judaism*. Bloomington, IN: Indiana University Press.

Gorlin, M. 1970. "Mental Illness in Biblical Literature." *Proceedings of the Association of Orthodox Jewish Scientists* 1, pp. 43–62.

Grazi, Richard V. and Joel B. Wolowelsky. 1992. "Donor Gametes for Assisted Reproduction in Contemporary Jewish Law and Ethics."

Assisted Reproduction in Reviews 2:3, pp. 154–160.

————. 1993–94. "New Halakhic Issues in Infertility Therapy." *Amit* (Winter), pp. 19–21.

Greenberg, Irving. 1986. "Toward a Covenantal Ethic of Medicine." In Levi Meier, ed., *Jewish Values in Bioethics*. New York: Human Sciences Press, pp. 124–149.

Greenberg, Simon. 1977. *The Ethical in the Jewish and American Heritage*. New York: Jewish Theological Seminary of America.

Grossman, Susan. 1992. "Feminism, Midrash, and Mikveh." *Conservative Judaism* 44:2 (Winter), pp. 7–17.

Grossnass, Lev. 1958. *Responsa Lev Aryeh*. London: L. Honig and Sons (Hebrew).

Hamel, Ronald P. and Edwin R. Dubose, eds. 1996. *Must We Suffer Our Way to Death? Cultural and Theological Perspectives on Death by Choice*. Dallas: Southern Methodist University Press.

Harlow, Jules, ed. 1985. *Siddur Sim Shalom*. New York: Rabbinical Assembly and United Synagogue of Conservative Judaism.

Hartman, David. 1979. "Moral Uncertainties in the Practice of Medicine." *Journal of Medicine and Philosophy* 4, pp. 100ff.

————. 1985. *A Living Covenant: The Innovative Spirit in Traditional Judaism*. New York: Free Press.

Hauerwas, Stanley. 1974. *Vision and Virtue*. Notre Dame, IN: Fides Publishers.

————. 1975. *Character and the Christian Life: A Study in Theological Ethics*. San Antonio: Trinity University Press.

————. 1977. *Truthfulness and Tragedy*. Notre Dame, IN: University of Notre Dame Press.

————. 1981. *A Community of Character: Towards a Constructive Christian Social Ethic*. Notre Dame, IN: University of Notre Dame Press.

Herring, Basil. 1984. *Jewish Ethics and Halakhah for Our Time*. New York: Ktav and Yeshiva.

Heschel, Abraham J. 1955. *God in Search of Man*. New York: Harper & Row.

Hodgson, Anita M. 1993. "The Warranty of Sperm: A Modest Proposal to Increase the Accountability of Sperm Banks and Physicians in the Performance of Artificial Insemination Procedures." *Indiana Law Review* 26:357–386.

Hull, Richard T. 1990. *Ethical Issues in the New Reproductive Technologies*. Belmont, CA: Wadsworth.

Hyamson, Moses, trans. 1970. Bachya ben Joseph ibn Paquda, *Duties of the Heart*. New York and Jerusalem: Feldheim.

Idel, Moshe. 1990. *Golem: Jewish Magical and Mystical Traditions of the Artificial Anthropoid*. Albany, NY: State University of New York Press.

Ingrassia, Michele, et al. 1993 [1]. "Standing Up for Fathers: The Troubling Case of Baby Jessica Focuses Attention on Paternal Rights in Adoptions. *Newsweek*, May 3, pp. 52–53.

————. 1993 [2]. "Daughters of Murphy Brown." *Newsweek*, August 2, p. 59.

Jacob, Walter. 1983. *American Reform Responsa*. New York: Central Conference of American Rabbis.

————. 1987. *Contemporary American Reform Responsa*. New York: Central Conference of American Rabbis.

————. 1992. *Questions and Reform Jewish Answers: New American Reform Responsa*. New York: Central Conference of American Rabbis.

———— and Moshe Zemer. 1995. *Death and Euthanasia in Jewish Law*. Pittsburgh: Freehof Institute of Progressive Halakhah.

Jakobovits, Immanuel. 1953. "Artificial Insemination, Birth Control, and Abortion." *ha-Rofeh ha-Ivri* 2:169–183 (English version) and 2:114–129 (Hebrew).

————. 1959, 1975. *Jewish Medical Ethics*. New York: Bloch.

Jakobovits, Yoel. 1989. "[Brain Death and] Heart Transplants: The [Israeli] Chief Rabbinate's Directives." *Tradition* 24:4 (Summer), pp. 1–14.

Kantrowitz, Barbara. 1996. "Gay Families Come Out." *Newsweek*, November 4, pp. 50–57.

Kaplan, Mordecai M. trans. 1936, 1964. Moses Ḥayyim Luzzato, *The Path of the Upright (Mesillat Yesharim)*. Philadelphia: Jewish Publication Society.

Katz, Jacob. 1961. *Exclusiveness and Tolerance: Jewish-Gentile Relations in Medieval and Modern Times*. New York: Oxford University Press. Reprinted by Schocken, 1962.

Kellner, Menachem, ed. 1978. *Contemporary Jewish Ethics*. New York: Sanhedrin Press.

Kimmelman, Reuven. 1992–1993. "Homosexuality and/or Family Centered Judaism." *Jewish Spectator* 57:3 (Winter), pp. 23–27.

————. 1994. "Homosexuality and Family Centered Judaism." *Tikkun* 9:4 (July/August), pp. 53–57.

Kirschenbaum, Aaron. 1970. *Self-Incrimination in Jewish Law*. New York: Burning Bush Press.

———. 1980. "The Bystander's Duty to Rescue in Jewish Law." *Journal of Religious Ethics* 8, pp. 204–226.

Klein, Isaac. 1975. *Responsa and Halakhic Studies*. New York: Ktav.

———. 1979. *A Guide to Jewish Religious Practice*. New York: Jewish Theological Seminary of America.

Kohl, Marvin, ed. 1975. *Beneficent Euthanasia*. Buffalo, New York: Prometheus Press.

Kolata, Gina. 1993. "New Pregnancy Hope: A Single Sperm." *New York Times*, August 11, p. C11.

Konvitz, Milton R., ed. 1972. *Judaism and Human Rights*. New York: W. W. Norton.

———. 1980. *Judaism and the American Idea*. New York: Schocken.

Krauss, Pesach. 1988. *Why Me? Coping with Grief, Loss, and Change*. Toronto and New York: Bantam.

Kubler-Ross, Elisabeth. 1995. *Death Is of Vital Importance*. Barrytown, NY: Station Hill Press.

Kushner, Harold. 1981. *When Bad Things Happen to Good People*. New York: Schocken.

Laan, E., W. Everaerd, M. T. Van Aanhold, and M. Rebel. 1993. "Performance Demand and Sexual Arousal in Women." *Behavioral Research Therapy*. 31:1 (January), pp. 25–35.

Ladd, John, ed. 1979. *Ethical Issues Relating to Life and Death*. New York and Oxford: Oxford University Press.

Lamm, Norman. 1971. *Faith and Doubt*. New York: Ktav.

———. 1974. "Judaism and the Modern Attitude to Homosexuality." *Encyclopedia Judaica Yearbook 1974*. Jerusalem: Keter, pp. 194–205. Reprinted in Kellner (1978), pp. 375–399.

Lasker, Daniel J. 1988. "Kabbalah, Halakhah, and Modern Medicine." *Modern Judaism* 8:1 (February), pp. 1–14.

Lauritzen, Paul. 1991. "Pursuing Parenthood: Reflections on Donor Insemination." *Second Opinion* (July), pp. 57ff.

Leitenberg, H., M. J. Detzer, and D. Srebnik. 1993. "Gender Differences in Masturbation and the Relation of Masturbation Experience in Preadolescence and/or Early Adolescence to Sexual Behavior and Sexual Adjustment in Young Adulthood." *Archives of Sexual Behavior* 22:2 (April), pp. 87–98.

Levado, Yaakov (a pseudonym). 1993. "Gayness and God: Wrestlings of an Orthodox Rabbi." *Tikkun* 8:5 (September/October), pp. 54–60.

LeVay, Simon and Ean H. Hamer. 1994. "Evidence for a Biological Influence in Male Homosexuality." *Scientific American* 270:5 (May), pp. 43–49.

Levenson, Jon Douglas. 1993. *The Death and Resurrection of the Beloved Son: The Transformation of Child Sacrifice in Judaism and Christianity.* New Haven: Yale.

Levine, Baruch A. 1989. *The JPS Torah Commentary: Leviticus.* Philadelphia: Jewish Publication Society.

Lewy, Hans, Alexander Altmann, and Isaak Heinemann, eds. 1960. *Three Jewish Philosophers.* Philadelphia: Jewish Publication Society.

Lieberman, Saul. 1955. *Tosefta Ki-Fshutah.* New York: Jewish Theological Seminary of America (Hebrew).

————. 1963. "How Much Greek in Jewish Palestine?" In Alexander Altman, ed., *Biblical and Other Studies,* Cambridge, MA: Harvard University Press.

Llewellyn, Karl. 1950. "Remarks on the Theory of Appellate Decision and the Rules or Canons About How Statutes Are to Be Construed." 3 *Vanderbilt Law Review* 395.

————. 1960. *The Common Law Tradition.* Boston: Little, Brown, & Co.

Machiavelli, Niccolo. 1950. *The Prince.* New York: Modern Library.

MacIntyre, Alasdair. 1981. *After Virtue.* Notre Dame, IN: University of Notre Dame Press.

————. 1988. *Whose Justice? Which Rationality?* Notre Dame, IN: University of Notre Dame Press.

Mackler, Aaron. 1993. *Jewish Medical Directives for Health Care.* New York: Rabbinical Assembly.

————. 1995. "An Expanded Partnership with God? In Vitro Fertilization in Jewish Ethics." *Journal of Religious Ethics* 25:2 (Fall), pp. 27–33.

Mahlstedt, Patricia P. and Dorothy A. Greenfeld. 1989. "Assisted Reproductive Technology with Donor Gametes: The Need for Patient Preparation." *Fertility and Sterility* 52:6 (December), pp. 908–14.

Maibaum, Matthew (Menachem). 1986. "A 'Progressive' Jewish Medical Ethics: Notes for an Agenda." *Journal of Reform Judaism* 33:3 (Summer), pp. 27–33.

Maller, Allen S. 1992. "Gilgul, Dybbuks, and the Afterlife." *Heritage,*

March 20, p. 5.

Mayeroff, Milton. 1971. *On Caring*. New York: Harper & Row [Perennial Library].

McClendon, James William, Jr. 1987. *Ethics*. Nashville, TN: Abingdon.

McClintock, Lon T. 1982. "Duty to Aid the Endangered Act: The Impact and Potential of the Vermont Approach." *Vermont Law Review* 7:1 (Spring), pp. 143–183.

McInnes, Mitchell. 1994. "Protecting the Good Samaritan: Defences for the Rescuer in Anglo-Canadian Criminal Law." *Criminal Law Quarterly* 36:3 (May), pp. 331–371.

Michael, Robert T., John H. Gagnon, Edward O. Laumann, and Gina Kolata. 1994. *Sex in America: A Definitive Survey*. Boston: Little, Brown.

Milgrom, Jacob. 1990. *The JPS Torah Commentary: Numbers*. Philadelphia: Jewish Publication Society.

————. 1991. *The Anchor Bible: Leviticus 1–16*. New York: Doubleday.

————. 1993. "Does the Bible Prohibit Homosexuality?" *Biblical Review* 9:6 (December), p. 11.

Money, J., K. S. Prakasam, and V. N. Joshi. 1991. "Semen-Conservation Doctrine from Ancient Ayurvedic to Modern Sexological Theory." *American Journal of Psychotherapy* 45:1 (January), pp. 9–13.

Monmaney, Terrence. 1997. "How We Die May Be Behind Assisted Suicide Debate." *Los Angeles Times,* January 8, pp. A1, A9.

Murray, Thomas H. 1996. "Organ Vendors, Families, and the Gift of Life." In Youngner, Fox, and O'Connell (1996).

Nevins, Michael. 1996. *The Jewish Doctor: A Narrative History*. Northvale, NJ: Jason Aronson.

Newman, Louis E. 1990. "Woodchoppers and Respirators: The Problem of Interpretation in Contemporary Jewish Ethics." *Modern Judaism* 10:1 (February), pp. 17–42. Reprinted in Dorff and Newman (1995), pp. 140–160.

Nielson, Kai. 1973. *Ethics Without God*. Buffalo, NY: Prometheus Books.

————. 1976. "Morality and the Will of God." In Peter Angeles, ed., *Critiques of God*. Buffalo, NY: Prometheus Books, pp. 241–257.

Nietzsche, Friedrich. 1914. *Beyond Good and Evil,* Helen Zimmerman, trans. New York: Macmillan.

————. 1956. *The Genealogy of Morals,* Francis Golffing, trans. Garden City, NY: Doubleday (Anchor Books).

Nijs, Martine, et. al. 1993. "Prevention of Multiple Pregnancies in an In Vitro Fertilization Program." *Fertility and Sterility* 59, pp. 1245–50.

Noddings, Nel. 1984. *Caring: A Feminist Approach to Ethics and Moral Education.* Berkeley, CA: University of California Press.

Novak, David. 1983. *The Image of the Non-Jew in Judaism.* New York: Edwin Mellen Press.

Numbers, Ronald L. and Darrel W. Amundsen, eds. 1986. *Caring and Curing: Health and Medicine in the Western Religious Traditions.* New York: Macmillan.

Oliner, Pearl and Sam Oliner. 1988. *The Altruistic Personality.* New York: Free Press.

1994. "One Size of Condom Doesn't Fit All." *Men's Health* (March), p. 27.

Oshry, Ephraim. 1983. *Responsa from the Holocaust.* New York: Judaica Press.

Paldiel, Mordecai. 1993. *The Path of the Righteous.* New York: Jewish Foundation for Christian Rescuers, and Hoboken, NJ: Ktav.

Payer, Lynn. 1988. *Medicine and Culture.* New York: Henry Holt.

Pinchbeck, Daniel. 1996. "Downward Motility." *Esquire* (January), pp. 79–84.

Pretorius, Diederika. 1994. *Surrogate Motherhood: A Worldwide View of the Issues.* Springfield, IL: Charles C. Thomas.

Preuss, J. 1978. *Biblical and Talmudic Medicine.* Fred Rosner, trans. New York: Sanhedrin Press.

Prouser, Joseph H. 1995. "*Chesed* or *Chiyuv?*: The Obligation to Preserve Life and the Question of Post-Mortem Organ Donation." Unpublished manuscript approved by the Conservative movement's Committee on Jewish Law and Standards, December 1995; ultimately to be published by the Rabbinical Assembly in its collection of the committee's responsa for 1995.

Reisner, Avram Israel. 1991 [1]. "A Halakhic Ethic of Care for the Terminally Ill," *Conservative Judaism* 43:3 (Spring), pp. 52–89.

————. 1991 [2]. "Mai Beinaiyhu [What Is the Difference Between Them]." *Conservative Judaism* 43:3 (Spring 1991), pp. 90–91.

————. 1995. "Peri- and Neo-Natology." Unpublished manuscript approved by the Committee on Jewish Law and Standards in September 1995.

Riemer, Jack and Nathaniel Stampfer, eds. 1983. *Ethical Wills: A Modern Treasury*. New York: Schocken.

————. 1991. *So That Your Values Live On: Ethical Wills and How to Prepare Them*. Woodstock, VT: Jewish Lights Publishing.

Rosenbaum, Irving J. 1976. *The Holocaust and Halakhah*. New York: Ktav.

Rosenfeld, Azriel. 1972. "Judaism and Gene Design," *Tradition* 13:2 (Fall), pp. 71–80. Reprinted in Rosner and Bleich (1979), pp. 401–408.

Rosner, Fred. 1970. "Artificial Insemination in Jewish Law." *Judaism* (Fall). Reprinted in Rosner and Bleich (1979).

————. 1977. *Medicine in the Bible and the Talmud*. New York: Ktav.

————. 1990. "Pregnancy Reduction in Jewish Law." *Journal of Clinical Ethics* 1, pp. 180ff.

————. 1991. *Modern Medicine and Jewish Ethics*. 2nd ed. Hoboken, NJ: Ktav, and New York: Yeshiva University.

———— and J. David Bleich, eds. 1979. *Jewish Bioethics*. New York: Sanhedrin Press.

Royte, Elizabeth. 1993. "The Stork Market." *Lear's* (December), pp. 52–55.

Rubenstein, Richard. 1974. "Jewish Theology and the Current World Situation." *Conservative Judaism* 28:4 (Summer), pp. 3–25.

Schachter, Melech. 1982. "Various Aspects of Adoption." *Journal of Halakhah and Contemporary Society* 4 (Fall), pp. 107ff.

Scherman, Nosson. 1986. *The Complete ArtScroll Siddur*. 2nd ed. Brooklyn, NY: Mesorah Publications.

Schochet, Elijah J. 1973. *A Responsum of Surrender*. Los Angeles: University of Judaism.

Schulweis, Harold. 1994. *For Those Who Can't Believe: Overcoming the Obstacles to Faith*. New York: HarperCollins.

Schur, Tsvi G. 1987. *Illness and Crisis: Coping the Jewish Way*. New York: National Conference of Synagogue Youth/Union of Orthodox Jewish Congregations of America.

Schwartz, Earl and Barry D. Cytron. 1993. *Who Renews Creation?* New York: United Synagogue of Conservative Judaism (Department of Youth Activities).

Sherwin, Byron L. 1985. *The Golem Legend: Origins and Implications*. Lanham, MD: University Press of America.

Sidorsky, David. 1975. "The Autonomy of Moral Objectivity." In

Marvin Fox, ed., *Modern Jewish Ethics*. Columbus, OH: Ohio State University Press, pp. 153–173.

Siegel, Seymour. 1971. "Ethics and Halakhah." *Conservative Judaism* 25:3 (Spring), pp. 33–40.

————. 1975. "Fetal Experimentation." *Conservative Judaism* 29:4 (Summer), pp. 39–48.

————. 1976. "Updating the Criteria of Death." *Conservative Judaism* 30:2 (Winter), pp. 23–30.

————. 1977. "Some Reflections on Telling the Truth." *Linacre Quarterly* (August), pp. 229–239.

————. 1980. "Reaction to the Modern Moral Crises." *Conservative Judaism* 34:1 (September/October), pp. 17–27.

Sinclair, Daniel B. 1989. *Tradition and the Biological Revolution: The Application of Jewish Law to the Treatment of the Critically Ill.* Edinburgh: Edinburgh University Press.

Singer, Isaac Bashevis. 1957. "From the Diary of One Not Born." In *Gimpel the Fool and Other Stories*. New York: Noonday Press.

Small, Meredith F. 1991. "Sperm Wars." *Discover* (July), pp. 50–52.

Smith, Lee. 1994. "The New Wave of Illegitimacy." *Fortune,* April 18, pp. 81–94.

Smith, Lynn. 1993. "Salvation or Last Resort?" *Los Angeles Times,* November 3, pp. E-1, 3.

The Soncino Talmud. 1936. London: Soncino Press.

Sperling, Abraham Isaac. 1957. *Sefer Ta'amei ha-Minhagim u'M'korei ha-Dinim.* Jerusalem: Eshkol (Hebrew).

Spero, Moshe Halevi. 1980. *Judaism and Psychology: Halakhic Perspectives.* New York: Ktav.

Spero, Shubert. 1983. *Morality, Halakha, and the Jewish Tradition.* New York: Ktav and Yeshiva University Press.

Spirtas, Robert, Steven C. Kaufman, and Nancy J. Alexander. 1993. *Fertility and Sterility* 59:2 (February), pp. 291–293.

Spitz, Elie. 1996. "On the Use of Birth Surrogates." *Journal of Religious Ethics* (Spring 1996), pp. 65–97.

Stevenson, C. L. 1947–48. "The Nature of Ethical Disagreement." *Sigma,* vols 1–2.

————. 1963. *Facts and Values.* New Haven: Yale University Press.

Stockler, Julie. 1993. "The Longing for Children." *Moment* 18:5(October), pp. 63–65, 93–95.

Struewing, Jeffrey P., Dvorah Abeliovich, Tamar Peretz, Naaman Avishai, Michael M. Kaback, Francis S. Collins, and Lawrence C.

Brody. 1995. "The Carrier Frequency of the BRCA1 185delAG Mutation Is Approximately 1 Percent in Ashkenazi Jewish Individuals." *Nature Genetics* (October), pp. 198–200.

Styron, L. Thomas. 1986. "Artificial Insemination: A New Frontier for Medical Malpractice and Medical Products Liability." *Loyola Law Review* 32:411–446.

1985. *Tanakh—The Holy Scriptures: The New JPS Translation According to the Traditional Hebrew Text.* Philadelphia: Jewish Publication Society.

Tannen, Deborah. 1990. *You Just Don't Understand: Women and Men in Conversation.* New York: Ballantine Books.

Tate, Julia J. 1992. *Artificial Insemination and Legal Reality.* No city indicated: American Bar Association, Section of Family Law.

Tec, Nechama. 1986. *When Light Pierced the Darkness.* New York: Oxford University Press.

Teitelbaum, Yoel. 1954. "Responsum on Donor Artificial Insemination." *ha-Maor* 15:9, pp. 3–13.

_____. 1981. *Sefer Divrei Yoel al ha-Torah.* 3rd ed. Brooklyn, NY: Bet Mishar. (Hebrew).

Trachtenberg, Joshua. 1939. *Jewish Magic and Superstition: A Study in Folk Religion.* New York: Behrman House. Reprinted: Philadelphia: Jewish Publication Society, 1961.

Tuchinsky, Yehiel Mikhal. 1960. *Gesher ha-Ḥayyim.* 2nd ed. Jerusalem: Solomon (Hebrew).

Twersky, Isadore. 1972. *A Maimonides Reader.* New York: Behrman House.

U.S. Congress, Office of Technology Assessment. 1988 [1]. *Infertility: Medical and Social Choices,* OTA-BA-358. Washington, DC: U.S. Government Printing Office (May).

_____. 1988 [2]. *Artificial Insemination: Practice in the United States: Summary of a 1987 Survey-Background Paper,* OTA-bp-ba-48.Washington, DC: U.S. Government Printing Office (August).

Unterman, Isaar Yehudah. 1970. "The Problem of Heart Transplantation from the Viewpoint of Halakhah." *No'am* 13, pp. 1–9 (Hebrew).

Waldenberg, Eliezer. 1951–1983. *Tzitz Eliezer.* Jerusalem: Mosad Harav Kook (Hebrew).

Waskow, Arthur. 1995. *Down-to-Earth Judaism: Food, Money, Sex, and the Rest of Life.* New York: William Morrow.

_____ and Ari Elon, eds. 1996. *The Tu B'Shvat Anthology.* Philadelphia: Jewish Publication Society.

Weinhouse, Beth. 1994. "Is There a Right Time to Have a Baby? The Yes, No, and Maybe of Pregnancy at 20, 30, 40." *Glamour* (May), pp. 251, 276, 285–287.

Wengrov, Charles, trans. 1988. *Sefer ha-Ḥinnukh: Book of [Mitzvah] Education.* 4 vols. Jerusalem and New York: Feldheim.

Weir, Robert F., Susan C. Lawrence, and Evan Fales, eds. 1994. *Genes and Human Self-Knowledge.* Iowa City, IA: Iowa University Press.

Winslade, William J. and Judith Wilson Ross. 1986. *Choosing Life or Death: A Guide for Patients, Families, and Professionals.* New York: Free Press.

Yeh, John and Molly Uline Yeh. 1991. *Legal Aspects of Infertility.* Boston: Blackwell Scientific Publications.

Young, R. V. 1987. "Constitutional Interpretation and Literary Theory." *The Intercollegiate Review* 23:1, pp. 49–60.

Youngner, Stuart J. and Edward T. Bartlett. 1983. "Human Death and High Technology: The Failure of the Whole-Brain Formulations." *Annals of Internal Medicine* 99, pp. 252–258.

Youngner, Stuart J., Renee C. Fox, and Laurence J. O'Connel, eds. 1996. *Organ Transplantation: Meanings and Realities.* Madison: University of Wisconsin Press.

Yovich, John and Gedis Grudzinskas. 1990. *The Management of Infertility.* Oxford, England: Heinemann Medical Books.

Zohar, Noam. 1991. "Artificial Insemination and Surrogate Motherhood." *S'vara: A Journal of Philosophy and Judaism* 2:1 (spring), pp. 13–19.

Index

Aaron ha-Levi (of Barcelona), 266

abandonment: protection from, 82; of terminally ill patients, 193

Abba (rabbi), 257

Abba Saul (rabbi), 332n.34

Abba, the bleeder, 299

ablution rituals, 118. *See also* personal hygiene

abortion: emotional impact of, 56–57; permissibility of, 56, 129–32, 315; to prevent genetic disease, 152, 153–54, 159, 161–62; to prevent pregnancy, 128–33; prohibition of, 56, 109, 123, 128–29; rate of, 132. *See also* selective abortion

Abraham, 121, 339n.15

Abraham ben David (of Posquieres), 335n.7

Abrams, Judith, 235

abstinence: dietary, 25; for homosexuals, 145; sexual, 122, 150, 252. *See also* self-denial

active euthanasia: contemporary issues about, 186–98; definition of, 176; medical and legal context of issues of, 176–80; prohibition of, 177, 187

Adam and Eve, 37–38, 322, 324

adoption: asymmetry in, 91, 99; biblical references to, 357–58n.79; confidentiality of, 65; and fatherhood, 74–75; by homosexuals, 141, 148; and incest, 50, 78–79, 108, 109; in Jewish law, 108–9; marriage between siblings by, 78–79; permissibility of, 41, 107–11; secrecy in, 88; single parenthood through, 114; as surrogacy analog, 64–65

adultery: definition of, 68–69, 99; and donor insemination, 67–69; forgiveness of, 15, 30; prohibition on, 50, 68, 181; punishments for, 69; and surrogacy, 62. *See also* licentious sex

Advance Directive for Health Care ("living will"), 169, 176, 192, 195, 207, 219, 226, 261

afterlife. *See* reincarnation; resurrection

Genesis Rabbah, 143

Aḥitofel, suicide of, 181

AIDS: avoidance and prevention of, 120, 122, 138, 150, 245, 252; testing of donated sperm for, 67, 86; treatment of, 296, 314

Akiba (rabbi): background of, 332n.34; on healing, 28; on healthful diet, 29, 30, 282; on preservation of a life, 17, 284, 300–301; on visiting the sick, 258

Alabama: donor records in, 355n.55

alcohol use and abuse, 162, 250–51, 265, 293, 303, 304

Alexandri (rabbi), 258

altruism, in surrogacy, 63

Alzheimer's disease, 208, 212, 215, 216, 265

American Association of Tissue Banks-Reproductive Council, 71

American Fertility Society, 53, 57, 66, 87

American Medical Association, 189

American Psychiatric Association, 144, 366n.16

Amir, Yigal, 396

amniocentesis, 130, 154–55

anal sex, 139, 288

anesthesia, 280

animals: cloning of, 310–11; prohibition on threatening the life of, 184; transplantation of organs of, 217–18

antibiotics, 5, 198, 202, 206, 252, 280

Antiochus (Greek king), 15

antiseptics, 280

antispermatozoal antibodies, 45

Aristotle, 20, 140, 395, 406

Arizona: surrogacy in, 347n.78

Arkansas: adoption laws in, 360n.98

artificial insemination: advantages of, 47–48; asymmetry in, 90–93, 98–99; by donors, 48, 49, 50, 55, 58, 66–115; by husbands (AIH), 47, 51–53, 55, 74; Jewish sources on, 47–51; lying about, 83–84; rate of, 340n.29; secrecy in, 83–90; as treatment for infertility, 46–47

artificial organs, transplantation of, 217–18

Artson, Rabbi Bradley Shavit, 142–43

asceticism, 20, 24–25

asexual reproduction, 321. See also cloning

Ashkenazic Jews: incidence of genetic

disease among, 152, 156–57

assimilation, 40, 336–38n.11

assisted suicide: definition of, 176; incidence of, 178; medical and legal context of issues of, 176–80, 182; motivation for, 178, 188–91; patient's right to, 18, 170; prohibition of, 177, 183–86; punishment for, 182

asthma, 253

athletics, 248–49

Augustine (saint), 20, 135

Australia: donor insemination in, 87, 92

autopsy, 224–25, 235, 238

Ayer, A. J., 407

ba'al tashḥit ("Do not destroy"), 330n.13, 370n.6

Baby Jessica case, 110

Babylonian Talmud. See Talmud

Baby M case, 64

Bahya ben Asher, 266

Bahya ibn Pakuda, 266

bar kayyama, 274

barrenness. See infertility

bathing. See ablution rituals; personal hygiene

Bebai (rabbi), 122

Ben Azzai, 290

Ben Betairah, 284

Benningfield, Anna Beth, 113

Ben Sira, midrash on, 48–49

Ben Zoma, 48

Bible citations: Genesis 1:26, 215; Genesis 1:28, 37; Genesis 2:6, 228; Genesis 2:15, 316, 318; Genesis 2:18, 37–38; Genesis 2:24, 37–38; Genesis 3:21, 264; Genesis 3:22, 322; Genesis 5:1, 290; Genesis 7:22, 228; Genesis 9:4, 210; Genesis 11:1-9, 318–19; Genesis 11:6, 319; Genesis 18:1, 264; Genesis 30:21, 100; Genesis 38:9-10, 52; Exodus 19:6, 247; Exodus 20:12, 79; Exodus 21:10, 37; Exodus 21:19, 201; Exodus 21:19-20, 27; Exodus 34:6, 222; Leviticus 11:44,

248; Leviticus 18:5, 15, 343n.43; Leviticus 18:9, 50; Leviticus 18:20, 50; Leviticus 18:22, 139; Leviticus 19:3, 79; Leviticus 19:14, 183; Leviticus 19:16, 16, 27, 29; Leviticus 19:18, 27, 29; Leviticus 20:13, 139; Leviticus 21:13, 48; Leviticus 22:24, 125; Leviticus 25:36, 17; Deuteronomy 4:9, 343n.43; Deuteronomy 4:15, 343n.43, 377n.58; Deuteronomy 5:16, 79; Deuteronomy 8:11-20, 319; Deuteronomy 11:22, 222; Deuteronomy 12:16, 210; Deuteronomy 13:5, 222, 263; Deuteronomy 14:21, 247; Deuteronomy 17:8-13, 403; Deuteronomy 20:19-20, 330n.13; Deuteronomy 22:2, 27; Deuteronomy 23:2, 125; Deuteronomy 30:19-20, 326; 1 Samuel 31:3-5, 181; Isaiah 51:2, 76; Isaiah 63:16, 76; Isaiah 64:7, 75, 76; Psalms 90:12, 322; Psalms 103:3, 258; Psalms 106:3, 78, 108; Psalms 116:6, 122; Psalms 145:17, 222; Proverbs 31:3, 117; Lamentations 5:3, 76; Ecclesiastes 12:3-8, 276–77

bikkur holim (visiting the sick), 194, 197, 202, 255–64, 375–76n.48

Bill of Rights, 273

biodiversity, 311–12, 316

bioethics: business decision making in, 6, 298; fundamental beliefs underlying, 14–33, 395–423; government decision making in, 6; insurance companies as decision-makers in, 6, 298; new questions posed by, 412–13, xiv–xv; personal decision making in, 6, 168–72, 298; as response to changes in curative medical practices, 6; social contexts of, xv; sources of guidance in, 6–7

birth control. *See* abortion; abstinence; contraception; masturbation; sterilization

birth control pills and implants, 123

birth defects, prevention of, 127. *See also* genetics, prevention of defects and disease

Bleich, Rabbi J. David: on artificial insemination, 56, 80, 101, 344–45n.56; on genetic screening, 152, 153; on preserving a life, 199; on scientific cadaver donation, 239

"blended" families, 91

bloodletting, 6, 30, 280

blood transfusions, 210

body: autopsy of, 224–25, 235, 238; and body-mind (soul) bifurcation, 20–24; commodification of, 314, 315; commodification of mother's, 60; cremation of, 223–24; honoring after death, 221–23, 225, 240; as integrated whole, 20–24, 135; moral neutrality and potential good of, 24–26, 135–36; and organ donation, 225–41; as property of God, 15–18, 125, 128, 151, 179, 180, 188, 223, 267; as property of self, 179, 187. *See also* cloning

body piercing, 267, 269–70

Bok, Sissela, 83

brain death, 213–17, 232

BRCA1 mutation, 156–57, 159, 163

breast cancer, 156, 158–59, 160

breath test, for life, 228–29, 232

Breish, Rabbi Jacob, 354n.35

Brown, Louise, 53

burial: affordability of, 223–24; appropriate customs for, 221, 223–24, 231; psychological benefits of, 241; for suicides, 181

cadaveric donations. defining moment of death for, 228–29; impediments to, 230–39; and issue of *hillul ha-Shem*, 229–30; permissibility of, 226–28; scientific, 239–41

Cahill, Lisa Sowle, 82

California: donor insemination laws in, 352–53n.19; donor records in, 88; managed care in, 393n.46; sodomy laws in, 406

Calvin, John, 20, 135

capital punishment, 289
captives, redemption of, 287, 288–89, 300, 301–2, 303–4, 305
Caro, Rabbi Joseph, 27–28, 303, 392n.38
celibacy, 145, 150, 252. *See also* abstinence
Centers for Disease Control and Prevention, 138, 252
charity: obligation to accept, 18, 249, 303, 304–5; physicians' donations to, 300; provision of health care as, 284–86. *See also* ḥesed (lovingkindness, fidelity)
children: as blessings, 40, 42, 124; conversion of, 108, 109–10; disabled, 273–76; education of, 339n.15; gender of, 44, 123, 155, 336n.9; Jewish identity of, 72–79, 108; as link to future, 40–41, 94, 321; obligatory number of, 40, 41, 44, 52, 123, 336n.10; passage to adulthood of, 160. *See also* conception; parent-child relationships; pregnancy; procreation
Christianity: and artificial insemination, 52; and bodily pleasure, 24–25; body/mind bifurcation in, 20; opposition to euthanasia in, 184–85; reaction to forced conversion to, 31, 181
chronic fatigue syndrome, 189
circumcision, 333n.45
cleanliness. *See* personal hygiene
Clomid, 46
clones, rights of, 318
cloning, 310–24; evaluation of results, 315–16; moral issues of, 313–18; recommendations for, 322–24; theological issues of, 318–22; uses of, 316–17
clothing, 267
coercive sex. *See* oppressive sex
colon cancer, 156, 157
Colorado: donor records in, 355n.55
commandments (mitzvah): of *bikkur ḥolim* (visiting the sick), 194, 197,
202, 255–64, 375–76n.48; on diet, 15, 25; of ḥesed (lovingkindness, fidelity), 85, 108, 111, 171, 221–23, 225, 264; on personal hygiene, 15, 25; on procreation, 52–53, 80, 85, 97, 102–3, 123
commitment ceremonies, 151
community: acceptance of donor insemination in, 89–90; obligations and social responsibility within, 29–30, 32, 33, 209, 222, 248, 249, 252–54, 281–82, 285, 299, 302–5, 307, 308–10; prayer within, 258; prioritizing of duties of, 286–88; role of health care in, 29–30, 252–54
compassion, 96–97, 99, 222, 411
conception: biblical description of partners in, 21–22, 359–60n.90; with donated genetic materials, 66–115; with one's own genetic materials, 37–65; prevention of, 116–33; social context of, 134–64. *See also* artificial insemination
condoms, 52, 121–22, 138, 150
Connecticut: donor records in, 355n.55
conscience, 405–6
Conservative Jewish tradition, 11, 402–3, 405, 415; on abortion, 57; on adoption, 109; on artificial insemination, 67; on assisted suicide, 375–76n.48; on beneficial therapies, 203; on calling people to Torah, 72–73, 263, 351–52n.17; on contraception, 132; historical analysis within, 96; on homosexuality, 151; on incest, 78; on Jewish identity, 101; on living wills, 169–70; on masturbation, 119; on moment of death, 213, 229; on moral decision making, 10; on organ donation, 171, 226; on organ transplants, 213, 227–28, 230, 381n.18; on resurrection, 235; on smoking, 249–50; on surrogacy, 62; on withdrawing life support, 185–86, 200

contraception: permissibility of, 120–21; reliability of, 123; social, religious, and personal issues in, 123–25; types of, 121–23

Cooke, S., 86, 88, 92

cosmetic surgery, 270–72

creation of human life. *See* conception; procreation

cremation, 223–24

Crusades, 396

Cruzan, Nancy, 171, 209, 214

cryopreservation: of embryos, 54, 57–58; of sperm, 67

cultic sex, 139, 142, 149

cultic tattooing, 268

curative medicine: effectiveness of, 7; history of, 6; new moral questions in, 6

cures. *See* healing

cystic fibrosis, 156, 157

danger, obligation to avoid, 17–18, 249–52

Danto, Arthur, 412

death: defining the moment of, 228–29, 232–34; influence after, 40, 321; loss of soul at, 21, 22, 199, 200, 215, 232–33; obligation of adoptive children to parents, 109; obligation to avoid, 26–29; obligation to avoid impeding, 198–202, 210–11; and persistent, vegetative state (PVS), 213–17; prayers for, 197–98; preparations for, 167–75; process of dying, 176–220. *See also* active euthanasia; life support; passive euthanasia; suicide

demographic crisis, Jewish, 40, 95–96, 99, 124, 132–33, 141, 336–38n.1

demons, creation of, 119

Dewey, John, 140

diaphragm, 123

diet: as commandment, 15, 25; personal responsibility for, 303; as preventive medicine, 6, 29, 30, 246; rules for *(kashrut),* 147, 217, 247, 423n.30. *See also* fasting

Dimi (rabbi), 257

Dinah, 100

disabilities: adoption of children with, 110; affirmation of, 187, 214, 272–73; in children and adults, 110, 274–76; in elderly, 177, 276–78; in newborns, 273–74; psychological issues about, 272–78; traditional blessing for, 19–20, 187, 275, 317

disease: communal measures to prevent, 29–30, 252–54; as divine punishment, 26–27, 292, 319; obligation to avoid and heal, 26–29, 158, 164, 281, 286, 296, 319; personal measures to prevent, 245–52

dissection, in medical education, 239–41

divorce: and child custody, 359–60n.90; infertility as grounds for, 102–3, 339–40n.18; prevention of, 97

DNA. *See* cloning

DNA analysis, 71

donor insemination (DI): history of, 66–67; legal concerns about, 66–79; moral concerns about, 80–97, 141; to prevent genetic disease, 154; rate of, 340n.29; using donated eggs, 98–107

Down's syndrome, 154, 207

drinking water, 5

drug therapy, for infertility, 46, 51, 55

drug use and abuse, 191, 251, 254, 265, 303

drunkenness, 162, 250–51

dual-career marriages, 336–38n.11

Durable Power of Attorney for Health Care (Health Care Proxy), 169

Dworkin, Ronald, 9, 202, 408

dying, process of, 176–220. *See also* death

eating habits, healthful. *See* diet

Edels, Rabbi Samuel, 100

Edwards, Robert, 53

egalitarianism, 289–91, 296

egg donation, 98–103, 106–7

elderly: disabilities in, 177, 276–78;

health care for, 168–72; Medicare for, 302, 309
electroencephalograms, 229
Eliezer (rabbi), 185
Elijah (prophet), 295–97
Ellenson, Rabbi David, 421n.18
Elohai neshamah, 22
Elohai neshamah she-natata bi, 331n.19
emergency room care, 308
environmentalism, 253–54. *See also* biodiversity
Ephraim, 76
epilepsy, 153
equality. *See* egalitarianism
ethical wills, 173–75, 195, 261
Ethics of the Fathers *(Pirkei Avot),* 266
eugenics, 94–95, 163, 317. *See also* genetic engineering
Eurotransplant, 230
euthanasia. *See* active euthanasia; passive euthanasia
Eve. *See* Adam and Eve
executions, 203, 378n.61, 410
exercise: as commandment, 15; as preventive medicine, 6, 246, 248–49
family planning, 121, 124, 128. *See also* contraception
fasting, 25
fatherhood. *See* parents
Feinstein, Rabbi Moshe, 48, 70
Feldman, Rabbi David M., 344–45n.56
female masturbation, 116–17, 120
First Amendment rights, 273, 409
Florida: adoption laws in, 360n.98; surrogacy in, 347n.78
forced sex. *See* oppressive sex
foster parenting, 74
Fourteenth Amendment, 178, 314, 330n.12
Freud, Sigmund, 267
furies *(dybbuks),* 264
"gag rules," 298, 309
gamete intrafallopian transfer (GIFT), 47, 54–58, 340n.29
gastrointestinal tube feeding, of terminally ill patients, 208–17

gay couples: parenting by, 114, 141–42
Gellman, Rabbi Marc, 62
gematria, 342n.37
gender: ability to select, 155; of children, 44, 123, 155, 336n.9
gene therapy, 161–64
genetic engineering, 95, 158, 161–64, 312, 316, 317. *See also* eugenics
genetics: prevention of defects and disease, 70–71, 72, 75, 86–87, 88, 95, 104, 130–31, 152–61; screening and counseling for, 152–61; theological underpinnings of issues of, 151–52
gentiles, acceptance of, 272. *See also* intermarriage
Georgia: donor insemination laws in, 352–53n.19; sodomy laws in, 406
Gesher ha-Ḥayyim (Bridge of Life), 179–80
gestational surrogacy, 47, 58–59
ghosts *(shedim),* 233–34, 264
Gilligan, Carol, 263, 411
Gnosticism, body/mind bifurcation in, 20
God: abstinence from sexual relations by, 43; body as property of, 15–18, 125, 128, 151, 179, 180, 188, 223, 267; goodness of, 398–99; as healer, 26–27; human beings in image of, 18–20, 43–44, 261, 271, 272, 290, 314; sanctification of name of, 30–32, 229–30
Goebel, P., 91
Goldfarb, Rabbi Daniel C., 229
Goldstein, Baruch, 396
golem, 312
Golinkin, Rabbi David, 163
"Good Samaritan" laws, 329n.4
Gordis, Rabbi Daniel, 60–62, 63
Gordis, Robert, 397
goses (moribund person; state of *gesisah*), 199–200, 232
Gouche's disease, 152
grandparents, 92, 93
Greek philosophy, body/mind bifurcation in, 20

Greenberg, David, 142
Greenfeld, Dorothy A., 89, 92
guardianship *(apotropos)*, 74, 75, 108
Haggahot Semak, 49–50
Halevi, Rabbi David (the "Taz"), 68, 348–49n.9
Ḥananyah ben Teradiyon (rabbi), 181, 199, 408
Handel, William, 64
handicaps. *See* disabilities
Hartman, David, 397
Ḥasidic Jewish tradition, 411
healing: by God, 26–27; obligation to provide, 26–29
health. *See* disease; injury
health care: access to, 249, 279, 280–99, 307–8; cost of, 279, 281, 299–310; for elderly, 168–72; fundamental Jewish beliefs about, 14–33, 395–423; gendered, 261–62
Health Ministry, Israeli, 62
heartbeat, 228–29, 232
heart disease, 162
Ḥelbo (rabbi), 258
Herzog, Rabbi Isaac, 224, 239–40
ḥesed (lovingkindness, fidelity), 85, 108, 111, 171, 221–23, 225, 264
ḥevrah kaddishah ("holy society"), 223–24
Hillel, 15, 246, 332n.34
ḥillul ha-Shem (desecration of God's name), 30, 31, 229–30, 240
HIV virus. *See* AIDS
Hiyya bar Abba (rabbi), 185, 258
Hobbes, Thomas, 395
ḥoleh lefaneinu (patient who will benefit immediately), 226–27, 239
holistic concepts, 20–24
Holland: assisted suicide in, 188–89
homelessness, 254
homicides, allowable, 177
homosexuality, 11, 139–51, 317. *See also* gay couples; lesbian couples
hopelessness, 193–95
hospice care, 172, 177, 190–91, 194, 201, 218–20, 279

Ḥovot ha-Levavot (Duties of the Heart), 266
human beings: cloning of, 310–24; as created in God's image, 18–20, 43–44, 261, 271, 272, 290, 314; as integrated whole, 20–24, 135
Huna (rabbi), 264
Hunter, Dr. John, 51
Huntington's disease, 155
hydrocephalus, curing of, 161
hygiene. *See* personal hygiene
Idaho: donor records in, 355n.55
idolatry, 15, 30, 76, 181, 203, 344n.52
illegitimacy *(mamzer)*, 48, 49, 67–69
Illinois: donor insemination laws in, 352–53n.19; donor records in, 88; sperm bank regulations in, 349–50n.14
illness. *See* disease
impurity, 118, 247, 361–62n.7. *See also* pollution
inception, Jewish terms of, 200
incest: between adoptive parents and children and siblings, 50, 78–79, 108, 109; between donors and parents, 99–100; forgiveness of, 15, 30; prohibition of, 50, 68, 77, 181, 203; unintentional, in next generation, 69–72, 77, 104
incubators, 274
Indiana: sperm bank regulations in, 349–50n.14
individuals: conscience of, 405–6; as decision makers in health care, 6, 168–72, 298; as divine and unique, 18–20, 261, 272, 290, 320–21; responsibility for paying for medical care, 300–302, 306–7, 309–10; rights of, 272–73
infertility: causes of, 45–46, 125, 336–38n.11; compassion about, 96–97, 99; definition of, 45; as grounds for divorce, 102–3, 339–40n.18; Jewish sources on, 42–45; and obligation to procreate, 41–42, 44, 73–79; rate of, 45, 46; treatment of, 45–65

inheritance, in donor insemination, 73, 76

injury: obligation to avoid and heal, 17–18, 26–29, 184, 249–52. *See also* disease

inoculations, 253

Inquisition, 396

insanity. *See* mental health and illness

institutional review boards and ethics committees, 323

insults, to other people, 19

insurance companies: as bioethical decision makers, 6, 298; expenditures on terminally ill, 178

intermarriage: and donor insemination, 70; and infertility, 40, 336–38n.11; and reproductive rates, 124

interrupted coitus, 118

intoxication, 162, 250–51

intravenous feeding, of terminally ill patients, 208–17

in vitro fertilization (IVF), 47, 53–58, 98, 129, 340n.29

Ishmael (rabbi), 28

Israel: abortion rate in, 132; autopsies in, 224–25, 235, 238; inheritance in, 73; organ transplants in, 229, 230; surrogacy prohibited in, 62

Israel, Chief Rabbinate of, 213, 224, 229, 239

Israel, Rabbi Richard, 174

Isserles, Rabbi Moses, 102–3, 199, 228–29, 302, 339–40n.18, 392n.38

Jacob, sons of, 76, 100, 121

Jakobovits, Rabbi Immanuel, 60, 80–81, 95, 113, 132, 226

Jefferson, Thomas, 397

Jerusalem Talmud. *See* Talmud

Jewish Big Brothers and Big Sisters, 111

Jewish Family Service, 251

Jewish law, moral guidance from, 7–8, 10–11, 96, 401–17

Jewish tradition: death in defense of, 31; flexibility of, xiii–xiv; fundamental beliefs of Jewish medical ethics in, 14–33; moral guidance

within, 5–13, 400–404; normative elements of, 12, 399, xiv; of preventive medicine, 5–6; reader's interpretation of, 9–11, 416. *See also* Conservative Jewish tradition; Orthodox Jewish tradition; Reform Jewish tradition

Johanan (rabbi), 265

Joshua (rabbi), 332n.34

Joshua ben Levi (rabbi), 295–97

Judah (rabbi), 23, 197–98, 292, 294, 332n.34

Judah ben Samuel (of Regensberg), 353n.28

Judah ha-Nasi (rabbi), 333n.45, 408

Kad ha-Kemah (Measure of Flour), 266

kadosh ("apart"), 68

Kahana (rabbi), 258

Kansas: donor records in, 355n.55

Kant, Immanuel, 281, 407

kavod ha-met ("honor of the dead"), 221, 225, 240

kedushat ha-mishpahah (laws of sanctifying the family), 342–43n.42

Kentucky: surrogacy in, 347n.78

Kevorkian, Dr. Jack, 178, 189

kiddush ha-Shem (sanctification of God's name), 30, 31–32

kiddushin (marriage), 136

kidney donors, 226

Klein, Rabbi Isaac, 240

Knaus, Dr. William, 192

laparoscopy, 54

Lauritzen, Paul, 82–83, 84–85, 90–91

Leah, 100

leprosy, 153

lesbian couples: parenting by, 111, 114, 141–42

lesbianism, 139

levirate marriage, 75, 338–39n.14, 356n.65

licentious sex: in donor insemination, 80–81, 99; in homosexuality, 142, 149–50; prohibition of, 38, 68

life expectancy: of clones, 311; of humans, 5, 167, 177, 252

life support: advance directives about,

170–71; permissible withdrawal of, 185–86, 198–202, 273–74, 330n.12

Likutei Maharil, 48–49

Lister, Joseph, 280

living donors, of organs, 226

living wills, 169, 176, 192, 195, 207, 219, 226, 261

Llewellyn, Karl, 9

Loeb, Rabbi Judah, 312

Lubke, F., 91

Luther, Martin, 20, 135

Luzzato, Moses Ḥayyim, 266

Machiavelli, Niccolò, 406

Mackler, Rabbi Aaron, 55

Madison, James, 397

Mahlstedt, Patricia P., 89, 92

Maibaum, Matthew, 414, 415

Maimonides (Moses ben Maimon): on adultery, 68; on bodily pleasure, 26; on charity giving, 302; on ensoulment, 215, 216; on good health, 5–6, 15, 188, 246–47, 328n.2; on human worth, 19; on masturbation, 117, 119; on mental health and illness, 265; on mind-body bifurcation, 21; on personality traits, 266; on preservation of a life, 16; on procreation, 40; on proper eating habits, 247; on resurrection, 237; on visiting the sick, 259

malpractice insurance, 299

malpractice lawsuits, 308

managed care, 303, 306–10

marital companionship, 25, 37–39, 136, 334n.1

marriage: blood tests before, 152–53; financial obligations imposed after, 301; as holy, 136. *See also* spousal relationships

marriage contracts *(ketubbah)*, 75, 109, 143

Marriage of Moschetta case, 64

martyrdom, 30, 31, 181, 182–83

Marx, Karl, 395

Massachusetts: adoption laws in,

360n.98

master-slave relationship. *See* oppressive sex

masturbation: for artificial insemination, 52; to prevent pregnancy, 116–20; prohibition of, 117; for sperm donation, 106

Medicaid, 302, 308, 309

medical care. *See* health care

medical ethics. *See* bioethics

medical research: cadaver donations for, 239–41; on cloning, 310–24; recommendations for, 322–24; support for, 253

Medicare, 302, 309

megalomania, 201

Meir (rabbi), 122

Menaḥem Meiri (rabbi), 294

Menashe, 76

menstruation, conception during, 49–50

mental health and illness, 186, 216, 264–67

"mercy killing." *See* active euthanasia

Mesillat Yesharim (The Path of the Upright), 266

Michigan: sperm bank regulations in, 349–50n.14; surrogacy in, 347n.78

Midrash: on fatherhood and guardianship, 75–76; and mind (soul)-body bifurcation, 21

mikveh, 118

mind-body bifurcation, 20–24

Minnesota: donor records in, 355n.55

miscarriages, 45, 128, 315

misnagdim, 411

Missouri: adoption laws in, 360n.98

Mizraḥi, Rabbi Israel Meir, 130

modesty, 270

monogamy, 149–50

Montana: donor records in, 355n.55

moral judgment: education about, 135–38; as human ability, 19

Moses ben Naḥman (Naḥmanides): on healing, 29; on mental health and illness, 266; on sexual intercourse,

50, 335n.7

motherhood. *See* parents

murder: assisted suicide as, 184; definition of, 176; of fetus, 128; forgiveness of, 15, 30, 410; prohibition of, 181, 203, 315–16; of unborn children ("wasting the seed"), 118–19

Musar movement, 266

Naḥman (rabbi), 122

narcotics. *See* drug use and abuse

Nazirite, and self-denial, 25

needle biopsies, 225

nefesh (soul, self-identity), 21

neshamah (soul, inner being, "breath"), 21, 22

Nevada: donor records in, 355n.55

New Hampshire: adoption laws in, 360n.98; surrogacy in, 347n.78

New Jersey: adoption laws in, 360n.98; donor records in, 355n.55; surrogacy in, 347n.78

Newman, Lewis, 9, 12

New Mexico: donor records in, 355n.55

New York (state): sperm bank regulations in, 349–50n.14; surrogacy in, 347n.78

Nietzsche, Friedrich Wilhelm, 406

Nodding, Nel, 262–63

nonmarital sex, 119–20, 136–38

North Dakota: adoption laws in, 360n.98

Office of Technology Assessment, U.S. Congress, 94, 112

Ohio: donor records in, 88

Oklahoma: donor records in, 355n.55

ona'ah (economic oppression), 313

185delAG mutation, 156

oppressive sex (master-slave relationship), 39, 142, 149

oral sex, 139

Oregon: access to health care in, 298, 309; donor records in, 355n.55

organ and tissue donations: for artificial or animal transplants, 217–18; cost of, 231; disfigurement from, 231; instructions for ("living wills"), 170, 171, 172, 226; as obligation, 227–28, 241; types of, 225–41

organ and tissue harvesting, 316–17

original sin, 349n.13

orphans, 108

Orthodox Jewish tradition, 8, 405, 414–15, 419–20n.12; on abortion, 57; on artificial insemination, 70; on autopsy, 235; on beneficial therapies, 203; on calling people to Torah, 72–73; on donor insemination, 89; on euthanasia, 409; on genetic engineering, 162; on masturbation, 119; on moral decision making, 10; Musar movement in, 266; on organ transplants, 227, 229, 230, 381n.18; procreation within, 90; on resurrection, 235; on smoking, 249; on surrogacy, 60

Oshry, Rabbi Ephraim, 182–83

"outcomes research" (effectiveness), 7

ovarian cancer: incidence of, 156; increased risks of, 55, 106; testing for, 158

overpopulation, 336–38n.11

ovulation, intercourse timed to, 46, 51

ovulatory dysfunction, 45, 53

ovum surrogacy, 47, 58–59

pain: obligation to avoid and relieve, 26–29, 177, 185–86, 191–93, 201–2, 218–19; as redemptive, 184–85

Pancoast, Dr., 66

parent-child relationships: asymmetry in, 90–93, 98–99; preservation of, 81–83; secrecy in, 83–90

parents: Jewish identity through, 72–79, 263; Jewish roles described for, 112; role in creation of human life, 21–22, 37, 39–42; surrogate, 58–64, 111–12. *See also* parent-child relationships

passive euthanasia, 177, 198–202

Pateman, Carole, 61

paternity. *See* parent-child relation-

ships; parents
patur aval assur (compulsion to violate laws), 146
Paul (saint), 20, 135
pelvic endometriosis, 45, 53
penicillin, 198, 280, 310
Peretz (rabbi), 342n.40, 348–49n.9
Perez ben Elijah (of Corbeil), 49–50
Pergonol, 46
peritoneoscopy, 225
persistent, vegetative state (PVS), patients in, 213–17
personal hygiene: celebratory, 25; as commandment, 15, 25; as preventive medicine, 5, 246–49
peter reḥem ("opening the womb"), 101
Pharisees, 236, 277, 338–39n.14
phenylketonuria, 59
Philo, 21
physicians: as decision makers in patient care, 168, 207–8, 297–98, 299, 308–9; fees for services by, 299; historical value of, 280–81; obligation to heal, 27–28
piety, 296, 297
pikuaḥ nefesh (preservation of one's own life), 15–18, 223, 225, 266, 325–26, 328–29n.3, 343n.43, 374n.37
Pittman, Dr. Frank, 113
Plato, 20, 395, 406
pleasure, bodily, 24–26, 38, 135
pneumonia, 206
pollution, avoidance and eradication of, 253–54
polygamy, 357n.70
Popenoe, David, 112
prayer: for death, 197–98; healing power of, 198, 257–58, 260
pregnancy: experience of, 98; ideal age for, 45–46, 124–25; and identity of the mother, 100–101; out of wedlock, 137; prevention of, 116–33. *See also* artificial insemination; conception
preventive medicine: communal, 252–

54; effectiveness of, 7, 245–46; in Jewish tradition, 5–6; personal, 245–52
priestly status, determination of, 72–73, 108
procreation, 37, 39–42, 52–53, 73–79, 80, 85, 97, 102–3, 123, 136. *See also* conception; pregnancy; sexual intercourse
promiscuity. *See* adultery; licentious sex
prostate cancer, 156, 157
Prouser, Rabbi Joseph, 227
public assistance. *See* charity
public baths and toilets, 29, 248, 282
public health: in Jewish tradition, 29–30, 252–54; modern movement toward, 5
"quality of life" issues, 18–19, 187–88
quarantine, 5
Quinlan, Karen Ann, 171, 214
Rabbenu Nissim, 146
Rabbenu Tam, 363n.20
Rabbinic Letter on Human Intimacy, 151
Rabin, Yitsḥak: assassination of, 398
Rachel, 43, 64, 100, 121
racism: in adoption, 110; in donor insemination, 70, 93–95
Rashi, 143, 363n.19, 390n.1
Rava, 146, 312
Rebecca, 43
Reform Jewish tradition, 8, 403, 405, 415; on calling people to Torah, 73, 263; on masturbation, 119; on moral decision making, 10; on organ donation, 226, 380n.11; on organ transplants, 230; on resurrection, 235; on smoking, 249
re'im ahuvim ("loving friends"), 39
reincarnation, 238–39
Reinhardt, Stephen, 330n.12, 370n.3
Reisner, Rabbi Avram, 185, 212, 215–16
religion: definition of, 395; and ethics, 397–400; in moral decision making, 395–404
reproductive rates, Jewish, 40, 95–96,

99, 124, 132–33, 141, 336–38n.11
Republic, The (Plato), 20
Resh Lakish, 294–95
resurrection, 21, 22, 234–39, 277, 332n.28, 338–39n.14, 393–94n.53
Rosenfeld, Rabbi Azriel, 162
Rousseau, Jean-Jacques, 406
ruaḥ ("breath"), 22
Saadiah Gaon, 236, 237, 239
Sabbath: dietary celebration of, 25; violations of, 16, 204, 266
Sadducees, 236
safe sex, 150, 251–52
Saks, Jane, 113
Samuel (prophet), 233
Samuel (talmudic rabbi), 5
Samuel bar Naḥmani (rabbi), 108
Sanhedrin, 402
Sarah, 43, 64, 121
Saul: mental illness of, 264; suicide of, 181
scientific cadaver donations, 239–41
secondhand smoke, 250, 254
second marriages, 105
secrecy, in artificial insemination, 83–90
secular philosophies, 395
Sefer ha-Ḥinnukh (Book of Education), 266
Sefer Ḥasidim, 199, 233–34
Segal, Rabbi Jacob Moellin, 48
selective abortion, 56–57, 101–2, 129–30
self-denial, 25
self-idolization, 321–22
self-pollution, 117–18
sex education, 135–38
sexual appetites, as gendered, 39
sexual intercourse: for marital companionship, 25, 37–39, 136, 334n.1; nonmarital, 119–20, 136–38; for procreation, 37, 39–42, 52–53; rate of, 138
sexually transmitted diseases, 120, 122, 138, 150, 252
sexual orientation, development of,

143–46
Shapiro, Rabbi Morris, 52
shem (name), 21
sheniyot (secondary relations), 78–79, 109
shtus (shtut, mental incompetence), 265
Shulḥan Arukh, 28, 199, 283, 284, 286–87, 288–89, 300, 301, 304–5, 392n.38
sickle cell anemia, 161
sickness. *See* disease
Siegel, Rabbi Seymour, 229
Sifra, 143
Simeon bar Judah (rabbi), 268
Singer, I. B., 119
single parenting, 47, 82, 111–15
slaves, body piercing of, 269
sleep: loss of soul during, 21, 22; as preventive medicine, 246; requirements for, 15
Smith, Lee, 112, 113
smoking: community responsibility to repair effects of, 304; obligation to avoid, 18, 249–50, 254; personal responsibility for, 293, 303, 304
Snowden, R., 105
social hierarchy, 283–84, 289
socialized medicine, 298, 303, 308, 309
Society for Assisted Reproductive Technology, 53
sodomy, 288
Sofer, Rabbi Moses, 109
soul, 20–24, 199, 200, 215, 232–33
"special needs" children, 41
speech, as human ability, 19
spermatozoal disorders, 45, 343n.45
sperm donation: acceptability of, 103–6; confidentiality of, 71–72, 85–89, 104; and fatherhood, 74, 86, 87; and insemination rates, 71, 349–50n.14; by non-Jews, 70; record keeping in, 71
sperm-mucus interactions, 45, 344n.46
Spero, Moshe Halevi, 265
Spitz, Rabbi Elie, 62, 63, 65
sports, 248–49

spousal relationships: asymmetry in, 90–93, 98–99; benefits of, 149–50; disclosure within, 105–6, 160–61; and marital companionship, 25, 37–39, 136, 334n.1

stealing, 16

stepparenting, 74

Steptoe, Patrick, 53

sterility. *See* infertility

sterilization, 125–27

Stevenson, Leslie, 407

suicide: definition of, 176; forgiveness for, 182–83, 203, 410; medical and legal context of issues of, 176–80; motivation for, 178; prohibition of, 18, 177, 179–83; as reaction to forced conversion to Christianity, 31, 181; as reaction to sexual violation, 181. *See also* assisted suicide

SUPPORT, 192

Supreme Court, U.S.: on sodomy, 406; on suicide and assisted suicide, 18, 178

surgery: to correct infertility, 46; cosmetic, 270–72; history of, 6, 280

surrogacy: description of, 58–65; with donated sperm or eggs, 58–59; and identity of the mother, 101; moral objections to, 60–65; for single male parents, 111–12, 141; types of, 47, 58–59

Sweden: sperm donation in, 86

takkanah ("fixing" of law), 402, 422n.28

Talmud: and abortion, 128; and adoption, 108; and adultery, 68; and alleviation of pain, 185; and artificial insemination, 48, 53; and assisted suicide, 184; and clothing, 267; and community obligations, 29–30, 281–82, 303; and donor insemination, 78; and egg donation, 100; and genetic screening, 153; and healing, 27, 29; and homosexuality, 143; and "life of the hour" (*ḥayyei sha'ah*), 203–4, 409; and

marital companionship, 41; and marriage between adopted siblings, 78; and mental incompetence, 265; and mind (soul)-body bifurcation, 21; and moment of death, 228; and paying for health care, 300–301; and personal hygiene, 5, 248; and physicians, 299; and prayer for healing, 260; and preservation of a life, 16–17, 30–31, 106, 283, 294–95, 300–301, 328–29n.3; and resurrection, 237–38; and Sabbath violations, 266; and suicide, 181; and tattooing, 268; tolerance expressed in, 273; and visiting the sick, 257–58, 259

Tannen, Deborah, 263, 359–60n.90

Targum Yonatan, 100

tattooing, 267–69

Tay-Sachs disease, 152–54, 156, 157, 161, 317

Teitelbaum, Rabbi Yoel, 50

temporary insanity, 181

terefah (an imperiled life), 154, 200–201, 207, 232, 294, 376–77n.56

terminally ill patients: affirmation of quality of life of, 187–88; artificial nutrition and hydration for, 154, 185, 186, 208–17; beneficial therapies for, 202–8, 211–12; deception of, 194–95; experimental therapies for, 217–18; futility of treatment for, 192; hopelessness of, 193–95; obligation to avoid prolonging life of, 198–202. *See also* hospice care

testicular cancer, 126

Thomas Aquinas (saint), 407

thought, as human ability, 19

throat cancer, 208

Tisha b'Av, fasting on, 25

tohorat ha-mishpahah (laws of family purity), 51

Torah: on active euthanasia, 196; on adultery, 50, 68; on blood transfusions, 210; commandment to follow and study, 23; on dietary rules,

247; on disabilities, 274; on disease as divine punishment, 26–27, 292, 319; on egg donation, 100–101; on healing, 28, 29; on homosexuality, 139, 140–41; on human worth (in divine image), 19, 261, 272, 290; on illegitimacy, 67; on impurity, 118, 247, 361–62n.7; on incest, 50, 68, 78; literal meaning of, 136; on marital companionship, 38, 39, 41; on preservation of a life, 17, 30–31, 106, 325–26, 328–29n.3; on procreation, 42, 43; on quarantine, 5; on resurrection, 236; on sanctification of God's name, 30; social hierarchy based on knowledge of, 283; on soul, 215; on tattooing, 267–68, 269

Tosafists, 204–5

Tosefta: on procreation, 338n.13; on welfare, 285

"traditional surrogacy," 47, 58–59

triage: application of, 291–99; criteria for, 282–91, 297

tubal disease, 45

tubal feeding, of terminally ill patients, 208–17

tubal ligation, 125, 126

Tuchinsky, Rabbi Yehiel M., 179–80

tzedakah ("justice," required charity), 221–22, 285, 286

tzidduk ha-din, 173

Ulla, son of Qoseb, 295–96

ultrasound, 54, 55

unconscious patients, artificial hydration and nutrition of, 212, 213–17

Uniform Parentage Act, 73, 86, 87, 114, 352n.19

Utah: surrogacy in, 347n.78

vasectomies, 125–27

vegetarianism, 217

venereal disease, avoidance and prevention of, 120, 122, 138, 150, 252

Vermont: "Good Samaritan" laws in, 329n.4

Virginia: adoption laws in, 360n.98; surrogacy in, 347n.78

visiting the sick (bikkur holim), 194, 197, 202, 255–64, 375–76n.48

Waldenberg, Rabbi Eliezer, 50, 67–68, 344–45n.56

washing. See personal hygiene

Washington (state): donor records in, 355n.55; surrogacy in, 347n.78

Washington, George, 397

"wasting the seed," 106, 118–19

water, cleanliness of, 5

welfare. See charity

wills: Advance Directive for Health Care ("living will"), 169, 176, 192, 195, 207, 219, 226, 261; material and ethical, 172–75, 195, 261

Wisconsin: donor records in, 355n.55; "Good Samaritan" laws in, 329n.4

Wyoming: donor records in, 355n.55

Yeh, John, 85

Yeh, Molly Uline, 85

yissurim shel ahavah ("afflictions of love"), 185, 332n.35

Yohanan (rabbi), 162, 185, 203, 267, 294–95, 332n.34

Yom Kippur, fasting on, 25, 144

Yose bar Halafta, 332n.34

Zionist movement, 249

Zohar, on visiting the sick, 255

zygote intrafallopian transfer (ZIFT), 47, 54–58